# CONFLUENCE

# CONFLUENCE

## Tools for Thinking about
## How Organized Plans
## and Self-organized Patterns
## Flow Together

Cynthia F. Kurtz

Kurtz-Fernhout
Publications

ISBN 978-0-9913694-1-6

For printables, errata, and other information, visit cfkurtz.com/confluence.

Typeset with LaTeX using the Cochineal font.
Cover image: Path in Plitvice Lakes National Park, Croatia. Licensed from 123rf.com.

**confluence**. a place where two rivers join, or a situation in which two or more things come together.

– Macmillan Dictionary

# Contents

# 1 Introduction

*What this book is about*

Here are some things.

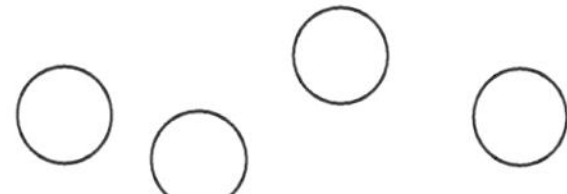

Let's say that these things interact with each other. Because they interact, we will call them *interactors*. How do they interact? Like this.

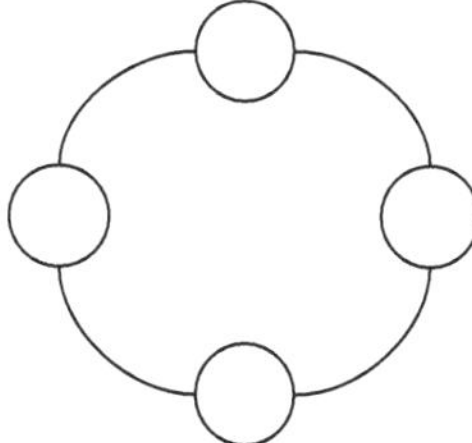

Notice that these particular interactors—for whatever reason—are connected *only* to their closest neighbors. Their interactions are *local,* not global.

Also notice that this particular group of interactors forms a circle. Nobody decided to form a circle, but a circle formed. Why? *Because of the way the interactors connected to each other.* Each one reached out to its closest neighbors in such a way that the entire group became circular.

When a *global* pattern (such as this circle) emerges out of the nature of local interactions, it's called *self-organization.* A self-organized pattern *looks* like somebody planned it, but nobody planned it. *It formed itself.*[1]

You can see examples of self-organization all around you. Did you ever sit on a beach and pile up grains of sand? The pile of sand got higher and higher, and then at some point, the top of the pile always came sliding back down, didn't it? That sudden, global collapse emerged out of many local interactions between each grain of sand and its closest neighbors. That was self-organization.[2]

Did you ever watch a flock of birds pass overhead? Did it seem like someone was calling out directions, telling them all to fly this way or that way? But of course nobody was. The global shape of the flock *emerged* out of many local interactions between each bird and its closest neighbors. Each bird kept saying to its neighbors, in effect, "Hey, keep your distance, I'm flying here," mixed together with, "Hey, where are you going? Wait for me!" And out of those many local interactions, the flock took shape. That was self-organization.[3]

Self-organization happens in people too. Once I was walking on a sidewalk in a big city along with about fifty strangers. Suddenly we all heard a loud bang. In half a second, the entire crowd of people collapsed into a dense clump on the side of the building. We stood there, close together, holding our breaths, for a few more seconds. Then, when nothing else happened, we dispersed and walked on. Nobody said anything. Nobody looked at anybody. It just happened. Each of us experienced a momentary impulse to minimize the distance between ourselves and our closest neighbors, and the crowd shrunk. But then the impulse passed and we regained our previous pattern. That was self-organization.[4]

You can probably think of a time when you saw self-organization happening. Traffic slowing down, a crowd rushing forth, bees swarming, patterns in the sand on the shore of a lake. You've seen it. Everyone has.[5]

## Organizers and their plans

Now let's add another thing to our diagram. This thing is a very different sort of thing. See if you can guess what it does from this picture.

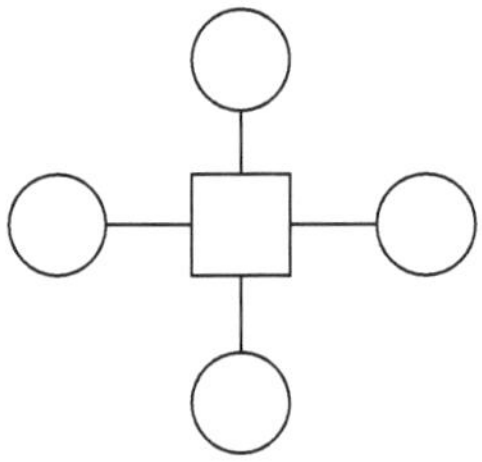

The square thing in the middle is an *organizer*. Organizers, unlike interactors, can see and reach *beyond* their closest neighbors. When an organizer wants to create a global pattern, it moves itself to a place where it can get hold of the interactors—as it has done here, by jumping into the middle of the circle—and it grabs hold of the interactors and puts them where it wants them to be.

Say you're standing in the lobby of a building. That building didn't grow there. Somebody built it, and somebody decided what its lobby should look like. The people who did those things were organizers. Now say you're standing in somebody's kitchen, and you open a cabinet. The food in that cabinet didn't grow there. Somebody put it there. Whoever did that was an organizer.

All humans are organizers, but not all organizers are human. Any being that is capable of intentionally arranging anything can be an organizer. In some species of fish, for example, the male builds a mating mound on the lake or ocean floor, spending days carefully arranging millions of sand grains and pebbles into a perfectly circular pattern. That's organization. *Self*-organization is what happens *after* the fish stops maintaining its circular construction.[6]

## Two forces flowing together

Now we get to why this book is called *Confluence*. If you look around in the world, you are almost *never* going to find pure organization or pure self-organization. In the real world, intentional plans and spontaneous patterns intermingle and interact, like two rivers flowing together.

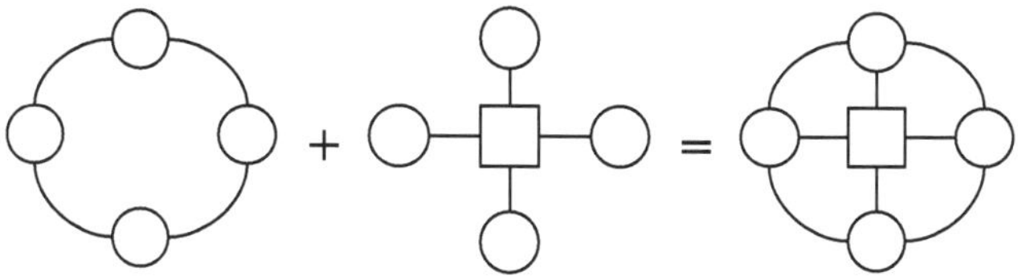

Picture yourself standing in a busy central plaza in a big city. You look around and see famous buildings, monuments, streetcars, taxis, trucks, street food, locals, tourists, photographers, pigeons, pets.

Some aspects of the situation you see were carefully planned: the building facades, the streetcar lines, the advertisements, the storm gutters, the police presence. Other aspects of the situation formed spontaneously due to local interactions. Three teenagers, strangers to each other, noticed that they were all carrying guitars, started talking, and struck up an impromptu music session. Some tourists gawking at the monuments gathered around to watch. A few locals saw the crowd and wandered over from their walk to the office to see what was up. The old folks on their usual bench watched it all happen while they fed their usual pigeons. The pigeons ignored everything except the bread.

A city center is the best place to see organization and self-organization come together. People-watching takes on a whole new dimension when you start thinking about interactors and organizers. You can learn a lot by watching the two forces mix together in kaleidoscopic combinations.

## Why I wrote this book

Every life, every group, and every effort is a long series of *situations*. Things begin; things happen; things change; things end. We all keep needing to make sense of the situations we find ourselves in, individually and collectively, over and over. That's how we know we are still alive.

We all develop *habits* of situational awareness: things we do, things we notice, things we ignore. The purpose of this book is to *help you develop a new habit* of situational awareness, one that pays particular attention to the ways in which organization and self-organization flow together.

Why develop this habit? Because it's useful. The two forces of organization and self-organization flow through all of our lives, whether we know it or not. Thinking about how they flow together can help us make sense of things that happen, think about how things got to be the way they are, weigh our options, consider risks and opportunities, and understand other points of view.

How do I know this? Because I have been relying on the habit for decades, and because I have helped other people use it to improve their own situational awareness. For example, these are some true stories of people who used the ideas in this book to think about situations they were facing.

- A group of first responders realized that they had been paying too little attention to a potentially important aspect of their work.
- A team of evaluators realized that the two forms of evaluation on which they had been relying—global measurement and local engagement—could support rather than conflict with each other.
- A group of military analysts compared aspects of organization and self-organization in recent and historical conflicts, then used the insights they gained to reconsider risks and opportunities in the current situation.
- A teacher found a new way to explain the reasoning behind some difficult-to-explain teaching concepts.
- A group of government policy makers saw that their assessments of risk were influenced by a surprising variety of factors, some of which worked against each other.

I believe this habit of situational awareness could be useful to every person, family, community, and organization. That's why I wrote this book.

## Who this book is for

You. It's for you. I wrote this book for anyone who is interested in this topic. It's not only for people in a specific field or with a particular background or level of education. It's for everyone.

If this is the first time you've encountered the concept of self-organization, you might be a little daunted by it. Don't be. I believe we all understand it intuitively. If you've ever watched a cloud or a crowd take shape, you know what self-organization is. Sure, there's plenty more you can learn about it. Mathematicians and scientists spend decades exploring its many fascinating details. But you don't need a mathematical or scientific background to think about self-organization at its most basic level. All you need is curiosity.

## What to expect in this book

The first part of the book introduces you to a tool you can use to think about how organization and self-organization flow together in situations that matter to you. The second part of the book describes six similar tools you can use to explore situations in more detail.

# Part One

## A Thinking Tool and an Exercise that Uses It

In this book we will use a type of tool I call a *thinking space*: a two-dimensional diagram defined by labeled axes. One thing increases in amount or degree from left to right, and another thing increases from bottom to top. Placing a situation into the space describes it with respect to those two things.

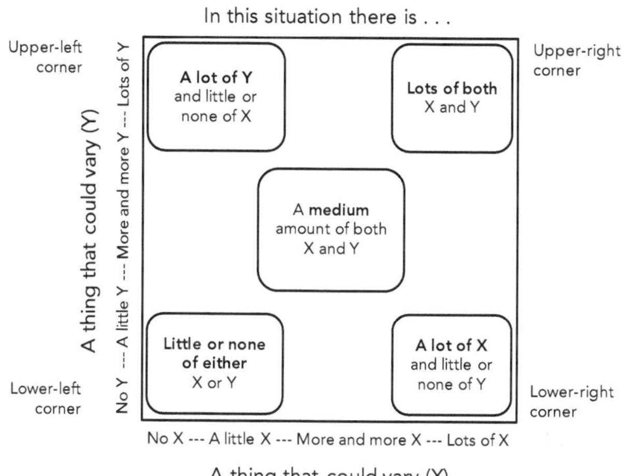


If your axes were tomatoes (X) and celery (Y), and your favorite soup had lots of tomatoes but no celery, you would place it in the lower-right corner.

*The axes of a thinking space aren't there to measure anything.* They are there to help you think. If you're working in a group, they are there to help you talk to each other. If you and I were neighbors, say, and we were talking about resilience in our community, we might use a thinking space to explore how mutual aid flows together with personal responsibility.

A thinking space always starts out empty, because it's waiting for you to fill it up. It's like an empty notebook or a blank canvas. Filling up the space helps you think about the situations you put into it.

Chapter Two describes a thinking space that explores how organization and self-organization flow together. To help you understand the space, the chapter goes through several example situations. Chapter Three shows you an exercise that helps you use the space to think about situations *you* care about.

# 2 The Confluence Thinking Space

*Thinking about how organization and self-organization flow together*

Here's our first thinking space. The amount of organization increases from left to right, and the amount of self-organization rises from bottom to top.[1] The corner diagrams describe the conditions at each corner point. Thin and thick lines represent weak and strong connections.

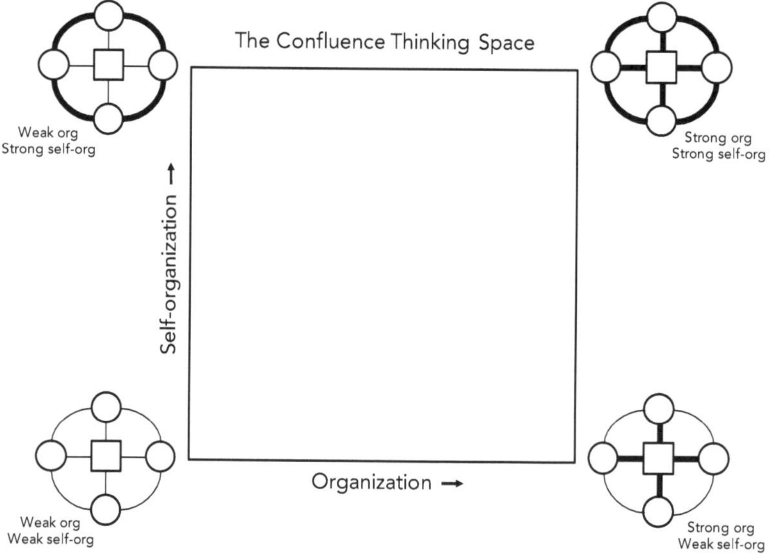


Now let's fill up the space. We'll start by thinking about situations that can be found near the four corners of the space. Then we'll consider some situations that range across the space.

### Weak organization, weak self-organization

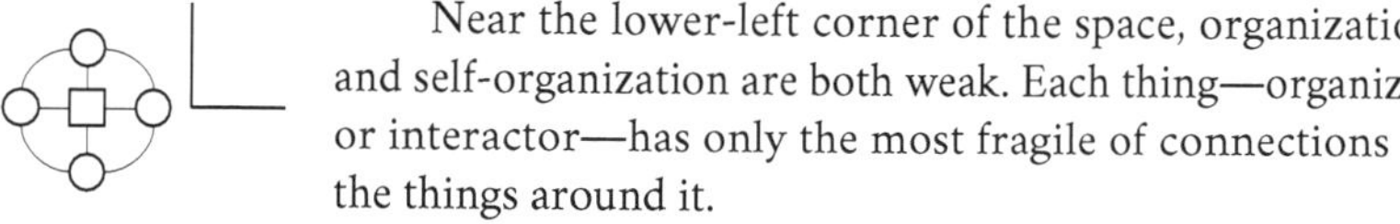

Near the lower-left corner of the space, organization and self-organization are both weak. Each thing—organizer or interactor—has only the most fragile of connections to the things around it.

This is where we find ourselves during natural disasters. Fires, hurricanes, tornadoes, and earthquakes are self-organized patterns, so they themselves are not in this corner; but they push *us* into it. During such disasters, the connections we normally rely on are torn apart. It's hard to get control of the situation, and it's hard to get new patterns to form, because the ongoing emergency keeps pulling apart any connections we manage to create.

Still, it's rare for even the most dire emergency to stay in this corner for long. People who work in disaster preparedness try their hardest to keep situations from approaching this corner of the space, and once a situation does land there, they try their hardest to pull it *back* out of the corner as quickly as possible. Every town has plans that help its first responders recover control. And people like you and me maintain multiple ways to reach out to our neighbors, friends, and family members in an emergency. The emergency kits we keep in our kitchens and garages help us to quickly rebuild severed connections.

Would a war zone be located in this corner? It depends on how narrowly you define the situation. Certainly there are few reliable connections in the midst of a pitched battle. But on a longer time scale, across many battles, the forces of organization (strategy, training, transportation) and self-organization (networks, negotiations) keep warfare some distance from this corner.

## Weak organization, strong self-organization

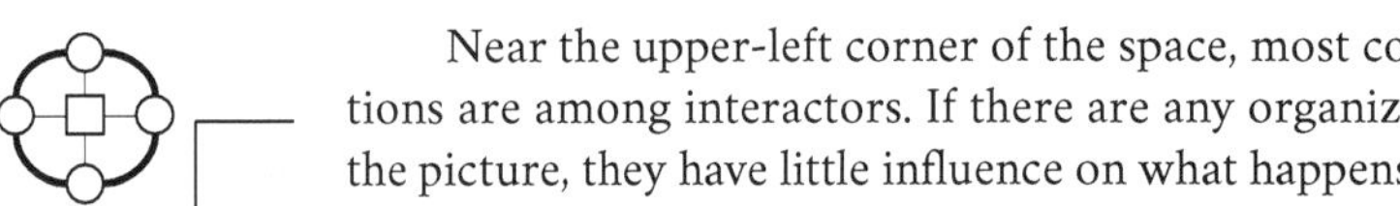

Near the upper-left corner of the space, most connections are among interactors. If there are any organizers in the picture, they have little influence on what happens.

This is what the earth looked like throughout the roughly four billion years before there were organisms that intentionally shaped their environments. Probably the first examples of organization in earth's history were spider webs, which date to about 300 million years ago.[2] Dinosaur nests, some communal and repeatedly used, began to appear about 200 million years ago.[3] Such weak organizers had relatively small impacts on their environments. Still, they moved the situation a baby step away from *pure* self-organization, because they created organized structures by intentionally manipulating objects around them.

What does an organizer need to be an organizer? By my reckoning, even a weak organizer must have three essential traits: awareness, intent, and access.

### Awareness

An organizer needs the ability to see beyond its closest neighbors. That's why the organizer in my diagram has plopped itself right down in the middle of the group: so it can see everybody. People in crowds get up onto rooftops, into trees, and onto the shoulders of their friends because they are trying to organize the space around them—even if it's just the square meter of space around them—to better suit their needs.[4]

### Intent

An organizer needs the ability to make plans and carry them out. Grains of sand can't be organizers. They can't see anything at all, but more importantly, they can't make plans. As soon as you start talking about *living* things, the question of whether they have awareness and intention becomes a matter of debate. An individual bacterium can't see the colony of which it is a part, and

*Confluence*

and Patricia Wynne, encourages young people to do just that: zoom in to [...] at which they can see self-organization at work, even in the middle [...] park or suburban back yard.[8]

Are there places where you can observe pure self-organ[...] people? Not really. Every place where you can find people [...] rules that were set up by organizers to control what hap[...] think people milling about in a public park are self-o[...] but only *partly*, because the park was designed, an[...] might think cars in traffic are self-organized, [...] because the roads were designed, and the ca[...] people in the cars are following schedul[...] Even the people in my crowd-bunchin[...] design of the building and the side[...]

So we in our human world [...] that's not a *bad* thing. Organ[...] of balance. That's what t[...] organization and self-[...] our needs in the sit[...]

## STRONG ORG[...]

Tuck[...] space i[...] pure [...]

empty at this point.[7] But there are still many situations that *approach* this corner.

One way to find such situations is to look where people aren't. Some of the places on earth that are thriving, ecologically speaking, are places in which human beings can no longer live, such as the area around the Chernobyl nuclear plant, or the Korean demilitarized zone. Of course, there are organisms in every human-deserted space that intentionally change their environments. But the *extent* to which they do this is so much smaller than what we do (in terms of energy, matter, and area) that the mix of organization and self-organization is much nearer this corner than in any place where you will find people.

Another way to find nearly-pure self-organized patterns is to focus on a smaller frame of reference. Where there are forests, fields, or seashores, self-organization is not hard to find. But even in a busy city park you can find small areas, perhaps in places that are difficult to mow or landscape, where traces of organization are weak or absent. These are great places to learn about self-organization. You can watch whole communities of tiny things interact with their closest neighbors, and you can see how their local interactions form global patterns. A series of books called *One Small Square*, by Donald M. Silver

scale
of a city

ization among
has structures and
pens there. You might
rganized, and they are—
d people watch over it. You
and they are—but only partly,
rs were designed, and most of the
es that were set up by other people.
g-up story were partly influenced by the
walk.[9]

never quite reach pure self-organization. But
ization is only bad when it's out of place or out
his book is for—*to talk about the balance* between
rganization and how to adjust it (when we can) to meet
ations we find ourselves in.

## ANIZATION, WEAK SELF-ORGANIZATION

ed into the lower-right corner of the confluence
where an organizer feels most at home. In a state of
organization, each interactor is connected *only* to the
rganizer, and not at all to the other interactors. Not a single
pattern forms unless the organizer has decided to create it.
The organizer has a place for everything, and it keeps everything in its place.

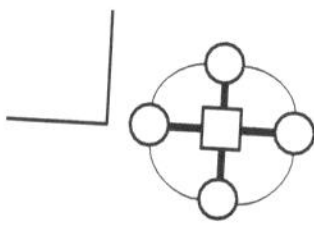

Because life itself is a self-organized phenomenon, pure organization is as impossible as pure self-organization. The places that come closest to this corner are cleanrooms: medical, industrial, and scientific spaces where every attempt is made to eradicate self-organized patterns. In an ISO 1 category cleanroom, for example, exactly ten airborne particles of 0.1 micrometers or larger are allowed per cubic meter of air.[10]

It takes a lot of effort to keep self-organization at bay. People who work in cleanrooms not only must wear special suits and masks; they must also *walk slowly*, because they spread more bacterial cells around when they move than when they stand still. Human beings *leak* self-organization.

When I think of this corner of this space, I always think of *Life After People*, a 2008 documentary series that explored what would happen to the buildings, power plants, and other organized structures we have built if we suddenly disappeared from the earth.[11] It was fascinating to learn how so many things we think of as permanent—not just buildings and power plants, but whole cities—require constant maintenance to prevent them from disintegrating.

The segments of that series I found the most interesting were its visits to ghost towns and abandoned structures, because I grew up in a ghost town. From around 1860 to 1880, my childhood neighborhood was a bustling oil boom town, one of many that "sprang up almost in a day," according to a local history book.[12] In the span of a few decades, "most of these towns disappeared, some leaving not even a sign to mark the spot where they once stood." Our town once had hundreds of inhabitants, a post office, two churches, two schools, a fancy hotel, a general store, factories, repair shops, and a "forest" of oil derricks connected via a network of pipes. (Our house, built in 1861, was the general store.) All of that organization is gone now. There's nothing left but a few dozen people in a handful of houses strung along a road.[13]

When we were children, my siblings and I spent many hours wandering the woods looking for "haunted houses," as we used to call them. (We thought every neighborhood was full of haunted houses.) We found several, and we kept visiting them over the decades, watching as they transformed from neglected but still livable houses to heaps of mangled wood and stone. Eventually the forest ate them up. But if you knew what to look for, you could still find a few traces of the old homesteads. You might come across a path that seemed too smooth to be natural, or a bit of barbed wire stuck to a tree, or a stone with chisel marks on it. Even the fact that the woods were still woods came down to a deed sitting in somebody's filing cabinet.

The structures we build never completely disappear, but they never stay the way we made them either. Not without effort. That's how it goes. We organize things, and the things self-organize as fast as we organize them. And I'm not just talking about bacteria or old houses now. I'm talking about people. Because we ourselves are interactors. We organize and self-organize at the same time. We build rules and we work our way around them. We build towns and we abandon them. We build cleanrooms and we contaminate them. Our nature pulls us both toward and away from pure organization. That's why nothing we do or create stays in this corner for long.

With all this talk of decay, you might be wondering why I haven't mentioned *entropy*, the universal tendency of things to fall apart into random disorder. Organization and self-organization are both anti-entropic forces, in the sense that they bring things together. You could think of entropy as a third dimension in the confluence space, but I'm not sure you'd get a lot out of doing that. Besides, I've noticed that people often mistake self-organization for entropy because of our tendency to ignore things *we* didn't make happen. When we think of something as decayed, it is often not actually falling apart, but coming together in a different way. The bacterial and fungal colonies that grow on our abandoned buildings are as anti-entropic, in their own way, as the buildings they replace.

### Strong organization, strong self-organization

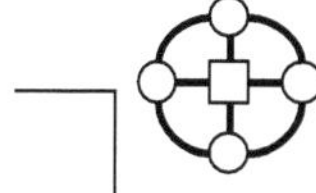

The upper-right corner of the confluence space, where organization and self-organization are both strong, is a special place. In the other three corners, though a situation might briefly approach the corner, it will rarely stay there for long.

Near the upper-right corner, however, you can find many situations that stay firmly in place for long periods of time.

We don't have to look far to find an example of a situation near this corner. Just go back several pages to the busy city plaza I mentioned before. Cities are perfect examples of places where strong organization meets strong self-organization. Responsible people spend their careers poring over maps and designing structures and procedures to preserve order in cities. And the structures and procedures they design are constantly washed over by waves of people and the self-organized patterns they form.[14] That's why I always recommend that people go to a city plaza if they want to see how organization and self-organization blend together, because that's where you can see the two forces interacting most strongly.

But a city is not the only such example. Any situation in which groups of people come together for any reason tends to work its way into this corner over time. If you take a close look at any corporation, government agency, military branch, or other organization, you are bound to find structures and procedures inextricably tangled up with self-organized patterns.[15] People in such organizations follow the rules, but they also know how and when to bend them. Everyone knows who gets to tell them what to do, but they also know who they can turn to when they need to do something else.[16] That's a good thing and a bad thing. Sometimes it leads to corruption and injustice, but sometimes it prevents the machine from crushing the people under it. As Eugene McCarthy famously said, "The only thing that saves us from the bureaucracy is inefficiency."[17]

## Crossing the confluence space

Now that we have explored the four corners of the space, let's consider a few situations that range across it.

### The life of a skyscraper

A modern skyscraper rises into the clouds. Its detailed design is based on its expert architect's global *awareness*, careful *intention*, and privileged *access*. The architect, and the small number of other professionals who are involved in building the skyscraper, are strongly connected to the city's rules, standards, and building codes. They are only weakly connected to the diverse community of people who will live in, work in, and visit the building. The situation is highly organized: near the lower-right corner of the confluence space.

Now let's visit the same skyscraper ten years later. Corporations have leased and customized some floors of the building. Popular restaurants have developed faithful followings. Extended families have moved in. Tenant groups have formed. Friends gather to walk together at lunchtime. City ordinances and building maintenance tasks still require constant attention to organization, but not as strongly as when the building was under construction. Self-organization has grown, and it has tugged the whole situation upward in the confluence space. Now the building is close to the middle of the space.

Fifty years later, the same skyscraper is the subject of contentious debate in the city council. One group wants to demolish the eyesore to make way for modern construction. Another wants to restore the building as a hallmark of the city's cultural history. Few people want to live or work in the building anymore, but those who do defend its unique character and community. The building itself requires constant repair to counter the forces of self-organization. Vines from abandoned balcony gardens have taken over entire walls. Alcoves meant to provide quiet meeting spaces proved in retrospect perfectly designed to attract rodents and trash. Charming patios that were once washed clean by sunlight are now shaded, damp, and covered with mold.

Now the city has a decision to make. Will it pull the situation back to the right side of the space by allocating time and money to *re-organizing* the building? Or will it pull the situation in the opposite direction, to the lower-left corner, by tearing the building down and removing all connections—organized and self-organized—and starting over with a clean slate?

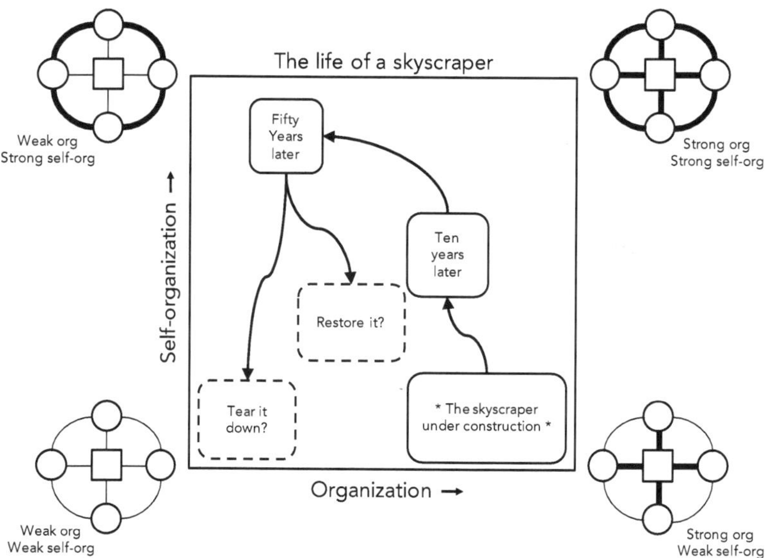


(Note that in this diagram, as in all of my diagrams that tell a story, the first situation is marked with asterisks, so you know where to start reading.)

### A beaver builds a dam

A young beaver is moving through the forest. It has recently left its birth home and is looking for a place to raise a family. As the beaver walks along, it hears water running through shallow streams. Where the sound of running water is loudest, the beaver begins to work. It pushes rocks, sticks, and mud into the stream. It chews through the trunks of small trees and anchors the cut tree trunks in the river bottom. All of these obstructions slow down the water flow as it approaches the dam. The leaves on the small trees provide food for the beaver, and the pond keeps them in cold storage under the water—which grows colder due to its increased depth.

Beavers build dams so they can escape from predators by diving under the water. When a beaver can find a building site next to deep water, it will build a burrow or lodge on the water's edge. But when a beaver can't find the conditions it needs, it will create them itself by building a dam.

Beaver dams are organized structures, though self-organization is involved in the form of instinct shaped by natural selection. The instinct to build where the water is loudest, for example, helps the beaver in two ways. First, streams are loudest where they are narrowest and shallowest, thus easiest to dam. Second, once the dam is built, the sound of running water is a sure sign of a leak.

But dam-building is not entirely instinctual. Beavers learn how to build better dams through imitation and experience. Young beavers watch older beavers build, and all beavers engage in a certain amount of site-specific problem solving as they shape their dams to suit the flow of water in each stream.

The impacts of a beaver dam on the surrounding forest are manifold. Sediment enters the pond with the incoming stream and is deposited, silting up the pond and reducing its utility as a cold storage facility. This can cause beavers to build extensions or additional dams over time. The water table under the dam changes, creating new water gradients that affect plant life for some distance around the pond. Impacts on fish populations are both positive and negative: water temperature is lowered, which increases oxygen content; but dams prevent movement through the stream. In fact, every species around a beaver dam is affected, from plants to invertebrates to birds to large mammals, and the impacts of these changes ripple out over a large area. This is why beavers are often called nature's engineers.

A beaver's decisions about its building site, materials, and methods are its own. It does not consult any local animals that may be living there. It simply makes the area inaccessible to them—or newly accessible to them, depending on the species. But as much as the beaver works to change the forest, the forest reacts in ways that change the beaver. A beaver dam requires constant monitoring and maintenance as self-organized forces encroach upon it. Deer walk across it; reeds grow through it; mice burrow into it; storms threaten it.

But the biggest force affecting beaver dams today is not self-organization. It is another source of organization: human habitation.

On our rural property we have a small pond. A beaver once tried to enlarge it. Unfortunately, the sound of running water leaving the pond did *not* mean that the stream was shallow. It meant that the pond emptied out through a culvert that ran under an old road. The beaver spent weeks trying to plug up the far end of the pipe with rocks, sticks, mud, and small trees, but nothing worked because the pipe emerged at the top of a hill. The beaver would have had to build up ten times as much material as it could collect to stop the water flow. Eventually it gave up and went off to look for a better site. I hope it survived.

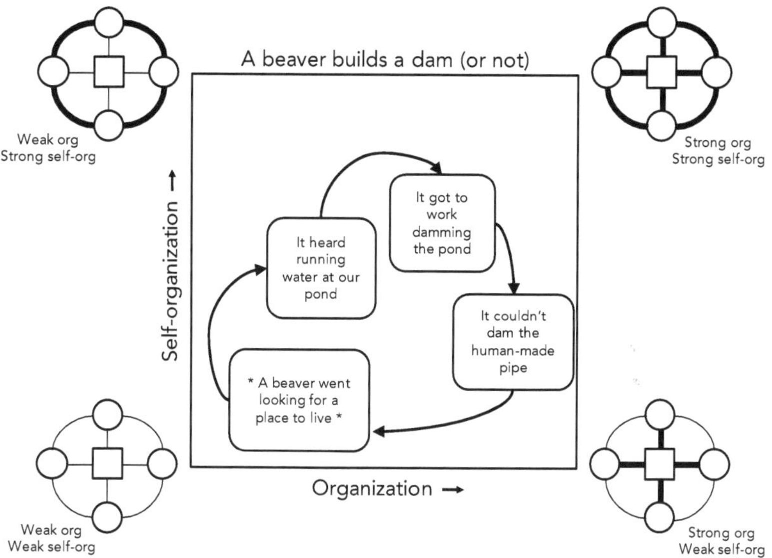


## Order and service in the medieval monastery

Medieval European monasteries were painstakingly designed to achieve perfect organization and to eradicate self-organization. The plentiful records they left behind show us that every moment of a monk's or nun's life was strictly regulated. Brothers and sisters in the monastic family were told when and where and how to sleep, eat, dress, speak, work, love, travel, fall ill, and die.[18] This was all done for a specific reason: to create an earthly model of the kingdom of heaven, which was believed to be perfectly ordered, with not a blade of grass out of place.

At the same time, however, monasteries were tasked with service to the community. They provided schools, infirmaries, orphanages, hostels, inns, nursing homes, laboratories, libraries, bakeries, baths, stables, farms, and eateries, all of which exposed the monastery to self-organizing forces. Even the fact that many well-to-do families chose one child to join the church meant that nearly every monk and nun had blood ties to the world outside the monastery's walls. Especially when such children came from powerful families, these connections had strong impacts on the way monasteries were run. Other connections were established when adult converts (especially widows and widowers) joined monasteries. And local lay people, servants and other workers, were employed or volunteered in monastery farms and workshops.

Possibly to counter these continual sources of worldly contamination, penalties for disturbing the monastic order were severe. However, the many tales of errant monks and nuns in *The Decameron* and other collections of tales show us that the mixture of organization and self-organization in the medieval monastery was deeply complex. As a result, cycles of secular involvement and isolationist reform passed in succession over the monastic world, and tensions between the ideals of purity and service were never completely resolved.

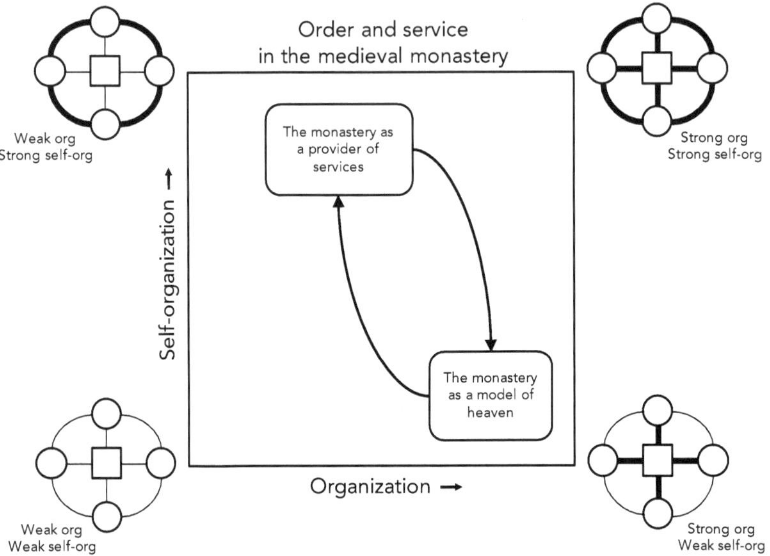


## A SELF-SUSTAINING TRAFFIC JAM

One day, about twenty years ago, I was driving to work. Just before I got to a curve in the road, I noticed that traffic was beginning to slow down.

*Oh boy,* I thought, *here we go again. Better switch to the local road at the next intersection.* I knew that to *get* to the local road at the next intersection, you had to turn left. So I worked my way into the left-turning lane.

A lot of other drivers had the same idea, and we all crammed ourselves into the left-turning lane, smug in our knowledge that we were smarter than the idiots inching past us on our right.

After a long wait, I finally arrived at the traffic light. I looked at the road ahead. It was empty. There *was* no traffic jam.

On that day I joined the ranks of the smart people who inched past the idiots turning left, creating the very traffic jam they were trying to avoid.

I have thought about that traffic jam many times over the past twenty years. It has such a fascinating blend of organized and self-organized elements in it.

Whoever designed that intersection must not have realized that they were setting up conditions under which a self-organized—and self-sustaining—pattern was bound to form. The curve in the road made it impossible for drivers to see the extent of the slowdown ahead of them, and the lack of access to a local road on the right side caused drivers avoiding the slowdown to pile up in the left-turning lane, causing the slowdown. As a result, small traffic jams kept forming and dissolving every day, probably for decades. There might be a traffic jam there right now.

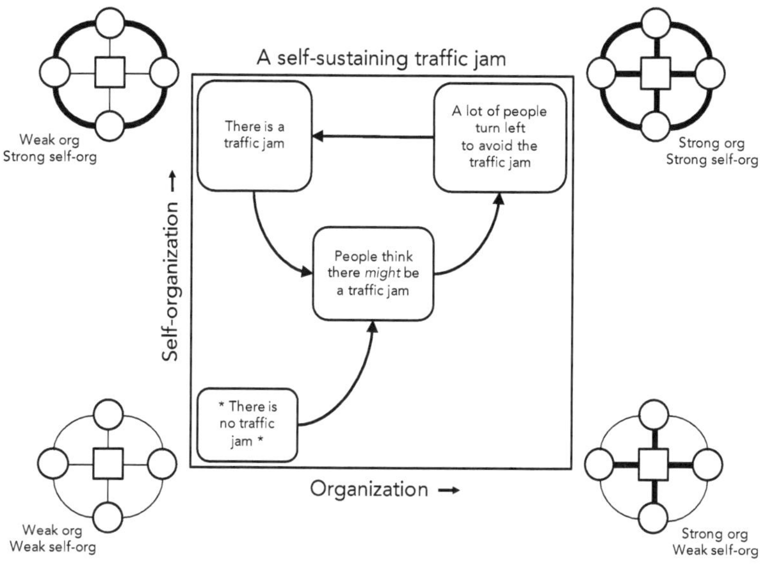


The pattern might have gone away if all the people who drove on that road saw what was happening and stopped trying to leave at the first sign of a slowdown. But membership on the road was too fluid to make that solution work. Drivers who learned their lesson, like I did, eventually moved away and were replaced by new drivers, who were doomed to repeat the same pattern several times before *they* realized what was causing it. With no way to communicate their insights to other drivers, enlightened drivers couldn't stop the pattern from forming.

How could an organizer, say the local government, have stopped that self-organized pattern from repeatedly forming? They could have accommodated people's instincts to get off the road by building a new local road to the right. They could have widened the left-turning lane so any jams that formed would dissipate more quickly. They could have added a temporary third lane so traffic could flow as people slowed down to consider their options.

Or they could have given people more information to work with. They could have put up a sign just before the curve with information about upcoming traffic. If drivers coming up to the curve saw a sign that said "traffic ahead is clear," they would be less likely to clog up the left-turning lane and cause a jam. Even a static sign explaining that turning left could cause traffic jams to form could have helped to stop the pattern before it got started.

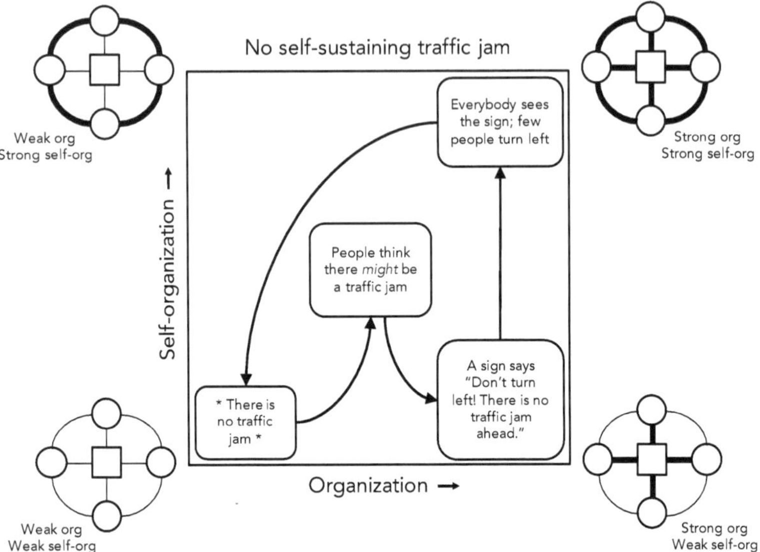


## Now you try it

So that's the confluence thinking space, and that's how you use it. You put situations into the space, and you think about what it means that you put them where you put them.

In the next chapter, I will tell you more about how you can use this space (and all of the spaces in this book) to think about situations that matter to you.

# 3 Using the Confluence Space

*An exercise in situational awareness*

In the previous chapter I introduced you to the confluence thinking space. Now I will show you an exercise that uses it (or any of the spaces in this book) to think about any set of situations.

## A thinking game

You can use a thinking space as a game, a lesson, a brainstorming session, or just a way to start a conversation. You can use it by yourself or in a group.

Thinking spaces always work better in groups. People think better when they think together. That doesn't mean you *can't* use a thinking space by yourself—I do it all the time—but it does mean you should at least *consider* asking other people to join you. If you are using the exercise by yourself, just *think* about each thing I say you should *talk* about in the instructions below.

Set aside at least an hour. You will need sticky notes, pens, and scissors. (You can also do this exercise online. See this chapter's end notes for details.)

### 1. Choose a topic

Agree on a subject you want to think about, like *resilience in our community* or *the way my career has been going* or *how our family communicates* or *equity in our workplace.* Describe your topic in a few words on a sticky note.

### 2. Choose a thinking space

What aspect of confluence do you want to think about? If you're not sure, use the main confluence space, as described on page 7. If you want to look more deeply into a particular aspect of confluence as it relates to your topic, choose a thinking space from the diagram on page 35.

### 3. Prepare your axis and/or corner labels

Look in the "Exercise Materials" appendix (page 263) and find the thinking space you chose. Do you see its axis and corner labels? You will use those to define your space. You can use both sets of labels (axes *and* corners) or just one.[1]

Photocopy the pages you need from the printed book, or download the materials from cfkurtz.com/confluence and print the pages you need, or copy the labels by hand. Cut them apart with scissors if necessary. Arrange them on a table or wall so they mark out a square roughly one meter tall and wide. Put the sticky note you wrote to describe your topic (in step one) above the space.[2]

### 4. Familiarize yourself with the space

If you are using this thinking space for the first time, take some time to get to know it. Look in the exercise materials and find its *example situations* and *proverbs*. Photocopy or print them and cut them apart, or write them on sticky notes. Then place them, one by one, into your thinking space where they seem to belong. Talk about *why* you put each situation or proverb where you put it. There are no right or wrong answers, just things to think about.[3]

### 5. Choose a time frame

Decide whether you want to look back over the past, consider the present moment, or imagine the future. Write your choice on a sticky note ("In the past," "Right now," "In the future"), and put it under the note that describes your topic.

### 6. Think of some situations

Sit quietly (each person alone) and think of some situations that relate to your topic and time frame. Use these questions to help you think.

| Past | Present | Future |
|---|---|---|
| What are some moments that stand out in your memory because they were especially *connected* or *relevant* to this topic? What happened in those moments? | *What's on your mind* right now with respect to this topic? What are some situations you are hopeful, confused, or concerned about? | With respect to this topic, what are some situations that could, could not, should, or should not happen in the future? What do you *wish* would happen? What do you *dread* happening? |

Summarize each situation you think of in a few words on a sticky note. Write down two or three situations (each) before you stop.[4]

### 7. Tell each other about the situations

When everyone has written down a few situations, take turns telling each other about them. Keep doing this—thinking of situations, writing them down, telling each other about them—until you have collectively described *at least twenty situations* related to your topic and time frame. (Thirty is better.)

### 8. Place the situations into the space

Now put all of your 20+ situation sticky notes into one pile.[5] Then place them, one by one, into the thinking space you created earlier. Place each note where it seems to belong. *Talk* about what you are doing. Decide where to place each situation together.

### 9. Look for patterns

After you have placed all of your situations into the space, you should start to see some patterns. These are some types of patterns you might see.

- ***Clusters*** are groups of situations you placed near each other that *seem to belong together* for some reason. You can always tell when you've found a cluster, because you can give it a *theme* that can stand in for the whole group of situations. It might be something like "when we have trust, everything works" or "in a crisis, we use whatever we can." Where do the situations on your space clump together?
- ***Gaps*** are spots where you placed few or no situations. When you find a gap, ask yourself *why* you didn't place any situations there. Could you be avoiding an issue? Or is that area not relevant to your topic? Why is that?
- ***Boundaries*** are dividing lines between areas in which situations seem to be *meaningfully different* from each other. Situations on opposite sides of a boundary might involve different people, places, perspectives, issues, or outcomes. If you *had* to divide up your space based on the situations you placed on it, where would you draw dividing lines? What would lie on either side of them? And what would that mean?
- ***Links*** are situations or clusters that connect through *lines of similarity* across the space, even though you didn't place them close together. For example, there might be two distinct areas in which problems are pressing or solutions are promising, but for different reasons.
- ***Contrasts*** are situations or clusters that connect through *lines of opposition* across the space. For example, one area might be filled with stable situations while another is volatile. What interesting or useful contrasts can you see between situations on the space?

You won't find patterns of every type in every space, but you are likely to find at least one of these types of patterns in every space. Describe the patterns you find (and what you think they might mean) using other sticky notes (in a different color, or circled, or written in ALL CAPS).[6]

### 10. Wrap up the exercise

When you are done finding and discussing patterns, it is time to bring the exercise to a close. Write these list names on sticky notes.

| I was **surprised** to see that . . . | I am **curious** about . . . | Here's an **idea** we could try . . . |
|---|---|---|

Now sit quietly (each person alone) and write down *at least one item for each of the three lists* based on the experience you just had. When everyone is ready, talk about what you wrote.[7]

## A FICTIONAL WALK-THROUGH

I wanted to give you an example of how this exercise plays out in practice. But though I have helped many groups use it, their stories are not mine to tell. So I decided to write a representative yet fictional story to show you what usually happens when people do the exercise.[8]

Imagine a group of managers at a small manufacturing firm. Let's call it FictCo. One day these managers decided to spend some time thinking about how FictCo could work better for all of its employees. First they agreed on a topic: "Working at FictCo: What it's *really* like." Then they chose their time frame: the recent past. Then they started thinking of situations. These are some of the situations they told each other about.[9]

- I will never forget the day I came into the building for the first time. Every single person there shook my hand. I was like—are these people strange, or what? It was only later I found out that new employees are always welcomed in that way. It's not an official policy or anything, but people around here just do that. Now I do it myself. What a wonderful way to start things out. It shows who we are.
- Why do they have those speed bumps in the parking lot? Do they think we will crash our cars? And at the same time they expect us to work long hours and do amazing things. These contradictory messages are demoralizing.
- You know what I'm proud of? I broke a machine. We got this new machine, and right away I could see that something was wrong with it. It was a tiny thing, but I knew what it would do once the machine got up to speed. I told the foreman, but he wouldn't listen. He didn't think the tiny thing mattered. So I broke something *else* on the machine, something *anyone* could see was broken. We had to send the machine back. A few months later, the foreman admitted that I probably prevented an accident.
- I used to be in this group that walked after lunch. There were maybe ten of us. People would see us and ask to join in. It was great for a few months, but then people started disappearing. I ran into one of the people yesterday, and I was like, hey, why don't you walk after lunch anymore? It's a great way to restart your brain before you go back to work. He was like, oh, my boss had a little talk with me. He said I could only walk after lunch if I stayed half an hour late. I have kids, you know, and I can't stay late. Wish I could. That's what he said.
- Have you heard of quality symptoms diagramming? No? You should look it up. I found it on the internet. We've been using it for months. Oh, no, of *course* we don't put it on our reports. We're not that stupid! If they found out we were using it to keep our quality high, we'd never hear the end of it. So we do both things: the thing they make us do, and the thing that works. Our work process is better, our numbers are up, and they leave us alone.

As the managers were talking through these situations, they noticed that some were more positive than others. So they started writing positive and negative situations on different colors of sticky notes. Once they got up to twenty situations, they put them into the space. It looked like this.

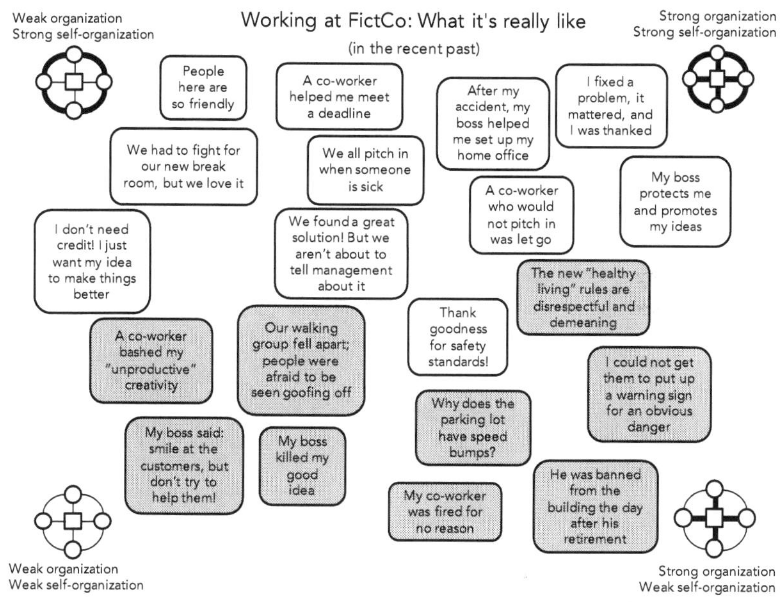


The first pattern they noticed was a *boundary*. The positive situations were closer to the top. "Self-organization is holding us together," they said.

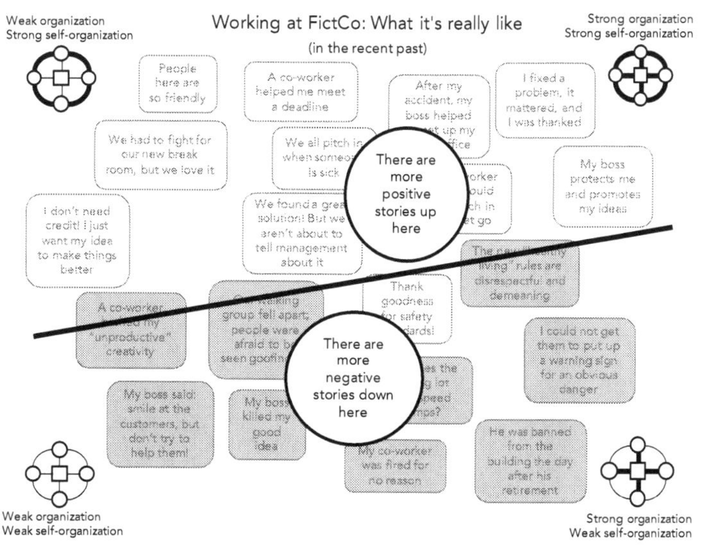

Next they noticed four *clusters*, each of which represented a different view of the company. All four views were worth exploring, they decided, but only the two on the top were helpful, at least as things stood.

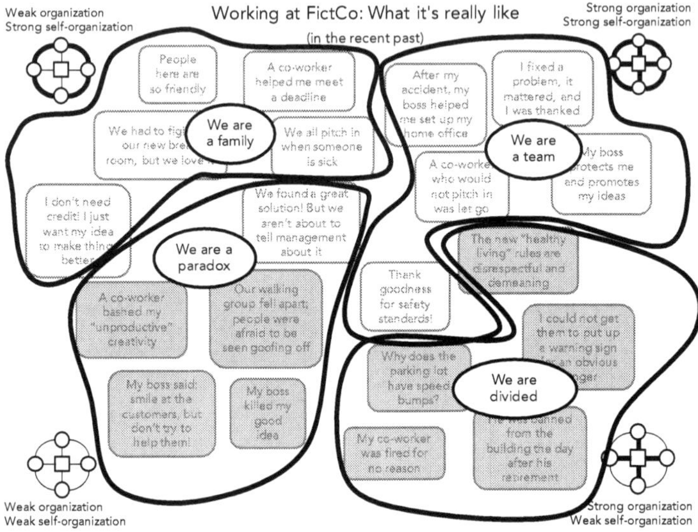


Then they noticed a *contrast* between managers. It seemed that whether people worked with or against each other had a lot to do with the behavior of whoever was in charge. That led them to notice a *link* between solidarity *among* the workers and solidarity *against* the rules. The two forms of solidarity seemed to reinforce each other.

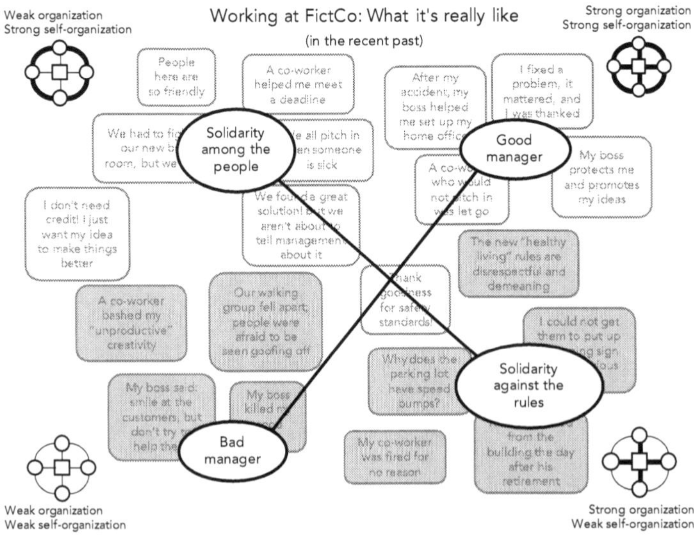

All of these patterns gave the managers much to discuss, and discuss they did. Finally they wrapped up the exercise by making some lists.

| I was **surprised** to see that . . . | I am **curious** about . . . | Here's an **idea** we could try . . . |
|---|---|---|
| Self-organization is keeping us together! | What this picture would look like from *other* points of view | Teamwork awards? |
| Who your boss is makes so much of a difference | Why people don't like the healthy-living program | Ask about the speed bumps? |
| It's so hard to change our safety rules | Where the shaking-hands ritual came from | Start a sanctioned walking program? |

The managers decided that a good next step would be to gather more situation descriptions from a wider variety of people. Each of them chose a different part of the company to visit. One said they'd go and see the people in charge of safety. Another wanted to talk to some of the oldest and newest employees of the company. A third planned to visit the famous new break room. The managers planned to reconvene in a month to see what they could learn from a broader range of perspectives.

## Obstacles you might get stuck on

These are some problems you might encounter while doing this exercise, along with some solutions that work to fix them.

**We don't see any patterns in our situations.**

Finding few or no patterns usually means your *coverage* of the topic is weak. Any of these issues can cause the problem.

- ***Volume***. You might just need more situations. If you have twenty situations and you can't see any patterns in them, think of ten more. If that doesn't work, think of ten more again. Give yourselves more material to explore.[10]
- ***Focus***. If your topic is too broad or vague, your situations will be too generic. Define your topic more precisely. Put aside any situations that don't match the new topic. Think of some more situations that do.
- ***Interest***. If your topic is not important to everyone in the group, your situations might be dull and featureless. Refine your topic until everyone is eager to talk about it. Use the new topic to think of more situations.
- ***Experience***. Maybe you don't know as much about the topic as you thought you did. You could learn more about it and come back to the exercise. Or you could see if you can get some more knowledgeable people to join you.
- ***Openness***. You could be dancing around an issue that you aren't ready to talk about. If you think that's the case, you can choose a different, safer topic. Or you can talk about what will help you open up your discussion. Maybe you need to break up into smaller groups, or set up some ground rules about what can and cannot be said.

- ***Understanding.*** If you aren't all thinking about the space in the same way, you won't be able to reach consensus on where situations belong in it. Talk about the space and what it means. Then see if you feel like moving any of your situations around, or if you think of any new situations to place.

Patterns always appear when you have addressed a topic with enough volume, focus, interest, experience, openness, and understanding. So if you don't see patterns, talk about these issues, then try again.

Anytime you get stuck doing this exercise, it will help to put it aside for an hour or a day. Stop for lunch or take a walk. This sort of reflective work always flows better when you can pause to contemplate the topic in other ways, then come back with a fresh perspective.

**We can't decide where to place a situation.**

Put it aside, then come back to it after you have placed some other situations into the space. You can *use the situations you have already placed* to think about where new situations belong. Ask yourself, "Does this situation belong above or below this other one? Does it belong to its right or left?"

You can also *move* situations you have already placed as you consider them in the light of new additions to the space. Sometimes a new situation will shift your perceptions of those around it.[11] Remember that it is the *overall pattern* of placements that matters, not whether each individual placement is perfect.

**We found a situation that could belong in more than one spot.**

Then put it in more than one spot—by copying it onto multiple notes. On each note, write specific details of the situation you want to consider. For example, you might add a *perspective* on the situation ("the traffic jam from a tourist's point of view") or a *cause* ("the game crowd flowed into the commuting crowd") or an *outcome* ("a traffic jam might affect work productivity").

**Should we start by drawing dividing lines on the space?**

No. Don't do that. Use the empty space as a *gradient*, not a set of boxes. You will get much more out of the exercise if you avoid drawing lines on the space until *after* you have placed all of your situations on it.

If you find yourself dividing the space—into quadrants, for example—ask yourself: *on a scale of one to ten*, how much organization (or strength, effort, etc.) do you see in this situation? If you ask that question for each axis, you've made a hundred boxes, and a hundred boxes are almost as good as no boxes at all.

**We are placing situations and we thought of another one.**

That's a wonderful problem to have. More situations means stronger patterns. Whoever thought of the situation: tell everyone about it, give it a name, write the name on a new note, and stick the note on the space where you think it belongs. (Just watch your time.)

**Only some people are placing situations.**

Ideally, your entire group should place each situation into the space together, talking about it as they do so. However, that doesn't always work. Sometimes one or two people end up doing all the placement because everyone else is confused or bored or intimidated.

If you see this starting to happen, use this workaround. Have each person *annotate* their situation notes with answers to two sliding-scale questions. For example: "On a scale from one to ten, how strong were the organized plans in this situation? How strong were the self-organized patterns?" Then *use the answers to place the notes* into the space. Talking about each note is better; but if that's not working, this will.[12]

## More things you can do

These are some optional things you can do to bring out even more interesting patterns. You might want to put these aside until you have done the exercise a few times. When you are ready for them, give them a try.

### To explore your topic more fully

#### Annotate the space

Build your thinking space on a large piece of paper. After you have placed your situations, use pens and markers to mark the patterns you see and to record your thoughts about them.

#### Add a third dimension

Answer a question about each situation that adds a height dimension to your space. Mark your answers using different colors of sticky notes or a consistent scheme of letters or numbers. You can answer the question as you write the situations, or you can add it later on. Here are some useful third dimensions.

- ***Value***. Is this a positive situation? Are things going well in it? Or is this an undesirable state of affairs? Or is it somewhere in between? (The managers in my fictional case study chose this option.)
- ***Stability***. Is this situation volatile and likely to change quickly? Or is it likely to stay this way for a long time?
- ***Behavior***. Did the people in this situation behave responsibly or irresponsibly? Or focus on a specific role: Did the doctor or parent or employee in this situation behave responsibly?
- ***Clarity***. Was this situation easy to place in the space, or was it hard? Did the note immediately jump to the right location, or did you only manage to place it after a lot of time and thought?
- ***Consensus***. To what extent does everyone in the group agree that this situation belongs where you put it? Is there a complete consensus that it belongs there, or did some people have misgivings? What about people outside the group? Would they agree that it belongs there?

There are many other questions you could use as a third dimension; these are just a few ideas. After you have annotated your situations, look for patterns in your third dimension. Do you see peaks and valleys? Do you see ridges and troughs? What do you think they mean?

### Create a timeline

For this option, lay out your thinking space on a big piece of paper. Think of situations as usual, but before you place any of your situations into the space, *spread them out in a line* in the order they took place (or *might* take place in the future). Write numbers on them to record the order you put them in.

When that's done, pick up the situations and put them into your thinking space where they seem to belong. Once you have placed the situations, *draw arrows* on the paper from each situation to the next, in order, so they make a timeline moving across the space. What do you see?

### Build a model

In some of the later chapters of this book, I develop abstract models using these thinking spaces. You can do that too. After you have considered all of the situations you thought of during the exercise, build a representation of "the way things are" (or were, or could be, or should never be) in relation to your topic. What does your model show you? What did you learn while building it?

## To widen the scope of your imagination

### Split into multiple groups

Don't do the exercise in one group. Split up into two or more groups (even if each "group" has only one person in it). When you are finished, show each other what you found out, and talk about it.

### Turn your notes

Square sticky notes lend themselves better to using pre-established categories of classification than to developing emergent clusters of similarity. But *diamond* sticky notes cluster pretty well. So if you notice that your clusters keep ending up as fixed categories, try *turning* your notes by forty-five degrees.

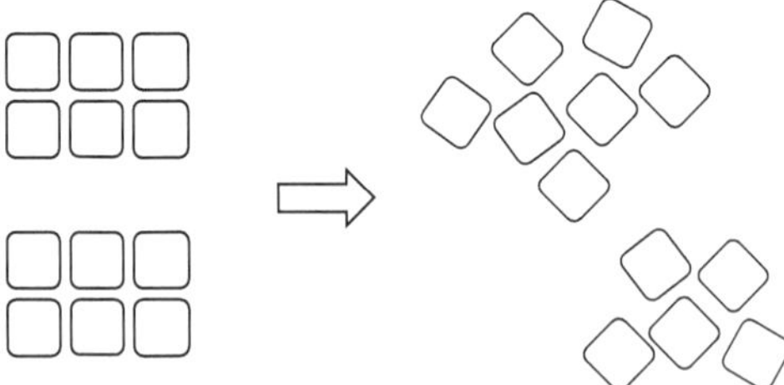

Choose a side where the sticky part will face (up and to the left works well), and turn each note before you write it. Remembering to turn your notes adds difficulty to the task, but after you have learned how to use a thinking space, you can try this tweak to improve your results.

### Consider multiple perspectives

You can use this exercise to step outside your own viewpoint and consider how other people see the topic you are exploring. Choose a person or group whose perspective you want to consider. Describe some situations from *their* point of view. Better yet, find some situation descriptions in their own words. Look for interviews, speeches, or other communications where they have described situations related to your topic. Find at least twenty such descriptions. Summarize each description on a sticky note. Place it into the thinking space *where you think that person or group would put it* if they were doing the exercise. Then look for patterns.

If you have enough people, you can ask each small group to explore a *different* perspective. Say your topic is "Revitalizing our town center." One group might consider how business owners see the situation, while another looks at the perspective of longtime residents, and a third group thinks about new residents or tourists. You can ask all of the groups to start with the same situations (and vary only in their placements), or you can have each group come up with their own situations, or you can combine the two approaches. Once each group has placed their situations and discovered some patterns, come back together as one group and look for patterns *across* the spaces.

### Consider multiple aspects

Another way to think more broadly about situations is to look at them from different angles, as you would turn a gem to look at its many facets. For example, you could list, for each situation:

- ***Elements***. What made up the situation in a *literal* sense? List the individual people, and groups of people, involved. What sorts of structures or objects were important to the situation? How about rules or procedures? Write a series of sticky notes that lay out the elements of the situation, then place each one into your thinking space. For each note, consider how the situation looks *when you consider only that element*, putting aside all others.
- ***Influences***. What forces were at play in the situation? What pushed it this way or that way? Was it affected by hopes, fears, expectations, stereotypes, confusions, miscommunications, rumors? How does the situation look when you consider *only that one influence?*
- ***Consequences***. How does the situation *affect* you? How does it expand or constrain your options? Place each note by considering *only that one consequence* of the situation.

These are just a few ideas for ways you can expand your situations into multiple aspects. You can probably come up with some more ideas of your own.

### Consider change

After you have placed each situation on the space, think about how it could change (or change further) in the future. If the situation changed for the better, where on the space would it move to? Draw an arrow on its note in that direction. What if it changed for the worse? Draw a second arrow in a different color. When you have done this for all of your situations, step back and look for patterns in the arrows you have drawn. What do they show you?

### Tell stories

In the basic instructions above, I said you should *think of situations* to place into your thinking space. Another option is to *tell stories.*

Every story has multiple situations inside it. For example, the situation at the beginning of a story is likely to be different than the situation at the end. So when you do this exercise, instead of thinking of situations, you can tell stories, then list the situations you see inside of each story.

Why didn't I say to tell stories in the basic instructions? Because when you ask people to tell *stories,* they tend to think of *interesting* or *entertaining* stories to tell. Those kinds of stories aren't very helpful in this exercise. Instead, you need *relevant* stories, which are not always interesting or entertaining. Using the word "situation" instead of "story" takes the emphasis away from performance and places it on reflection.

However, once you have done the exercise a few times, and you understand what sorts of stories you need to tell, you can draw your situations out of stories instead of listing them directly.

### Consider fiction

Another option is to explore a fictional scenario. Set it up *before* you start thinking of situations. Here are some ways to find scenarios you can explore.

- ***Assumptions.*** List everything you take for granted about your topic, like "it rarely floods in our area" or "people need the product we sell." Choose one assumption to break. Think of situations that could happen if that assumption was no longer valid. (Or have each small group break a different assumption.)
- ***Alterations.*** Think of a specific change that could have affected the present situation, like "if the war had never happened" or "if a different mayor had been elected." Imagine some situations that could have happened (or could be happening right now) in that altered reality.
- ***Extremes.*** Make up some situations that could happen in a perfectly utopian or horribly dystopian future. Or consider both extremes.

Go through the exercise *as if* the scenario you chose was actually happening. Then talk about what you discovered. By moving out of reality and into fiction, you can change the patterns you see and the insights you discover.

## To explore your topic in even greater depth

### Use another thinking space

After you have thought about your topic using one thinking space, you can go through the exercise again with a different space. For example, say you used the confluence space, and you found yourself focusing on the upper-right corner, where organization and self-organization are both strong. You might want to go through the exercise again with the "Mix" thinking space (page 143). Or if situations kept coming up in which people said other people were lying, you might want to use the "Connecting the dots" space (page 195).

You can use the same situations again (copy your sticky notes), think of new situations, or do both (reuse some situations and think of some new ones).

### Use all of the thinking spaces

If the topic you want to ponder is very important to you, or if you want to learn to use this whole book, explore the same topic with all seven spaces. Use every tool in the toolbox. Start with the first space, then work your way through all of them, in whatever order suggests itself to you.

### Use your own terms and images

As I have developed these thinking spaces, axes, and diagrams, I have tried to use terms and images that I think will be useful and understandable to everyone. You are not everyone. After you have been working with the spaces for a while, you might find that other terms or images work better for you—or for your family, community, or organization. I invite you to *translate* my terms and images into ones that work better for you.

### Create your own thinking spaces

You can move beyond the thinking spaces in this book by building your own. Start by gathering a working group of at least three people who have plenty of experience in the area you want to think about. Commit to spending at least twenty hours (each) on the project. You are going to be building something you may use for decades, so be prepared to take your time and get it right.

#### *Dive into your experiences*

Begin by asking each person to remember and recount several stories from their experiences related to the overall subject you want to address. You can use the questions on page 20 to get stories flowing. If someone tells a story and it reminds someone else of another story, that's great—let the stories flow. Give yourself plenty of time to talk, at least two hours.

As each person finishes telling each story, ask them to *think of three situations* that were important to the story, things like, "people trusted each other" or "it began to rain." Ask them to summarize the situations on sticky notes. Keep piling up sticky notes until you feel that you have covered the subject well.

Now look at your situation sticky notes. What *varies* across the situations? What is there in them that is sometimes more present and sometimes less present? List every potential axis of variation you can think of.

#### *Remove value-laden axes*

Next, go through your list of potential axes and discard any axes that contain evaluations of value. If situations on one side of the axis are consistently more or less positive or desirable than situations on the other side—from any perspective—remove the axis from your list. When people use a thinking space, they must be able to negotiate value on a *third* axis, as the height of the landscape they are building. A thinking space that embeds value into either of its space-defining axes prevents people from using it effectively.

***Test your axes***

Once you feel like you have arrived at a good set of potential axes, *test* each one by drawing it along a table or wall and placing your situation notes along it. (You can also do this on a computer screen.) How much does the placement of situations on the line tell you? A lot? Or a little? How *useful* does the axis seem to you? Try this with every axis on your list (copy or reuse your situation notes). Which axes tell you the most?

If you feel like you don't have enough potential axes to choose from, pump some more stories into the process. Have everyone tell a few *more* stories, find a few more situations in each story, and look for more axes of variation. (You might also find it useful to *pause* your work, let a day or two go by, and see if more stories and situations come to mind.)

You can use one good axis to find another one. Draw your good axis along a wall or table (or on a computer screen), and place your situations along it. Then think about how your situations seem inclined to "rise up" or "fall down" into a second dimension. List each potential second dimension, then rank them. Again, watch out for value-laden axes.

***Evaluate axis pairs***

At some point you should arrive at a small number of good axes, say six or eight. Now start looking for good axis *pairs*.

The two axes that make up a thinking space must be *independent*. Knowing an item's placement on one axis must not tell you anything about its placement on the other. If the axes are connected, any patterns that appear in the space will be correlated, and that will make it harder to discover surprising insights.

Think of all the independent axis pairings you can. Write each pair as the X and Y axes of big empty spaces on big sheets of paper (or big empty spaces on your computer screen). Then gaze into each space, let your minds go receptively blank, and *wait for situations to come to mind*. When somebody says, "Hey, I know what would fit here," or "This reminds me of the time," write the situation on a sticky note and put it in the space.

Keep doing this. Use your thoughts to evaluate the generative potential of each thinking space. The axes, and axis pairs, that bring the most plentiful and diverse situations to mind are the best ones to keep.

## Use other methods and frameworks

I wrote this book because some people have told me that this way of thinking about situations has been useful to them. But I am fairly sure that it will not be equally useful to everyone. I think this is true for *every* thinking method or mental framework, whether its creators admit it or not. Every mind has its methods, and every method has its minds. Our diverse minds work best when they can work with a corresponding diversity of methods.

Each of the following methods and frameworks has the potential to be useful to your thinking about how organization and self-organization flow together. If you search the internet for any of these terms, you are likely to find ideas you can use.

- The American Indian Medicine Wheel[13]
- The Chinese Five Elements
- The Tipu Ake ki te Ora Maori Organic Leadership model
- The Yin-Yang symbol[14]
- Jurgen Appelo's simplicity model
- Robert Freed Bales' dimensions of social interaction (power, safety, utility)
- Stafford Beer's Viable Systems Model
- Manuel de Landa's concepts of hierarchy and meshwork
- Emery and Trist's Causal Textures model
- Dan Epp's Relational Paradigm
- Tom Graves' Context-Space Mapping
- Dee Hock's writings on Chaordic systems
- Luc Hoebeke's Work Systems Model
- Claes Janssen's Four Rooms of Change model
- Iain McGilchrist's writings on right and left-hemisphere perspectives
- Will McWhinney's Paths of Change model
- Olson and Gorall's Circumplex model of marital and family systems
- Sarbo, Farkas, and van Breemen's Knowledge in Formation theory
- Herbert Simon's theory of bounded rationality
- Dave Snowden's Cynefin framework
- Ralph Stacey's Agreement & Certainty Matrix
- Strum and Latour's social link model
- Harold van Garderen's SenseCanvas
- Harrison White's species of identity interaction

Most of these frameworks are lists of categories, not open spaces for mapping; but they are all useful in their own unique ways.[15]

You can use the diversity of these frameworks to increase the diversity of your own thought processes. Why not, for example, use the exercise described in this chapter to explore your topic with a different framework each month? What can you learn from looking at your topic through many different lenses?

# Part Two
## Six More Thinking Tools

There are seven thinking spaces in this book. The six remaining spaces fit inside the first one, like this.

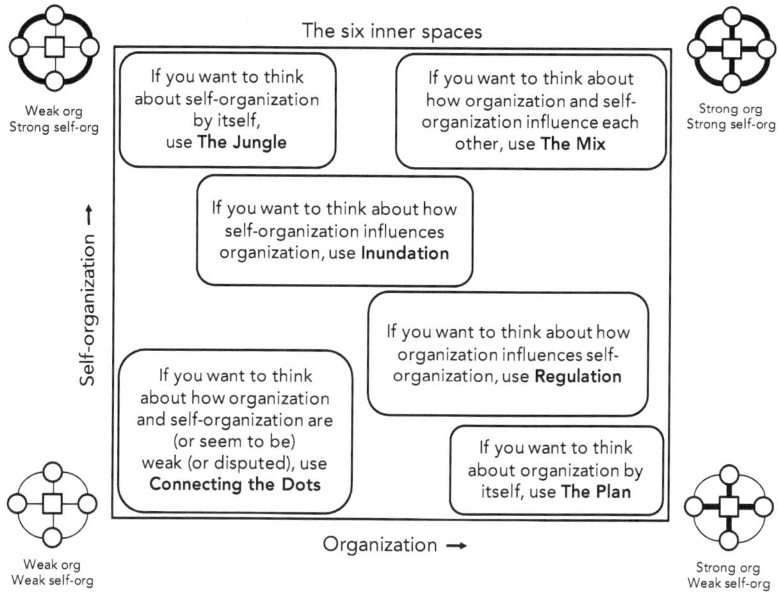

The six inner spaces
Weak org
Strong self-org
Strong org
Strong self-org
If you want to think about self-organization by itself, use The Jungle
If you want to think about how organization and self-organization influence each other, use The Mix
If you want to think about how self-organization influences organization, use Inundation
If you want to think about how organization influences self-organization, use Regulation
If you want to think about how organization and self-organization are (or seem to be) weak (or disputed), use Connecting the Dots
If you want to think about organization by itself, use The Plan
Self-organization →
Organization →
Weak org
Weak self-org
Strong org
Weak self-org

Where did the seven spaces come from? It's simple. If you have two forces, A and B, you can look at either force alone (A, B), both forces intermingling (A+B) and interacting (AxB), neither force (O), and how each force pushes on the other (A on B, B on A). That's all there is to it.

Each of the following chapters introduces one thinking space and uses example situations to explore it. Each chapter stands on its own and can be read separately. However, if you're skimming, be aware that I arranged the chapters in order of increasing difficulty. The last chapters are the longest because the last spaces are the most difficult to use—and the easiest to use wrongly.

### About the chapter examples

As I worked on this book, I tried to choose examples that would best help you understand the spaces. I looked at each space and thought, "What are some examples that will help people explore this space?" And certain examples came quickly to mind.

At first I convinced myself that I chose my examples solely based on their objective potential to help you understand the spaces. After all, I put aside many more examples than I used. But eventually I realized that the objective potential of each example was only *one* of the factors that influenced my choice. My own interests and personality played a part as well.

That's not to say the examples I chose aren't useful to explain the spaces. They are. But they are not the most useful of *all* possible examples. They are the most useful of the examples *I* like to think about. To my surprise, the book turned out to be somewhat autobiographical.

As a result, some parts of the chapters that follow read less like instructions for improving your situational awareness and more like digressions into my various nerdy obsessions. I tried to describe multiple points of view on each topic, and I trimmed back many of the hey-look-at-this sections I couldn't help but write. But like everyone else, I have my own point of view, and I find it hard to shut up about the things I like to think about.

In fact, I think I can guarantee that at least one section of this book will bore you or even annoy you—though by the same logic, at least one section is bound to interest or even fascinate you. (Each of the readers who sent me early feedback on the book liked a different part best.)

Is this a problem? No, not at all. In fact, it's the opposite of a problem. It means the spaces are working as they should. A thinking tool *should* tell you as much about yourself as it tells you about the topics you are exploring. The fact that you can see me in my examples means that when *you* look into these spaces, *you will see yourself* in the examples that spring to mind for you. And if you are using the spaces in a group of people, *you will see each other* in the examples that spring to mind for each of you.

## We are the situation

People often describe situational awareness as knowing "where you are," but that's only half of the picture. Knowing *who* you are is at least as important, because *your own mind is part of the situation you are facing,* as are the minds of those around you. If you don't understand every relevant perspective, your situational awareness will be incomplete.

Remember that when you use these spaces. If you see someone put a situation in a different place than you would have put it, don't rush to correct them; think about what you learned from what you saw.

And if—no, when—you disagree with the way I have placed any of the situations I describe in this book, that's a good sign! It means you are using the spaces along with me. I invite you to *redraw each of my diagrams* the way *you* think it should be drawn.

Also, if any of my examples don't resonate with you, come up with your own examples, and place them on the spaces in ways that make sense to you. You might even want to fill up a notebook with diagrams as you read. That's what this book is for: *to help you practice* using the spaces.

# 4 The Jungle

*Thinking about self-organization*

Picture yourself in a dense jungle, machete in hand. The path to the next village has grown over again, and it's your job to clear the way. As you survey the task before you, two questions rise to your mind. Which of these vines is strongest? And which will grow back first?

Picture yourself in the midst of a demonstration, arms locked with fellow protesters, ready to protect vulnerable people from a ruthless dictator. As you watch the army approach, two questions rise to your mind. Who will hold on tightest? And who will stand back up first?

Whether you want to destroy or promote a self-organized pattern, the *strength* and *resilience* of its connections matter. We can create a thinking space that combines these two dimensions. Here connection strength (the outside, obvious line) increases from left to right, and resilience (the inside, hidden line) increases from bottom to top.

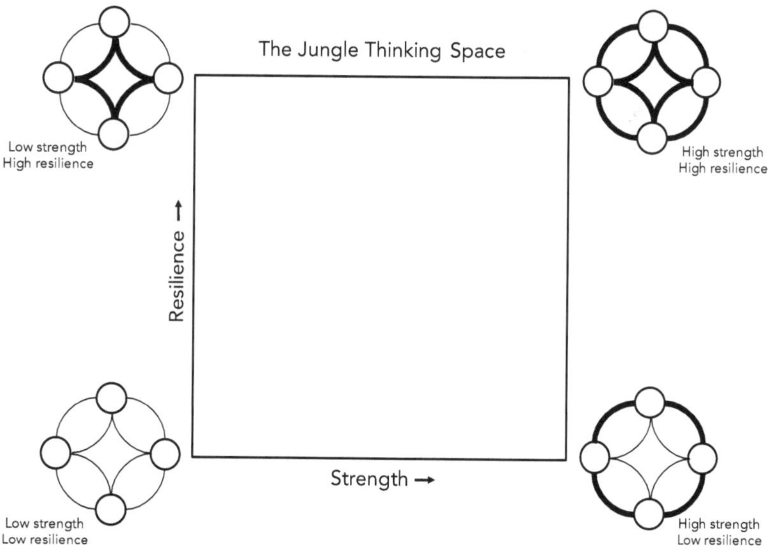


Before we start looking at the corners of this space, let's take a moment to think about what lies *outside* it.

Self-organized patterns depend on moderate amounts of *interaction* and *iteration*. When things are too tightly coupled to move around, or too spread out to encounter each other, they cannot form patterns. When things get stuck together on their very first encounter, or when things snap back to their previous positions after every interaction, they cannot form patterns. It's only in the sweet spot where patterns can form, dissolve, and reform that self-organization has a chance to develop.

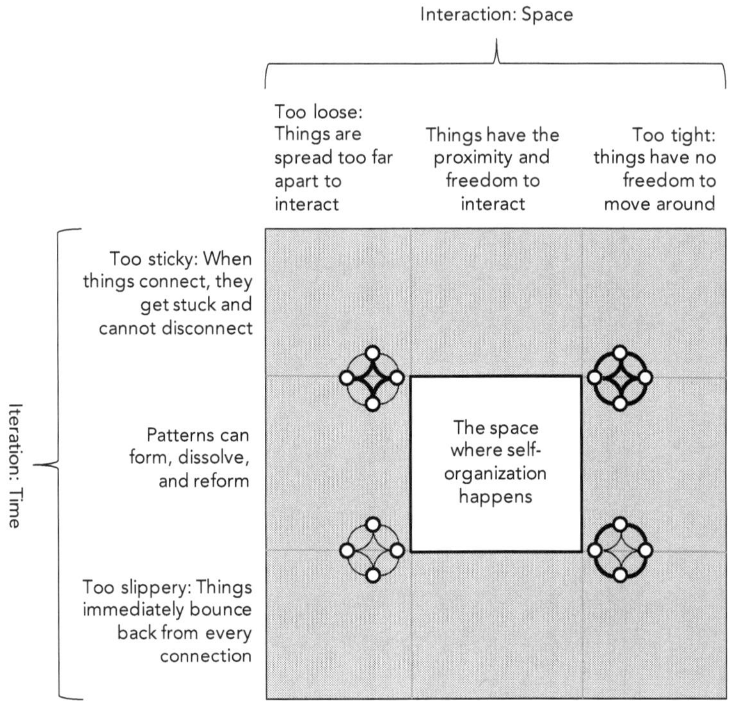
Interaction: Space
Too loose: Things are spread too far apart to interact
Things have the proximity and freedom to interact
Too tight: things have no freedom to move around
Iteration: Time
Too sticky: When things connect, they get stuck and cannot disconnect
Patterns can form, dissolve, and reform
Too slippery: Things immediately bounce back from every connection
The space where self-organization happens

Within this sweet spot, connection strength relates primarily to interaction. Resilience, which is a response to change, relates primarily to iteration.

You may be wondering what I mean by connection strength. Those who study self-organized networks talk about *tie strength* (how hard it is to break connections), *tie density* (how many connections each network member has), *multiplexity* (how many different types of connections exist), and *network closure* (whether A being connected to B and C leads B and C to become connected). Let's lump all of those measures together into a general sense of how tightly a self-organized network is held together.[1]

To better understand connection strength, picture three different visits to the countryside. On your first trip, you stand in a farm field watching a dense flock of starlings wheel and turn overhead in perfect unison. It's amazing how the birds seem to share one mind.

On your second trip, you travel to the ocean shore and watch seagulls. These birds behave very differently from those you saw before. They still pay attention to each other, but their movements are more individual and less coordinated. In fact, one particular bird seems a lot more interested in you and what you have to eat than what the rest of the seagulls are doing.

On your third trip, you sit beside a lake watching a solitary hawk perch on a high branch, paying no attention to the activities of its neighbors miles away (as long as they *stay* miles away). Connection strength is highest in the starling flock, lower among the seagulls, and lowest for the hawk.

By the way, have you noticed what is *missing* in the four corner diagrams of this thinking space? Something we talked about in the second chapter? That's right, there's no organizer in this chapter. We can't turn off the organization in our lives, but we can *turn our attention* away from it, for a while and for a reason. Let's do that now.

## The jungle (self-organized) thinking space

Now let's go around the space and think about some of the places on it.

### Weak, fragile connections

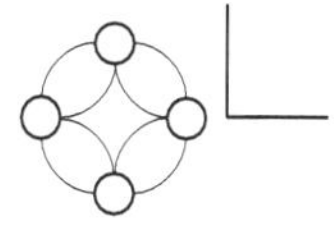

In the lower-left corner of the self-organized space, connections are both weak and fragile. This is like a newly planted garden, right? You prepare your soil, plant your seeds, and wait for the weak connections you have created—among seeds, soil, moisture, and warmth—to grow stronger. Right?

Sure, that's what a newly planted garden *looks* like. But what you *can't* see are all the *other* connections: among *weed* seeds, soil, moisture, and warmth; between mice and seeds; between fungus and seeds; between cats and . . . what cats use garden beds for. Some of those other connections might be stronger and more resilient than the connections you are trying to create.

Experienced gardeners know that no garden can ever be a blank slate, and that the things they want to grow will always be mixed in with a lot of other things they didn't want to grow. That's the biggest danger we face when we think we are in the weak, fragile corner of the self-organized space: we might not be as close to the corner as we seem to be.

#### An accidental garden

Three summers ago, I planted some sunflower seeds in my garden. Because "my garden" is actually just several of those half-barrel planters sitting on the grass, I had a lot of seeds left over in the packet, so I scattered them around for the mice to eat. I had a wonderful garden that year: tomatoes, beans, cucumbers, arugula, spinach, and several very nice sunflowers.

The next year, a few weeks after planting my garden, I noticed some strange plants growing nearby. I had no idea what they were, so I waited to see. By the time I figured out that they were the sunflower seeds I had discarded the previous year, they were shoulder-high and as strong as little trees. Eventually my garden was transformed into a four-meter-high thicket of sunflowers. I searched for the vegetables I had planted, but I couldn't find them.

I thought this was funny. I took pictures of it. I left the sunflowers alone. After all, they had been marked as annuals on the seed packet.

The next spring they came back. This time I knew what they were right away, and I was no longer amused. Three times I rampaged through the growing sunflowers, cutting and pulling, but they kept on coming, and the fourth wave covered up my garden all over again. I got a few cucumbers out of the garden that year, but that was about it.

The next year I moved my planters and conceded the space to the sunflowers. They had earned my respect, and I looked forward to having them as neighbors. In fact, I regretted our conflict, and I was a little worried they might not come up again. But they did, and I was glad to see it.

The whole thing reminds me of something my husband said he learned from growing things in an aquarium. He said that if you try to grow something *specific* in an aquarium, you are going to have to work very hard to get it. But if you set out to grow something *interesting*, it's almost impossible to fail.

**Pioneer species and personalities**

Some species of plants, called pioneers, thrive specifically in weak, fragile environments. For example, some seeds can only germinate after they have been through a fire. It seems a strange requirement—to be baked before you can live—but there is a good reason for it. After a fire there are few competitors, for a while anyway, and seedlings that develop at such a time face little opposition when it comes to gathering food from sunlight.

Just as there are pioneer species, there are pioneer personalities among people. Have you ever met a person who seems to come alive just when everything is falling apart? Such people can be uniquely helpful. They can keep a cool head when connections are difficult to rely on. But sometimes, pioneer personalities can enjoy the mayhem a little too much—enough, maybe, to consider *causing* it. The superheroes and super-villains of our comic books are *all* comfortable with low-strength low-resilience situations; the only difference is whether they want to move the situation *out of* the corner or further *into* it.

## Strong, resilient connections

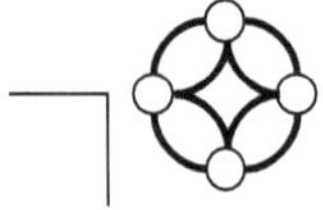

Now let's look at the upper-right corner of the space. Here self-organized networks are so strong and resilient that no organizer can break them apart. Such a network acts as a single entity within which individuals are indistinguishable. In the rare event that a bond does break, it reforms instantly, and the identity of the group is practically constant.

I had a hard time finding examples to describe this corner. Every example I thought of slid away when I considered what could happen to its apparent strength if we organizers decided to counter it. Human beings have so much power today, with our massive machines and our weapons of mass destruction, that it's hard to find an example of a network we can't overrule.

Or so it seems. There is still one self-organized network that could enter into this extreme corner of the space: antibiotic-resistant bacteria.

### A post-antibiotic world

For millions of years, pathogenic bacterial strains coevolved with humans in the same way they coevolved with every other species: their self-organized networks were strong and resilient, but never overwhelmingly so. Parasites that eradicate their hosts eradicate themselves. That's why epidemics always leave survivors behind. It's an evolutionary survival strategy.

People have been using natural antibiotics (such as the tetracyclines in ancient beers) for thousands of years. But historical uses made relatively small nudges to the coevolutionary situation.

The first strong antibiotics came into wide use in the 1930s and 40s. They devastated pathogenic bacterial networks, giving them a brute-force shove into the lower-left corner of the self-organized space. Immediately and inevitably, as thousands of generations of bacterial cells were sifted and sorted by natural selection, bacterial strength and resilience began to recover. The coevolutionary cycle was turning, as it had turned many times in evolutionary history. In this instance, however, the turn was accelerated by two factors.

First, the early twentieth century saw a dramatic increase in the pace and volume of global transportation, both of people and of goods. Bacterial spores had always been world travelers, wafting along on high-altitude winds. But these new modes of transportation boosted the global connectivity (thus resilience) of bacterial strains.

Second, starting around the 1950s, a general belief spread that we had won the coevolutionary game. At that time, most people would have placed pathogenic bacteria near the lower-left corner (weak and fragile) when they were actually rising upwards (still relatively weak, but increasingly resilient).

Some of the scientists who developed antibiotics knew what they were dealing with, and they tried to warn people that underuse *or* overuse of antibiotics could breed resistant bacterial strains. But their voices were largely ignored by people in search of easy answers—or easy money. The idea at the time was that, yes, of course resistance would form, but we would just keep developing new and shinier silver bullets.

This widespread over-confidence in the power of organization to corral self-organization led to the massive overuse of antibiotics, both in medicine and in agriculture. As a result the situation moved, in zig-zagging lines, to the right and high up into the space of resilience.

Worse, while antibiotic resistance has continued to grow, the development of new antibiotics has shrunk due to its increased difficulty, cost, and uncertainty. Some scientists warn that we are *already* living in a post-antibiotic world, where a simple cut or scrape can lead to an unstoppable infection and an early death. It is estimated that 700,000 deaths each year are being caused by antibiotic-resistant bacteria, with a predicted rise to ten million deaths per year by the middle of the century.

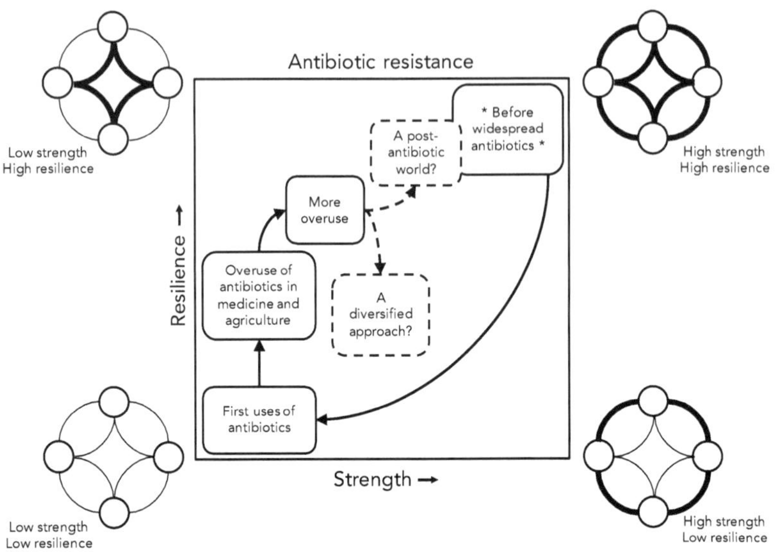


Our resilience as a species has been compromised by over-reliance on a single organized solution. If we can diversify our response, we can improve our resilience while reducing theirs, restoring the coevolutionary balance. For example, scientists today are working on bacterial vaccines (killed or weakened bacteria that activate the immune system), bacteriocins (proteins bacteria use to kill other bacteria), probiotics (bacteria that make us healthier), bacteriophages (viruses that kill bacteria), genetic analyses (which might lead to more focused uses of antibiotics), hygiene and nutrition (to strengthen our immune systems), and biosecurity measures (to reduce the spread of infections once they start). If we can build connections among these organized yet diverse solutions, we can meet bacterial resilience with resilience of our own.

## Strong, fragile connections

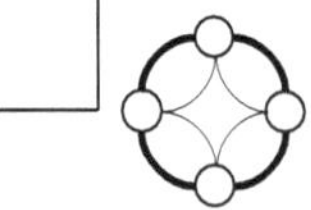

Now let's look at the lower-right corner, where strength is high but resilience is low. Every time I think of situations like this, I remember a song I used to sing when I was little:

> There was a little girl
> Who had a little curl
> Right in the middle of her forehead.
> When she was good
> She was very very good,
> And when she was bad she was horrid.

Supposedly, Henry Wadsworth Longfellow composed this poem while carrying his infant daughter, who I'm going to guess was adorably quiet, right up until the moment when she started screaming.

Like babies, strong yet fragile self-organized patterns are paradoxical. They can repeat and repeat for such long periods of time that it seems like they will go on forever—until they suddenly *stop* repeating.

Network strength is obvious, but network *resilience* is hidden and can only be understood in retrospect. Lacking awareness, we sometimes substitute what we can see (strength) for what we cannot (resilience) and rely on stability that does not exist. This unsettling truth lies behind some of our scariest stories, in which something we depend on to be safe turns deadly. The tagline for the horror movie *The Shining* captures the contradiction well: "Check in. Relax. Take a shower."[2] We tell stories like these to remind ourselves to keep our senses sharp even when—especially when—things seem the most stable.

**Reefs in danger**

The Great Barrier Reef is one such paradox. Its origin is ancient, and its future is uncertain. It was built by tiny organisms, and it is visible from space. It teems with life, and it is intensely vulnerable to destruction.

The symbiotic relationship between coral polyps and the photosynthetic algae that inhabit them is a high-maintenance one. When it works, it works beautifully; but it works only within a narrow range of conditions. To produce photosynthate, algae require abundant light, thus clear water. In the ocean, where nutrients are suspended in the water column, clear water is nutrient-poor. Thus the symbiosis is fragile by definition, with few options for the survival of either polyp or algae beyond optimal photosynthesis.

Coral reefs may be able to adapt to some degree of climatic change; but climate is only one part of the problem. In many coastal areas, agricultural and development-caused runoff of excess nitrogen and other pollutants has clouded formerly crystal-clear waters. Runoff also can upend nutrient balances, starving coral organisms while supporting the growth of competitors and predators. Positive feedback cycles can come about as crumbling reefs fail to hold back storm surges, leading to further crumbling. Scientists claim that coral reefs are in danger of dying out worldwide by mid-century.

It's hard to believe that coral reefs could be so huge, so long-lived, so beautiful, and so vulnerable. How could a "wonder of the world" like the Great Barrier Reef, twenty million years old and over 300,000 square kilometers in size, really be in danger? The answer is that it has *always* been in danger; we just didn't see it. Fossil evidence shows that there have been several mass die-offs of coral reefs over the past 400 million years. Temperature fluctuations, nutrient imbalances, reductions in sunlight, and changes in circulation patterns have devastated these fragile ecosystems time and time again.

Coral reefs keep reappearing in the fossil record, millions of years after each die-off, so you could say that they *are* resilient on a geological time scale. On the other hand, never before have corals faced as many compounding dangers as they do today. And even if they do reappear, it seems—here's a good scary-movie word for you—*apocalyptic* to think that coral reefs could disappear from the earth within a single human lifetime.

## Weak, resilient connections

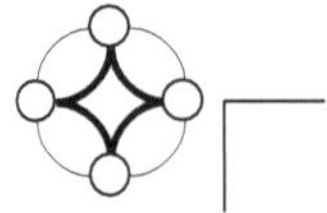

Finally, let's consider the last of the four corners of our self-organized space, the upper left, where networks are weak but resilient. When I picture this corner I always think of the tortoise who, slow and steady, wins the race. It's an image as reassuring as the previous one was unsettling. If at first you do not succeed, try, try again. The strength of self-organization, you could say, lies more in resilience than in strength.

In the previous section we considered a symbiotic relationship between a photosynthesizing organism (microscopic algae) and a non-photosynthesizing partner (coral polyps). Now let's consider another such symbiosis, one as robust as coral symbiosis is fragile.

### The fungal matrix

The tips of plant roots search the soil for water and nutrients. Fungal hyphae, single-cell-wide filaments, do the same; but being roughly thirty times thinner, they can push their way into soil micro-pores that plant roots cannot reach. The fungi release water and nutrients near plant roots and absorb sugars the roots exude into the soil.

There is no organizer in this exchange. Neither party is "farming" the other. But both participants have benefitted, evolutionarily speaking, from the association, and so it has persisted, apparently for at least 400 million years. Such mycorrhizal associations (*myco*, fungus; *rhiza*, root) can be found in more than ninety percent of plant species.

So why is this particular symbiosis so resilient? Well, to begin with, it's remarkably flexible. A single fungal individual can associate with a variety of plant individuals and species, and a single plant can associate with a variety of fungal individuals and species. For example, a tree may belong to as many as a dozen separate fungal networks, each of which covers tens of square meters with tens of kilometers of hyphae. In other words, mycorrhizal connections are multiplex and redundant, and that makes them resilient.

Another source of resilience is the way fungi buffer potentially dangerous environmental fluctuations. Carbon, water, nitrogen, phosphorus, and trace minerals move through fungal networks from sources to sinks, and these flows support growth, repair, and maintenance of fungal structures throughout the networks. For example, carbon absorbed from established plants is transported to fungal structures in or near the roots of seedlings, which can as yet supply little carbon to the network but nevertheless need help reaching water and nutrients. Thus fungal networks effectively subsidize the growth of new symbionts. Whether this is an adaptation or a side effect (on the part of plants or fungi) is not yet clear. But in any case, connecting plants into a larger symbiotic community distributes risk and increases resilience for both plants and fungi.

Along with carbon and nutrients, fungal networks also distribute chemical signals. For example, in one experiment, tomato plants bolstered their chemical defenses soon after a plant connected to the same fungal network was attacked by aphids.[3] Again, this could be an adaptation, but it could also be a simple side effect of the growth of fungal connections. It doesn't much matter which explanation is correct, because the effect is the same in either case: the network of symbiotically connected fungi and plants is more resilient as a result.

If you compare this mix-and-match carnival to the simple tête-à-têtes of coral polyps and the algae that live inside them, you can see why the self-organized network in this situation is more resilient than the other.

Why did I say mycorrhizal networks were *weak* and resilient? Because they are literally as thin as tissue paper. Did you ever take a plant out of its pot and see little clusters of fuzzy white hairs near the bottom, like clumps of fine cotton threads? Those were mycelia, networks of fungal hyphae. Every time a farmer tills a field, they rip up hundreds of kilometers of these intricate networks. Every time you disturb the soil of your garden, you reduce the resilience of the plants you want to grow in it.

Freshly tilled soil was once seen as a blank slate, a controlled medium for optimal growth, free of the tangled remains of history. But in light of new evidence about fungal networks, plants grown without the benefit of mycorrhizal symbiosis are starting to seem dangerously isolated. More and more farmers are practicing *conservation tillage*, disturbing the soil as little as possible. Low-till and no-till methods were originally developed to combat soil erosion and reduce the effects of drought. But they also preserve mycorrhizal networks, which help crops weather fluctuations in temperature and rainfall.

## Crossing the jungle space

Now that we've poked our fingers into the four corners of the space, let's look at a few examples that range across it.

### The amazing life of a slime mold

Cellular slime molds are made up of cells, and they are slimy, but they are not molds. They were thought to be molds long ago. Today they are considered members of the kingdom *Protista*, a sort of catch-all for organisms that are not animals, plants, bacteria, or fungi (molds are fungi). These tiny blobs of goo are found in forests, under rotting logs and in leaf litter. They have been extensively studied by evolutionary biologists because their collective behaviors put them on the border between individual cells and multi-cellular organisms. Plus, they're *totally* fascinating.

When food is plentiful, cellular slime molds exist as free-roaming populations of single-celled individuals. They wander the forest floor, propelling themselves with their flagella, and look for bacteria to engulf and ingest. Once in a while, they split in half and become twins. That's all normal.

But when food grows very scarce, something amazing happens. The starving cells begin to secrete a series of signaling chemicals that coordinate a complex cooperative process. When a slime mold cell encounters a signal gradient, it responds in two ways: it swims up the gradient, and it releases its own burst of the same chemical. As a result, the cells gather in flowing, pulsing streams until they form a single blob that contains hundreds or thousands of individuals.

The crowd then begins to look and act as if it were one organism. It forms a finger-like "slug" that moves toward greater light, warmth, and humidity. As a sort of temporary pseudo-organism, a slug can do things individual cells cannot. It can travel faster than a single cell (and the more cells it has, the faster it moves). It can push through barriers and bridge gaps. It can protect itself against predators with a slimy sheath.

At some point the slug seems to make a decision. It stops moving and rises up, waving and swaying like a tiny arm holding up a tiny flag. Now the assembly is called a "fruiting body." Some of its cells form the stalk; some anchor the stalk to the ground; and some form the flag itself—a tiny ball of spores.

Eventually the ball bursts open, and the spores are carried by air currents and passing animals to new locations. The spores are hardy and can survive long periods of cold, heat, drought, and even ingestion by predators. So they are likely to survive, even if they have to wait a long time to start over. Once they find themselves in suitably warm, moist, nutrient-rich environments, they hatch and begin to forage again as individuals—until the food runs out.

For spore cells, this is a story of renewal and rebirth, a second chance at life. Not so for the twenty percent of cells that form the stalk of the fruiting body. They stiffen and die. It is through their sacrifice that the spore cells gain the ability to travel to new and better worlds.

Are stalk cells altruists, sacrificing themselves for the good of others? Or are they losers in a competitive struggle for survival? Do they volunteer to leave the fallout shelter, or do they get pushed out? The evidence so far indicates that a cell's fate is fixed at the moment the call comes to aggregate. Cells that have most recently divided (and so are the smallest, weakest, and hungriest) tend to become stalk cells, mostly because they are the least able to fend off the "we need some volunteers to be stalk cells" signal, which apparently takes some energy to ignore. So the stalk cells are losers, but in a lottery nobody can control. They just happen to be in the wrong place at the wrong time.

But not every slime mold cell turns into a stalk cell or spore cell. Some "loner" cells ignore the call to join up and continue to behave as if nothing is going on. For a long time researchers ignored loners, assuming they died. But it turns out they don't *always* die. The whole assemble-move-rise-travel-hatch process takes quite a bit of time, and it sometimes happens that new food arrives while the process is ongoing. And when that happens, the loners win. They never get a chance to travel to new lands, but they never run the risk of turning into a flagpole either.

Another group of cells do join the slug, but are sloughed off while it is moving to a new area. These are called "sentinel cells" because their position near the slug sheath gives them the job of engulfing bacteria and toxins the slug encounters as it moves. Still, sentinels sometimes fall off the slug in better places than where they started. They gain the benefits of movement without running the risk of ending up in the stalk.

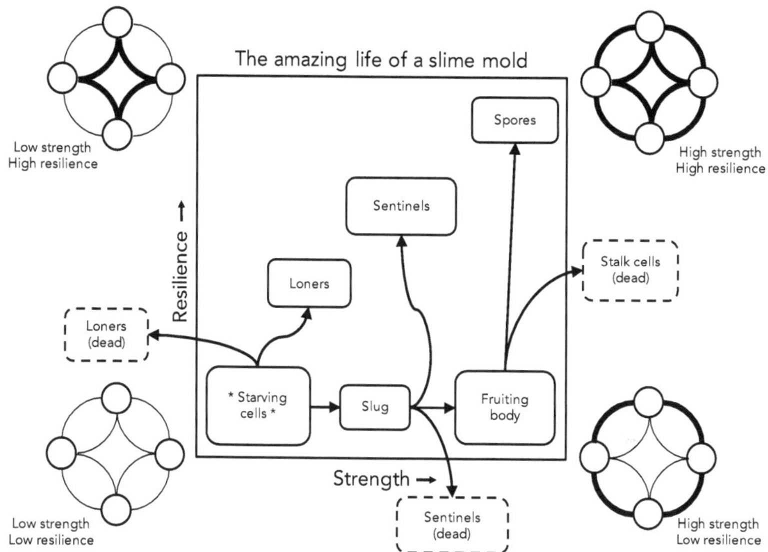


Whenever I think about these tiny cells joining up and forming a single-minded pseudo-organism, I can't help thinking of stories I've read about people coming together after natural disasters. Neighbors who have been minding their own business for decades, living next to each other without exchanging more than a few words, find a new sense of community when the town gets hit by a flood or a cyclone and everyone has to pull together to survive.

Of course, the difference between people and slime mold cells is that, because we are organizers as well as interactors, we can *choose to continue* to work together to improve our common conditions through planning and deliberation long after the crisis is over. (I will come back to the topic of disasters in Chapter Six, on page 80.)

## Life in the deep

The first deep sea hydrothermal vent was discovered in 1977. A group of geologists studying tectonics had towed a submersible fifteen meters above the seafloor to look for temperature spikes. As they pored over 3000 photographs taken by the submersible, they saw something strange in just thirteen of the photos: hundreds of white clams and brown mussels. At a depth of 2500 meters, this was simply impossible.

Within hours, three scientists descended to the site in a manned submersible. What they saw was something no human being had ever seen before: a hydrothermal vent pumping out warm, shimmering water, like an underwater geyser. Even more surprisingly, they discovered a thriving community of living organisms—clams, mussels, crabs, bright red tubeworms, and a purple octopus.

There is no sunlight at such depths. This entire biological community was supported by chemosynthetic bacteria that lived on hydrogen sulfide rushing up out of the earth's crust. Scientists around the world were enthralled by the discovery, and research on deep sea vent communities began immediately.

The first question that puzzled scientists was: how do such communities persist? Some vents appear to have been active for thousands of years; but others seem to start and stop venting every decade or two. How do the organisms found at deep sea vents persist after their sources of energy disappear? Scientists knew that many of the organisms released larvae into the water, but they wondered how such tiny larvae could survive voyages of possibly hundreds or thousands of kilometers to the next active vent.

It turns out that the distance is not as vast as it seemed. Scientists have now mapped more than 500 deep sea vents and found that many of them are connected in lines along tectonic plate boundaries. Studies of larval dispersal have verified that larvae drift upward into higher and stronger currents than they can access at the ocean floor, making it easier to travel long distances than was originally thought. Today, deep sea vent communities are seen more as participants in a vast and resilient meta-community than as isolated, fragile oases in a vast desert.

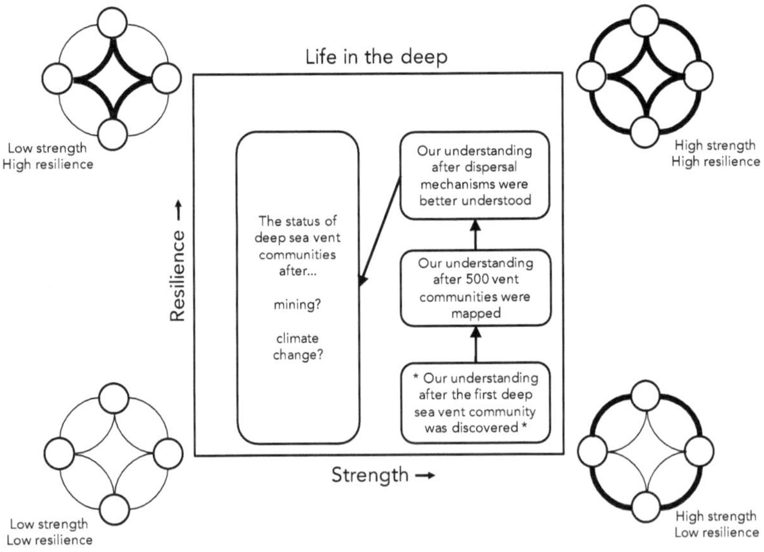


However, the vent meta-community may now be in danger. Climate change has been altering ocean currents, and that could affect larval dispersal and the re-establishment of vent communities.

Deep-sea mining is another concern. The hot water pumping out of deep sea vents carries elements it picked up during its rush through the earth's crust. Among them are copper, cobalt, gold, and rare earth metals, which sometimes pile up in tall chimneys. The prospect of mining these concentrations of valuable metals is now being explored, and the first whole-scale mining operation recently took place in Japan (on an inactive vent).[4]

It is too soon to say what effects climate change and mining will have on deep-sea vent communities. However, it is possible that the resilience of the vent network depends on a critical yet invisible threshold.

## Kudzu: The vine that ate the South

Kudzu. It's a monster; it's a marvel; it's a mystery. This perennial climbing vine in the genus *Pueraria* is native to Asia, where it grows in the mountains, competes with other vines, and dies back every winter. In the southern United States, it's another story.

Kudzu was first introduced to the United States at the 1876 Centennial Exposition in Philadelphia. The vine was considered exotic and beautiful, and its ability to grow in partial shade made it an attractive option for shading porches in the hot South. Warm winters, plentiful rainfall, and few native competitors or predators caused this invasive species to spread rapidly, eventually coming to cover vast tracts of land.

Southern towns and cities spend millions each year removing kudzu vines from power lines, street lights, and other structures. Where the plant is well established, it can take five to ten years of mowing (or close clipping by goats or llamas) to reduce its spread. Kudzu can be kept under control, but complete eradication is considered by most land managers to be practically impossible.

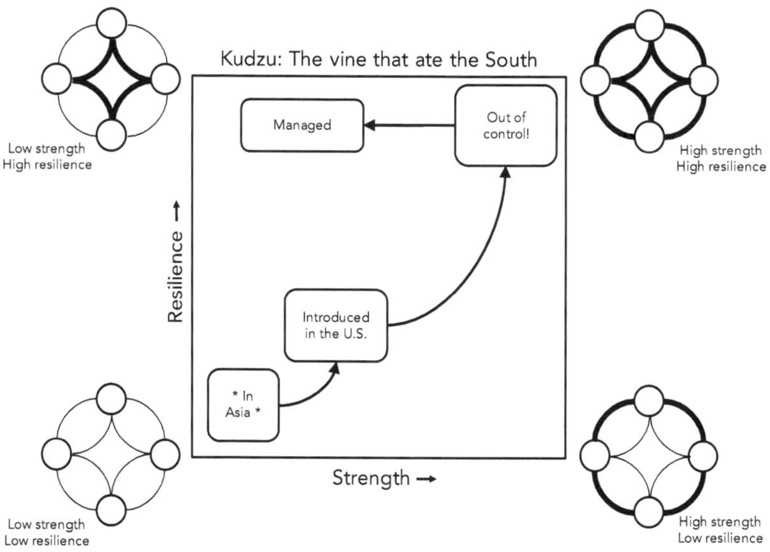


Several features of kudzu make it an exceptionally resilient competitor. Because it is a legume (*Pueraria* is in the pea family, *Fabaceae*), kudzu fixes atmospheric nitrogen. This means it can grow on poor soils. And it grows fast, as fast as ten to thirty meters per year. As a climbing vine, kudzu can take hold of virtually any structure—porch, tree, telephone pole—and use it to reach higher into the sunlight without expending energy on building woody stems.

So far kudzu doesn't sound that different from a bean plant, which also fixes nitrogen and grows on trellises and other structures. However, kudzu is an amazingly effective structural parasite. A kudzu vine doesn't just grow up a tree; it smothers it. The large, dense leaves of the kudzu form a blanket that shades the tree's own leaves. Eventually the weakened tree is felled by the great weight of its parasite. Imagine a bean plant felling a tree.

Gardeners know that most plants can be propagated by placing a cutting (a piece of stem with a leaf node) into moist soil and waiting for root hairs to appear. In most plants, adventitious roots such as these form naturally, but not often. In kudzu, almost every node that happens to touch the ground forms a new adventitious root. Each root develops into a knobby base called a *crown* that can grow new shoots. Each crown extends downward to a deep taproot, which stores water and sugars in a starchy tuber, like a potato. Kudzu tubers can grow to several hundred kilograms in weight and are key to the plant's long-term resilience. They help it regrow after periods of bad weather or predation.

Finally, the kudzu plant has one more ace up its sleeve. When it flowers, it produces seed pods that can survive for several years. But kudzu seeds do not germinate until they have been heavily damaged, such as by a fire or a heavy storm. After such an incident, kudzu seedlings are well positioned to dominate the landscape in the absence of competitors. (Remember the pioneer species I mentioned on page 40? Kudzu is one of them.)

All of these aspects of kudzu growth—nitrogen fixing, structural parasitism, adventitious root growth, root storage, and seed dormancy—contribute to its high resilience. It's like somebody took the superpowers of five different plants and put them all together into one powerhouse of a plant. It's no wonder they call kudzu "the vine that ate the South."

### Miracle to menace

But that's not the whole story of kudzu. The plant did not *immediately* dominate the landscape on its first introduction into the United States. It did survive winters in the warm south, and it did get a few steps ahead of native predators and competitors. But its viability was only moderately enhanced over what it had been in Asia.

Around the turn of the twentieth century, farmers began to experiment with kudzu as a forage crop, since it was known to thrive on poor soils. They found it hard to work with. It produced very few seeds, they had a low germination rate, and its seedlings did not grow well in compacted or poorly drained soil. Its starchy roots took years to develop, and before they were established, the vines were easily destroyed by even moderate grazing. And it was hard to harvest, partly because the vines were difficult to form into bales, and partly because it retained too much water.

In 1935, American farmers were faced with massive losses of topsoil, brought on by years of drought and excessive tillage of fragile prairie soil. In response, the U.S. Congress created the Soil Conservation Service, which immediately began testing ground cover plants that could reduce soil erosion.

Kudzu did so well in their tests that they grew more than 70 million kudzu seedlings—and paid farmers eight dollars an acre to plant them.

The effect of these plantings was dramatic. Many acres of severely eroded land were restored to agricultural use. "What, short of a miracle, can you call this plant?" said Hugh Hammond Bennett, head of the SCS. Everyone was talking about kudzu, the "savior of the South," the "miracle vine."[5]

While this was going on, railway companies also had an erosion problem. They often had to cut steeply through hillsides to lay out their rail lines on minimal grades, and they needed a way to stabilize embankments and prevent landslides. Following the lead of the Soil Conservation Service, they planted kudzu seedlings next to hundreds of miles of railroad tracks. Cities and towns also planted kudzu next to their newly built highways. By 1945, more than a million acres (400,000 hectares) of kudzu had been planted.

Ten years later, perceptions of kudzu could not have been more different. The vines grew much faster than anyone expected—or desired. The problem was not so much in the farms; most of the fields that had been planted with kudzu were plowed under when the subsidies ran out. It was in the railroad and highway plantings that kudzu got out of hand. The sides of roads and railways were like kudzu nurseries: cleared, well-drained, sunny soils, often at forest edges, with lots of trees to climb and few predators to eat the young leaves. The vines grew and grew, and people stopped calling them a cure and started calling them a disease.

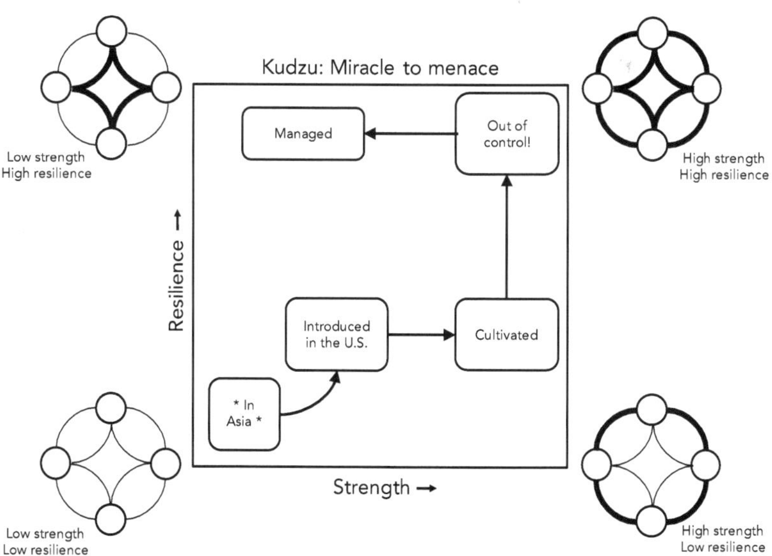

**Hero, villain, both, or neither?**

But again, that's not the whole story of kudzu. It turns out that its monstrous growth may have been exaggerated.

People have been claiming for decades that kudzu covers nine million acres (3.6 million hectares) of land and consumes an additional 150,000 acres (60,000 hectares) per year—the size of a small city! But according to a recent article by horticulturist Bill Finch in the *Smithsonian* magazine, such claims may never have been correct.[6] The nine-million-acres claim, he says, came from "a small garden club publication" which was never fact-checked.

Indeed, a comprehensive 2010 survey by the U.S. Forest Service has estimated that kudzu covers a mere 227,000 acres (92,000 hectares) of Southern land and grows by only 2500 acres (1000 hectares) a year.[7] That's *two percent* of previous estimates. It is unclear whether this wide discrepancy means that kudzu has been dying off or that the numbers were always wrong. (It could mean both.) But if the current estimate is correct, given that there are 200 million acres (81 million hectares) of forested land in the Southern U.S., there's not actually very much kudzu out there.

So why do people still think kudzu ate the South? According to Bill Finch, it's because people drive cars, and you can see a lot of kudzu from cars. All of the highways and rail lines in the South—including the rail lines that became highways—are flanked on either side by thriving communities of kudzu. But if you park your car and walk through the wall of kudzu, you will find that it doesn't extend very far. When you get into the deep shade of the forest, where deer are no longer in danger of becoming road kill, you stop finding kudzu.

The truth is, several other invasive species, such as privet, oriental bittersweet, and non-native grasses, have damaged Southern ecosystems more than kudzu has. And kudzu is not that much harder to eradicate than other species. It has its vulnerabilities. For example, if you destroy a kudzu crown, you can leave its three-meter-long taproot in the ground, because the root cannot grow new shoots on its own. A group of volunteers practicing "surgical crown removal" can destroy a small stand of kudzu in a few hours.[8] The method requires patience, care, and coordination, but it's possible. (And yes, seed pods will remain, but that's a smaller problem that can be dealt with later on.)

In his *Smithsonian* article, Finch suggests that kudzu may have grown into a Southern bogeyman because the way it happens to grow connects it to a widespread sense of poverty and hopelessness in the South. That makes sense to me. If you look on the internet at pictures of kudzu draped like a heavy blanket over trees, cars, and houses, you'll see what he means. It looks post-apocalyptic. It's easy to feel overwhelmed at the very sight of it, like something sinister and alien has taken over the world. And I don't even live in the South. I can't imagine what it would feel like to see such a thing in person everywhere I drove.

On the other hand, there's something weirdly appealing in the idea of kudzu and the way it lives. Mixed among mentions of kudzu as a scourge, it's easy to find people saying things like "You have to admire its persistence" and "I think of it as an old friend." Kudzu seems to possess an indomitable spirit that literally rises above every obstacle. Its wealth of resilience, its spunk in the face of adversity, is something every one of us would like to have for ourselves.

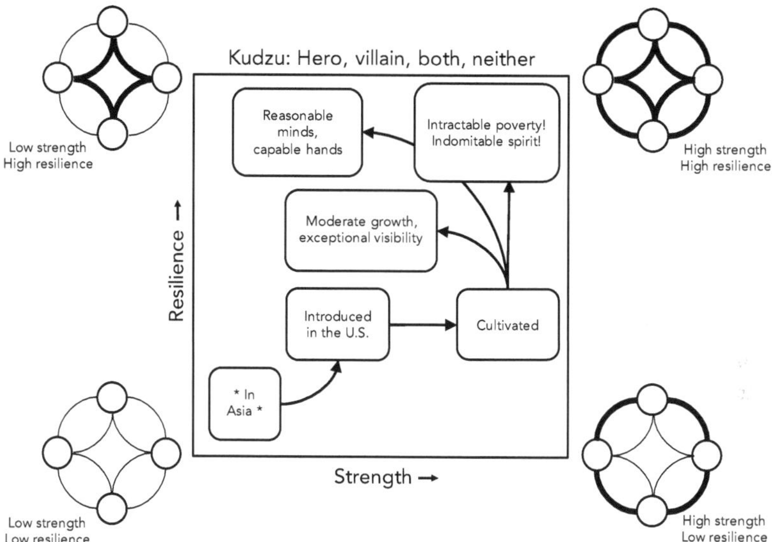


And in fact, kudzu has many uses. Some people eat it. You can eat every part of the plant, and it's tasty and nutritious. It has been used for centuries in traditional medicine (though many of those claims have not been scientifically tested). Some people build beautiful baskets from its vines.

But seeing kudzu as either a villain or a hero disregards its actual history. In truth, it has only attained its great powers of resilience because of a considerable investment of energy on the part of *organizers*—people who put it where they wanted it to be. See, I said organization would work its way into this chapter whether we wanted it to or not; and so it did. In the next chapter, organization will be our focus.

# 5 The Plan

*Thinking about organization*

From a spider building a web to a suburbanite mowing a lawn, many living things shape their surroundings to suit their needs and desires. I call this activity *organization*, and in this chapter we will focus exclusively on it. Let's start our exploration with a story.

> It was a busy day at the factory. All of a sudden the most important machine in the place stopped working. Everyone tried their hardest, but nothing could coax the machine back to life.
>
> Finally an experienced engineer was called in. The engineer walked in, looked, listened, looked some more, then took out a little hammer and made three little taps on a pipe. The machine sprang back to life, and the factory got back to work.
>
> A week later, the factory manager received the expert's bill—for ten thousand dollars. It seemed like a lot of money for a few minutes of work, so the manager asked for an itemized account. In a few more days it came:
>
> Tapping machine with hammer . . . . . $10
> Knowing where to tap . . . . . . . . . . . $9990

Have you heard that story before? If you have, I'm not surprised. It's over a hundred years old. The reason it keeps getting passed around, I think, is because it has so much to say about organization. Our modern lives are so tied up with organization that stories like this one matter more than they ever did before.

Details of the story vary from telling to telling. Sometimes the machine is a ship boiler or a car engine, and sometimes the expert is Edison or Tesla. But two aspects of the story never change. First, the expert's action is always tiny. Sometimes they turn a nut or bolt, and sometimes they simply mark a little chalk "x" on the spot where the problem is. Second, the bill *always* contains the phrase *knowing where to* do whatever the expert did.

In the first chapter of this book, I said an organizer "grabs hold of interactors and puts them where it wants them to be." To do that, an organizer needs the same two items as are listed on the expert's bill. It needs to *know where* the interactors are, and it needs to apply some *effort*—at least a little.

Let's combine awareness with effort to create a thinking space.

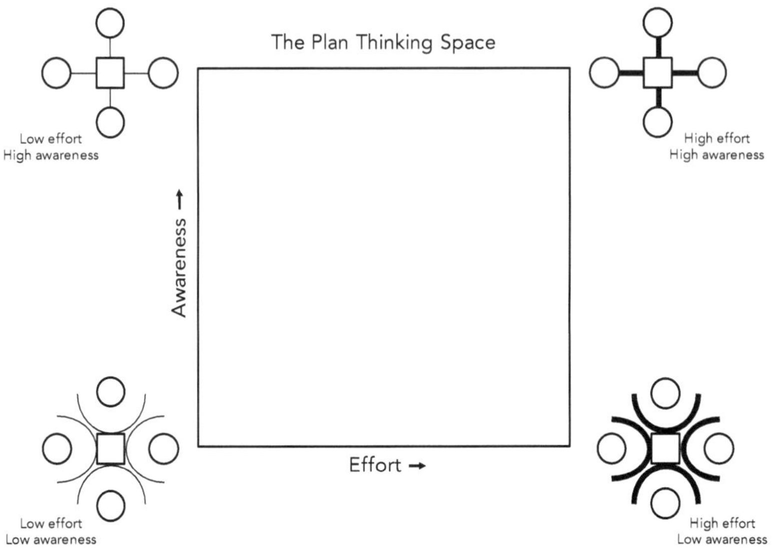


At the top of the space, where awareness is high, the organizer *knows* where the interactors are, so it simply reaches out and grabs them. At the bottom, the organizer has to *guess* where the interactors are—or just flail around hoping to hit them. So on the bottom corner diagrams I've drawn curved lines, which could represent either satellite dishes or flailing arms.

On the left side of the space, the organizer applies very little effort. On the right, the organizer applies as much effort as they possibly can.

## The journey to where we want to be

The natural state of human beings is near the bottom of the space of organization, far from omniscience. We forget more than we remember, so we have a tendency to keep sliding down. Necessity, exhaustion, and the boredom of repetition keep us away from either perfect ease or boundless energy.

But where we are is not where we *want* to be. We want to be in the upper-left corner, like the engineer in the story. We want to take out a little hammer, make a few little taps, and get everything to work.

Ancient Chinese philosophers, both Confucian and Daoist, thought a lot about the situation in that upper-left corner. They called it *wu wei*, or "action without action." You could say they cornered the market on thinking about it, because nobody else has studied it as explicitly or completely as they did.

Still, you can find references to similar situations in every culture. The idea of big changes coming from tiny but perfectly-placed actions is all over the place. It's in stories, like the one about the Dutch boy who saved his village by plugging a tiny leak in a dike.[1] It's in songs, like the one about the trapeze artist who "flies through the air with the greatest of ease." When people say "keep your mouth shut and your eyes open," they're talking about *wu wei*.

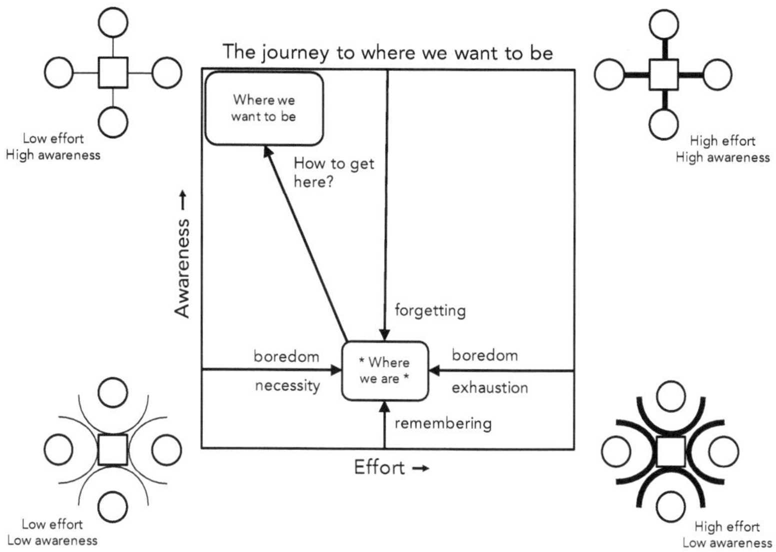


My favorite example of *wu wei* is a story told by the ancient Daoist scholar Zhuangzi about a butcher who has honed his craft to perfection. When the king praises his skill, the butcher puts down his knife and says (in part):

> A good cook changes his blade once a year: he slices. An ordinary cook changes his blade once a month: he hacks. I have been using this same blade for nineteen years, and yet it is still as sharp as the day it came off the whetstone. For the joints have spaces within them, and the very edge of the blade has no thickness at all. When what has no thickness enters into an empty space, it is vast and open, with more than enough room for the play of the blade. . . .
>
> Nonetheless, whenever I come to a clustered tangle, realizing that it is difficult to *do* anything about it, I instead restrain myself as if terrified, until my seeing comes to a complete halt. My activity slows, and the blade moves ever so slightly. Then all at once, I find the ox already dismembered at my feet like clumps of soil scattered on the ground.[2]

If you think about something you know how to do very well, you can recognize the feeling of looking down and finding the thing "already" done.

There is a second, even more compelling reason to want to be in the upper-left corner of the space: to get along with each other. Edward Slingerland, in his book *Trying Not to Try*, puts forth a theory that makes a lot of sense to me.[3] Ten thousand years ago, when we started forming large groups, we were thrown together with strangers in a way we had never been before. We needed a way to *signal* to each other that we were trustworthy and competent without having years to prove ourselves.

So here's a question. Would you say that the engineer in the factory story proved themselves to be trustworthy and competent? If *you* were the factory manager, would you bring them back the next time there was a problem?

Of course you would. A person who shows effortless ability, who can do much with little, has a charismatic quality that is impossible to fake. It's a *reliable sign of reliability*, in the same way that a peacock's tail is a reliable sign of good genes. Lying requires conscious effort, so if a person is doing something in a way that seems effortless, they are probably telling the truth. The ancient Chinese called this charismatic quality "de." The ancient Greeks called it "virtue." In popular culture today, we call it "cool." You know what makes somebody *uncool*, right? Trying to be cool. That's the paradox of *wu wei*.

## Divergent paths

So we want to be in the upper-left corner, and we have reasons to want to be there. *How* do we get there? That's a question people have been asking and answering for thousands of years. The answers can be grouped into two general categories, with a third answer that falls between.

### The path of mastery

One answer is to look within ourselves and improve our skills through diligent practice. To do this we must first focus on effort, on moving ourselves to the right side of the space.

As we practice, we make use of information, disciplines, and rituals that have been built up over decades or centuries—but as masters of our own fates, we do not *depend* on these things. Masters by definition manage on their own, eager to use what they can find but ready to make do when they find nothing.

After much practice, we develop good habits and internalize our skills to the point that they become automatic. Then it is time to "level up" and practice even more difficult tasks. Eventually we reach a state in which we understand so much that we can organize the world around us with minimal effort.

Practitioners of the Aikido path of *Shuhari* move through three stages: *shu* ("obey"), in which they memorize traditional forms; *ha* ("detach"), in which they begin to question and modify the forms; and *ri* ("depart"), in which they understand the art so well that they can do whatever they like while remaining true to its essence. Similarly, the educational framework known as Bloom's taxonomy helps students walk the path of mastery as they learn to remember, understand, and apply (that is, memorize traditional forms); analyze and evaluate (question and modify the forms); and create (do as they like).

Confucius described his own journey on the path of mastery. At fifteen, he says, "I had my mind bent on learning." At thirty, he "stood firm" in his efforts to learn and grow. At forty, he "had no doubts" about his place in the universe. At fifty, he "knew the decrees of Heaven," meaning that he not only understood his part in the universe but also knew what he had to do to fulfill it. At sixty, he says, "my ear was an obedient organ for the reception of truth." I take this to mean that he was able to look beyond the commotion of daily life to its deeper meaning. At seventy, Confucius arrived at a place where, he says, "I could follow what my heart desired, without transgressing what was right."

The last stage of Confucius's path reminds me of Saint Augustine's decree to "Love, and do what thou wilt"—meaning that when you really and truly understand what it means to love, you need no other instruction.

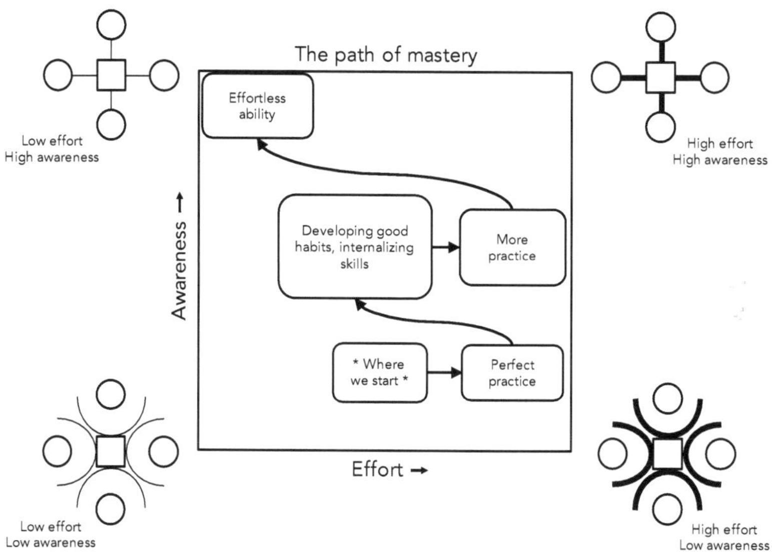


## Tricksters lead the way

The path of mastery is paved with stories. As far back as the bronze age, trickster figures such as Coyote, Anansi, and the Monkey King have beckoned to us from the place of effortless action every time they changed the world with a simple, smart trick. They have also warned us away from the opposite corner when they acted as blundering idiots. It's a curious fact that tricksters everywhere seem to dance between mastery and idiocy. They will come up with a brilliant solution only to overturn it with a new act of stupidity, sometimes within the same story. Why do they do this? My guess is that it helps us understand that the path of mastery includes—indeed, requires—mistakes. Every movement we make to the right of the space, each effort, is simultaneously a chance to succeed and a chance to fail, and we can learn from either outcome.

Tricksters treat everything that happens to them as a joke, a farce, a game; and they are as ready to laugh at themselves as they are at everyone else. When you bounce down the path of mastery laughing at everything—life and death, joy and sorrow, wealth and want—it is easier to keep picking yourself up and starting over. If you think the object of the game is to win, you have already lost. But if your object is to *keep playing*, you cannot lose.[4]

However, breaking the rules is only half of the cultural function of trickster figures. In every culture, tricksters create and enforce rules as often as they break them. Tricksters know how to laugh, but they also know when to *stop* laughing and do what must be done. In many creation stories, tricksters make wise but difficult decisions for the people.

In one American Indian tale, for example, the first people who lived on the earth did not die.[5] After a time, they grew too many for the earth to sustain. The tribal chiefs met to talk about what should be done. Coyote said he believed people needed to die forever, so new generations would have enough to eat. The chiefs disagreed. They decided that when a person died, that person would exist as a wind-carried spirit for a time, then would return to life in a special medicine house. When the time came for the first spirits to be revived, Coyote snuck into the medicine house and *closed the door* so the spirits could not enter. Ever since that time, the dead have stayed dead. Coyote knew that the wishes and needs of his people were at odds.

**Tales of wit and wisdom**

Another type of story often told on the path of mastery pits one master organizer against another. Such tales of intellectual combat search for signs of mastery through tests and contests. A sure sign that a story is of this type is the mention of *proof* or authenticity. Only a *true* princess can feel a pea under many layers of mattresses. Only the *rightful* king can pull the sword from the stone. Only a man *fit* for his position can see the Emperor's new clothes. The hands of a killer will never wash *clean*. The truth will always come out.

In a Mayan folk tale, a huge jaguar was devastating the countryside, devouring livestock and villagers alike.[6] A man tracked the jaguar, used his slingshot to hit it in the eye, and stabbed it dead. He brought the dead jaguar to the king. Then a second man stepped in to claim that *he* had killed the jaguar. The king asked for the slingshot. Then he gave it the second man and asked him to *prove* that he killed the jaguar—by hitting the first man in the eye. The pretender, who could not prove his claim, was punished, and the true hero was rewarded.

Here is a contemporary folk tale in the same category. A young woman was leaving the supermarket when an old woman, stooped and burdened with groceries, asked her for a short ride home.[7] As the old woman put her groceries into the back seat, the driver noticed that she had a very hairy and very strong arm. She distracted the "old woman" with a ruse and drove off. Later, she saw a news report that a man had raped a young woman—after posing as an old woman burdened with groceries. This and many other "killer in the back seat" stories pit one organizer against another, each vying for control of the situation.

The everyday stories we tell in conversation—the *accounts* we use to establish *accountability*—often include statements of proof. If you listen to any group of people sharing stories in conversation, you will hear such proof statements passing back and forth. Did you ever hear someone say, "You can talk the talk, but can you walk the walk?" That's a *request* for a proof statement, and most people know how to reply to it. They tell a story of mastery—a story that shows a deep and lengthy association with the subject about which they have been challenged. Their story proves that they have earned their place on the path. Being prepared to provide proof is an essential part of walking the path of mastery. It's a check that prevents us from straying into ignorance.

## The path of deliverance

Now let us consider a second path. To start on this path, we must take the opposite approach. We must *decrease* our efforts, forget what we know, and retreat to the lower-left corner, where everything is still and silent. It is only in this quiet corner that we can prepare ourselves to accept the aid of someone or something bigger and more powerful than ourselves.

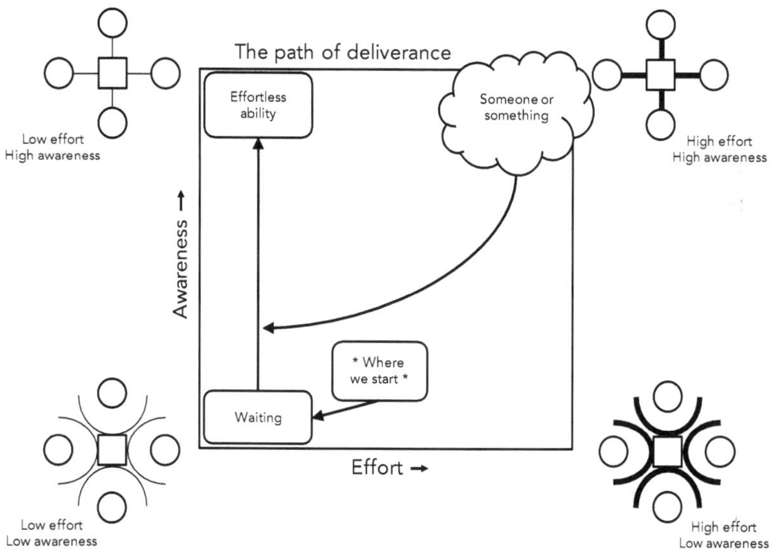


Note that I drew the "someone or something" as a cloud rather than a rectangle because, depending on our beliefs, it may or may not be an organizer. The path of deliverance does not require intention; it only requires aid.

### Organized sources of deliverance

When the "someone or something" on which we rely is an organizer, we can place that organizer into the space along with us. We have many organizers from which to choose, and we can choose more than one. The same person can be a student, citizen, patient, and parishioner, and they can draw strength from all of these relationships.

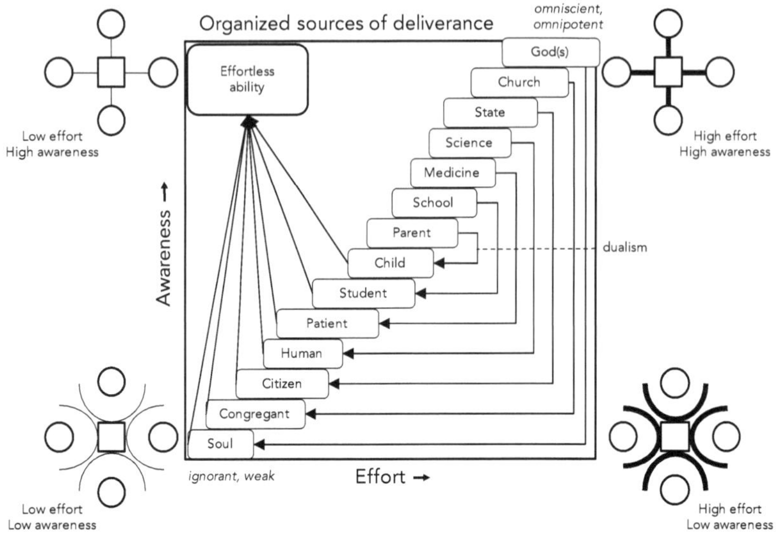


Notice the line between the upper and lower halves of the space. When deliverance comes from an organized source, there must be an impenetrable barrier between ourselves and our benefactors. If they were no stronger or smarter than we were, there would be no point in waiting for them to save us; we could save ourselves. Thus the path of deliverance is inherently dualistic: someone waits, and someone (or something) comes.

There is peace and joy in the act of waiting patiently for deliverance that is sure to come. Think about that moment when you are opening a gift from someone who knows you and loves you; it's *that* feeling. You can hear it in this passage from François Fénelon, a sixteenth-century Christian quietist:

> God never ceases to speak to us; but the noise of the world without, and the tumult of passions within, bewilder us, and prevent us from listening to him. . . . [The voice of God] is a still small voice, and is only heard by those who listen to no other.[8]

Fénelon was later forced to recant those beliefs, and the leader of the quietist movement, Miguel de Molinos, was imprisoned for heresy. The suppression of quietism involved many factors, from ecclesiastical politics to clashes of personality. But to a large extent the movement failed because its growing popularity put the livelihoods of thousands of people at risk. Fénelon's "still small voice" threatened to render obsolete all but *one* deliverer—and overturn an organized structure that had taken hundreds of years to construct.

This example highlights the fact that every organizer can function as a deliverer *or* as a provider of optional resources to those on the path of mastery—and that organizers don't always like being optional. The tension plays out in every sphere of life, from governance to education to health care. Every teacher wants to be more than a workbook, and every doctor wants to be more than a dispensary. Deciding how to respond when those you support prefer to walk another path is a challenge for every helper.

## Non-organized sources of deliverance

Those who don't believe in (or don't choose to rely on) organized sources of deliverance often believe in (or at least rely on) other powerful forces such as nature or the cosmos. Such forces have no intentionality, so they can't be organizers—but they can work *as if they were organizers*, in the same way that self-organization works *as if* someone were in charge.

Because these forces are not organizers, they cannot be placed *into* the space of organization. They can, however, lie *beneath* it, as an aspect of reality itself. Such sources of aid do not *come* to us; we live *in* them. They are the air we breathe and the ground on which we stand. We cannot be distinguished from them because we are part of them.

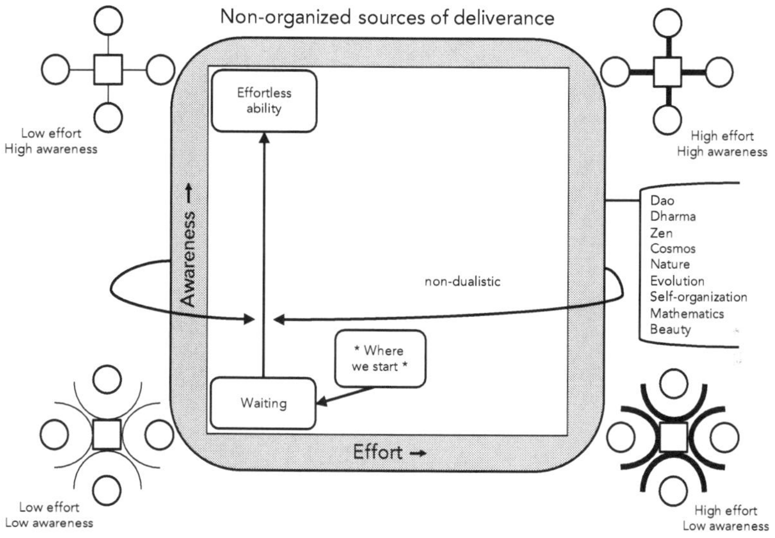


Non-organized forces are non-dualistic in a second sense as well. Unlike organized forces, which always work against something (God against the Devil, science against pseudo-science, governments against anarchy), non-organized forces work against nothing, because there is nothing outside them. If the cosmos is everything there is, how can it counter anything?

In Daoism, for example, the yin-yang symbol represents opposing forces, but each force contains some of the other inside it. It is not meant to evoke a dualistic contest; its meaning is closer to the way in which the seasons turn into each other as the year goes by. In fact, the symbol is meant to *turn* like a wheel to represent the fact that in life, change is the only constant. One day's blessing might be another day's curse; behavior that seems kind in one century might seem cruel in the next (or vice versa); and whether a piece of luck turns out to be good or bad depends on what happens next.

From this perspective, we move into the lower-left corner not to wait for deliverance but to draw energy from a source that helps us find beauty and joy in a world that *includes* suffering and pain. We tap into that energy by withdrawing from the tumult and clutter of everyday life to a simpler place, such as the one described in one of my favorite passages from the *Daodejing*:[9]

> Thirty spokes
> meet in the hub.
> Where the wheel isn't
> is where it's useful.

As I get older, I understand better and better why that quiet place, where the wheel isn't, is exactly where I want to be.

Like many others, I find beauty and joy in the contemplation of nature. I spent a lot of time in the forest as a child, and I still spend as much time there as I can. My rule is: wait fifteen minutes. When I can walk or sit quietly in the woods for at least fifteen minutes, something *always* happens.

Once, I was walking down a path when a grouse suddenly jumped in front of me and showed me its "broken" wing. I felt so honored to be included in the community of the forest that I did my best to play my part and pretend to be "taken in" by the trick. I followed the grouse until it took off, all in a rush of wings, having successfully drawn me away from its nest. That experience was the best I've ever had in the woods—better than watching a deer give birth—because *an animal came to me with a message*. (The message was a lie, but it was exciting all the same.)

Most of the time, nothing so dramatic happens. Usually I just listen to the squirrels chattering and watch the trees swaying in the breeze. Sometimes what happens is in my mind. I can't tell you how many insights I've had while waiting in the woods to see what would happen. The forest is a force that gives me strength and understanding, and it has never disappointed me. I'll bet *you* believe in something that gives you strength and understanding, and I'll bet you don't mind sitting and waiting for it either. Say what you like about the path of mastery; the path of deliverance is worth considering.

***Stories of deliverance***

I said before that the path of mastery is paved with stories. Are there stories on the path of deliverance as well? Yes, but they are different stories. On the path of mastery, stories stimulate, challenge, and enrich our exploration. On the path of deliverance, stories assure us that help is close at hand.

The "Footprints" story is one such tale. In a dream or in the afterlife, a person is walking with God on a beach. As they walk, they look back at a line of footprints in the sand that represents the course of the person's life. For most of the path there are two sets of footprints, but at one point only one set of footprints is visible. The person remembers that the time in question was a hard time for them, and they wonder if God abandoned them during it. God gently explains that those are *his* footprints. That was when he carried them.

Interestingly, several writers claim to have originated this story, on dates ranging from 1936 to 1964.[10] We will probably never know where it really came from, but its sense of reassurance and comfort is profound.

### The path of supported growth

In practice, most people wander through life on a middle path, one that blends elements of mastery and deliverance. Those on this path rely on someone or something, in part; but they also rely on practice and the refinement of skills.

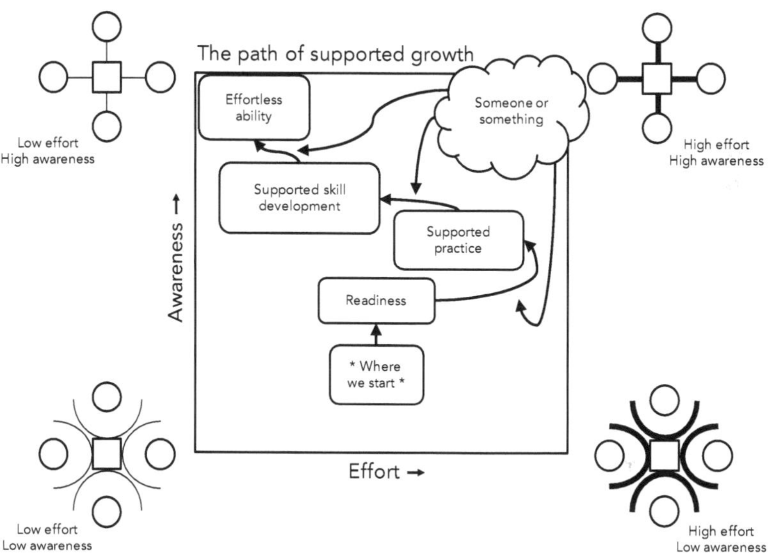


The starting direction of the middle path goes neither to the right nor the left. It doesn't require you to adhere to a strict schedule or hide in a dark room. You just go about things as you were; but you are *ready to pay attention* to what you can do and how you can get help to do it. As the ancient Greek playwright Euripides wrote, "He who strives will find his gods strive for him equally."

## Three paths, one destination

One way to sum up the three paths is to consider how a person might learn to play a musical instrument—say a guitar.

A person who followed the path of mastery would practice playing the guitar every day. They would think about how they wanted to play the guitar in ten years' time, and they'd figure out which exercises would help them get there. They would make up rules for themselves, such as "Twenty minutes a day, without fail" or "Once I have played my scales and my chords, I can play whatever I want." They might or might not look for a teacher, but if they did, they would pepper the teacher with questions and pick their brain for ideas. In time they would amaze everyone with their mad skills.

A person who followed the path of deliverance with an organized benefactor would *definitely* go to a teacher. In fact, choosing the right teacher would be the last decision they would make. Once they were sure of their choice, they would put themselves entirely into that person's hands and do whatever they were told to do. They would say, "What sort of guitar player should I be?" and "How often should I play?" and "Should I play my scales first?" They wouldn't make up rules for themselves; they would hope that their teacher—the person who was going to make a guitar player out of them—would do that for them.

A person who followed the path of deliverance with a non-organized source of support wouldn't go to a teacher; they'd go to a *guitar*. And they wouldn't *play* the guitar; they'd *play with* the guitar. They would explore it, get to know it, figure it out. They would learn about the physics of sound and the acoustical properties of strings. They would learn how guitars are made and how guitar music has changed over the years. They'd look at how people they admired played the guitar, hang out with other guitar players, and think about their own style and talent. They would make no up-front decisions; they would just start playing and see where it led them. Eventually, they would evolve a way of playing the guitar that made sense to them deep inside, and they wouldn't mind if nobody else in the whole world played the guitar that way.

A person who followed the middle path of supported growth would do *all* of these things. They would practice diligently, seek out guidance, and explore.

I wonder if you're laughing right now because I've just described everybody you know. There's no doubt that the path we choose has a lot to do with the way we are, with our individual personalities. That's a good thing. All of these paths are equally valid and honorable. The problem comes in when we think everyone *else* should learn and think the way we do.

## The plan (organized) thinking space

You may have noticed that I have broken my previous chapter structure, which considered each of the four corners of the space *before* giving examples that range across it. I know. It bothers me too. I did *try* to write the chapter that way, but those three paths wouldn't let me take them apart. Let's see if I can make it up to you now.

### Low effort, low awareness

In the lower-left corner of the space, as we have seen, nothing much happens. The organizer sits waiting for help or instructions.

Waiting is not the only thing that happens here, though. Sometimes we need to retreat to quietude just to gather our strength and reboot our cluttered minds, even if we're not waiting for anything in particular. Sometimes we need a break before we head back out into the storm.

## High effort, high awareness

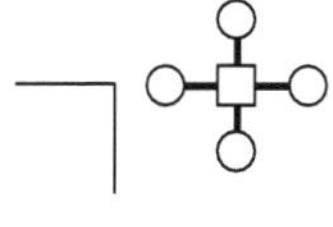

In the upper-right corner, effort and awareness are both at their highest. This is where you can find the benefactors: clergy, government workers, scientists, doctors, teachers, parents. If you are one of these people, this is where you work. Exhausting, isn't it? (Every teacher reading this just sighed.)

Are there reasons to be in this top right corner *other* than to act as a benefactor? I can't think of any. Generally the better anyone gets at anything, the less effort they need to use to do it. So as people rise up in awareness they tend to work themselves over to the left. Of course, that comfy place can also be a danger, because it's easy to ooze back down without realizing it. It's almost like the top of the space—peak awareness—keeps receding, so the whole thing is more like a treadmill than a static space.

That's why benefaction benefits benefactors. It moves them over into a place where they exert more effort, and that effort causes them to re-assess where they are on the space, which may not be as high up as they thought. I've been working in my field for either twenty or thirty-five years, depending on how you define "my field," and I am absolutely grateful for every question I get from novices—and every criticism, no matter how ill-founded. I always respond to such queries with effort, because I believe that if I don't, I will wake up one day to find myself obsolete and confused in a world I don't recognize.

Of course, it goes without saying that some supposed benefactors are actually parasites or monsters. The state in Orwell's novel *1984* is a perfect example of an all-knowing, all-powerful villain—to the extent that even the resistance to the plan is part of the plan. It's a nightmare scenario. (When I read *1984* to my son, I had to stop near the end; I couldn't say those things out loud.) Thankfully, though, such aberrations are few, and most helpers do help.

## Low effort, high awareness

The most important thing to remember about the upper-left corner is: if you think you're here, you're probably not.

In Plato's *Phaedro,* Socrates tells the story of how his friend Chaerephon asked the oracle at Delphi if anyone was wiser than his friend Socrates. The priestess replied that no one was wiser.

On hearing this, Socrates set out to correct the oracle by finding someone wiser than himself.

> I went to one who had the reputation of wisdom . . . and tried to explain to him that he thought himself wise, but was not really wise; and the consequence was that he hated me, and his enmity was shared by several who were present and heard me.
>
> So I left him, saying to myself, as I went away: Well, although I do not suppose that either of us knows anything really beautiful and

> good, I am better off than he is—for he knows nothing, and thinks that he knows. I neither know nor think that I know.

When I find myself thinking I'm an "expert" in anything (usually after someone says I am), I remember that story. I like to place myself into the character of the person "who had the reputation of wisdom" and laugh at how ridiculous I look. It's energizing, like a bracing dip in a cold mountain stream. I highly recommend the remedy. (It also helps to type "Dunning-Kruger effect" into a search engine a few times a year.)

### High effort, low awareness

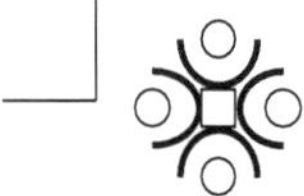

The lower-right corner is a *calamity*. It's a bull in a china shop, the blind leading the blind, the fools who rush in. We have so many stories and so many proverbs about this corner because *we should never go there*. But the very first step you take on the path of mastery leads you near this corner. That's why it's a hard path to walk. To succeed, you must be ready to teeter on the edge of disaster.

Once I was hired for a job, and I asked my boss why he chose me. He said, "Because you failed in business. That means you know something." He was right, but the failing part wasn't much fun.

The price of mastery is that you have to make your own mistakes. More importantly, you have to *own* your mistakes. You have to pay attention to them, even when you don't want to, so you can learn what you need to move forward. That's why they call this path "the school of hard knocks"—because it hurts.

What's the price of deliverance? Well, though your benefactor *probably* has your best interests at heart, they might not. You could end up far from where you want to be without a return ticket.

The price of the middle path is that the greatest potential benefits of the other two paths are closed to you. You hedged your bets, and you're safe; but you might have turned away from a source of help that could have made things easier for you. At the same time, you might have developed better skills and understandings if you had worked things out on your own.

## Crossing the plan (organized) space

Now, having described the four corners of the space, I will go through some examples that range across it.

### The wu-wei spider

Web-building spiders spend most of their time waiting for things to land in their webs. When something does get caught, it might not be something they can eat. So spiders have evolved a way to conserve effort in the face of uncertainty. When a spider senses a disturbance in its web, it grabs a few strands of the web and *plucks* them like the strings of a violin. Then it waits to see what will happen next.

If there is no response, the spider knows that the disturbance was probably just a twig or something else it can ignore. If there *is* a response, the spider can tell from the pattern of vibrations on the strings (each of which is "tuned" to its own frequency) what type of prey has been caught; and it can use that information to decide what to do next. For example, large or energetic prey could be dangerous, so the spider might wait for it to calm down before moving closer. Or the disturbance might be a mate rather than a meal. By using its web to amplify its awareness, the spider reduces its effort.

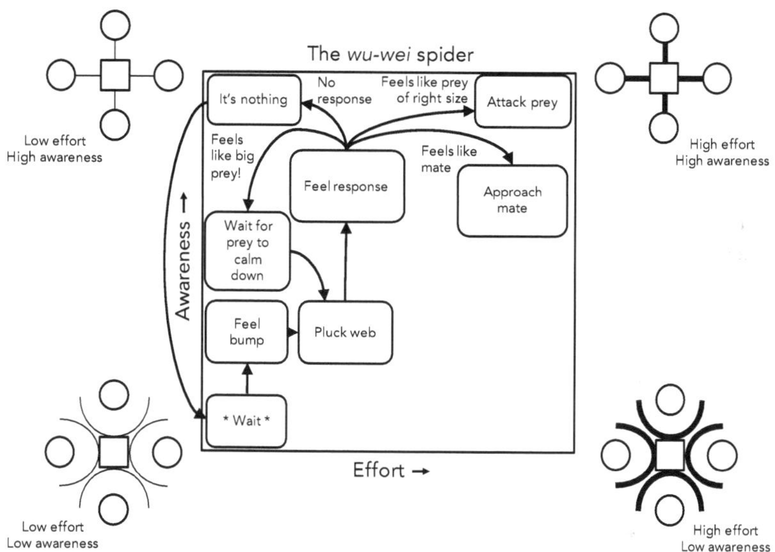


## Effort and awareness in Chekhov's *The Duel*

Anton Pavlovich Chekhov was, in my opinion, one of the finest writers who ever lived. His 1891 novelette *The Duel* is one of my favorite stories. Recently I read it for the sixth time, and this time I think I finally understood it—just in time, it turns out, because *The Duel* is a treatise on the paths of mastery and deliverance.

If you haven't read *The Duel*, you have three choices at this moment: read it, then come back (it's short, and you can find it on the internet[11]); spoil your reading with my summary; or skip this section and come back to it another time. Passing over this example won't ruin the chapter for you. Just skip down to the heading past the next diagram, then start reading again.

### Escape from escape

Ivan Andreitch Laevsky moved to a sleepy little town on the Black Sea with his mistress, Nadyezyhda Fyodorovna, two years ago. Both are in their late twenties. She happens to be married to someone else.

Laevsky is a government functionary, but he barely works. He spends most of his time shuffling around in slippers, drinking, playing cards, and complaining. He describes himself as a "superfluous man" caught up in the "degeneration" of the Russian upper class after the emancipation of the serfs.

Laevsky's closest friend in the Caucasus is an army doctor named Samoylenko. As the story begins, Laevsky shows Samoylenko a letter with the news that Nadyezyhda Fyodorovna's husband has died. This has put Laevsky into a difficult position, because "To show her this letter would mean: let's kindly go to church and get married."[12] The problem is that Laevsky has fallen out of love with Nadyezyhda Fyodorovna, "as it happens," he says.

The move to the Caucasus was supposed to be the start of a new life for Laevsky. He and Nadyezyhda Fyodorovna were going to buy a plot of land and start a lovely vineyard. But, thinks Laevsky, it's *hot* here, and everything is *boring*, and there might be *snakes*. Also, Nadyezyhda Fyodorovna doesn't seem half as exciting in the Caucasus as she did in Moscow. Now the only thing Laevsky can think of is escape—back to Moscow, and alone. "To the pines, to the mushrooms, to people, to ideas. . . ."

Meanwhile, Nadyezyhda Fyodorovna's enthusiasm for their plan has also dwindled. In her boredom she has taken lovers and run up debts, and she has also begun to think of escape.

**Another point of view**

Samoylenko has another friend: the zoologist von Koren. This young man has a strong head on his shoulders—too strong. He's an intellectual and a scientist, and he is well versed in the theories of Herbert Spencer and the other social Darwinists of the day. Von Koren knows his function in society, works hard to fulfill it, and expects everyone else to do the same. He constantly pesters Pobyedov, an empty-headed young deacon who never seems to stop laughing, to work harder and to plan his career with more vigor.

One day von Koren tells Samoylenko that he considers Laevsky so worthless that if he saw him drowning he would "help him along with a stick." Samoylenko says that's not true, and von Koren responds, "Why don't you think so? I'm as capable of a good deed as you are." He then counts off the ways in which Laevsky has spread dissipation and debauchery among the locals. Because natural selection no longer weeds out such cancerous growths on society, he says, "we ourselves must take care of destroying the feeble and unfit" before they multiply. At the very least, he says, such "incorrigible" people should be isolated from society and put to "common labor."

I am sure you have guessed by now that von Koren represents the path of mastery and Laevsky the path of deliverance. Von Koren, certain that his path is the right one, tries to convince everyone around him to join him on it. Laevsky doesn't try to change anyone's mind. It's true that he taught the locals dissipation and debauchery, but he did it accidentally. What Laevsky wants is deliverance. He escaped from home to school, then from school to the arms of a woman, then from Moscow to the Caucasus. Now it is Moscow that will deliver him from the Caucasus and the woman. He comes to Samoylenko, distraught, and begs him to lend him the money for the trip right away.

Samoylenko has little cash on hand, so he needs to borrow money from von Koren to give to Laevsky. Von Koren guesses what Samoylenko needs the money for, and . . . it doesn't go well. Insults are traded, the situation escalates, and a challenge is declared and accepted. There will be a duel.

**The abyss**

The night before the duel, Laevsky is led by one of Nadyezyhda Fyodorovna's jealous lovers to discover her in the arms of yet another lover. Believing that he has now lost his chance at a "beautiful, pure life," whether or not he survives the duel, Laevsky undergoes a storm-tossed night of soul-searching in which he finally sees himself for what he is.

> He had never planted a single tree in his own garden, nor grown a single blade of grass, and, living amidst the living, had never saved a single fly, but had only destroyed, ruined, and lied, lied. . . .
>
> "What in my past is not vice?" he kept asking himself, trying to clutch at some bright memory, as someone falling into an abyss clutches at a bush.[13]

By the next morning, Laevsky is a changed man, ready to turn over a new leaf. Von Koren, however, slept soundly and made no such plan. He shoots directly at Laevsky, whose life is spared only by a desperate cry from the deacon, who had been hiding in the bushes nearby.

**You know best**

The point at which von Koren begins to question *his* beliefs comes in the moments immediately after the duel. He has this exchange with the deacon—who, remember, he has been bullying throughout the story:

> "I was strongly tempted to finish the scoundrel off," said von Koren, "but you shouted right then, and I missed. However, this whole procedure is revolting to someone unaccustomed to it, and it's made me tired, Deacon. I feel terribly weak. Let's go . . . "
>
> "No, kindly allow me to go on foot. I've got to dry out, I'm all wet and chilly."
>
> "Well, you know best," the weakened zoologist said in a weary voice, getting into the carriage and closing his eyes. "You know best."[14]

This is von Koren's moment of reckoning, when he realizes how much he doesn't know about life and death. After all, the duel was as dangerous to him as it was to Laevsky. If the deacon had not called out, von Koren would almost certainly have been sent to hard labor in Siberia, and he might not have returned from such a sentence.

**Two steps forward, one step back**

The action then skips ahead three months to von Koren's previously scheduled departure. Laevsky and Nadyezyhda Fyodorovna, quietly married, have moved to more modest lodgings and are working hard to pay off their debts. Von Koren visits them one last time and makes a concession that shows how much he has changed:

> "I was mistaken concerning you, but one can stumble even on a smooth road, and such is human fate: if you're not mistaken in the main thing, you'll be mistaken in the details. No one knows the real truth."[15]

This refrain—no one knows the real truth—is echoed twice more by Laevsky as he watches von Koren leave the shore in a small boat on a stormy sea. "The boat is thrown back," he says, and "So it is in life. . . . In search of the truth, people make two steps forward and one step back."

The duel forces both Laevsky and von Koren to re-assess their positions and discover that they are lower in the space of organization than they thought. Laevsky realizes that he and Nadyezyhda Fyodorovna must stop waiting for deliverance and save themselves. Von Koren realizes that his attempts to organize others have been turning him into the social cancer he sought to eradicate. The fact that both men receive deliverance from their brush with death makes the fascinating point that deliverance does not always wait to be sought.

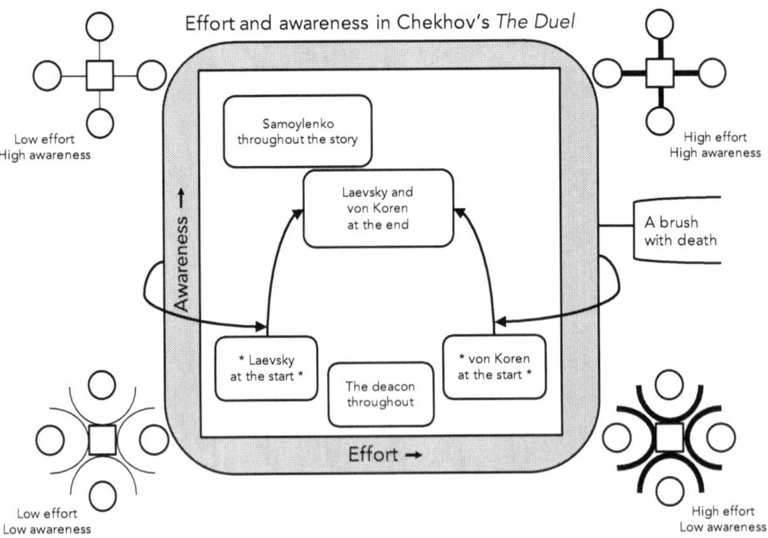


Samoylenko's position stays the same throughout the story. Indeed, he sits out the entire duel, and he has almost nothing to say in the last chapter. I take this to mean that though Samoylenko has more awareness than either Laevsky or von Koren (this is clear in his conversations throughout the story), he senses that his awareness is not transferable, so he does not try to save his friends. My guess is that he represents Chekhov himself, and his refusal to intervene speaks against well-meant but futile attempts to direct the lives of others.

I once thought the deacon existed merely to cry out from the bushes; but I am beginning to suspect that Chekhov meant him as an example of a person living a simple but balanced life. The deacon proves that, even for someone who is almost absurdly unaware, it is possible to neither insist on deliverance nor burden others with unwelcome attempts at it. We can each make our way to enlightenment by any path we choose, Chekhov seems to be saying, but we should do it with responsibility and compassion.

### Two views of childhood

Of all the organized things people do, arguably the most important is raising children, because it has a ripple effect on everything else. At different times and in different places, the questions "What are children?" and "What do children need?" have been answered by every organizer in human life: religion, culture, government, science, education. Across all of these organizers, two fundamental beliefs about childhood have competed, each waxing and waning in influence as the years have gone by. See if you can pick up the parallel threads in the following descriptions.

From a religious perspective, children have often been portrayed as angels whose state of grace we should protect and even emulate. In the Bible, for example, Jesus says, "It is to those who are childlike that the Kingdom of the Heavens belongs." On the other hand, religious leaders have long warned that children are uniquely vulnerable to attack by the devil, so they must be watched over (and kept in line) while they are being taught right from wrong. For example, the fourth-century theologian Jerome gave this advice to a young monk: "Always have some work on hand, that the devil may find you busy."

Some cultural scholars have argued that children are authentic human beings whose innocent wonder can save us all—if we can allow them to develop naturally, without force. In the words of Friedrich Fröbel, the German pedagogue who coined the word "kindergarten,"

> [T]he child in his quiet diligence tells us that he must know the properties and uses of all the things he finds, but we dismiss his activity as childish because we fail to understand it . . . We shout at him and say he is clumsy, but he is much wiser than we are.[16]

Others have seen children as uncivilized brutes who must be taught how to behave among others if we are to avoid societal collapse. Said John Locke:

> He that is not used to submit his will to the reason of others when he is young, will scarce hearken or submit to his own reason when he is of age to make use of it.[17]

To governmental bodies, children are people with rights, which we must defend; but they also have responsibilities, to which we must see that they attend. The 1959 UN Declaration of the Rights of the Child protects children when it says, "[T]he child, for the full and harmonious development of his or her personality, should grow up in a family environment, in an atmosphere of happiness, love and understanding." But the very next clause hints at responsibility: "[T]he child should be fully prepared to live an individual life in society."[18]

Scientifically speaking, attachment theory portrays young children as vulnerable beings dependent on unconditional love and support. Psychologist John Bowlby recommended that caregivers take on the role of "being available, ready to respond when called upon to encourage and perhaps assist, but to intervene actively only when clearly necessary."[19] On the other hand, behavioral psychology demonstrated that the careful shaping of behavior through conditioning could produce socially desirable outcomes. Behaviorism itself has faded from view, but many of its conditioning techniques are still in use.

From an educational perspective, some have portrayed children as resilient, creative learners whose innate enthusiasm helps them face challenge after challenge—when adults can get out of their way. Said Jean Piaget: "Every time we teach a child something, we keep him from inventing it himself."[20]

Other educators have portrayed children as heedless drifters who must be taught to apply themselves if they are not to wander through their lives ignorant and feckless. Those with this view would agree with Thomas Henry Huxley when he said:

> Perhaps the most valuable result of all education is the ability to make yourself do the thing you have to do, when it ought to be done, whether you like it or not.[21]

Do you see the pattern? In each of these comparisons, the first perspective focuses on the needs of children to develop *awareness*, and the second focuses on their need to exert *effort*. It is remarkable to what extent these two visions of childhood have persisted, from ancient times to the present day, across many economic and cultural conditions, and through many waves of influence.

**An awareness-based view**

The first approach to raising children we will consider is focused on awareness. From this point of view, children are *born ready to make an effort*, full of curiosity and enthusiasm. What they lack is awareness. It is the role of caregivers to help children satisfy their curiosity and develop their awareness. If we show children the world, say proponents of this view, they will rise up to meet the challenge. What we *don't* want is for them to fall into ignorance, thoughtlessness, and vulnerability to manipulation.

In a child's early years, caregivers who focus on awareness provide freedom to explore by meeting the child's needs with unconditional and unrestricted support. When children cry, they are held; when hungry, they are fed; when afraid, they are comforted. When they need a helping hand, it is there.

Because awareness-focused caregivers consider it their primary duty to help children explore the world, they spend a lot of time talking to children and answering their questions. Nothing is hidden; everything is explained, even things that are complicated or frightening. Fred Rogers was a famous proponent of talking frankly to children about difficult things. He believed they deserved to know the truth—and could handle it.

Awareness-focused caregivers don't *encourage* effort; they *assume* it. They allow children to set goals that are difficult or even impossible to achieve, not because they don't care, but because they believe that whether children succeed or fail in any particular goal, they will learn something. As the old saying goes, *everything is grist that comes to the mill.* When you hear someone say that children are like sponges, soaking up everything around them, that's a focus on awareness.

Working from this assumption, awareness-focused caregivers invite children to explore perplexing issues and allow ambiguities to remain unresolved. For example, the educator John Holt suggested that caregivers follow this rule: *Never ask a child a question whose answer you already know.* Thus instead of asking, "What color is the cat?" you might ask, "What do you notice about the cat?" The second question invites the child to forge their own path of discovery.

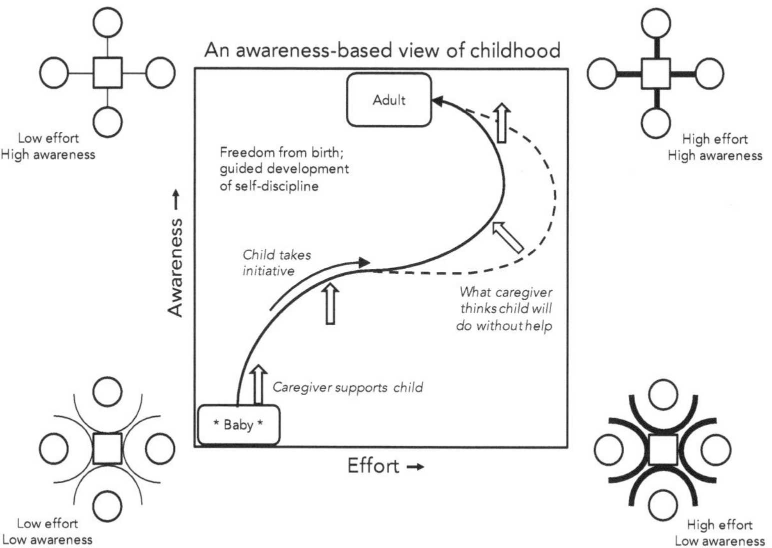


When a child begins to make an effort toward learning about a topic, awareness-focused caregivers meet them halfway, helping them find and evaluate learning resources, seek out answers to their questions, and discuss their options. But they carefully avoid structuring the experience. They stay in the background, as resources and helpers, because they want the child to develop their own skills as an organizer. Their goal is to help the child learn from the attempt, whether it succeeds or fails, so they can move on to bigger challenges in the future.

**An effort-based view**

The second approach to raising children is focused on effort. From this perspective, children are born eager to learn, but they are hampered by their inability to *apply themselves* to tasks. It is the role of caregivers to help children learn how to do this. Teach children *industry*, say proponents of this view, and they will be empowered to obtain awareness—and every other goal they want to achieve. What we *don't* want is for them to end up weak, idle, dependent on others, and unable to take on adult responsibilities.

In a child's early years, effort-focused caregivers help them achieve control over their bodies, minds, and emotions with scheduled feedings, sleep training, and other managed activities. The goal is not to confine or punish children but to teach them how to regulate themselves. The push towards effort continues as the child grows, with increasingly complicated schedules to keep, projects to complete, procedures to follow, and chores to carry out.

These caregivers want children to develop confidence in their abilities, just like those with an awareness-focused perspective. But because of their fundamental belief that *all children will slide into helpless inaction* if left to their own devices, effort-focused caregivers see unconditional freedom as a danger rather than a benefit. So instead of *waiting* for children to show interest in topics, they bring the topics to the children. They design experiences that fit each child's current awareness and move them one step closer to understanding—through the application of effort, proving that *you can do anything you set your mind to.*

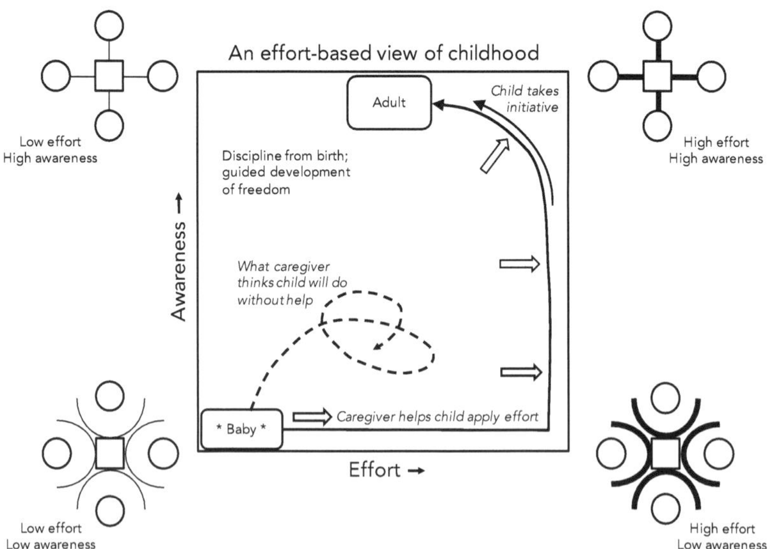

Effort-focused caregivers believe that complicated or sensitive topics should be kept away from children until they are better equipped to understand them. They measure out freedom *and* information in ever-expanding circles, as children prove themselves ready to handle them. Awareness-focused caregivers, by contrast, believe that children are ready to handle everything all the time. They see no problem, for example, with letting children puzzle out adult-level reading material, if they are so inclined. An effort-focused caregiver would find this not only ill-advised but cruel, *because it could cause the child to apply effort without achieving success*, and that would deplete the child's limited supply of effort. The child should instead be given age-appropriate reading material.

Eventually, effort-focused caregivers feel that young people have successfully learned to apply effort on their own, so they "give over the reins" and let them assume responsibility for their own learning.

### Comparing the two views

We can compare these approaches by looking at how they help children learn new skills. If an effort-focused caregiver wanted to help a child learn, say, how to bake a pie, they would first demonstrate—or *model*—the baking of a pie. Then they would lead the child through an organized pie-baking experience whose instructions were carefully designed to reward effort with success. Only after this exercise would the caregiver allow the child free access to the kitchen.

An awareness-focused caregiver would simply bake pies, making sure to work in plain sight; and they would let the child use the kitchen right away. If the child started baking a pie, they would offer to help, answering questions and fetching ingredients. If the pie came out badly, they would offer to help the child figure out what went wrong. But they would not find it necessary to make sure the child succeeded, because they would assume the child would *eventually* want to try again. From the awareness-based perspective, effort is a renewable resource.

If the child *never* expressed an interest in baking a pie, an awareness-focused caregiver would simply assume that the child wanted to apply effort elsewhere. If they felt for some reason that the baking of pies was an important part of life, they would *talk* to the child about pie-baking in their own life, and they would discuss what happens when a person does or does not bake pies. In the end they would leave it up to the child to decide whether or not they would like to be a pie-baking sort of person—but they would make sure that the child was fully *aware* of the consequences of that decision.

### Combining the two views

Few children are raised with either of these approaches in its pure state; most experience some mixture of the two. The balance tends to lean towards awareness in indigenous cultures and effort in non-indigenous cultures.[22] Still, only in rare cases is the other approach completely disregarded. Often the balance changes as children grow through different phases of childhood.

Also, most children have multiple caregivers who help them in different ways. A child's parent might focus on effort while a grandparent sets them off-balance with puzzling challenges. Or they might benefit from different learning environments at home and at school. Even within one person's care the two approaches can intermingle. A caregiver might be awareness-focused about academic learning, for example, but effort-focused when it comes to chores.

The most important source of variation lies in children themselves. Some do better with open space, and some do better with structure. But these needs are relative, not absolute. A child who does better with structure does *even better* with *mostly* structure and a *little* open space. This, I think, is why the presence of multiple caregivers who can offer a *diversity* of approaches is such a beneficial environment for learning. The saying "it takes a village to raise a child" may be true not because of the effort involved but because of the diversity we need *among ourselves* to provide our children with the help they need.

# 6 Inundation

*Thinking about how self-organization influences organization*

In Chapter Two, we considered how organization and self-organization happen together (or don't). In Chapters Four and Five, we looked at each force on its own. Now we will focus on how the two forces *influence* each other. We'll start with how self-organization influences organization.

This is our thinking space. The vertical axis shows the amount of self-organization: low at the bottom, high at the top, just as in Chapter Two.

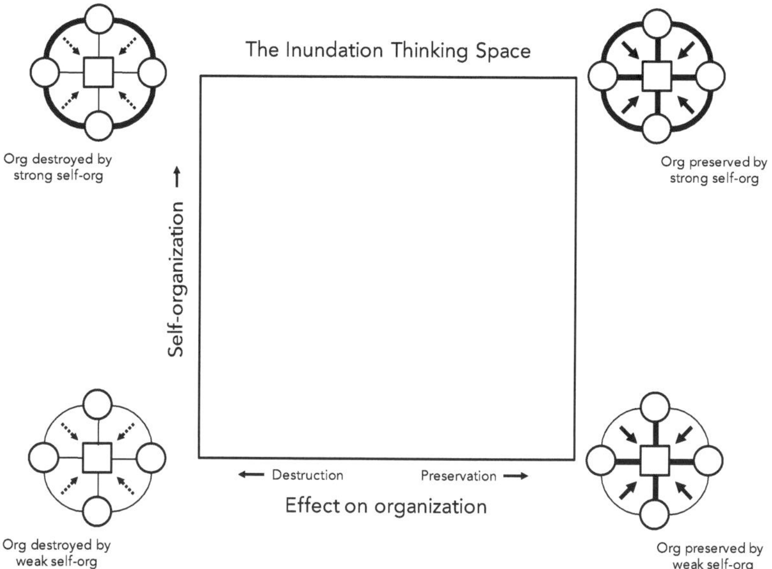


The horizontal axis of this space is different from any of the axes you've seen thus far. This is a *causal* relationship. In the previous chapters, the things on the two axes either happened together or they didn't, but they didn't *influence* each other. Here the amount of self-organization *pushes on* the amount of organization in the situation, driving it up or down. That's why the arrows point both ways: because influence can be positive or negative.

On the left side of the space, the amount of self-organization—the fact that it is strong or weak, high or low—*tears apart* organized structures and plans. On the right side, strong or weak self-organization *preserves* existing structures and supports the creation of new ones. Halfway across, the amount of self-organization in the situation has no impact on the amount of organization—or the forces of preservation and destruction are perfectly balanced.

## The inundation thinking space

Where can we get some good examples to help us think about how self-organization influences organization? When I asked myself this question, my mind went directly to the topic of ghost towns. (Maybe *your* mind would have gone somewhere else, but that's what I thought of. Remember, these thinking spaces are not about exploring reality in a general sense; they are about exploring reality from specific perspectives.)

Ghost towns are paradoxical places: beautiful yet broken, silent but filled with history. I count twelve factors that contribute to the development of ghost towns. In ten of them, self-organization influences organization. As we work our way around the space, we will meet with each of the factors.

### When strong self-organization destroys organization

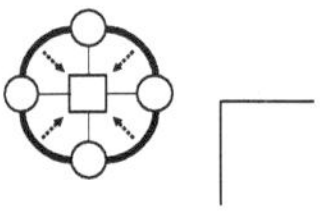

In the upper-left corner of the inundation space, self-organization is a force of destruction. Here I place two of the twelve factors that contribute to the formation of ghost towns: natural disasters (obviously) and industrial accidents (not so obviously, but I'll explain why when we get there).

**Factor 1: Natural disasters**

Natural disasters are the clearest examples of self-organized patterns that destroy organized plans: tornadoes, hurricanes, earthquakes, tsunamis, avalanches, floods, fires, volcanic eruptions. During such a disaster, if anything *can* be done, first responders work to limit the scope of damage.

When you listen to first responders talk about their work, you can tell they operate in an environment of high self-organization. They don't talk about fixed plans. They talk about forces, and they talk about boundaries. They talk about "reading" the situation—the room, the fire, the herd, the crowd, the waves—to assess risks and options. They rely more on tacit intuition drawn from lived experience than explicit knowledge of processes and structures. They know they can't *stop* the disaster, but they can mitigate its damage by sensing its forces and maintaining boundaries that protect the most vulnerable people and places.

After the storm ends, the situation moves to the lower-left corner, to the aftermath. The self-organized force that caused the disaster has been spent, and nearly all connections, organized and self-organized, have been broken. People search for relatives or wander through the remains of their homes.

In response to the disaster, people come to the site from all around, ready to help. This welcome surge of social adrenaline increases the amount of both organization (as temporary structures and plans are put in place) and self-organization (as new connections form and old ones are rebuilt).

But the response phase is usually short-lived.[1] The outsiders rush off to the next disaster, and the locals are left with a depleted sense of energy. Conditions in the secondary aftermath are not as bad as they were at first, but they can *feel* worse. It's harder to cope without outside help, and the true scope of the loss begins to set in as people start thinking beyond the next few hours or days.

It is in this secondary aftermath that people sometimes turn away from each other in their despondency. Thus self-organization falls a second time—and support for organization falls with it, as people lose the energy to maintain structures that were erected during the time of outside support.

If self-organization falls far enough, the town can simply disappear as people are drawn away to stronger connections outside it. Some go to live with relatives and never return. Some find new work elsewhere. Some are just too overwhelmed to remain. It is not uncommon for devastated towns to empty out, leaving only a small number of people to pick up the pieces.

If there are enough inhabitants left, or if new people come, new connections may form. Then, over the months and years, survivors may heal and lay down new layers of experience. Only when self-organization recovers is it possible to rebuild the structures and plans of an organized town.

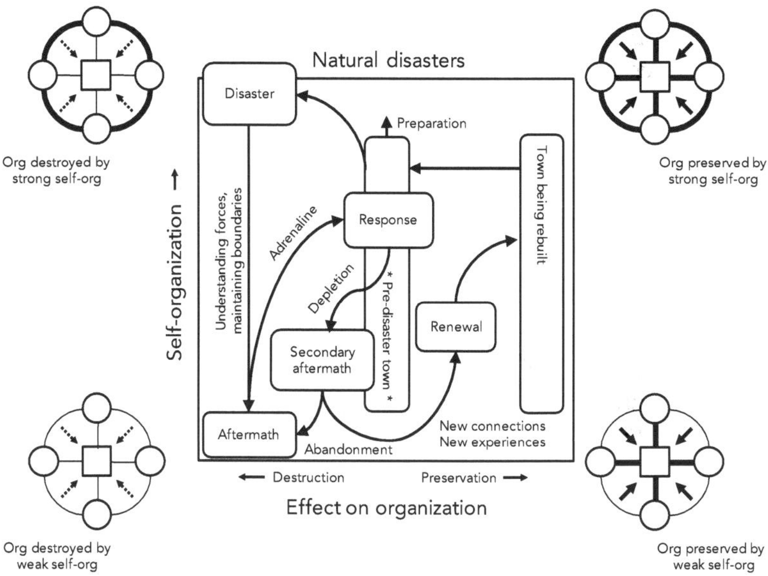


What determines whether self-organization will recover? Why does one town rebound while another disappears? It has a lot to do with what each town was like *before* the disaster came. People almost always come together and help each other at first—but even as they do, tensions that existed before the disaster come into play. A town with strong, resilient connections is likely to recover more quickly and completely than a town with weak or brittle connections.

That's why I drew the town, both pre-disaster and during rebuilding, as two *tall* boxes along the height of possible self-organization. Anything a town can do to increase the strength and resilience of its self-organized connections will increase its chance of coming through its next disaster intact.

You've probably seen Maslow's pyramid of needs: basic needs at the bottom (food, water, shelter); then safety (health, security, resources); then belonging, esteem, and self-actualization. After a natural disaster, basic needs come first, of course. But it is belonging and esteem—being a proud part of a strong community—that matter most in rebuilding long-term support for basic needs. Those who study disaster response are increasingly recommending that outside helpers allocate some of their resources to helping victims strengthen the bonds of community *immediately* after a disaster. They might, for example, set up meeting places where survivors can find friends and family members, share knowledge and experiences, and coordinate group efforts. In this way, responders can help communities maintain their self-organized connections so people will have a *reason* to stay and rebuild the town.

***Build back better?***

Should devastated towns be rebuilt? Throughout history, natural disasters have warned us that certain locations are best avoided—until the disasters fade from memory, that is, and people build there anyway.

In *Thinking in Time*, Richard Neustadt and Ernest May explain that memories of events in one's own generation and the one just before it tend to have an exaggerated influence on decision making.[2] Such "folk memories," they claim, cause people to make choices that are not always in their best interest. In the years immediately following a natural disaster, traumatic folk memories push people away from devastated sites. But after a few decades have gone by, memories of the *town* may become stronger than memories of the *disaster*. It seems like such a peaceful, quiet place. Why not rebuild it?

The Italian countryside is dotted with thousands of abandoned hillside towns destroyed by earthquakes over the past few centuries. One of the more interesting examples is Bussana Vecchia. The town was hit by a severe earthquake in 1887, killing hundreds. Survivors built a new city in the valley below, and the old city sat empty for decades. In the 1940s, a handful of immigrants tried to settle in the ruined town. Police evicted them in the name of safety. To discourage other potential residents, they removed the town's first-floor stairways and rooftops.

In the 1960s, a small colony of artists formed in the abandoned town. Calling themselves the "International Artists' Village," they rebuilt some of the town's buildings using materials they drew from the rubble. Another confrontation with police in 1968 led to a long court battle, which led to a 1998 eviction order—and to an appeal, which (at the time of writing) is still pending. As the years of stalemate went on, residents added running water, electricity, and a septic system, and the population rose to about a hundred people.

The legal state of Bussana Vecchia is still precarious. The Italian government, to whom the site officially belongs, continues to consider residence in the town illegal as well as unsafe. The residents, however, claim that the site is no more dangerous than any other place in the earthquake-prone area. They point out that the nearby town of San Remo was also hit by the 1887 earthquake but was not abandoned. They suspect that the government wants to evict them not for their safety but because it wants to tax tourism at the popular site. Whether the site is *truly* unsafe is difficult to prove or disprove.

Should people be allowed to rebuild towns that have been devastated by natural disasters? Who will help them when disaster strikes again? And what if disaster *doesn't* strike—for decades? For centuries? Who gets to say what's safe enough? Difficult questions such as these have been asked and answered by millions of people over thousands of years.

One answer can be found in the Japanese countryside, which is littered with "tsunami stones"—warnings to avoid building in areas where tsunamis have obliterated towns in the past. Some of the stones are over a hundred years old. Their warnings are poignant: "Remember the calamity of the great tsunamis. Do not build any homes below this point." Some of the tsunami stones were ignored when new construction surged after World War II. But others were heeded, and they are credited with saving lives in the 2011 tsunami.

**Factor 2: Industrial disasters**

The ghost town of Wittenoom in Western Australia owes its origin to a slow-moving industrial disaster. The town's asbestos mine exposed some 7000 workers to toxic levels of asbestos dust between 1939 and 1966. Health officials raised concerns as early as 1948, but the mine continued to operate for nearly two decades longer. Roughly 2000 cases of fatal lung cancers have been attributed to working in the mine—or simply living near it. Residents were encouraged to leave the area in the 1970s because asbestos had permeated every area of the town. In the early 2000s, the town was officially "degazetted"—removed from all official maps. Tourists are warned that the area is still too dangerous to visit.

The impact of a human-made disaster such as at Wittenoom is similar to that of a natural disaster, but with one important difference: someone is to blame. Justified anger can boost helpful energy in the response period, but it can worsen the secondary aftermath. Psychologists have found that people in chronic pain who see themselves as victims of injustice (rather than simply unfortunate) tend to develop a pervading sense of powerlessness, which can prevent them from reaching out to seek help.[3]

To make things worse, *getting* help after an industrial disaster requires a higher burden of proof. If a tree falls on your house during a storm, the cause of the damage is obvious and irrefutable. Maybe you should have cut the tree, but nobody can say it didn't *fall*. If you were sickened by an industrial disaster, you are likely to have to prove that you were not sick beforehand, that the sickness has had serious effects on your health, and so on. Survivors can be trapped in a double bind: just when they should be healing and looking toward the future, they have to keep revisiting the disaster to prove the extent of their injuries—sometimes for decades. (The first court settlement that awarded compensation to Wittenoom victims was in 1988, forty-nine years after the mine opened.)

The burden of proof can have community-wide effects as well. Those who cause such disasters often claim that no lasting harm was done. Some even claim that victims are gaming the system to get unfair compensation. If some people in the community believe them, the resulting conflict can do more damage than the disaster itself. Of course, some small percentage of people probably *are* gaming the system—and that makes things even harder for those who are legitimately suffering. The fear (or the reality) of *not being believed* might be the worst thing survivors of human-made disasters go through.

***How are industrial accidents self-organized?***

You might be surprised to see that I have placed industrial disasters near the same high-self-organization, high-danger corner of the inundation space as natural disasters. Isn't industry an *organized* activity? Yes, it is. But most of the *accidents* that cause industrial disasters have to do with an excess of self-organization—more than was *expected*, that is.

Once I was at an open house event at our local fire department. The firefighter who led the tour asked if anybody had a question. My husband asked what was the most important thing homeowners should learn about house fires. The firefighter said, "Candles. I wish I could get rid of all the candles in the world! They cause *so* many fires. People start candles going, then just walk away as if they'd switched on a lamp!"

That's what I'm talking about. When we act as if self-organized patterns (like open flames) were organized structures (like electric lamps), our sense of control over the situation can become dangerously inflated. This can cause us to drift into the high-self-organization, high-danger corner of the inundation space—not because self-organization is particularly high (as in a hurricane) but because it's *higher than we imagine it to be.*

Charles Perrow, in his book *Normal Accidents,* described the situation well:

> What distinguishes these interactions is that they were not designed into the system by anybody; no one intended them to be linked. They baffle us because we acted in terms of our own designs of a world that we expected to exist—but the world was different.[4]

Why do people mistake self-organization for organization? Dietrich Dörner explains, in *The Logic of Failure,* that workers who have caused industrial accidents have shown "an inability to think in terms of nonlinear networks of causation rather than chains of causation."[5]

In a causal *chain,* each component influences the next in a linear sequence. It's easy for an organizer to see and manage all of the interactions. In a causal *network,* each component influences two or more components. Organizers have a hard time keeping track of all the interactions, especially those they can't see—or don't believe are possible.

Consider the fact that in most industrial plants, fluids and gases circulate through pipes and valves and hoses. Industrial designers map out where these fluids and gases *should* flow, but they can't always anticipate every situation. When conditions are right (or wrong), fluids and gases can flow into unexpected places—backwards, or up instead of down, or out of places where they must be and into places where they should never be.

The 1979 partial meltdown at the Three Mile Island nuclear power plant in Pennsylvania started when water from a high-pressure water line leaked into a lower-pressure air line. Why were the two lines connected? Because employees had been using the air line to clean out a stuck filter connected to the water line. They forgot to disconnect the lines when they were done with their work. If they had used an independent source of pressurized air, the leak would not have mattered. But they wanted more air pressure, so they tapped into the "instrument air" system—which happened to be connected to critical cooling-water valves. The air line lost pressure, the valves snapped shut, and a chain of events began that almost led to a disaster.

Ironically, the plant's designers *did* anticipate the possibility of water getting into the instrument air system. They planned to set up the cooling-water valves so they would "fail as-is"—that is, stay in place if the air pressure dropped. Unfortunately, the wiring for their improved design was never connected.

### *A matter of scale*

Industrial accidents are as old as industry. The Sumerian legal code of Ur-Nammu, in use 4000 years ago, contains such statements as "If a man knocked out the eye of another man, he shall weigh out half a mina of silver." Some have interpreted this and similar laws as an early form of worker's compensation, because at least some of those eyes must have been knocked out at work.

Consider a water-powered industrial facility, used as long ago as the third century BCE to grind grain, saw wood, and crush stone (and later to weave, print, and sew). A running stream turned a wheel, which turned a shaft, a gear, a belt, and a variety of machines. That sounds like a causal chain, right? But even in such simple situations, unexpected connections routinely appeared. For one thing, workers had clothing and hair, and those "components" sometimes interacted with the gears, shafts, and belts. For another, grain mills, textile factories, and paper mills generated fine mists of dust and lint that could suddenly burst into flames. The history books are full of accounts of workers burned, scalped, and crushed by causal networks industrial designers failed to anticipate.

The difference today is in scale. Technology amplifies, and powerful technology amplifies powerfully. When the self-organized pattern you fail to take into account is a massive, very hot, high pressure, toxic chemical reaction, you're not just talking about a fire. You're talking about a disaster like the 1984 Bhopal gas leak, an event that killed thousands and sickened half a million, and whose impact continues to be felt nearly forty years later.

I will have more to say about self-organization in industrial settings at the end of the chapter, but for now let's move on to the next corner of the space.

## When weak self-organization destroys organization

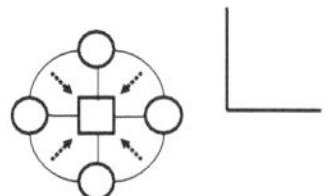

In the lower-left corner of the inundation space, it is the *absence* of self-organization that has a destructive effect on organized plans and structures. In this corner I will place two more of the factors that make a ghost town: resource depletion and anticipatory development.

### Factor 3: Resource depletion

Here we can find countless stories of boom and bust, of people who chased after self-organization that ended too soon. The absence of self-organization in this case is not absolute, but relative to an initial abundance.

A typical boom-bust story goes like this. A self-organized resource is discovered. It could be natural (a vein of gold, a deposit of gas, a good place to fish), cultural (an enchanting tourist destination), medical (healing mineral springs), economic (the perfect spot for a shipping port or trading post), or military (the best place to defend a border). People rush to the spot and build a town. Organization and self-organization rise together in a great cloud of excitement and activity. Then the resource runs out and the self-organization drains away, both in the resource and in the people who rushed to exploit it.

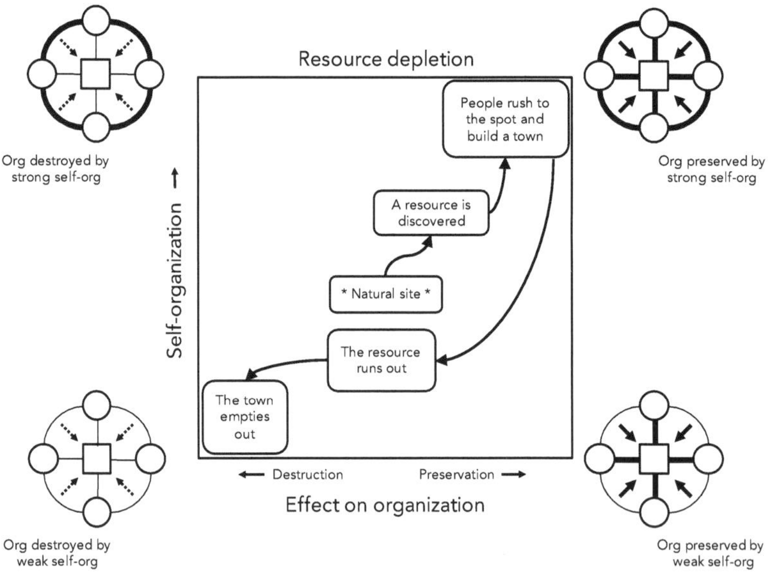


As the town empties out, it loses its collective ability to plan and carry out organized activities. First the town government gets smaller and smaller, until it's down to one part-time employee. Then the post office closes, then the school, then the food market. Finally the town's buildings lose value to the point that they are not worth maintaining—or even demolishing. So they are left behind, and a ghost town is born.

### Factor 4: Anticipatory development

Some ghost towns are abandoned before they are inhabited. This strange situation can happen when someone builds structures in anticipation of a self-organized resource that does not yet exist. Examples are colonial settlements, commercial housing developments, tourist destinations whose creators hope they will become the next big thing, and new-idea political communities that people believe are "waiting to happen" if given the right nudge. Organizers of anticipatory development might be governments, corporations, religious groups, or individuals who simply refuse to give up on something they believe is meant to happen.

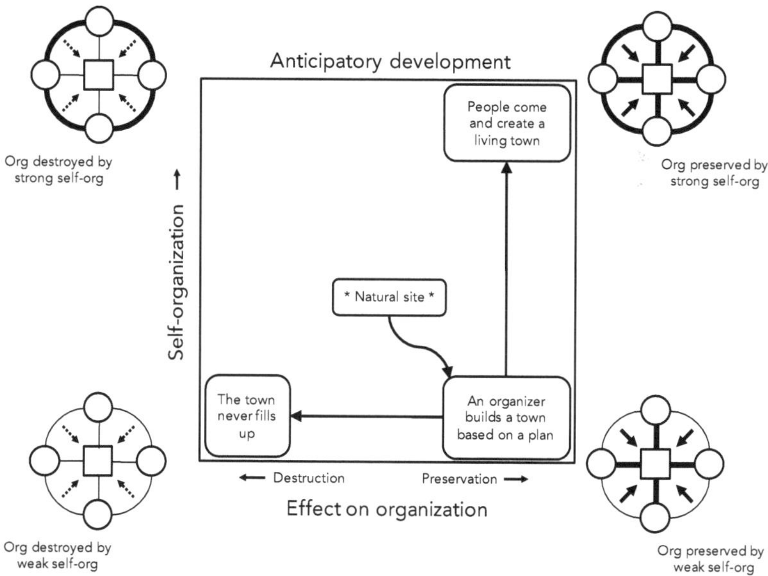


Sometimes anticipatory organizers guess correctly, and the structures they build fill up with people and become lively places, full of energy. But some anticipatory developments sit empty for decades, slowly turning into cautionary tales. When this happens, organizers sometimes *pretend* to have succeeded. They showcase their "thriving" (empty) planned cities, "viral" (ignored) tourist destinations, and "popular" (abandoned) new-idea towns. No one is fooled by such charades, not for long.

That's one of my favorite things about self-organization. No matter how much money or power you have, "if you build it, they will come" can *never* be a statement of fact. It can only ever be a gamble. You can lead a horse to water, but you can't make it drink. Self-organization is the great equalizer. I can't control it, but neither can you, and that makes us the same.

#### *A view from the summit*

At the top of Cambodia's Bokor Mountain stands a group of French colonial buildings with a long and strange history. They were built in the 1920s as a pleasure resort for French soldiers. The site offered stunning views of jungle and sea ("as if atop a huge Elephant"), plus a welcome break from the heat of the city. The Bokor Palace Hotel and Casino, with its grand ballroom and opulent terraces, was accompanied by villas, shops, a post office, and a church. Construction of the buildings, and the long road to the top of the mountain, took a heavy toll on local laborers, with reported deaths nearing a thousand. Some locals say the place is still haunted by the ghosts of those who perished during its construction.

The French abandoned the site in the 1940s during the first Indochina War. The site was soon reopened by King Norodom Sihanouk, and it continued to be used as a retreat for the rich and powerful. But by the 1970s the site was abandoned again. The Khmer Rouge used the mountain as a military base, defending it from the Vietnamese in 1979. By the late 1990s, the area had become a ghost town a third time. In the 2000s, a parade of photographers, travel writers, and tourists made the long journey up the mountain road to take haunting photos of the empty buildings with their creepy-beautiful coverings of bright red lichens and dense black mold.

In 2012, a Chinese investment group leased the area from the government. They renovated and reopened the hotel and casino—at the end of a new modern road. "Honestly," said a travel blogger, "I'm surprised the road doesn't go straight through the middle of the casino with a compulsory stop at the roulette table."[6] The site's new managers have completely resurfaced the old buildings, "ruining the ruins," as some have said. When you look at before-and-after photographs of the hotel, it's hard not to feel a sense of loss, a sense that the voices of the past have been out-shouted by the demands of the future.

This ghost-town story has elements of both resource depletion (economic and political) and anticipatory development. Whether the site will thrive in its new incarnation or go through the cycle a fourth time remains to be seen.

## Two factors that don't belong in this chapter

At this point I have gone through four of the twelve factors that lead to the development of ghost towns: natural and industrial disasters, resource depletion, and failed anticipatory development. Two more destructive factors don't belong in this chapter because they don't have to do with the influence of self-organization on organization. I'll just mention them briefly.

### Factor 5: Deliberate attack

War involves intricate combinations of organization and self-organization, which is why the "Mix" space (Chapter Eight, page 143) fits it best. For now we can simply say that a deliberate attack has a similar destructive effect to a natural disaster. There is the same aftermath, response, secondary aftermath, and gradual recovery, with the same possibility of abandonment.

### Factor 6: Central planning

Sometimes governments or corporations make plans that eradicate or displace towns. A city might destroy a neighborhood to put in a train line, or a country might relocate the population of a town that will be submerged after a dam is built. The dominant force in these situations is organization, so either the "Plan" space (Chapter Five, page 55) or the "Regulation" space (Chapter Seven, page 105) would be most useful for thinking about them.

## The other half of the paradox

No destructive factor can create a ghost town by itself, because destruction is only half of the paradox. A ghost town must be *preserved* as well as destroyed. There are plenty of places in the world where towns once stood, but they are not ghost towns; they are just places. Remember when I said (on page 10) that I grew up in a ghost town? I did, but that was half a century ago. I don't think anyone considers that stretch of roadway a ghost town anymore. The "haunted houses" I used to visit in the woods are all gone now, and if there's no *town*, there's no ghost town. That's why we call them ghost towns: because, like ghosts, they *seem* to be alive when they aren't.

So to fully explore the phenomenon of ghost towns, we need to work through the *right* side of our thinking space: situations in which the amount of self-organization (much or little) *preserves* organized structures and plans.

### When weak self-organization preserves organization

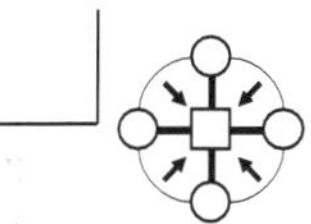

In the lower-right corner of the inundation space, organized structures are preserved by weak self-organization. This is not a surprising place. We expect the things we build to continue to exist when nothing encroaches upon them. Here we can find two factors: protection due to environmental conditions, and protection due to social isolation.

### Factor 7: A protective environment

Some ghost towns are preserved by environments in which there is little non-human self-organization. Intense cold or dryness prevents the usual self-organized patterns—mold, grass, rodents, freeze-thaw cycles—from damaging its structures. This type of ghost town looks like it is stuck in a time warp. There are whaling stations in Antarctica and mining towns in the Chilean Atacama desert where you can find buildings that look as though their inhabitants stepped away from them minutes ago instead of more than a century ago.

The same absence of self-organization can preserve underwater structures. Ships that sank in deep, dark, cold, still waters have been found nearly intact hundreds of years later. Ships that sink in surface-level, light, warm, turbulent waters rot and fall apart over the span of decades.

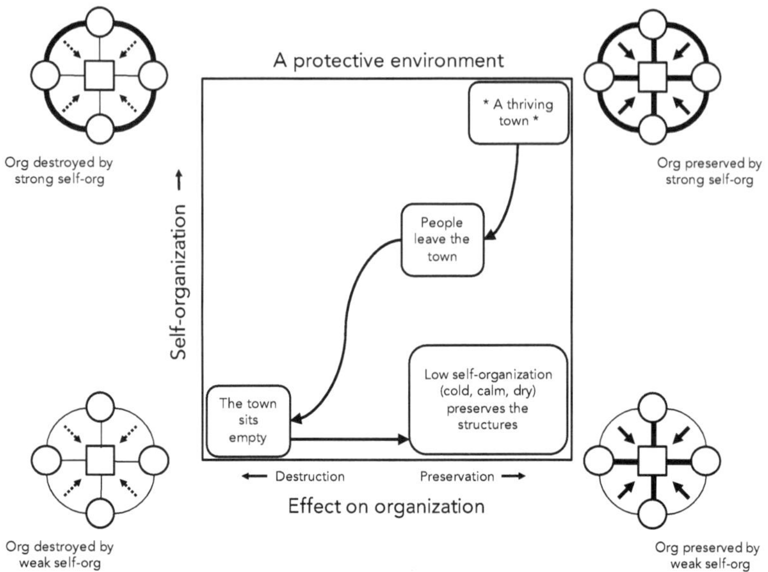


## Factor 8: Protective isolation

The longevity of an occupied town depends primarily on maintenance. Homeowners and building managers regularly check for problems and fix them as soon as they can. When a town is abandoned, it loses much of its coherence because people are no longer taking care of it.

Once a town has emptied out, however, it tends to last longer when people stay away. Maintenance, after all, is only *partly* about protecting buildings from the elements. The other part is protecting buildings from *people*. Wherever we go, we leave behind hair, oil, flakes of skin, and bits of food. These attract molds, fungi, insects, birds, rodents, and other agents of decomposition.

Thus some of the best preserved ghost towns are the most forgotten—that is, the lowest in *human* self-organization.

Some ghost towns are hard to find or hard to reach. Some are in inhospitable environments. Few people want to visit them because they are very wet, dry, hot, or cold. Some are in dangerous places: near volcanoes, on cliffs, under water, in disputed territories. Some are contaminated with nuclear or chemical waste. Some ghost towns develop reputations as taboo, haunted, or sacred: places people ought not to go. Some are owned or managed by governments or corporations that forbid visitors or require hard-to-obtain permits.

And some ghost towns are just unpopular. Being labeled "not worth seeing" might be the best preservative of all.

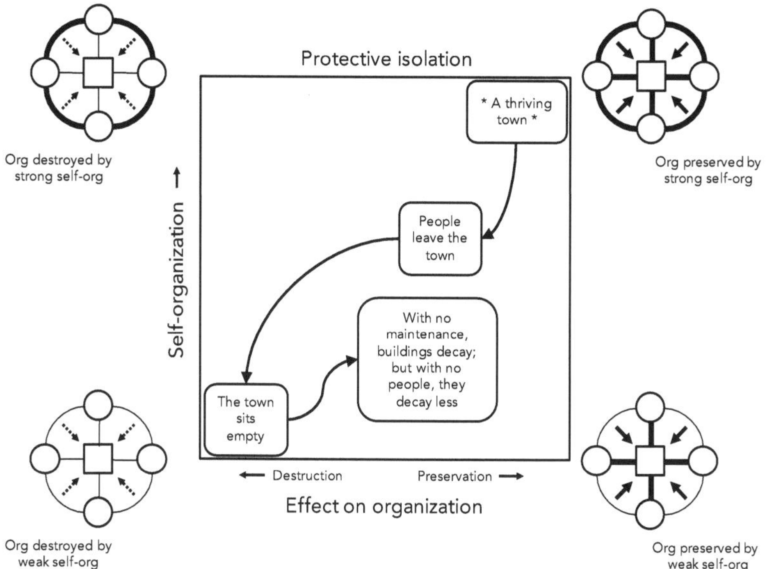


## When strong self-organization preserves organization

In the upper-right corner of the inundation space, strong self-organization preserves organization.

### Factor 9: Protective action

Only one preservative factor is completely positive and consistently high in self-organization. It is collective action. Some ghost towns are preserved because a community of citizens comes together in a groundswell of support. People contribute money, sign petitions, and vote. Of course, there has to be *some* organization involved in such a campaign. Someone has to gather money, write petitions, run for office, and propose legislation. But without self-organization, it's hard to gather the momentum to make preservation a reality.

It may surprise you to learn that historical preservation is a modern invention. Until fairly recently, it was considered perfectly acceptable to tear apart old, beautiful buildings and reuse their materials elsewhere. As Peter Larkham writes in *Conservation and the City*,

> In 1450 alone, Pope Nicholas V is supposed to have removed two thousand cartloads of marble from the Colosseum in a single year, while in about 1500, Pope Alexander VI leased the ruins for exploitation as a commercial quarry. [7]

The Roman Colosseum a *quarry*? It's hard to believe. But similar examples are abundant in the historical record. At the Karnak temple complex near Luxor, Egypt, several of the pharaohs who commissioned work at the site gave orders to *destroy* the exquisite works of art commissioned by their predecessors—*for use as rubble* inside new walls. (Ironically, we can now study some of these earlier creations *because* they were used as rubble.)

Can you imagine a city council voting to incorporate pieces of a beautiful old building into the walls of a new building *as rubble*? I can't. Well, I can't imagine such a thing happening in a *prosperous* city. In a desperate city plagued by poverty? Maybe.

Historical preservation has long been the sole concern of wealthy elites. In most countries today, a concern for history has worked its way down into the middle class, but preservation still relies on economic stability. International bodies such as UNESCO have attempted to address the imbalance, but inequalities remain. According to a 2010 report of the Global Heritage Fund:

> Of the approximately 500 global heritage sites in 100 of the lowest-income countries of the world . . . over 200 are facing irreversible loss . . . While Italy and Spain have 44 and 41 cultural UNESCO World Heritage designations, respectively, Peru—with 4,000 years of history and hundreds of important cultural sites—has only nine. Guatemala, the cradle of Mayan civilization with the world's largest pyramids and ancient cities, has just three. [8]

The writer William Gibson famously said, "The future is already here—it's just not evenly distributed." In the same way, the ghost towns of the past are all fading, but their disappearance is not evenly distributed.

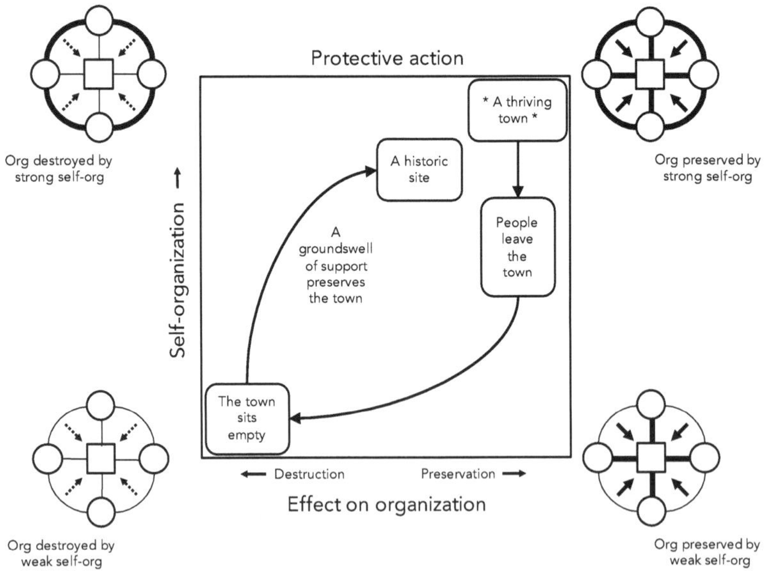

## Three factors that don't fit into a corner

There are three additional factors in the development of ghost towns that don't fit, or don't *stay*, in any of the corners of the inundation space.

### Factor 10: A protective shield

Some ghost towns are created when a temporary surge of self-organization seals them inside a boundary that prevents the formation of new self-organized patterns. In the short term this is always a disaster, but in the long term, under the right conditions, the effect can be preservative. The most famous example is the eruption of Mount Vesuvius, which buried the cities of Pompeii and Herculaneum in a layer of volcanic ash that prevented new self-organization from disturbing their structures for thousands of years.

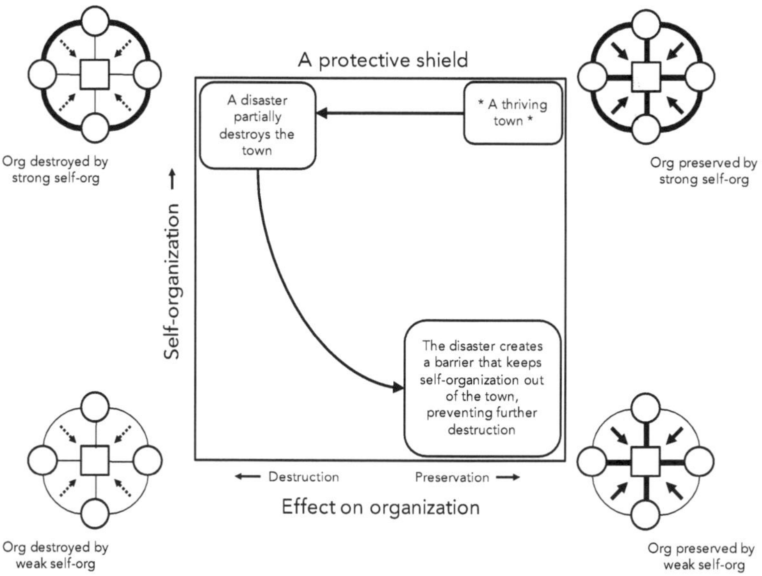


The destruction of the ancient city of Helike (he-LEE-kee) is believed by some scholars to have inspired the myth of Atlantis.[9] Helike was a prosperous port city, a cultural and religious center, and the leader of the Achaean League of Greek city-states. One winter night in 373 BCE, the city was struck by an earthquake and tsunami. The ground shifted and sank, the ocean rushed in, and the entire population perished in minutes. No survivors were found.

For a few centuries afterward, tourists visited the submerged city and wrote about what they saw. Fishermen told tales of nets snagged on the arms of underwater statues. Eventually the city was lost and forgotten.

In the twentieth century, archaeologists began to look for Helike in the Gulf of Corinth, where ancient writings seemed to say it could be found. But they kept coming up empty. In 1988, the archaeologist Dora Katsonopoulou realized that when ancient writers said Helike "sunk into a *poros*," they could have been referring to an inland lagoon that has since silted over with river sediment. In other words, the submerged city might now be buried underground.

She was right. Excavations in the former lagoon have now revealed *three* distinct layers of well-preserved buildings: Early Bronze Age dwellings, a Hellenistic industrial complex that was probably part of Helike, and a Roman road, straight as an arrow. In 2012, a "destruction layer" of scattered cobblestones, clay roof tiles, and pottery was found that dates to the time of the Helike earthquake. It is possible that *each* of these three settlements was preserved by the same type of disaster, each in its own time.

Protective shields can also be created by surges of *human* self-organization (as always, mixed with organization). Some of the best-preserved Roman theaters were buried by early Christians, who saw them as sites of immorality. As at Luxor, these theaters were preserved *because* people sought to destroy them.

The word *armageddon*, synonymous with destruction, comes from a real city, Megiddo, which was destroyed dozens of times between 6500 and 600 BCE. "Har" means "hill" in Hebrew, so "armageddon" is "the hill of Megiddo"—though, strictly speaking, there is no *hill* at Megiddo. The mound consists entirely of cities, each built on top of the last, in a sort of layer cake of habitation.

Megiddo was ideally situated at the entrance to a mountain pass where trade and military routes crossed. For this reason it was the site of many famous battles. For the same reason, the city was rebuilt each time it was sacked. Excavations have uncovered over twenty stacked cities, some with nearly intact tombs, temples, and palaces, as well as many gold, silver, ivory, and bronze artifacts from Canaanite, Israelite, Egyptian, and Assyrian cultures. If Megiddo had never been attacked (or rebuilt), its treasures would have been lost to history.[10]

### Factor 11: A protective menace

If a protective shield is created by a quick pulse of self-organization, a protective menace is created by a long, slow wave. In the Cambodian jungle, the trees that grow over, around, and through the ancient temples of Angkor Wat hide them from human notice, protect them from sunlight and erosion, *and* are slowly pulling them apart. The long-term effect falls ever so slightly on the side of preservation.

Another example of a slightly-more-preserved-than-destroyed ghost town is Kolmanskop in Namibia, an abandoned mining town whose buildings have been slowly filling up with sand since the 1950s. The built-up sand prevents exposure to sun and wind, but at the same time, it is unstable and can shift its weight, pressing on walls and roofs until they collapse.

When I first read about Kolmanskop, I thought it would fit into the "protective shield" category, because it seemed like the sand would settle in like concrete and *support* the buildings of the town. So I looked to see if desert sand makes good concrete. Turns out it doesn't. Wind-blown sand has two properties that make it a poor candidate for use in concrete. First, its grains are rounded and polished by constant movement. They're little spheres instead of all sorts of shapes. That makes it hard for them to fit together in compact assemblages. Second, grains of wind-blown sand tend to be fairly uniform in size. That also stops them from fitting together tightly.

So a building that has filled up with wind-blown sand is a more actively self-organizing environment than a building that has filled up with—well, buildings *don't* fill up with other kinds of sand, do they? The very fact that the sand makes its way into the buildings means that it must be relatively high in self-organization—and that makes it a protective menace.

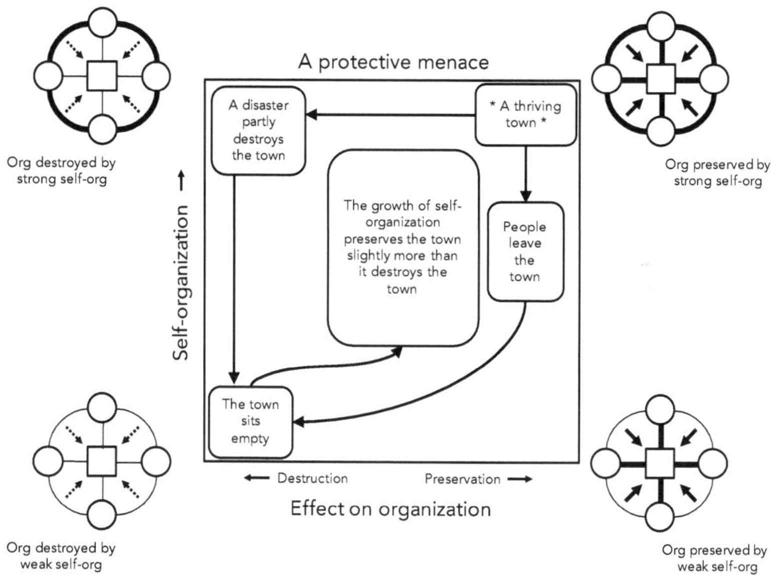


## Factor 12: Protective overuse

People who want to preserve historic sites need to generate maintenance funds, and to do that they need supporters. Few supporters are willing to help preserve places they can never visit, so most supporters are also tourists.

But tourists are a mixed blessing. Too many tourists can love a site to death, destroying the very structures they are helping to preserve. Even the *breaths* of too many tourists can erode ancient stones and damage fragile paintings. Still, it's better for tourists to love a site too much than not at all, because it might end up turning into a parking lot.

As a result, popular ghost towns tend to go through *cycles* of high and low human self-organization. When a town is first abandoned, the absence of people degrades, then preserves its structures. As the decades go by, the town becomes more interesting and beautiful. Tourists start to notice it, and its level of self-organization begins to rise again. Word gets out, and the town gets popular. Flocks of tourists damage the fragile structures, driving them further into the space of destruction. Eventually the buildings fall apart enough to lose their allure to any but the most determined tourists, and the site reverts to the vacant land it was before the town was built.

Those who maintain historic sites try to keep public interest high enough to maintain support for the site, but low enough to avoid overwhelming it.

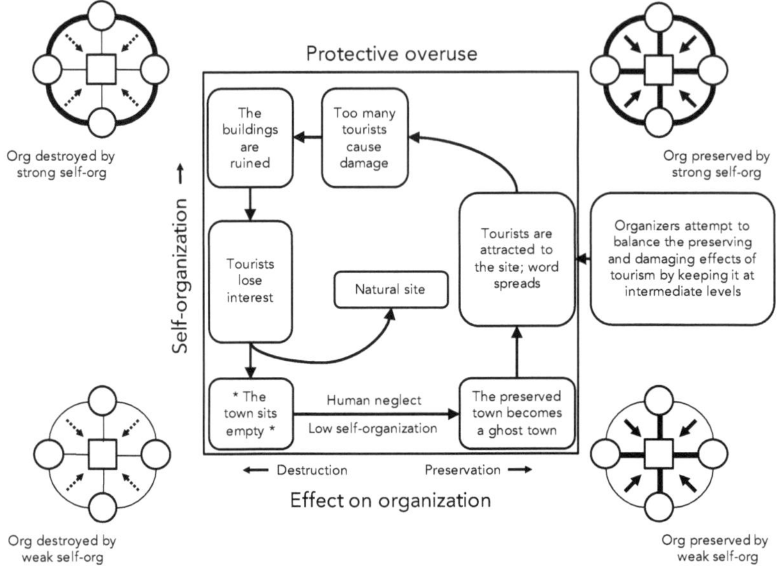
Protective overuse
Org destroyed by strong self-org
Org preserved by strong self-org
The buildings are ruined
Too many tourists cause damage
Tourists lose interest
Natural site
Tourists are attracted to the site; word spreads
Organizers attempt to balance the preserving and damaging effects of tourism by keeping it at intermediate levels
Self-organization →
* The town sits empty *
Human neglect
Low self-organization
The preserved town becomes a ghost town
← Destruction
Preservation →
Effect on organization
Org destroyed by weak self-org
Org preserved by weak self-org

## What we can learn from ghost towns

So that's how ghost towns are made. One or more destructive factors combines with one or more preservative factors, and you get a place that wanders between a town and an empty space, as a ghost wanders between life and death. What can ghost towns tell us about how self-organization encroaches on organization? You may have picked up a few common threads that ran through these examples.

### Take the good with the bad

Self-organization can never be said to have a completely positive *or* completely negative effect on organization. Even a disaster can have long-term benefits, such as a chance to rebuild using better construction methods. Where there is risk there is hope.[11]

For the same reason, self-organization can never be the panacea some claim it to be. If you think crowds are full of wisdom, you are likely to find that they have an abundance of stupidity as well. If you think self-organization has brought you "order for free," you may find that the cost has not disappeared, but tucked itself away in a place where you have not yet thought to look.[12] If you think complex systems are adaptive, it won't be long until you find out how *maladaptive* they can be. Beware simple solutions based on self-organization. It is *never* simple, and it rarely provides a solution without a problem nested inside (or vice versa).

## What goes up must come down

Another thread you may have noticed in these examples was the presence of *fluctuations*: pulses of destruction and preservation, waves of habitation and abandonment, cycles of growth and decay. Any situation that involves self-organization is bound to go through some sort of periodicity. Even our most robust institutions go through cycles of activity as their passionate founders and energetic volunteers pass the torch to new generations.

There are two ways to deal with the pulsations of self-organization. One is to try to slow them down or dampen their intensity. People do this by "reading" self-organized patterns, guessing what they will do next, and establishing boundaries to mitigate the damage they can cause. Yes, that's what I said emergency responders do during a natural disaster (on page 80). People who want to preserve their towns and cities do the same thing, only in slow motion.

The second method is to encourage *and* discourage the emergence of self-organized patterns—in time with their natural rhythms. In the same way a child "pumps" a swing by pushing it at just the right times (and *not* pushing it at the wrong times), community organizations can "pump up" the preservative factors that keep their neighborhoods alive (and pump *down* the destructive factors) by working together at just the right times. *Finding* the right times requires the same attention as it does for the child on the swing. The more you know about your community, the better you will know when and in what direction to push.

## Never a dull moment

A third thing you may have noticed about ghost towns is how *surprising* they are. Nobody sets out to build a ghost town. It's a surprise when they appear and a surprise when they linger. This is another way in which stories about ghost towns are like stories about ghosts. In both situations, unseen forces glide beneath the surface, and we see only what emerges. That's bad: hopes are dashed and treasures are lost. And it's good: wonders emerge where we least expect to find them.

Every time I think about how surprising self-organization can be, I keep getting this mental image of a man being pulled from the water. Let me explain. Charles Dickens, in his book *American Notes,* recounts a time when he was standing on a wharf watching passengers come and go. Some soldiers walked up with a new recruit who was far from sober.

> The soldiers rather laughed at this blade than with him: seeming to say, as they stood straightening their canes in their hands, and looking coolly at him over their glazed stocks, 'Go on, my boy, while you may! you'll know better by-and-by:' when suddenly the novice, who had been backing towards the gangway in his noisy merriment, fell overboard before their eyes, and splashed heavily down into the river between the vessel and the dock.

> I never saw such a good thing as the change that came over these soldiers in an instant. Almost before the man was down, their professional manner, their stiffness and constraint, were gone, and they were filled with the most violent energy. In less time than is required to tell it, they had him out again, feet first, with the tails of his coat flapping over his eyes, everything about him hanging the wrong way, and the water streaming off at every thread in his threadbare dress. But the moment they set him upright and found that he was none the worse, they were soldiers again, looking over their glazed stocks more composedly than ever.[13]

The "violent energy" of self-organization always seems to come out of nowhere. But later on, when you have time to think about it, its antecedents are all there, laid out for anyone to see. The influence of self-organization on organization is obvious in retrospect, but hidden before the fact.

## Crossing the space of inundation

Now, having described the four corners of the space, I will go through some examples that range across it. Note that there are only two (not the usual three) crossing-the-space examples in this chapter. That's because, as you may have noticed, some of my corner examples refused to *stay* in their corners. (That's self-organization for you, influencing the organization of my chapter.)

### Ivy on walls: Helpful or harmful?

The very first example that came into my mind for this chapter, before the ghost towns, even before I was sure what the dimensions of the space should be, was ivy growing on walls. I thought: what's something organized? A brick wall. Somebody builds it, on purpose, for a reason. And ivy grows on a wall, and ivy is self-organized. The ivy encroaches on the wall and tears it down. Right?

As you should be able to guess by now, the situation is nowhere near that simple. In many cases, the net effect of ivy on walls is slightly more *preservative* than destructive. That's right, it's a protective menace.

When ivy covers a wall, it acts as a thermal blanket, buffering the local microclimate and reducing freeze-thaw cycles.[14] A wall's worst enemy is not ivy; it's ice. Water can seep into the tiniest crack, freeze, expand, and push open the crack—further each time the temperature dips below freezing. Ice pulls walls apart like a crowbar, and ivy keeps the crowbar away.

In the same way, ivy reduces *haloclasty*, a form of weathering in which salt crystals repeatedly dissolve into solution and precipitate out of it, expanding tiny cracks into larger crevices. Ivy also protects walls from heavy rain and strong winds. And it absorbs pollutants, such as vehicle exhaust and road salt, which can corrode exposed stone, brick, and mortar. So in fact, removing ivy from a wall can do more harm than good.

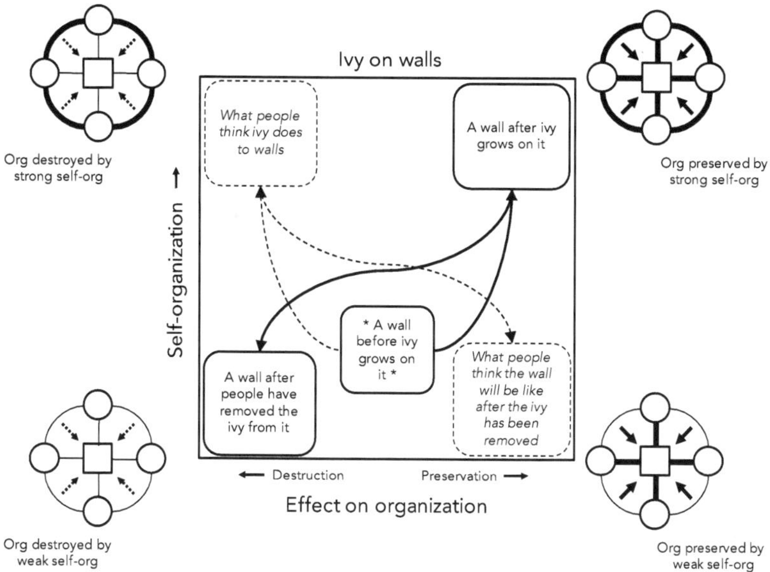


But ivy breaks walls apart with its roots, doesn't it? Not always. Ivy puts out two kinds of roots: tiny, thin *adventitious* roots that cling to the wall like gecko feet, and long, thick, probing *primary* roots that seek out moisture and nutrients. Only primary roots damage walls.

When areas of a deteriorated wall seem like they will provide water and nutrients to the plant—that is, when they are dark, wet, and weathered enough to seem like good soil (or if some actual soil has drifted into such areas), the plant will explore them by growing primary roots in those areas. If there are no such areas on a wall, primary roots will not appear on it.

However, primary roots will force themselves into a wall wherever they can if the ivy's main source of water and nutrients (usually in the soil below the wall) has been cut off—say, by a homeowner who has read that it's a good idea to cut the trunk of an ivy plant so it will die off. That's exactly the *wrong* thing to do. The ivy will pull the wall apart in its struggle to survive.

So what should you do if you have ivy on your wall? First, find out what *species* of ivy you have (or other climbing plant; not every climbing plant is an ivy). Second, find out what the wall is made of. Third, assess the condition of the wall. Are the bricks or stones intact? Is the mortar crumbling? Fourth, consider your microclimate. Do you have regular freeze-thaw cycles? Is the area wet or dry? What direction does the wall face? Is the area sunny or shaded? Is there traffic nearby? Use all of this information to think about what benefits your ivy might be providing and what negative effects it might be having.

One of the best ways to find out whether you should keep or remove ivy is to remove a *little* of it and see what you find underneath. Starting at the top, gently pull back some of the adventitious roots and examine the wall surface. Do you see any primary roots—that is, longer, thicker roots that reach into pockets of soil? If the wall is in good condition and you see no primary roots, the ivy may be having a net positive effect. Keep it away from gutters, downpipes, roof tiles, and window casings, but you don't need to remove it just because it's there. Ivy can be your friend—or at least your frenemy.

## What can we do about self-organized industrial accidents?

Now let's return to the topic of self-organization in industrial accidents. If industrial accidents are caused by treating self-organized patterns as if they were organized plans, what can we *do* about it?

Organizers need three things: awareness, intent, and access. They need to be able to *see* every element of a situation, *think* about those elements, and *move* them around. So let's consider industrial accidents with respect to those three things.

### Industrial awareness

As industrial facilities have gotten bigger and more dangerous, operators have increasingly come to rely on remote sensors to provide critical information. But sensors aren't always reliable. For example, this quote from Perrow's *Normal Accidents* sent a chill down my spine:

> A warning signal came on. . . . Operators reduced power and checked; nothing seemed wrong, so they supposed it was a faulty signal (it possibly was; they are common).[15]

When warning signals are nothing more than educated guesses, that's not a good sign. But since *Normal Accidents* and a slew of other complexity-in-industry books were written, people have been working on the awareness issue, and things are getting better. For one thing, self-diagnostic sensors frequently and automatically test their own functions, so faulty signals can be replaced *before* a problem occurs (and trusted when it does).

Also, many sensors today have built-in testing systems that allow operators to check their function by sending prescribed signals. If the signal doesn't match the expectation, the operator can tell that the sensor cannot be trusted. This is like what you do when you push that little button on your smoke detector. You want to know that it *can* go off when it should.

Another solution is redundancy. Two sensors are as bad as one, because it's impossible to say which is correct. But *three* sensors create a majority that can "out-vote" the faulty signal. In today's factories, triple redundancy often extends beyond sensors to information transfer devices and industrial computers.

### Industrial intent

When manufacturers, designers, and operators have little contact with each other, unaligned intentions can work at cross purposes. One group might prioritize safety, while another looks to cut costs, and a third favors efficiency. Often such misalignments are apparent only *after* an accident has taken place, as each group places blame on the others.

In December 1986, at the Surry nuclear plant in the U.S. state of Virginia, a pipe containing hot pressurized water suddenly burst. The water exiting the pipe flashed to steam, scalding several nearby workers. First responders tried to get into the room, but the door wouldn't open. The computer card reader that controlled the door lock had been shorted out by water from the fire suppression system, which had been activated by the heat of the steam.[16]

The designers of the Surry plant failed to integrate their systems well, and they failed to conduct thorough risk assessments. But another factor was a lack of interaction among the suppliers of the various system components. If they had talked more to each other, the possibility of dangerous interactions could have come up—especially if they had brainstormed about what could happen in extreme conditions. When competitive marketplaces lead suppliers away from discussions of interoperability, organized standards and regulations can compel them to work together to improve safety.

**Industrial access**

Last year I bought one of those electronic pressure cookers. I like it. Instead of spending half the day hanging around the kitchen so I can stir soup, I throw everything in, press a few buttons, and walk away. When I come back hours later, the soup is ready to eat. The only problem is: I used to *taste* the soup while it was cooking. I used to make little adjustments when I thought the soup needed a little of this or that. With the pressure cooker, I can't do that. The moment I close the lid, I lose access to the soup.

Actually, that's not quite true. I *could* open up the cooker mid-process, but I'd have to wait while the pressure ramped down, taste the soup, make my adjustments, then wait again while the pressure built up. It's not worth the bother to do that, so I just throw everything in and hope for the best.

Many industrial processes are like my pressure cooker. Once the cooker starts, you can't stop it, at least not without a lot of bother. In the industrial world, bother means cost. Stopping an ongoing industrial process can cost thousands of dollars every minute the system is down. The bigger the process, the bigger the expense—and the bigger the disaster if you *don't* stop to check the process once in a while. Some of the world's worst industrial accidents have been caused by deferred maintenance.

One way to improve access is to *downscale* industrial structures and plans into smaller units, which can be "loosely coupled"—swapped out, moved around, and switched on or off as needs change. For example, the Rolls-Royce company recently announced plans to roll out a series of small, factory-built, modular nuclear power plants across the United Kingdom.[17] The plan is to reduce costs and risks by building many small plants instead of few huge ones. In fact, some have argued that the era of *big* industry, with its massive unstoppable processes, is on its way out, and that the era of *smart* industry—small, agile, modular, flexible, just-in-time—is coming soon.

But there are still many massive unstoppable processes, and they rely on shutdowns. An industrial shutdown is a temporary uptick in access caused by a temporary reduction in self-organization. When a power plant shuts down, a chemical reaction is halted, or workers leave a building, the degree of self-organization goes down, and organizers can organize. (The same thing happens during school breaks.)

Before the shutdown starts, specialized crews prepare to service machines and facilities with the same intensity that pit crews prepare to service racing cars. (That's another time when self-organization goes down: when a racing car stops moving.) A shutdown's every moment is examined to see where it can be streamlined to maximize productivity in minimal downtime. *Between* shutdowns, when self-organization again hampers access, crews review and strategize, so their next shutdown will be even more efficient.

**Building helpful self-organization into industry**

Improving our awareness, intention, and access increases our ability to act as organizers. But there's another way to look at the problem. What if we could make self-organization work *for* industry instead of *against* it?

This is the thinking behind a set of new ideas called "Industry 4.0." In some factories today, components are being fitted with wirelessly connected microprocessors. (Industry 1.0 was steam; 2.0 was electricity; 3.0 was computers and automation; 4.0 is networked devices and machine learning.) In other words, people are building self-organization into factories *on purpose*.

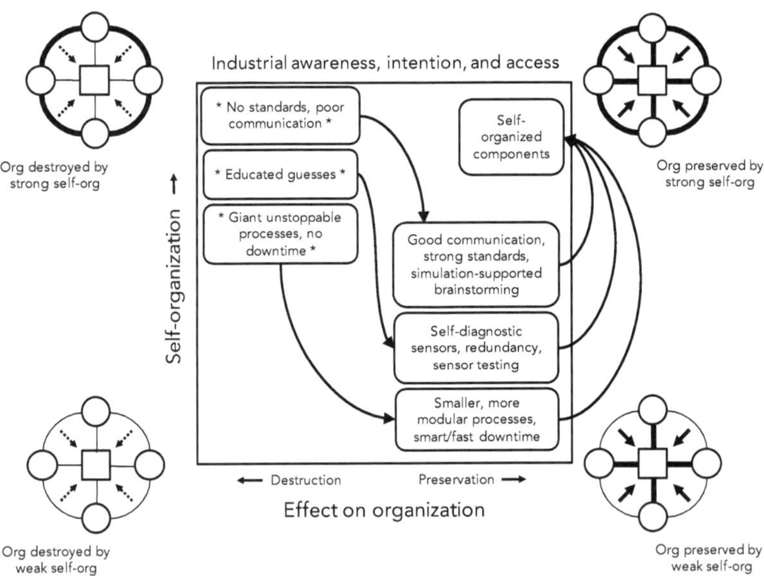


To show you how this could work, imagine the following fictional scenario, set in a self-organized factory.

### *A story of industrial self-organization*

Meet C128. C128 is an industrial component. It exists in a factory surrounded by other components in an interconnected "Industrial Internet of Things." C128 could be something very simple, like a rolling supply bin; or it could be something complicated, like an industrial oven or a printing press.[18]

C128 collects data about everything: how fast it is working, how much power it is drawing, its temperature, moisture, supply levels, and so on. It constantly checks this data against its *rules engine,* a set of if-then statements that tell it how to behave. Whenever its collected data matches the if-part of a rule, C128 does the then-part of the rule. It can speed up, slow down, heat up, cool down, turn parts of itself on or off, or even shut down completely.

To give an example: an operator walks by, and C128 notices. One of C128's rules says that if an operator's badge marks them as a visitor or a trainee, it should switch to "safe" mode; so it does, until they pass out of range again.

C128 often sends messages to its neighbors. It might send a report ("I have finished my print run"), an offer ("I have ten products ready for packaging"), a request ("Could someone check my cutting blade?"), a warning ("My operating temperature has gone above the normal range"), or an emergency ("My supply pipe has burst"). Every message indicates its danger level and describes the type of data involved: temperature, moisture, voltage, air pressure, and so on.

Every one of C128's messages has an intended audience. Some messages are sent to physical neighbors (components in its vicinity) or process neighbors (to which it is connected in an industrial process). Some messages are sent to all components in a category, like all printers, or all components that need to know about temperature. And some messages are sent to human operators: specific operators, or all the operators in the vicinity, or operators in a particular role. When a message is sent to an operator, it might include a chart showing a recent trend or a video showing an important event.

When C128 *receives* a message, it uses its rules to decide what it should do in response. It might take some kind of action, like adjusting its speed of production. It might send the message on to other components, or to operators, or to both. It all depends on what its rules say it should do.

Where did C128's rules come from? Originally, they were written by factory designers and component manufacturers, who worked out how C128 and its neighbors should behave in a series of planning and brainstorming sessions. They used a simulated factory, with a "digital twin" for each component, to think about what might happen and how the components should interact.

But C128's rules haven't stayed the same since it was installed. Its operators keep changing them. They "walk through" the simulated factory as they walk through the physical factory, checking to see what messages are being sent, how components are responding, and whether any self-organized patterns need to be reinforced or suppressed. Sometimes they temporarily set up global conditions like "stress test" or "slowdown," and the factory's components, C128 among them, detect the conditions and respond to them.

In addition, the messages exchanged by C128 and its fellow components accumulate into a body of collective experience that helps the factory make its own educated guesses. When an anomaly comes up, for example, the factory can consult its body of experience to determine what actions should be taken.

The other day, a new operator came into the factory and set down a fuel can right next to a very large, very hot industrial dryer. C128 noticed this right away, because the fuel can had a smart tag on it. C128 checked its rules. It found a rule that caused it to send a message directly to the operator's smartphone. The message asked the operator to move the can, explained that the location was unsafe, and directed the operator to a training video about fuel cans and where you can safely put them down. The operator was glad to get the message.

***Will smart factories be smart enough?***

Is cultivating industrial self-organization safer than squashing it? It's hard to say. In the last part of my scenario, for example, when C128 prevented an industrial accident, a skeptic might say that you could achieve the same goal by installing a barrier around the industrial dryer. The problem is that barriers have costs, both literally and in terms of production efficiency. Factory designers can't afford to invest too much effort in preventing unlikely scenarios.

On the other hand, unlikely scenarios happen all the time. Charles Perrow tells about a power plant containment building that was flooded with river water. The flooding went unnoticed for days because the building's sensors were designed only to detect the presence of *hot* water.[19]

In a system of networked components, dealing with even the most unlikely of scenarios requires only a few more lines of software code. And once the system is set up, that's essentially free. It's like how digital cameras changed the way we take pictures. I enjoy taking nature photos, and I remember the days when I would interrogate every picture: is this shot worth a dollar for the film and a dollar for the development? Now I just snap away. I might take 200 pictures on a single walk. This doesn't necessarily make my pictures any better, but it does give me the freedom to experiment with new ideas. In a factory setting, the difference can be transformative.

But wait—what if the fuel can isn't in the system? Aren't you setting up a reliance on information that might be missing? Yes, that's a valid concern. Incorporating self-organization into industrial processes does require additional attention to *boundaries*. At plant entrances, for example, components must be checked to make sure they have smart tags with working microchips. But maintaining boundaries is something people have been doing for a long time. If a big box store can do it, a factory can.

If smart factories live up to their hype, someday they will run themselves with minimal supervision, and their workers will be more like farmers tending crops than workers operating machines. Will this mean the industrial accidents of the future will be smaller and easier to contain? Or will Industry 4.0 unleash an even greater potential for disaster? If we have learned anything from our explorations in this chapter, we can guess the answer: probably some of both.

# 7 Regulation

*Thinking about how organization influences self-organization*

In the previous chapter, we thought about how self-organization creeps into organized plans. Now we'll do the opposite and think about how organization works to control self-organized patterns. Here is our thinking space.

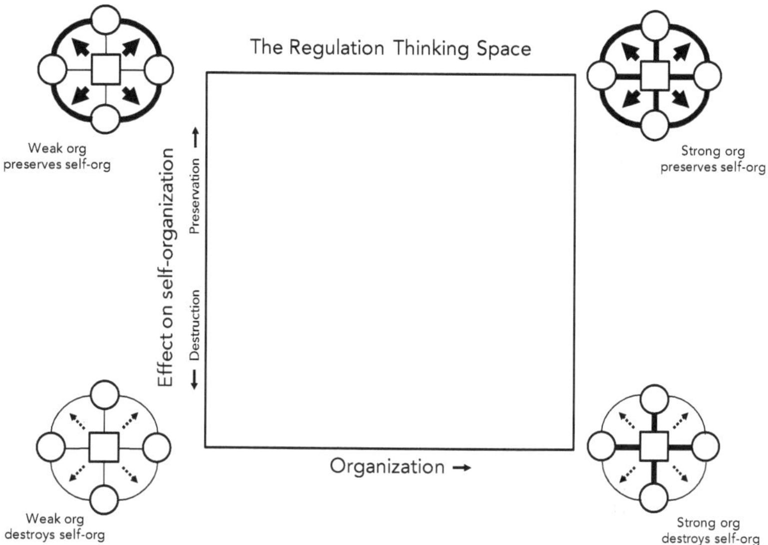


As you can see, this space is the mirror image of the one in the previous chapter—but it's rotated by ninety degrees so organization can march from left to right, as it did in Chapter Two.

The *extent* to which organizers organize the world around them increases from left to right. This does not necessarily mean that the amount of *effort* applied to organization increases from left to right. A situation could be on the left side of the space because organizers have *reached the limit* of their ability to organize the world, or it could be there because organizers have chosen to *limit the reach* of their organization. Those distinctions are not defined by the space itself. They are things we can think about as we fill up the space.

Near the top of the space, the amount of organization—the fact that it is weak or strong—*preserves* self-organized patterns. Near the bottom, weak or strong organization *destroys* self-organized patterns. Halfway up the space, the amount of organization has no impact on the amount of self-organization—or the forces of preservation and destruction are perfectly balanced.

## The regulation thinking space

Human life depends on self-organized patterns that convert sunlight into plants and animals we can eat. Thus the history of food in human society is a compendium of organized attempts to regulate self-organization. That makes it an abundant source of good examples to use in this space.

Now I will show you a model of how people get food to eat, a model I built using the regulation space. *My goal in showing you this model is not to explain how people get food to eat.* My goal is to *use the space in front of you* so you can see how you can use it to develop your own models. (You should be able to guess by now that this topic suggested itself in part because my academic background is in ecology and because I've always enjoyed growing my own food.)

## A model of how we get food to eat

My model defines five general strategies people use to get food to eat. (When I say "people," I mean any number of people who get food for any number of people to eat, from one hunter to an entire agricultural industry.)

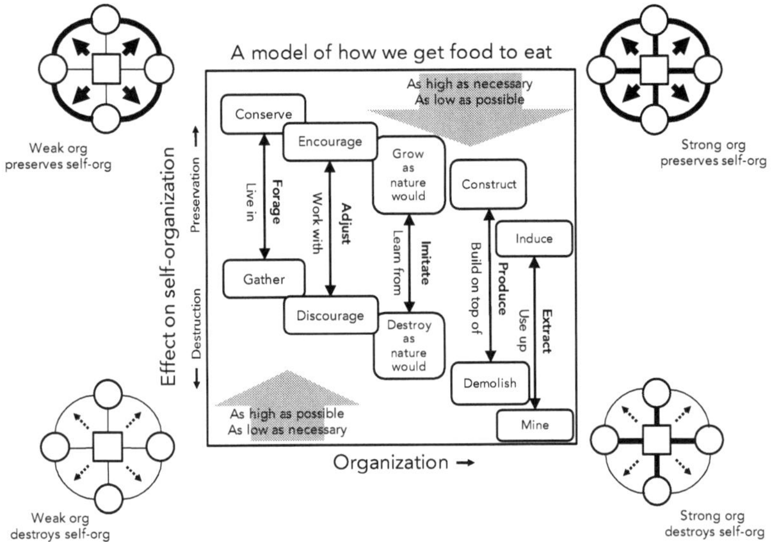


### Foraging

On the far left of the regulation space, where organization is lowest, people get food by *knowing where to find it*. They spend their time making detailed observations and building encyclopedic knowledge about self-organized patterns of food availability in space and time. For example, a forager might know where to find a particular edible plant, but they will also know when it should be picked, what parts of it can be eaten, how those parts should be prepared and preserved, and how much they must leave behind so they can harvest it again the next year.

From a foraging perspective, the world is a farm that grows itself, as long as we don't get in the way. Foragers depend on self-organized patterns in the world around them, but because they know everything there is to know about those patterns, and are quick to notice and adapt to changes, they are not worried about the future; they know they will find what they need.

Foraging does include *some* level of organization; anything that involves people involves some level of organization. However, foraging is the least organized of the five food-getting strategies, and deliberately so. If we were to place foraging on the plan (organized) thinking space, we would place it in the upper-left corner, where low effort meets high awareness.

Foragers aim to carefully limit their use of available resources, never taking more than is sustainable. After all, there's no point in knowing where to find food if you remove it from where you found it. For this reason, foragers destroy only as much self-organization as they must and conserve as much as they can. They may not always *succeed* in limiting their use of resources—they are as capable of making costly mistakes as anyone else—but that is their goal.

In a community of foragers, knowledge about food *is* food. Everyone is expected to pass on what they know to the next generation, so the community's collective knowledge—its food supply—can accumulate over time.

On the other hand, foraging knowledge is deliberately limited in both space and time. This may seem strange to you and me, but from a foraging perspective, it makes perfect sense. What would be the point of knowing where to find food you can't get to? And since nature continually changes, shouldn't knowledge change as well? A forager would never expect a solution that worked ten generations ago to work in exactly the same way today; that would be nonsensical. Foragers expect the best solutions to change over time, so they hold their solutions loosely.

### Adjusting

At a slightly higher level of organization, people get food by *modifying existing food sources*. Like foragers, adjusters spend a lot of time finding and studying self-organized patterns of food availability. Unlike foragers, they are not content to do all of the adapting themselves. Rather, they adapt the food sources they find to better suit their needs.

From an adjusting perspective, the world is a farm that grows itself, but we can make it grow a little better. Adjusters selectively encourage some self-organized patterns and selectively discourage others, introducing a small amount of organization into the self-organized patterns around them. For example, an adjuster might scatter fruit seeds in a forest clearing, or trim back trees that threaten to shade a growing fruit tree.

Like foragers, adjusters try to limit their impact on the environment. Their ultimate aim is still to live on the food they find around them, even though they themselves had a hand in putting it there. So they discourage self-organization as much as they must and encourage it as much as they can.

Adjusting does require a certain amount of trial and error, so it tends to drag the overall level of self-organization down—at least until adjusters come to a deeper understanding of the environment in which they are working. Expert adjusters can influence their environment so subtly that their changes are nearly invisible to the uninformed.

In a community of adjusters, knowledge is passed on from generation to generation. But the organized aspect of the knowledge is greater than in a community of foragers, since it involves making changes to nature. So the traditions of adjusting communities change more slowly than the fluid knowledge bases of foraging communities.

### Imitating

Sometimes people get food not by *interacting* with nature but by *copying* it. Like foragers and adjusters, imitators spend a lot of time observing the world around them. But they don't do this to learn where food sources can be found. Imitators observe the environment so they can learn how best to design the food sources they create.

From an imitating perspective, the world is a farm that grows itself, but it doesn't grow enough, even with adjustment. So imitators use what they know about the world to create their own version of it, one that produces more food than the world can by itself. Like adjusters, imitators encourage some self-organized patterns and discourage others. But unlike adjusters, they start with a blank canvas—or as blank of a canvas as they can create.

Imitators stand on the other side of the threshold between working with *existing* self-organized patterns and encouraging the formation of *new* self-organized patterns inside organized plans. Copying and pasting what works best from the world outside the farm, imitators create assemblages that are as much like the natural world as they can make them—within the constraint that their primary goal is to meet their needs. For example, a farmer might build a "bee house" that mimics the cavities in a dead tree in a way that attracts a particular species of bee to pollinate a specific crop.

In a community of imitators, a deep understanding of how the natural world works is considered a critical asset. However, unlike in foraging and adjusting communities, this understanding must be *global*, not local, to ensure the success of whatever type of farm needs to be built. Thus imitators rely more on context-free experimentation than on context-sensitive knowledge.

### Producing

Sometimes people get food by *creating it themselves*. Producers seek to draw neither food nor insight from their environment. In fact, they'd rather not have an "environment" at all. What they want is a *substrate* on which to organize their production of food as efficiently as possible.

The self-organized patterns producers encourage to grow are not copied from nature. They are *designed* from first principles—from the atoms up, you could say—as much like a *Star Trek* replicator as possible. If producers could grow food without *any* self-organization, they would gladly do so; but they can't, not yet. So they encourage the formation of just as much (and just the right kind of) self-organization as they need for the purpose they need it for. When the production process is complete, producers dismantle the self-organization they previously encouraged; it has served its purpose.

From a producing perspective, a farm is a factory, and it should operate as efficiently as possible. It should minimize its inputs of energy and raw materials and maximize its outputs of assembled products. The soil of a farm, like the floor of a factory, should be clean of contaminants, and it should support the machines and processes that are used on top of it. Nothing more is required.

Because producers fear contamination from the environment, they erect barriers between their production line and the world outside it. These attempts at exclusion can have the paradoxical effect of *enabling* self-organization that lies outside the production process. For example, some of our most thriving wildlife habitats today can be found in land left undeveloped (usually as sound or pollution buffers) near sites of industry, including industrial agriculture.

In a community of producers, the focus is primarily on engineering. Producers do not so much pass down knowledge as they record and reference it. Still, because ingenuity and creativity are highly regarded in this problem-solving culture, human self-organization has a moderate level of influence.

## Extracting

Sometimes people get food by *taking it out of the world.* Extracting is like foraging, but with a blindfold and a sledgehammer.

From an extracting perspective, the world is a mine, and a farm is a vein of ore. When a vein has been tapped out, it is time to move on to the next one. Extractors don't necessarily believe the amount of ore in the world is infinite; they just believe the supply will last long enough to meet their current needs.

Extractors are risk-averse, short-term, crisis-driven thinkers. They don't believe they can afford the luxury of learning about the world, improving their methods, connecting with others, or passing on knowledge. And they certainly don't believe they can rely on nature to provide them with anything or teach them anything. They see nature as an enemy, not a benefactor. Extractors take everything, observe nothing, and impose no limits—not because they are evil, but because they believe they have no other choice.

From an extracting point of view, it makes no sense to speak of "improving" the soil. Can a coal miner "improve" a vein of coal? The resource is there or it isn't. Good soil produces good harvests. If an extractor doesn't find good soil in one place, they look for it somewhere else. If their soil fertility is declining, they either find another place to farm or stop farming. What else can they do?

Extractors know that they must *induce*, or switch on, certain processes that are required to draw food out of the ground. Planting seeds, for example, is as necessary as drilling through layers of rock to get to ore deposits. They try to get through these necessary tasks as quickly as they can. Obstacles such as weeds and pests can also get in the way of extracting food from the soil.

Extractors don't try to understand why these obstacles exist; they just remove them as fast as they can so they can get back to mining.

Why are extractors so destructive to self-organization? There are a few possible reasons. They might not know it exists. They might know it exists but don't believe it matters. Or they might know it exists and believe it matters, but don't believe they can spare the time or energy to pay attention to it—at least not right now. Whether or not they are correct in this belief depends on the situation in which they find themselves.

In a community of extractors, tools and tool makers are highly valued. The primacy of survival leads extractors to favor packaged solutions guaranteed by powerful authorities—because there's less risk involved.

## Mixing the strategies

Each of these food-getting strategies has a different impact on self-organization. Foraging is the most preservative, because it expects to *continue to depend* on the self-organized patterns it finds. Extraction is the most destructive, because it expects to *stop depending* on any particular self-organized pattern after it has moved on to a new one.

This does not mean that foraging is better than extraction. Whether a food-getting strategy is better or worse, right or wrong, depends on the context in which it is used. A strategy can only be right or wrong in the right or wrong time, place, or proportion. The right strategy for a group of people facing starvation on a fertile flood plain is the wrong strategy for a well-fed group of people facing the loss of their last remaining wilderness.

All around the world, abandoned cities and farms tell the tales of those who chose the wrong strategy at the wrong time. Sometimes a strategy became impossible to sustain due to changing climatic or social conditions. At other times people slid from one strategy into another without realizing it—and without realizing how the change would affect their ability to get food. Some 2500 years ago, Plato mourned the loss of fertile Greek farmland when he said, "[W]hat now remains [of the soil] is like the skeleton of a sick man, all the fat and soft earth having wasted away, and only the bare framework of the land being left."[1] It's all just a little bit of history repeating.[2]

To avoid such a fate, people often mix the five strategies together. Sometimes they string them into sequences or cycles that are passed down as traditions. Sometimes they simply keep all five strategies in mind, as tools are kept in a toolbox, to be used when needed. Throughout history, subsistence farmers have foraged, adjusted, imitated, produced, and extracted food in the various aspects and seasons of life.

At times, however, a particular mix of strategies has come to dominate all others. Thus it has often happened that one group of people has misunderstood or condemned another group who used a different strategy mix, calling them "primitive" or "ignorant." Recently in Thailand, for example, some traditional farmers were arrested for farming the way their ancestors farmed.[3] Whether you think this is a problem or a solution depends on the mix of food-getting strategies you think (or your group thinks) is best.

This mix-and-match game has gone on since the beginning of human society and will continue far into the future. You might think that in our industrial age we have left foraging and adjusting behind, but that is only true in a limited sense. Not only do millions of people still depend in part on foods they find in nature, but the number rises every time a war or economic crisis comes up. None of these strategies are off the table, not yet.

## The history of getting food to eat

Why did prehistoric people switch from foraging to farming? There is no simple answer to that question—because the question is too simple. In recent decades it has become clear that agriculture developed in more locations, over a longer timespan, and in more diverse ways than was originally understood.

In 2015, archaeologists described their excavations at Ohalo, a well-preserved hunter-gatherer camp near the Sea of Galilee. There they found evidence that people were harvesting, grinding, and possibly cultivating precursors of today's staple grains (such as wheat and barley) 23,000 years ago. That's 11,000 years *before* the Neolithic agricultural revolution supposedly began.[4]

This does not mean the Neolithic revolution never happened, of course; clearly there were big changes afoot in human societies 12,000 years ago. However, the *roots* of agriculture may go back much further into the past, perhaps even to 50,000 years ago, when people first began to use symbolic language—though the starting date of that "revolution" also keeps getting pushed back.

As the story of agriculture gets longer, it keeps getting more complicated. In at least some locations, the transition to agriculture seems to have been more of an *addition* to an already complex repertoire of food-getting strategies. For example, archaeologists using LIDAR[5] have discovered that huge tracts of South American forest were shaped by an ancient Mayan system called *milpa*—a mix of foraging and cultivation that some Mayan people still practice today.

Still, even with all of this complexity, most of the human beings on this planet 50,000 years ago were foragers, and today, most of us depend on agriculture. How did that happen?

Archaeologists have come up with dozens of hypotheses to explain the rise of agriculture. They can be (and generally are) grouped into three larger explanations: crisis, opportunity, and coevolution.

### A story of crises

The story of agricultural development as driven by crisis is probably the one you are most familiar with. At the start of the story, everyone is hunting and gathering, and things are going along as well as can be expected. Hunter-gatherer lives are brutal and short, and the people often go hungry, but they carry on as best they can.

Then a rapid decrease in self-organization eliminates essential food sources. Recurring glacial periods shorten growing seasons and deplete critical sources of fruits, nuts, leafy plants, roots, and grains. Giant animals that once fed hundreds of people for months—woolly mammoths, cave bears, giant boars, giant elk—disappear from the earth. The effect is devastating.

Organizers cannot *create* self-organized patterns, so they have to *replace* them with organized plans.[6] After harrowing years of trial and error, some of the organized plans prove to be life-saving. The people remember that they were saved by the superior power of organization.

As the years go by, fears of a returning crisis keep this superior power in mind. Eventually self-organization comes to be seen less as a beneficial force, a source of life, and more as a dangerous menace, a source of death. (It is both.) Anyone who proposes a return to the old methods is shamed into silence. "Do you want to be the one who kills us all?" People ask.

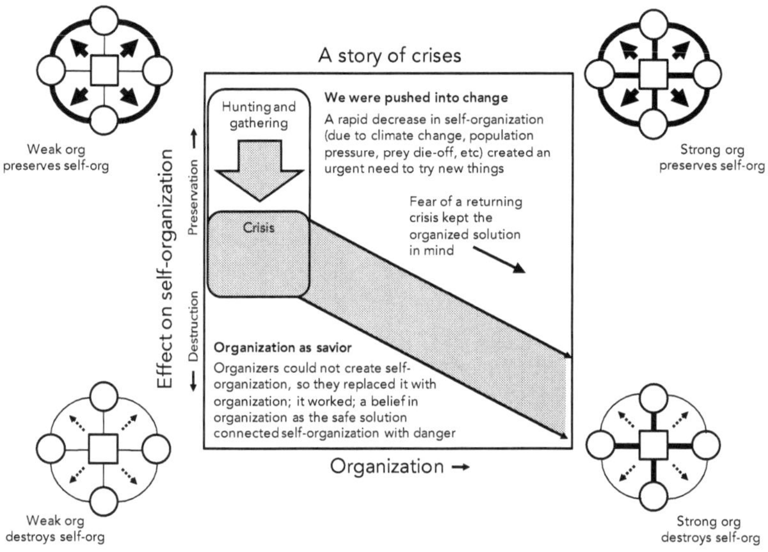
A story of crises
Weak org
preserves self-org
Strong org
preserves self-org
Weak org
destroys self-org
Strong org
destroys self-org
Effect on self-organization
Preservation →
← Destruction
Organization →
Hunting and
gathering
Crisis
We were pushed into change
A rapid decrease in self-organization (due to climate change, population pressure, prey die-off, etc) created an urgent need to try new things
Fear of a returning crisis kept the organized solution in mind
Organization as savior
Organizers could not create self-organization, so they replaced it with organization; it worked; a belief in organization as the safe solution connected self-organization with danger

## A story of opportunities

According to the second story of agricultural development, hunters and gatherers lived in "the original affluent society," surrounded by abundant food, blessed with free time, ready to play with new ideas. Yes, the giant animals died off; but there were plenty of smaller animals to eat. Yes, the cold winters were hard; but the people knew the land, and they still had enough to eat. What got the agricultural ball rolling in this version of the story was the fortuitous appearance of new, attractive, and interesting opportunities.

At the end of the last glacial period (roughly 12,000 years ago), stands of wild annual grains, precursors of today's staple foods, began to appear in abundance on the flood plains of rivers in several places around the world. As people gathered these wild grains, they accidentally dropped some near their cooking areas and garbage heaps. The grains grew into newly harvestable stands. Noticing this, people tried scattering grains in other places, *et voilà*—agriculture was born.

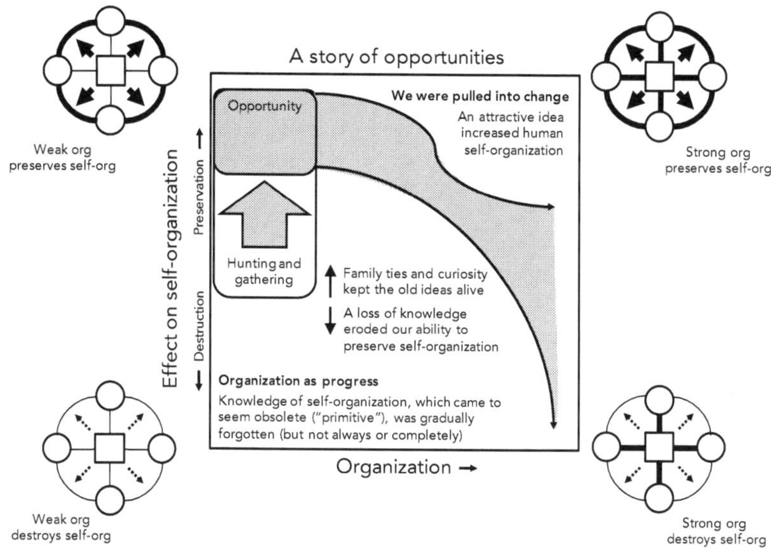
A story of opportunities
Weak org
preserves self-org
Strong org
preserves self-org
Weak org
destroys self-org
Strong org
destroys self-org
Effect on self-organization
Preservation →
← Destruction
Organization →
Opportunity
Hunting and
gathering
We were pulled into change
An attractive idea
increased human
self-organization
Family ties and curiosity
kept the old ideas alive
A loss of knowledge
eroded our ability to
preserve self-organization
Organization as progress
Knowledge of self-organization, which came to
seem obsolete ("primitive"), was gradually
forgotten (but not always or completely)

In this scenario, the birth of agriculture came about through an *increase* in self-organization—in human society. Someone had a great idea, and they told their neighbors about it. Their neighbors told their neighbors, and the idea spread until it became the next big thing. That's why agriculture developed so quickly and in so many places: because that's how new ideas spread in human societies. We're a social species, so agriculture must have developed socially.

A similar opportunity may have arisen in places where animal populations were easily domesticated: big enough to provide meals, small enough to enclose, not too nasty, and capable of surviving and reproducing in captivity. Hunters had been surrounding animals in coordinated group hunts for a long time, sometimes using natural corrals such as hollows or cliffs to herd the animals into place. It would have required only a small burst of insight to think of keeping animals in place for longer periods of time before killing them. Thus the group hunt became the "larder on the hoof," which grew into animal husbandry.

Because it is based on self-organization, the opportunistic story of agricultural development is fuzzier than the crisis story. Fads come and go, and old ways can become new again. So it's harder to account for a widespread transition to cultivated agriculture based on this version of the story. Unless, of course, you take into account the fact that the very idea of widespread cultivated agriculture is an over-simplification. While it is certainly true that only a few tiny fragments of hunter-gatherer societies remain, millions of people still practice complex local mixtures of foraging, adjusting, and cultivation.

## A story of coevolution

Lying between these extremes, the coevolution story claims that hunter-gatherer societies added cultivation to their food-getting repertoires carefully and gradually, over tens of thousands of years. Even though there were some periods of rapid change, they occurred against a background of constant accommodation between people and their environment.

From this perspective, early humans were neither pushed into agriculture by crises nor pulled into it by opportunities. Agricultural practices simply *evolved* as part of the process of natural selection working on our species, as it works on the species of plants and animals around us. The reason we added cultivation to our food-getting strategies is because diversity is an integral part of the evolutionary process. What's more, agriculture never *stopped* developing. We are still negotiating our place in the world, and we will continue to do so as long as our species exists.

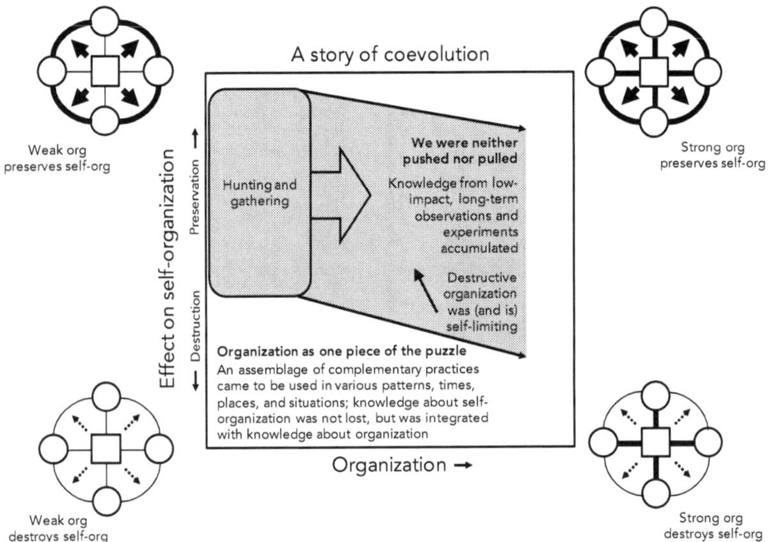
A story of coevolution
Weak org
preserves self-org
Strong org
preserves self-org
Weak org
destroys self-org
Strong org
destroys self-org
Effect on self-organization
Preservation
Destruction
Organization
Hunting and gathering
We were neither pushed nor pulled
Knowledge from low-impact, long-term observations and experiments accumulated
Destructive organization was (and is) self-limiting
Organization as one piece of the puzzle
An assemblage of complementary practices came to be used in various patterns, times, places, and situations; knowledge about self-organization was not lost, but was integrated with knowledge about organization

According to this scenario, natural selection has allowed us to increase our level of organization up to the point where it threatens the self-organization we need to survive, and it will support no further expansion.

As we sit in our modern cities, it may *seem* to us that organization has won out. But that is only because we have such a limited view of space and time.[7] Human organization has always been and will always be balanced in such a way that its destructive impacts to self-organization are kept in check. Our species may have lost its balance in recent times, but it will rebalance itself. Or it will die out. That's how evolution works.

### A blended story

Each of these explanations for the rise of agriculture has supporting evidence in the archaeological record. Each makes sense if you look only at particular times and places. But they make the most sense, I think, if you put them all together.

For the past 12,000 years we have been living in a remarkably stable climate. Things were different for our distant ancestors, as they may be for our descendants. Within the current Quaternary ice age (yes, we live in an ice age), which began 2.58 million years ago, we are living in the Holocene interglacial period, which began 11,500 years ago. The previous glacial period (the Weichselian glaciation), which began 115,000 years ago, was punctuated by at least 25 rapid temperature fluctuations known as Dansgaard-Oeschger (D-O) events. During these events, average annual temperatures sometimes rose or fell by as much as 10°C (18°F) over the course of a few decades.

Such rapid changes were not new to the planet, of course. Older ice cores suggest that similar events took place in previous glacial periods. But about 50,000 years ago—right in the middle of a series of D-O events—human beings started using symbolic language to work together in groups. Instead of *pointing* at a tree, for example, they began to *use words* to describe it. That meant they could talk about the tree *whether or not they could see it*. They could also talk about trees in general, or trees in a particular area, or trees of a particular species. Symbolic language helps us make plans, exchange knowledge, and solve problems in groups.

Consider a group of early humans living through any one of these D-O events. A rapid change in temperature, up or down, could have presented a crisis in the availability of one food source while simultaneously presenting an opportunity to exploit a different food source. These changes would have taken place against a background of ongoing concerted efforts to understand (and probably manipulate) the food sources in their environment. Much like our ancestors, we continue to face crises and encounter opportunities, and we are always trying to get our food in the best way we can.

## Food-getting in the inundation space

Now, keeping this model in mind, let's look into the four corners of the regulation space and see what we find there.

### When strong organization destroys self-organization

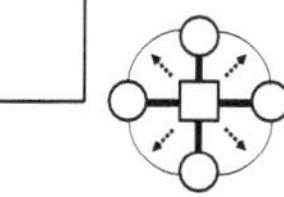

Let's start in the lower-right corner, where strong organization destroys self-organization. Six extractive farming practices can be found here: tillage; monoculture; continuous grazing; and synthetic fertilizers, pesticides, and herbicides. Each of these practices is simple, easy, and wondrously beneficial in the short term. Each, if used continually, sets in motion a creeping long-term disaster that is hard to detect and harder to stop.

Of course, the long term doesn't matter if you don't *survive* the short term; so these practices *can* be life-saving. On the other hand, if you do survive, relying on them will plant the seeds of your next crisis. And if you can't see *that* crisis coming, you may have no choice but to use another extractive practice, which will plant the seeds for another crisis after that. And so on.

But *why* are these practices extractive? And what's the long-term disaster? To answer those questions, we need to think about soil.

### Self-organization in the soil

A healthy soil is a bustling marketplace. Bacteria, viruses, fungi, protozoa, worms, snails, insects, plants, and mammals chatter and jostle as they strike deals and exchange resources. Supply and demand rise and fall as goods and services are exchanged. Market-goers, large and small, compete, cooperate, and seek advantage. This sprawling, brawling free-for-all opened its doors hundreds of millions of years ago, and it has been thriving ever since. Let's take a tour.

Soil-dwelling bacteria and fungi transform *organic matter*—the bodies of dead animals and plants (and dead bacteria and fungi)—into *humus*: a spongy jelly of chemical compounds (starches, proteins, acids) that plants can draw up through their root tips. Some bacteria also pull nitrogen from the air and transform it into forms plants can use. Bacteria and fungi produce glue-like substances that bind soil particles together into *aggregates*, leaving open spaces like tiny passageways through which air and water can circulate. Soil with more of these natural glues holds more water and is less susceptible to erosion.

Growing plants enter the marketplace eager to cultivate beneficial associations. They promote bacterial and fungal growth by handing out free carbon compounds derived from photosynthesis, exuding them from their root tips. Why do they do this? Because, in the same way that we can't absorb energy from the sun and need plants to do it for us, plants can't absorb nutrients from intact organic matter. So they feed bacteria and fungi, which convert organic matter to humus, and everybody gets what they want.[8]

But if the soil contained only bacteria and fungi, it would not support plant growth as well as it does. Too many of the nutrients plants need would be bound up in the bodies of living bacteria and fungi. Enter the protozoa—amoebae, flagellates, ciliates. These tiny animals roam the soil grazing on bacteria and fungi as well as organic matter. Their excretions (and bodies) contribute to the breakdown of organic matter and the creation of humus.

Above protozoa in the soil food web are worms, insects, and small mammals, which feed on protozoa, fungi, bacteria, and organic matter. These larger animals aerate and stir the soil as they move around, creating larger passageways and transferring nutrients from place to place. Plants provide these larger participants in the soil ecosystem with food by feeding bacteria and fungi, much as we provide food for domesticated animals by growing plants.

This complex network of relationships generated all of the fertile soil on the planet. Now let's look at what we've been doing to it.

## Tillage and self-organization

Tilling the soil provides an obvious and immediate boost to crop growth. It aerates and breaks up compacted soil, promotes nutrient availability through the short-term growth of aerobic bacteria, kills weeds, buries crop residue, mixes fertilizers into the soil, and prepares the soil for planting.

At the same time, the long-term effects of tilling are devastating. Tilling the soil is like setting off a bomb in the marketplace. It splinters populations, shatters relationships, shreds fungal networks, destroys aggregate stability, shrinks pore spaces, decreases the soil's water-holding capacity, and reduces its ability to hold on to nutrients. A freshly tilled field may *look* neat and clean, but it's in grave danger. Its complex ecosystem has been torn apart, and its topsoil is in a precarious state, unprotected from erosion and drought.

Tilled soil loses organic matter quickly. Promoting nutrient availability through the short-term growth of aerobic bacteria does wonders for plant growth, but it burns through organic matter faster than it can accumulate. And as the organic matter content of soil drops, the soil becomes compacted and less able to absorb and retain rainfall.

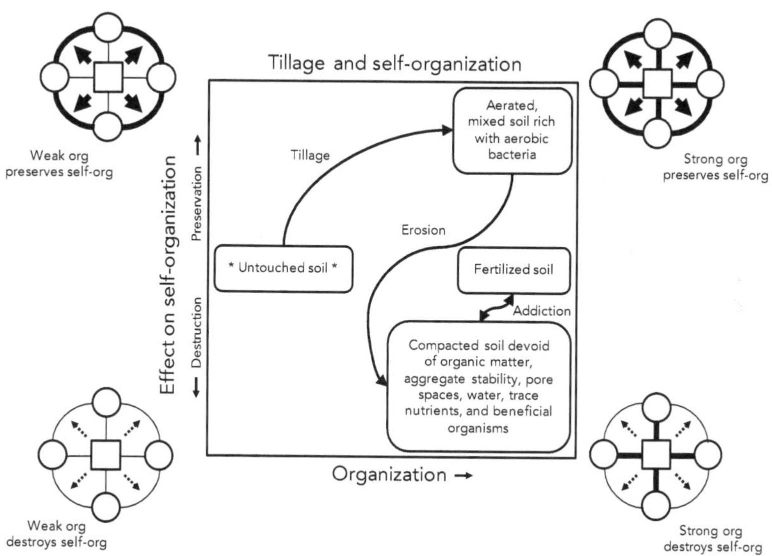


Agriculturally speaking, a drought is not a weather event. It is a lack of water in the soil. A lack of water in the soil *can* be caused by a lack of rain, but it can also be caused by the soil's inability to retain the water that falls on it. A farm with depleted organic matter can be in a state of drought one fence away from a farm with abundant organic matter and plenty of water in the soil.

Unfarmed soils vary from less than one percent organic matter in deserts to as much as eighteen percent in fertile lowlands. On most farms today, organic matter levels have fallen below three percent, and half of our productive topsoil has been lost to erosion.

It's hard to believe that the plow, which has always been seen as a symbol of success, has been sowing the seeds of failure for so many generations. But it's true nonetheless. As plows got bigger and more efficient, they depleted topsoil and organic matter more efficiently as well.

### Monocultures and self-organization

Now let's reset our bustling marketplace to its healthy state and see what happens when we grow enormous fields of single crop species.

Generally speaking, the amount of food any ecosystem can produce is strongly affected by the diversity of its plant community. Biological diversity is nature's insurance policy. It minimizes the impact of weather variations and disturbances. Just as a diverse stock portfolio will outperform a less diverse set of holdings, a diverse plant community will outperform an impoverished one.

Monoculture plantings tear up nature's insurance policy. All of the plants in a monoculture plot want the same things, so they can't exploit complementary niches with different nutrient profiles, growth heights, root depths, and relationships with bacteria, fungi, and beneficial insects. Worse, a huge single-species crop field is a giant EAT ME sign, an invitation to opportunistic pioneers—which are normally kept in check by a diverse plant community—to feast and multiply. If you wanted to design a farming practice that would *breed* weeds, pests, and diseases, monoculture would be a good way to do it.

So why do people plant monoculture crops? It's easier, simpler, and cheaper. With only one crop to plant and harvest, you only need one type of machine. And monoculture crops *can* provide better yields than polyculture crops—at first. It is only in the longer term, over the course of decades, that monocultures fail to stack up. Even with crop rotation, monocultures are more vulnerable to pests, diseases, and climatic conditions, and they deplete the soil more severely—because more consistently—than mixed plantings. In a crisis, this may be an acceptable burden. But there will be a price to pay later on.

### Continuous grazing and self-organization

Now let's go back to our bustling marketplace and kill it again, this time with continuous grazing.

For hundreds of millions of years, the land mass of the earth was shaped by enormous animals called megafauna. These giant ecosystem engineers maintained grasslands by knocking over trees and browsing on woody saplings. In forested areas, they regularly opened up clearings that created habitat mosaics. They also created natural fire breaks that decreased the impact of forest fires.

A few tens of thousands of years ago, the last of the megafauna vanished, probably due to a combination of climate change and hunting by newly organized human groups. As a result, the spread of grasslands was diminished, forest patches filled in, and fires became more devastating. Still, many grasslands remained due to the presence of smaller animals such as buffalo, camels, deer, bears, boars, and big cats. As recently as 500 years ago, for example, some 30-60 million bison covered the plains of North America. Today, wild populations of large herbivores, and the grassland ecosystems they depend on, continue to shrink. Within a century, there may be no grasslands and no large mammal populations left on the planet—except for those maintained by farmers.

The life of a wild herbivore has a rhythm to it, a rhythm driven by fear. Predators constantly stalk the perimeters of the herd, picking off the sick, the injured, the young, and the old. Most herbivores that make it to adulthood live relatively long lives by staying close to other adults, who help them fend off attacks from predators.

Because herbivores are pressed close together, they have no choice but to eat what is directly under their hooves. And because they eat what is directly under their hooves, they have no choice but to move frequently. Centuries ago, tens of thousands of animals would pass over grassy areas within the course of a few days and return to the same spot only months or years later. This pattern of intense cropping combined with frequent movement shaped the grassland ecosystem and all of its inhabitants.

When an herbivore tears off the leaves of a plant, the plant attempts to discourage further destruction by generating secondary plant compounds that are toxic in high concentrations. Herd animals minimize their intake of toxins by eating a variety of plants. They learn which plants to eat and in what proportions by observing what their mothers eat, first in utero, then through their mothers' milk, then by observing their mothers as they themselves begin to eat solid foods. They also learn from older members of the herd who are grazing close by. Later, they pass on what they have learned to others. Thus herds that stay together throughout their lives pass on survival knowledge in a learning culture.[9]

When people first started keeping domestic livestock, their grazing patterns were similar to those of wild herds: bunched up and moving. Shepherds used dogs and temporary fences (hurdles) to keep their herds packed tightly together, and they often moved their herds from place to place.

But these practices gradually fell away, and people started letting livestock range freely over large areas. Continuous grazing seems to have arisen through a combination of three factors: fewer predators; the greater ease of putting up permanent fences instead of moving hurdles and training dogs; and the establishment of extensive ranch lands, especially in Australia and the Americas.

When a herd spreads out over a large area, animals are free to ignore most of the plants under their hooves and seek out only the plants they like best. As a result, favored plants become over-grazed and die off, leaving some patches of soil bare. Soil fertility declines, the water-holding capacity of the soil is reduced, topsoil washes off, and invasive, opportunistic pests and weeds move in. In a few decades, a healthy ecosystem can become simplified and unproductive.

Things get worse even faster when calves are taken from their mothers at birth and when all of the animals are slaughtered at the same young age, because the herd loses its ability to transfer knowledge from one generation to the next. Eventually, ranchers become trapped in a downward spiral, with no choice but to use synthetic fertilizers, herbicides, pesticides, and grain feeds, all of which reduce the health of the soil, the plants, and the herd—and the nutritional content of the meat and milk they supply to people.

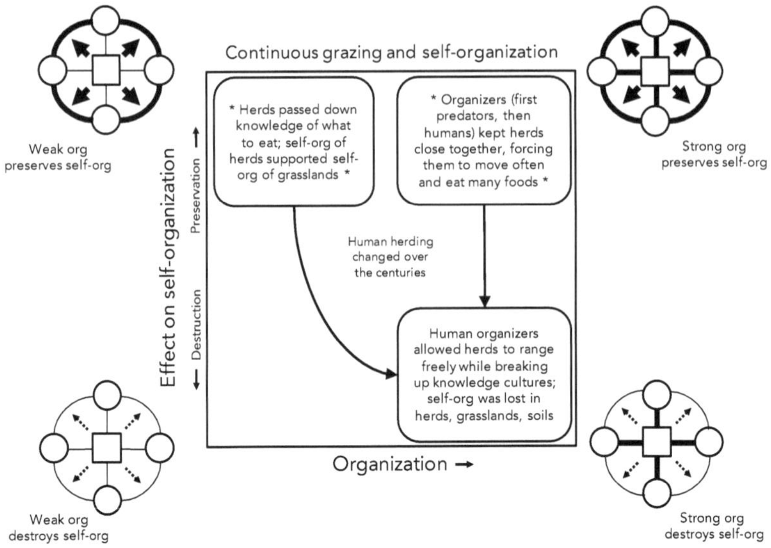
Continuous grazing and self-organization
Weak org
preserves self-org
Strong org
preserves self-org
Weak org
destroys self-org
Strong org
destroys self-org
Effect on self-organization
Preservation →
← Destruction
Organization →
* Herds passed down knowledge of what to eat; self-org of herds supported self-org of grasslands *
* Organizers (first predators, then humans) kept herds close together, forcing them to move often and eat many foods *
Human herding changed over the centuries
Human organizers allowed herds to range freely while breaking up knowledge cultures; self-org was lost in herds, grasslands, soils

## Agrochemicals and self-organization

Now let's kill off our thriving soil community one more time with synthetic fertilizers, pesticides, and herbicides.

When soil is bathed in readily available free-flowing nutrients, plants stop feeding the bacteria and fungi in the soil. The bacteria and fungi die of starvation, and so does everything that eats them, from protozoa to earthworms. There may still be some organic matter in the soil, but plants can no longer make use of it because there are too few decomposers left to turn it into humus. Thus the plants become addicted to synthetic inputs and unable to grow without them.

Even if there is still some humus left, the relatively few chemical elements found in synthetic fertilizers overwhelm and displace the diverse micronutrients held in the humus, causing them to leach out of the soil. Plants grown in this way may look healthy, but they are deficient in micronutrients, and this affects the health of the people who eat them. Some synthetic fertilizers attempt to counter the problem by incorporating micronutrients, and that does help, but not much, for reasons that will become clear in a moment.

As the bacterial and fungal glues that once bound soil particles into aggregates disappear, the structure of the soil begins to break down. Some soil erodes away, and what remains becomes compacted. Water runs off instead of sinking in, and drought becomes a problem even when rainfall is adequate.

Farmers who find themselves in this situation often feel that they have no choice but to keep applying fertilizers, *even though yields are declining*, because yields will plummet even further without them. So they keep spraying. Most of what they apply runs off the compacted soil—micronutrients and all—polluting downstream watersheds, endangering people and ecosystems. Eventually no amount of fertilizer can stop the downward spiral, and the soil is rendered barren and unusable.

Now let's talk about pesticides. For every insect species that eats a particular crop, hundreds of other insect species *support* the growth of the same crop, with benefits ranging from pest predation to weed-eating to pollination. Pesticides kill harmful and beneficial insects alike. Ironically, pest populations often rebound faster than their predators[10]; so spraying pesticides can actually give pests a competitive *advantage*. Says Gabe Brown in his book *Dirt to Soil*:

> Most farmers use insecticides to kill pests, but what they don't realize is that they are killing predator insects, too. Thus, they ensure that they will never have the population of predatory insects they need to kill the pests.[11]

A farm that is regularly dosed with pesticides becomes addicted to their use because the natural enemies of the pests—the natural *friends* of the farmer—are being killed off along with the pests.

Pesticides become concentrated as they move up the food chain, poisoning larger animals and harming human health. In contrast, plants grown without synthetic pesticides produce more secondary plant compounds (such as flavonoids) in reaction to stresses such as leaf damage. Secondary plant compounds, especially those that act as antioxidants, play a part in preventing human diseases such as heart disease, diabetes, and cancer. We might be healthier if we let insects take a few bites out of the foods we eat.

Now herbicides. As they kill weeds, they also kill many other plants, some of which provide food sources for beneficial insects, some of which eat the very weeds herbicides are meant to kill. Herbicides also kill soil bacteria, fungi, and invertebrates, cause soil compaction, and—yes, it's the same story all over again. And once again, a dependency can develop in which farmers feel that they have no choice but to keep spraying herbicides because every other option has been ruled out. As David Montgomery said in *Growing a Revolution*, "It was not lost on me that almost all the weeds I'd seen were in herbicide-treated fields."[12]

All of these forms of extractive farming destroy self-organization through the heavy hand of organizational control. All are good choices when we *must* produce the most food in the shortest time. In emergency situations they can save lives. But they have been used too long and too widely, and they are depleting the quantity and quality of the life-saving food our earth can provide.

## When weak organization destroys self-organization

In the lower-left corner of the regulation space, it is not the presence of organization but its *absence* that causes self-organization to be destroyed.

When I first started working on this chapter, I couldn't think of a single example to put here. How could a *lack* of organization cause self-organization to be destroyed?

When I mentioned the empty corner to my son, he said, "Oh, I can think of something that fits there. A fish tank."

"A *fish* tank?" I said. "What do you mean?"

"A fish tank when nobody is taking care of it," he said.

And he was right. In this corner are situations in which organizers seized control of self-organized patterns *to the extent that the patterns could not exist without their help,* then walked away from them, causing the patterns to collapse. Like a fish tank when nobody is taking care of it. Like a farm that has become dependent on synthetic inputs that have stopped coming.

Don't get me wrong; self-organization *always* bounces back. But it could take a year, or it could take a thousand years. Self-organization doesn't care how long it takes. We do.

Are we in this corner of the space already? Yes and no. The farmers of the world produce enough food to feed ten billion people right now. Everyone else just does a bad job of *distributing* what they grow. A third of the world's food is wasted between farm and fork.

However, we are *approaching* a global agricultural crisis due to soil degradation. A third of the farmable land on the planet has been lost in the past forty years. Some of the loss has been caused by urban and suburban development, but a substantial portion of farmland has been eroded away or rendered unusable by destructive farming practices. If those practices continue, our ability to feed ourselves will not be able to keep up, even if we improve distribution and reduce waste.

If you don't believe me, believe the farmers. David Montgomery, in his book *Growing a Revolution,* says:

> Time and again, at one farming conference after another . . . farmers would share stories about how their soil quality had gone downhill over their lifetimes, too slowly to notice year to year, but plain as day in retrospect. One after another piped up to say that they'd noticed their soil decline under the now-conventional marriage of the plow and intensive fertilizer and agrochemical use.[13]

But the problem is not confined to our agricultural soils. It's as big as the whole world. *Ecosystem services* are the things we get from the natural world that we cannot get without it (at least not without a lot of effort): clean air to breathe; clean, safe water to drink; safe, nutritious, abundant food (which requires healthy soils and healthy populations of pollinators); medicinal resources; building materials; waste processing services; moderation of extreme weather events; relief from pest and disease outbreaks; recreational spaces for the restoration of physical and mental health; places for families and communities to come together; inspiration for artistic, cultural, and scientific achievements; spiritual growth.

Many of the things we take for granted would not exist without these ecosystem services. Even from a purely organized perspective, the way we are living on the earth doesn't make sense. The continuation of our species depends on the vitality of the ecosystems in which we are embedded. *It doesn't matter if we don't believe we are embedded in them.* When we degrade them, we strike at the root of our own existence.

I'd like to take a moment to remind you of what I said at the start of the second part of this book (page 35)—that I allowed some of my own personality to show through in my choices of examples. This is the sort of thing I meant. Obviously, ecology is important to me. It might not be important to you. That's fine. The point of this book is not to convince you to believe what I believe or care about what I care about. It is to show you how you can use these thinking spaces to explore what you and other people believe and care about, whether or not you agree. With that understanding, let's continue.

### The tide is turning

The good news is that a quiet agricultural revolution has been going on for decades. It has a lot of different names, and few people agree on exactly what should happen. But most people agree that in a few decades from now, we are going to be growing food very differently than we did just a few decades ago. In fact, so many solutions have been proposed that to tell you about them I've had to corral them into four groups. Let's work our way through them.

### Isolation

The first group of solutions I want to consider seeks to address the agricultural crisis by switching from extraction to production. In this group are *hydroponics* (growing plants in water), *vertical farming* (growing plants in stacked trays, usually with water in them), and *cellular agriculture* (growing microorganisms and cell cultures in vats). All of these methods produce food indoors, away from weather, weeds, and natural habitats. Collectively they are called *Controlled Environment Agriculture* (CEA).

Growing food in a bubble protects self-organized patterns both inside and outside the bubble. Inside the bubble, farmers seed self-organized patterns that grow food (lettuce, tomatoes) while preventing undesirable self-organized patterns (molds, diseases). Outside the bubble, other self-organized patterns (trees, streams, deer) can thrive because the space they occupy is no longer needed to produce food for people. Thus food security and environmental health (and ecosystem services) can improve at the same time.

Tests of CEA farms have demonstrated yields at least ten times greater than conventional farms. They use far less water, don't leach nutrients, and require little or no herbicides or pesticides. They operate year-round and are relatively safe from weather events. Working indoors allows farmers to control things they could not possibly control outside, like the mix of gases in the air (more $CO_2$ makes plants grow faster) and the quality of the light plants receive.

CEA farms can be built anywhere: in skyscrapers, in abandoned buildings, in shipping containers, underground. This means they can be hyperlocal, delivering fresh food cheaply and in minutes everywhere people live. Ruined, barren land can be transformed into productive farms. If all of the farms in the world were converted to vertical farms, the amount of land required for food production could be drastically reduced, leaving vast areas available for ecosystem restoration.

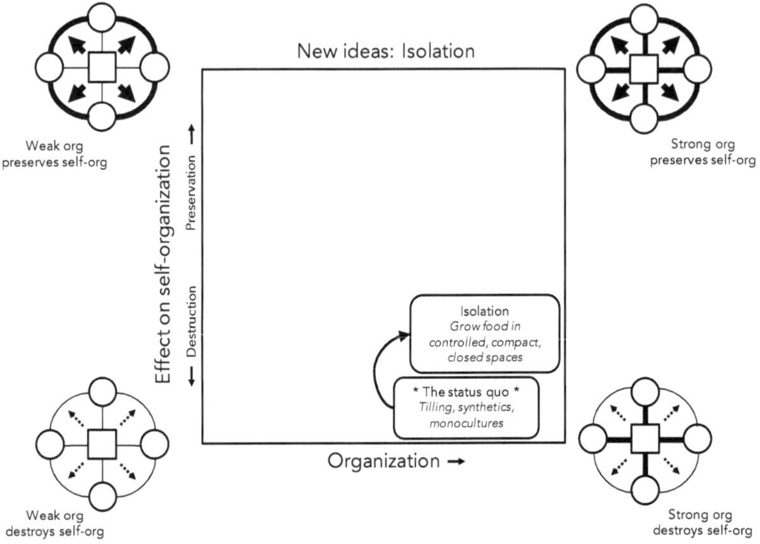


However, CEA farms require a lot of energy. Even with large windows, plants in the lower levels of vertical farms require supplemental lighting. If the energy to power vertical farms comes from burning fossil fuels, this is hardly better for the environment. On the other hand, as renewable energy technologies become more efficient, we might someday farm sunlight and wind on the roofs of eco-city skyscrapers, then channel that power into concentrated plant growth on the many floors below. Imagine a self-sufficient tower that looks out over a forest full of wildlife, like a giant tree filled with people living lightly on the land.

But the biggest obstacle to a CEA future still has to do with gaining control over self-organization. Preventing undesired self-organized patterns from growing inside the CEA bubble could prove to be an arms race no more winnable than fighting pests and weeds on a conventional farm.

People say that CEA installations are closed systems, but no biological system can ever be completely closed, and no environment can ever be completely controlled. If our vertical farms must someday be fumigated regularly, we may find ourselves back in the same predicament as we are in now. That doesn't mean CEA can't work, and it doesn't mean it isn't an improvement over traditional farms. It just means that CEA is not exempt from the laws of biology to which life on this planet has been subject for billions of years.

## Mitigation

A second group of agricultural solutions asks: if current agricultural practices take a sledgehammer to the self-organized patterns we need to survive, why not use a smaller hammer? In this category I place no-till farming, integrated pest management, and precision agriculture.

***No-till farming*** avoids disturbing the soil by (obviously) not tilling it. That's the theory, anyway. In practice, most no-till farming is actually *low*-till farming. Tilling kills weeds, so if you aren't going to till, you need a different way to kill weeds. Many no-till farmers use a tool called a *roller-crimper,* a heavy cylinder with dull blades that kills weeds by pinching their stems, leaving their dead bodies behind as green manure.

But roller-crimpers aren't perfect. If the timing is wrong and weeds have been allowed to grow strong stems, they are not so easily killed. And some invasive perennials have very tough stems. Uneven fields full of rocks and ruts make it hard to squash every stem. Besides, roller-crimpers are still heavy pieces of equipment, and they compact the soil. Farmers are experimenting with lighter, smaller machinery, including autonomous robot swarms. Designs are improving, but more work remains to be done.

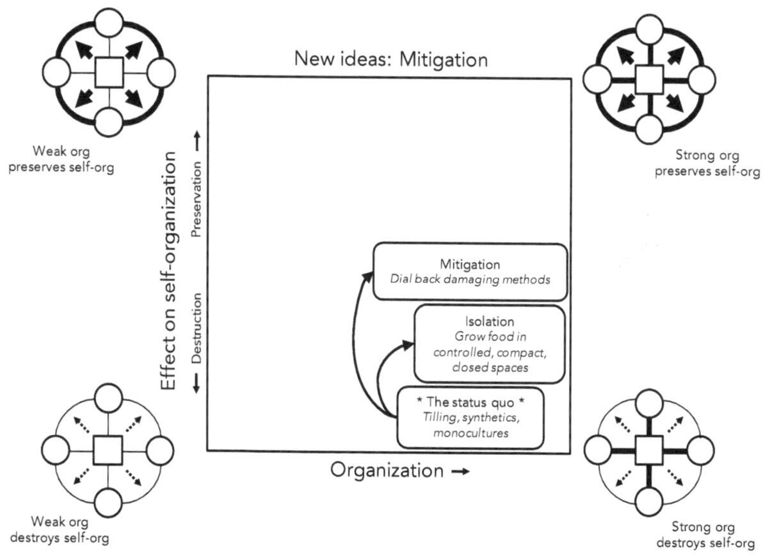


In the meantime, many no-till farmers use herbicides to kill weeds, which cancels out some of the benefits they achieve by not tilling the soil. Organic farmers can't use herbicides, so many of them till the soil, which cancels out some of the benefits *they* achieve by not using herbicides. Many no-till farmers have settled on a mixed strategy for the time being: use a roller-crimper most years, but fall back to tilling periodically, say every five years, to clear out tough weeds the roller-crimper can't kill.

***Integrated pest management*** (IPM) is a lot like no-till farming: its aim is as admirable as its application is variable. IPM aims to reduce the use of pesticides and other killing agents through the sciences of ecology, entomology, biochemistry, and plant breeding. IPM solutions include mechanical methods (such as picking pests off plants and building screens), quarantining affected fields, introducing new predators, breeding pest-resistant plant strains, and sterilizing pest populations. Pesticides and herbicides are not ruled out, but they are used as a last resort. Which option is best for any particular infestation is determined based on detailed monitoring and analysis. Spraying pesticides on a fixed schedule for no particular reason is something an IPM practitioner would never do.

In practice, however, IPM can be difficult to accomplish. It requires farmers to either make a heavy investment in training or depend on experts whose recommendations can be opaque. It depends on constant monitoring, and farmers must be ready to implement a variety of solutions, some of which require special equipment.

In short, IPM is a high-cost, high-benefit, high-organization solution. For farmers who can afford to educate themselves, and for farmers who have plenty of support, IPM can and does reduce the use of synthetic inputs while improving soils, increasing yields, and benefiting the environment. For many others, IPM is out of reach, at least for the moment.

In ***precision agriculture*** (PA), farmers use sensors, satellites, and drones to record yield, soil fertility, microclimate—everything that can be measured—in great detail. Millions of data points are used to build precise plans, which are fed into automated machines that deliver optimal amounts of seeds, water, fertilizers, pesticides, and herbicides to each square meter of soil. Much like IPM, PA aims to increase profitability and sustainability at the same time by using exactly what is needed exactly where and when it is needed.

PA has been shown to help farmers reduce their synthetic inputs by twenty to forty percent, sometimes with increased yields. However, most PA systems require the use of proprietary equipment, software, advice, and even seeds. Many farmers chafe at these terms, and industry watchers have pointed out the dangers of concentrating power over food production in ever fewer hands.

But these issues only matter on large farms. Most of the world's farmland is on large farms, but most of the world's *farmers* farm small farms. According to the UN's Food and Agriculture Organization, only *three percent* of the roughly 570 million farms worldwide are larger than sixty acres (ten hectares).[14]

Thus the best thing about precision agriculture, to my mind, is that it has no *inherent* dependence on technology. After all, farmers have been saying "the best fertilizer is a farmer's footsteps" since ancient times. To the many small farmers of the world, most of whom are also the poorest farmers of the world, it is the *ideas* of precision agriculture, not its tools, that may be of the greatest benefit in the years to come.

## Regeneration

The first two groups of solutions I described (isolation and mitigation) reduce the destruction of self-organized patterns by moving even further to the right side of the space, intensifying organized plans.[15] Regeneration moves in the opposite direction. By reducing the intensity of organized plans, it reduces the destruction of self-organized patterns.

Remember ecosystem services, and how we need them, and how they are in danger? One way to restore them is to *ask farmers to help*. Farmers are uniquely positioned to regenerate ecosystem services because *they care about their land* and the life that grows on it.

The idea of rethinking agriculture as a means of producing both food and ecosystem services goes by many names. My favorite is *regenerative agriculture*. To regen-ag advocates, the term "conservation" is no longer appropriate. What we need is *restoration*, and not only of the land: of a farmer's ability to make a good living, which depends on the fertility of soils. We can restore farming ecosystems and farming livelihoods at the same time by rebuilding soil fertility.

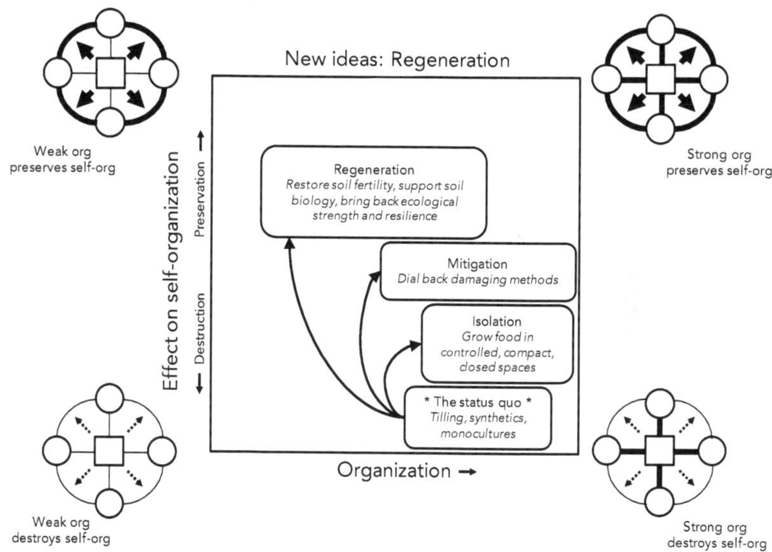


Here's an example of regen-ag at work. In the Burren region of Ireland, a government program supports farmers who improve the soil health and biodiversity of the fields on their properties. In a recent article in *The Guardian*, program director Brendan Dunford said that in the past:

> What defined farmers was how much food they can produce. The biggest challenge was to get them to take on a new role — to convince them they have a broader destiny than just food.[16]

Fifteen years after it started, with more than 300 farmers taking part, the Burren program has transformed both the landscape and the relationships between farmers and nature in the Burren.

Proponents of regenerative agriculture say it brings a new enthusiasm and even joy to farming. In *Growing a Revolution*, David Montgomery recalls what Gabe Brown (author of *Dirt to Soil*) told him about his new farming practices:

> "When I was farming conventionally," he said, "I'd wake up and decide what I was going to kill today. Now I wake up and decide what I'm going to help live." [17]

Asking farmers to see nature as a monster they must destroy puts them in a double bind, because *they themselves are part of the monster they must destroy*. It's no wonder that the ranks of farmers have declined so precipitously. When farmers are given the chance to see nature as a partner in a dance rather than an adversary in a battle, farming becomes an adventure, a font of energy, a gift.

Let's look at some of the regenerative practices in use today.

***Cover-cropping*** is the practice of growing crops not for food but to restore soil fertility. The method has been used since ancient times, but was mostly abandoned in the mid-twentieth century in favor of synthetic fertilizers. Cover crops are cut or mowed and left on the soil to decay. When cover-cropping is combined with no-till farming, it has been shown to restore organic matter content on farm fields by as much as—well, that number depends on whom you ask and how they measure organic matter; but everyone agrees that it goes up significantly. Cover crops crowd out weeds and provide habitats for insects that feed on weeds and pests. And keeping the soil covered reduces erosion.

Some farmers swear by cover-crop mixes with dozens of species; some prefer to plant just a few. Regenerative farmers tend to experiment until they find something that works for their farm—and then they *keep* experimenting, because they know that the best solution will keep changing. This is one of the tenets of regenerative farming: that the only organized plan worth having is a willingness to adapt to constant change. In other words, regenerative farmers deliberately limit the reach of their organized plans.

***Intercropping*** is the practice of growing multiple crops close together. Intercropping reduces weeds, pests, and diseases by increasing plant diversity and providing habitats for beneficial organisms. Closely spaced plants shade out weeds, retain soil moisture, and reduce erosion. Some intercropping mixes even include trap or sacrificial crops grown specifically to attract pests and keep them away from more valuable crops in the mix. And intercropping helps farms perform better economically as well as ecologically, since it's unlikely that every crop in the mix will fail at the same time.

The most famous intercropping mix is the "three sisters" combination of beans, squash, and corn planted by indigenous American farmers for hundreds or thousands of years. Bean plants cooperate with bacteria to fix nitrogen; corn plants provide trellises on which bean plants can grow; and squash leaves shade out weeds. A fourth sister, usually sunflowers or bee balm, is sometimes grown to draw birds away from the corn and to attract pollinators.

The main drawback of intercropping is that it is difficult to reconcile with mechanized farming. Most farming machines in use today were designed for use with monoculture crops. This is why a lot of farmers who intercrop work in strips or rows, because they can drive their tractors down the rows. It can also be difficult to find the right mix of crops for a particular location, and mistakes can be costly. Growing crops together requires greater attention to timing and makes the harvest more complicated. All of these things can make the transition to intercropping a daunting prospect. Still, farmers who have been intercropping for years swear by the method, reporting that it brings them better yields, better soil quality, and the ability to reduce or eliminate their use of synthetic inputs.

***Perennial grain crops*** can be harvested every year without replanting, removing the need to till the soil. Several varieties of perennial grains have been bred and are now being tested. The effort is being led by The Land Institute, an organization that seeks to establish "ecologically intensified polycultures that mimic natural systems."[18] If these new perennial grains succeed and are taken up widely, grain farms could be transformed into prairies on which farmers gather food instead of growing it.

***Mixed crop-livestock farming*** is another form of agricultural diversity that is ancient in origin, was recently abandoned, and is now being rediscovered. The advantage of raising animals and plants on the same farm is that they feed each other. A mixed farm mimics the food web of an ecosystem in which the wastes of one group become the food of another, in a cycle that goes from plants to herbivores to carnivores to decomposers and back to plants. This makes mixed farms more efficient than specialized farms. Raising animals requires land, but land that cannot support crops grown for human consumption can be used to pasture animals.

Mixed farming is more complicated than specialized farming. There is more to learn, more to handle, more to buy, and more to go wrong. On the other hand, when something does go wrong, other sources of income are there to make up for it. The same kind of natural insurance policy created by mixed-species plantings can be created by raising plants and animals together.

***Rotational grazing*** mimics the way herds of wild herbivores once roamed the grasslands of the world—and the way shepherds once moved their flocks. Farmers pack herds of cattle, sheep, and other herbivores close together on grassland pastures. Electric fences break fields into dozens of small paddocks, and livestock are moved out of a paddock as soon as its grass has been grazed to a desired amount. Grazed paddocks are left alone until their grasses have recovered enough to be grazed again—even if they must be left alone for months or years, and even if leaving them alone requires the use of supplementary fodder. Most rotational-grazing farms keep fodder banks ready for such contingencies so they don't have to sacrifice the restoration of their grasslands.

Practitioners of rotational grazing say that they have been able to increase the organic matter content and water-holding capacity of their soils, reduce the prevalence of weeds, pests and diseases, and reduce or eliminate their use of synthetic inputs. Rotationally grazed pastures have been transformed from near-monocultures to diverse ecosystems with hundreds of native plant species.

Some rotational grazers are bringing learning cultures back to their cow herds. Allowing calves to stay with their mothers, and allowing some herd members to live longer lives, helps animals pass on what they learn, which builds healthier grasslands. Not long ago, cows, pigs, sheep, and even chickens were slaughtered much later in life than they are today. Younger meat is cheaper meat, but price is not the only driver of consumer choice. There is value in living a healthier (and longer) life by eating tastier meat less often. The strong, gamy flavor of mature meat has been praised by chefs and connoisseurs, and "aged on the hoof" meat is growing in popularity. In Spain, the tradition of eating older meat never went away. Prized *txuleton* steaks come from cows that were slaughtered at twelve to twenty years old. Letting domesticated animals live longer lives could improve the health of people, animals, and ecosystems.

### New strategy mixes

Regenerative farmers are also exploring many new ways to mix the food-getting strategies of extraction and production together with foraging, adjusting, and imitating, such as the following practices.

- ***Pollinator-friendly zones*** are plantings of wildflowers and other native plants farmers establish around their fields to boost biodiversity, reduce pests and weeds, improve pollination services, and develop diverse sources of income by selling wild herbs, flowers, and seeds.
- ***Riparian forest buffers*** are areas near streams that farmers fill with trees and shrubs to filter pollutants, reduce erosion, grow nuts and fruits, and provide refuges and corridors for wildlife, including beneficial insects.
- ***Alley cropping*** is the practice of planting trees in wide rows, then planting a variety of shrubs and annual crops in the shaded, wind-free alleys between them. The trees grow nuts, fruits, and high-value lumber. The shrubs grow nuts, fruits, and fodder. Crops such as wheat, corn, and soybeans thrive in the protected alleys. The practice reduces erosion, improves soil and water quality, controls weeds and pests, provides habitats for wildlife, and produces more diverse economic benefits for farmers.
- ***Silvopasture*** is the practice of grazing animals in wooded areas, either by allowing animals into woodlands they were previously kept away from or by planting trees where animals have traditionally grazed. Silvopasture reduces heat stress on animals and provides them with a diversity of food sources, and the animals contribute organic matter to the forest.
- ***Integrated multi-trophic aquaculture (IMTA)*** is a method of growing fish, shellfish, and aquatic plants together so that the different parts of the system (the trophic levels, *trophic* meaning "eating") complement each

other. Waste feed and fish feces are eaten by worms and shellfish, and the nutrients their excrements release into the water feed seaweed and other aquatic plants—which are eaten by herbivorous fish, which are eaten by carnivorous fish. IMTA systems can be established in the ocean or in freshwater ponds. Some forms of IMTA include cultivated plants such as rice and domestic animals such as ducks.

And finally, gardeners and communities are getting in on the act, using regenerative practices to grow food outside of farms. For example:

- ***Food forests*** are permaculture plantings that incorporate human-usable plants at several levels: tall trees, shorter trees, understory shrubs, climbing plants, standing plants, and ground cover plants, plus mushrooms that grow in the soil. Each layer plays a part in growing food and providing ecosystem services. The high-density, self-sustaining biodiversity of a permanent food forest blends farming with forest management.
- ***Hügelculture*** is a traditional German farming method in which a mound of carefully layered logs, branches, sticks, leaves, wood chips, manure, grass clippings, kitchen waste, and other organic matter is covered with soil and planted with vegetables. Hügelculture mounds mimic the process of decomposition on forest floors, where fallen logs decay and become sponge-like, holding on to water and feeding bacteria and fungi that provide nutrients to nearby plants. Hügelculture mounds in back yards and town parks turn waste materials into free fertilizers and free food.
- ***Urban agriculture*** is the practice of growing food in cities. You might think this means mini-farms on rooftops, and it does mean that. But it can also mean much more. Imagine if every park in every city was a food forest, planted and managed to provide food for the people who live around it. Now imagine if every roof and every street was a food forest. (Let's throw some hügelculture mounds in there as well.) As a volunteer at the Beacon Food Forest in Seattle, Washington, put it: "Food provided free to the people, by the people, and for the people. It's unprecedented."[19] Actually, food forests are not at all unprecedented. They are how we once got our food. Someday they may be a part of how we get our food again.

### Another look at the old ways

The rise of regenerative agriculture has prompted the re-evaluation of traditional farming methods practiced by indigenous peoples, many of which seem a lot smarter than they did in the days of plowing and dosing.

Consider, for example, the practice of shifting cultivation. Also known as slash-and-burn farming, shifting cultivation has been labeled primitive, unscientific, and destructive, and it has even been banned in some countries.

Remember how I said (on page 110) that some farming traditions connect multiple food-getting strategies in sequences? Shifting cultivation does exactly that. The cycle of shifting cultivation moves through all five food-getting strategies. First a plot of land is chosen from the forest and burned. This is a purely *extractive* activity, done to clear the land and to free up nutrients for quick plant growth. Next the land is cultivated to *produce* food, in part by *imitating* nature with a no-till, inter-cropped, mulched planting of annuals and perennials. As time goes by, the dominant strategy shifts from imitation to *adjustment*, as cultivators guide the recovering forest plot into a mature state, ideally over two to five decades. During this time the forest increasingly supports *foraging* for food and other products.

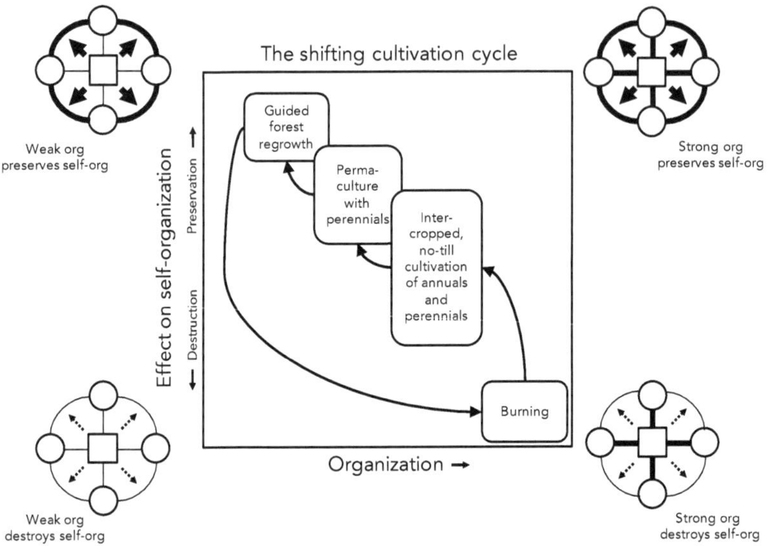


Critics of shifting cultivation have focused exclusively on the burning portion of the cycle. Stark photographs of burned lands accompany declarations that this "evil" practice has caused mass deforestation in the developing world. To my mind, it seems hypocritical to focus on a brief destructive stage in a mostly-restorative cycle when industrial agricultural practices consist of almost nothing *but* destruction. Why not call extractive agriculture "till-and-kill"?

Descriptions of shifting cultivation often claim that farmers "abandon" tracts of land after the cultivation of annual crops. This is not true. The forest is not abandoned; it is nurtured. Logging and continuous livestock grazing have deforested far more land than has shifting agriculture, and few logging and cattle-raising companies have decades-long plans for land stewardship.

In their book *The Maya Forest Garden,* Anabel Ford and Ronald Nigh counter the belief that the ancient Mayan civilization died out due to deforestation caused by the *milpa* tradition of shifting cultivation. Not only did the ancient Mayans preserve rather than destroy the forest, but they never died out, either, nor did the *milpa* tradition. Say Ford and Nigh:

> Our review of the evidence supports the hypothesis that the Maya forest ecosystems are essentially anthropogenic, the result of mil-

> lennia of selective management. . . . Far from threatening their tropical habitat, the skills and practices of the traditional Maya today provide valuable options for the conservation of the region and the survival of the forest and its people.[20]

The *milpa* system is just one system of shifting cultivation. There are many such systems, with dozens of local names, such as *jhum* in India, *chitimene* in Zambia, *proka* in Ghana, *rai* in Thailand, *ladang* in Indonesia. All of these systems involve long "bush fallow" periods in which people create permacultures that mix human-usable trees and shrubs with ecologically important species. If this sounds like the "food forest" concept I mentioned above, that's because *it's the same thing*. Shifting cultivation just doesn't get the same amount of respect, mostly because it is practiced by impoverished and often illiterate indigenous groups. To quote the anthropologist Malcolm Cairns:

> '[A]groforestry' is often touted as a wonderful, cutting-edge technology, while 'shifting cultivation' is condemned as a remnant of the Stone Age. . . People seem to forget that shifting cultivation is probably one of the oldest forms of agroforestry.[21]

Shifting cultivation is often described as a cultural relic, as if it was abandoned centuries ago by an enlightened world. But this is not true. In fact, the practice was prevalent in some parts of Europe (where it was called *swidden* cultivation) as recently as the middle of the twentieth century.

***Distortions of the regenerative cycle***

Having said all of that, however, there are some serious problems with shifting cultivation *as it is being practiced today* that do not bode well for its future. Even though the practice has supported human populations for thousands of years, it is no longer working as well as it once did.

When shifting cultivators can maintain at least an eight-to-one ratio of forest regrowth to cultivation, soil fertility recovers well, and the system is sustainable over long periods of time. Recently, however, due to pressures from increasing populations, changing climates, and social and political upheavals, many farmers have been forced to shift their recovery ratios into the unsustainable range, in some places to four-to-one or even two-to-one. Such distortions of the regenerative cycle can quickly deplete soils to the point that forests cannot recover, no matter how skilled their management.

The long-term sustainability of shifting cultivation rests heavily on its ability to work with self-organized patterns, and this requires the careful passing down of knowledge and skills from one generation to the next. For a host of reasons, the traditional knowledge required to make shifting cultivation work is being slowly lost in many parts of the world. For example, the practice of polyculture during the cultivation period has been abandoned in some places, as farmers grow monoculture cash crops rather than crop mixes chosen to minimize soil depletion. Also being lost are the nuanced understandings required to guide a forested plot into regeneration in a way that restores ecosystem services as well as food production.

Expertise has also been lost in the careful burning of plant matter. Managing controlled burns in a way that returns the great majority of carbon and nutrients to the soil (instead of releasing them into the atmosphere) is difficult. In the Mayan tradition, say Ford and Nigh:

> The Yukatek Maya employ specialists known as "wind-tenders" (yum ik'ob), who control milpa fires by burning against the prevailing winds and spreading the bush out to achieve an even, low-temperature burn throughout the process. . . . [S]uch practices result in a significant cumulative input of black carbon to the soil and the enhancement of other physical and chemical characteristics of anthropogenic dark earths. [22]

Negative views of shifting cultivation have arisen in part due to this gradual loss of expertise—but they also played a part in causing it. Many shifting cultivators have been forced into shorter forest regeneration periods because tracts of forest they once managed have been designated off-limits for the protection of the environment—as if their ancestors had not been managing those tracts of forest without harming the environment for thousands of years.

In most communities that practice shifting cultivation, the allocation of plots to families has long been managed by knowledgeable elders, who choose which plots should be cultivated and which should be left alone each year. The elders take into account the condition of each plot, the skills of each family, and the needs of the community. Each family is granted a right of *usufruct*—the right to farm the land—but the land itself belongs to the community. "Shifting cultivation is resource and land management at landscape scale," says researcher Christian Erni. "This has enabled the sustainable use of and equitable access to land and resources, thus ensuring livelihood and food security for all."[23]

Recently, however, governments have pushed many of these communities into individual land ownership, destroying carefully tended balances between the needs of communities and the health of their soils and forests.

### *A marriage of science and tradition*

Fortunately, attitudes towards shifting cultivation are changing. Instead of asking "How can we force people away from shifting cultivation?" people have begun to ask "How can we help people make shifting cultivation more sustainable?" To that end, thousands of farmers and researchers have been working together to update and revitalize this ancient practice to meet the needs of today's world.

Part of this work lies in valuing the traditional knowledge and expertise that does still exist—in the minds of the oldest and wisest of the shifting cultivators. Listening to knowledgeable elders with respect, helping them share their knowledge, and working with them to find new solutions—as indigenous groups have been doing for thousands of years—can still turn things around.

For example, *slash-and-char* is a burning process similar to what Ford and Nigh describe in the *milpa* system, but with less expertise required. *Biochar* is plant matter that has been burned under cover, with minimal ventilation, under a layer of soil or in a facility that scrubs exhaust gases. Biochar production returns far more carbon and nutrients to the soil than open burning, and biochar releases its compounds slowly, feeding the bacteria and fungi in the soil. By switching from open burning to biochar production, farmers can burn only a fraction of their plant matter, leaving the rest on the ground to protect the soil during planting and seedling growth.

*Inga alley cropping* marries traditional methods with new ideas in alley cropping, specifically the use of leguminous trees to rebuild soils. Trees in the *Inga* genus host nitrogen-fixing bacteria. Planting *Inga* trees during the cultivation and regrowth stages of the shifting cultivation cycle improves soils while providing food for consumption and sale, leaves for mulches and green manures, branches for firewood, shade for growing seedlings, and habitats for wildlife. Every region has leguminous trees that can be used in this way.

In short, every idea in the regen-ag world is being examined to improve soils under shifting cultivation. But the most important thing shifting cultivators need is freedom from persecution. Given enough land to practice their traditional methods without disturbance or distortion, shifting cultivators can thrive. They can even help reduce the impact of climate change. A recent paper summarizes twenty-five years of research into shifting cultivation thus:

> Our results suggest that policies imposing land-use transitions on upland farmers so as to improve livelihoods and environments have been misguided; in the context of varied land uses, swidden agriculture can support livelihoods and ecosystem services that will help buffer the impacts of climate change in Southeast Asia.[24]

Shifting cultivators are not the villains they were made out to be, and neither are they romantic heroes. They are simply people trying to survive in the best way they can, just as we are, and they deserve our help and respect.

The same can be said of the many farmers who are exploring ways to transition away from extractive farming. As Nancy and John Hayden said in their book *Farming on the Wild Side*, "We occasionally think back with a bit of guilt at all the plowing, rototilling, and oxidizing of the soil we did in the early years."[25] It's easy to blame each other for the current state of affairs, but there's no future in it. The future of food depends on collaboration.

## When weak organization preserves self-organization

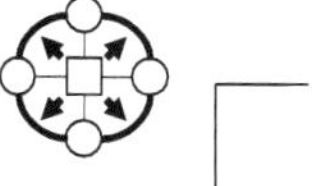

In the upper-left corner of the regulation space, self-organization is perfectly preserved because organization is completely absent. It is here that we can place the last group of solutions to the agricultural crisis: *leaving the land alone.*

Human beings are organized beings. Wherever we go, we take organization along. So one way to preserve self-organized patterns is to keep our organized selves out of them. The biologist E. O. Wilson made the perfectly serious recommendation that we *remove ourselves from half of the earth,* on land and in the sea. Says Wilson:

> [B]y destroying most of the biosphere with archaic short-term methods, we are setting ourselves up for a self-inflicted disaster. . . . Earth's shield of biodiversity is being shattered and the pieces are being thrown away. In its place is being inserted only the promise that all can be solved by human ingenuity. . . . Can the planet be run as a true spaceship by one intelligent species? Surely we would be foolish to take such a large and dangerous gamble.[26]

In his book *Nature's Best Hope,* Douglas W. Tallamy put forth a suggestion. If every homeowner in the United States would let half of their land grow up into native grasslands and forests, we could create a "Homegrown National Park" larger than all of the national parks in the lower forty-eight states combined. The impact on the natural world would be huge. If we can do this, says Tallamy:

> We will not be living with less; we will be enriching our lives with more—more pollination services; more free pest control; more carbon safely tucked away in the soil; more rainwater held on and within land for our use in a clean and fresh state; more bluebirds, orioles, and pileated woodpeckers in our yards; more swallowtails and monarchs sipping nectar from our flowers.[27]

As you can probably guess, I like this idea very much. In fact, almost two decades ago, my husband and I bought fifteen acres (six hectares) of forested land for the sole purpose of leaving it alone. (We had hoped to buy a hundred acres, but for the price we could pay, we could either get a hundred acres and a tent or fewer acres and a house.) Other than fencing some land near the house to keep our dogs from bothering the neighbors, we have left most of the land alone. We did clear a walking trail through the woods, but we've noticed that the deer and bears use the trail as much as we do.

Obviously, not everyone can or wants to do this. Plus, the fact that we have to drive forty minutes to get to the grocery store means that the preservation of our land depends on the destruction caused by our car, not to mention the delivery trucks that make living "out here" a lot easier. Also, somebody has to *put* food at the grocery store. If we ever actually faced starvation, "leaving the land alone" would go out the window in a heartbeat.

Still, Tallamy's idea is one way to achieve what E. O. Wilson was talking about. Millions of people and thousands of towns could set aside some of their land for nature, and such combined actions could have a dramatic effect on ecosystem services. Even if the only change we made was to *stop mowing the places we visit only to mow*, it could make a big difference. Sure, a mowed lawn looks nice, but is it worth the cost? Here are Nancy and John Hayden again:

> Our focus on biodiversity, ecology, and wildness as integral components of our farm has been interpreted by some as unkempt and messy. We say society needs to rethink "pretty," shed the cultural conditioning, and celebrate the wild, especially in the face of current environmental problems.[28]

What about existing parks and preserves? Well, right now, somewhere between ten and fifteen percent of the planet's surface area is protected from human influence. If that percentage was doubled, there is no doubt that it would improve the long-term survival odds of our species.

Life on earth is not in any danger. It will rebound no matter what we do. Some species will go extinct and others will take their places. The only question is which group *our* species will belong to.

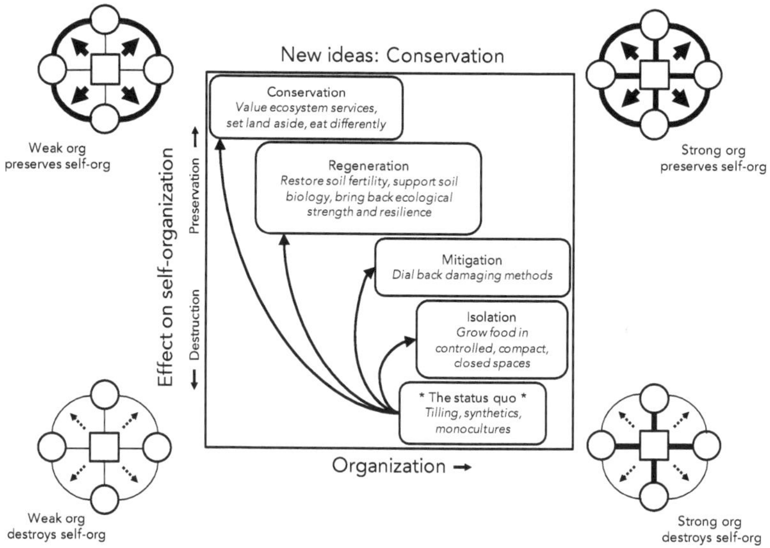


## A world without domesticated animals

Another way to leave nature alone would be to stop raising domesticated animals. Some people have envisioned a vegan world in which the entire human population subsists on a completely plant-based diet.

In such a world, only wild animals (and pets) would remain. Wild animals would face predation, of course, but most of their lives would be longer and less stressful than the lives of most domestic livestock today, especially those on factory farms. Of course, how *many* wild animals could live out their lives would depend on how much land people would let them use. In a vegan world, not every ranch and dairy farm would automatically turn into a forest. People might just spread out over the land and create a million paved-over suburbs, leaving wild animals nowhere to live.

There is no doubt that greenhouse gas emissions would decrease if people stopped raising domesticated animals. But the overall effect on the climate might be more complicated. Over half of the agricultural land on the planet is unsuitable for growing plants meant for human consumption. Most of it lies in grassland ecosystems. Grasslands need grazers, but few wild herbivores remain. So most of the grasslands of the world would be left ungrazed. This could cause dry, combustible plant matter to accumulate, creating tinder for massive fires that could pump enough smoke into the atmosphere to create a climate crisis, which could hamper our ability to grow food. To avoid this outcome, it would be necessary to raise some livestock for the sole purpose of stabilizing grassland ecosystems until wild populations could grow large enough to take over.

The effects of worldwide veganism on human health would also be mixed, especially if the transition was abrupt. Eating too much meat causes a variety of diseases, but it is also true that animal products contain micronutrients that are absent in plant-based staples such as grains. If everyone on the planet suddenly and entirely stopped eating meat, the nutritional profile of plant-based farming would have to improve significantly to avoid widespread malnutrition. We would have to grow fewer grains and more vegetables and beans. That's doable, but it would require effort to avoid suffering.

Also, we derive many more things from domesticated animals than just food. Animal products are used in the manufacture of hundreds of everyday materials such as glues, solvents, paints, cleaners, vitamins, and medicines. We could develop replacements for all of these products, but they would most likely require the use of fossil fuels, which (unlike domesticated animals) are non-renewable resources. Developing plant-based replacements would help, but that would cut into our ability to grow plants to eat.

None of this means we should keep eating too much meat. Clearly our current levels of meat eating are unsustainable, and factory farming is cruel as well as dangerous. But raising some domestic animals, whether we eat them or not, might be more environmentally sustainable than raising no animals at all, at least until we can free up enough habitats to support wild populations.

### Strength in diversity

I have now described over twenty potential solutions to the agricultural crisis—and those are just the ones I found interesting. I could easily have doubled the number. What's the *best* solution? All of them. People love to argue about how we should get our food. Everyone has a favorite solution. But it is the *diversity* of biological networks that makes them robust. The more diverse our food-getting repertoire, the more likely we will be to survive to tell the story of agricultural development ten thousand years from now.

## When strong organization preserves self-organization

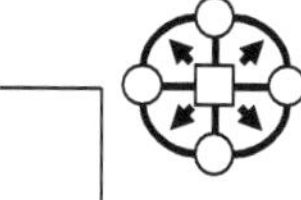

In the extreme upper-right corner of the regulation space lies a magical place where purely organized plans perfectly preserve purely self-organized patterns. Cue the flute-over-bubbling-brook soundtrack.

The reality is that nobody has ever succeeded in perfectly preserving a self-organized pattern within a perfectly organized plan. Every time we think we have understood and controlled some self-organized network or process, it veers away and does something we never expected. The only method that has been reliably proven to preserve self-organization has been to step *back* from this corner and give self-organization some room to grow.

Even if we *could* organize perfect support for self-organization, it might not be the best idea. A self-organized pattern can flip-flop from opportunity to crisis and back in an instant. A hearth fire can become a house fire. A revolution against tyranny can turn into genocide. An erupting volcano can smash a town in one year and support an abundant crop in the next. *Is* this the best corner? It depends on when and where (and of whom) you ask the question. The smartest move might be to keep a safe distance.

### Sharing the land

Let's finish the chapter with one more example that ranges across the space. I told you before about how we bought fifteen acres of forested land so we could stay out of them. Of the acre and a half we fenced, most of it lies under the trees, and we have left that part alone, aside from allowing our dogs to run in it. The quarter-acre (tenth of a hectare) of sunny land just around the house is where we have spent most of our time. That quarter-acre was mowed down to a centimeter once a week by the people who owned the property before us, probably for thirty years. For about fifty years before that, the land was in slow recovery from decades of extractive farming.

When we moved into the house, I was determined to return the sunny clearing to a natural, healthy state. So we left the land alone. It was *wonderful.* Wildflowers sprang up everywhere. I counted twenty, thirty species of native plants growing all over the yard. I finally had the nature preserve I had always wanted. I bought some books on edible wild plants and started foraging.

But the honeymoon didn't last. I now believe that if we had never mowed our yard, we would no longer be able to live in our house. The forest started trying to close the gap right away. That first summer, hundreds of tiny saplings appeared. Then the brambles started up. A few years later, most of the quarter-acre had turned into a thicket of thorny vines. I mowed a tiny postage-stamp space in front of the house so our son could have a place to play, but outside that space, we walked on narrow paths between banks of thorns.

Then one spring morning, about five years after we moved in, I hit my limit. Like an avenging angel, I rampaged through the yard, clipping the young trees and brambles, mowing the grass, clearing the land.

You should have seen our dogs. They ran and ran like they had just been let out of a cage. I hadn't realized how dangerous the eye-level thorns and woody saplings were to them—or to my son, who ran right after them. The truth is, *we wanted to live there too*. We had to find a way to *share* the land with nature—no, with the *rest* of nature.

After nearly twenty years, I think I have found a pretty good balance. In the spring, I walk around with a clipper and snip off most of the young saplings. But I identify each one before I decide whether to cut it. If there are lots of trees of that species in the forest, I snip away. If there are few like it, or if it's a fruit tree, I let it grow. And I let the brambles grow—in patches, not all over. I mow a few times a year, but in patches, leaving about half of the clearing for wildflowers and tall native grasses. And I give the brambles some competition by reseeding the area with clover, native grasses, and wildflower mixes.

Switching from a lawn mower to a string trimmer has helped me to mow more mindfully. The lawn mower was such a hassle to get started that I would always mow more than I intended and regret half of it later on. Once you have a weapon of mass destruction in your hands, it's tempting to forget your plans to selectively encourage and discourage particular species and just mow down everything in sight. (I mean, it's in the *name* of the thing.) A string trimmer is easy to pick up and put down; I can direct it at this or that plant and leave its neighbor alone; and it doesn't tempt me into overkill. It helps me destroy as much as I have to and preserve as much as I can.

And the yard is doing well. When we first moved in, we never saw fireflies near the house; now they are everywhere. I love to sit and watch the butterflies, moths, bees, birds, and bats. It's a thriving place. But if we want to keep living here, I have to keep asking the forest to accommodate us. Last year, hundreds of new ferns came up where the brambles used to be. I have no idea why that happened, but I like ferns, so I left them alone. If those brambles come back in the wrong place, though, they will have me to reckon with.

Even so, I keep making mistakes. A few years ago, when I was out walking one day, I saw some beautiful little green flowers growing beside the road. I thought they might help to stabilize a sandy area where nothing seemed to grow, so I scooped some up and transplanted them. The experiment was a rousing success. In two years my three or four transplants expanded to a thriving stand of thirty or forty plants.

So one day I thought, why not look up my new friends and see if they would be good candidates for gathering to eat? Well. Not only were they poisonous, but I had unwittingly abetted a nasty invader, *Euphorbia virgata*, leafy spurge, which outcompetes and displaces a variety of native plants. The internet says it "can be hard to eradicate." Oops. No wonder my experiment worked so well.[29]

The next day I rampaged through the leafy spurge (there were not thirty or forty plants; there were hundreds) and scattered some native seeds in the area. I will probably have to do this several times before I fix the problem.

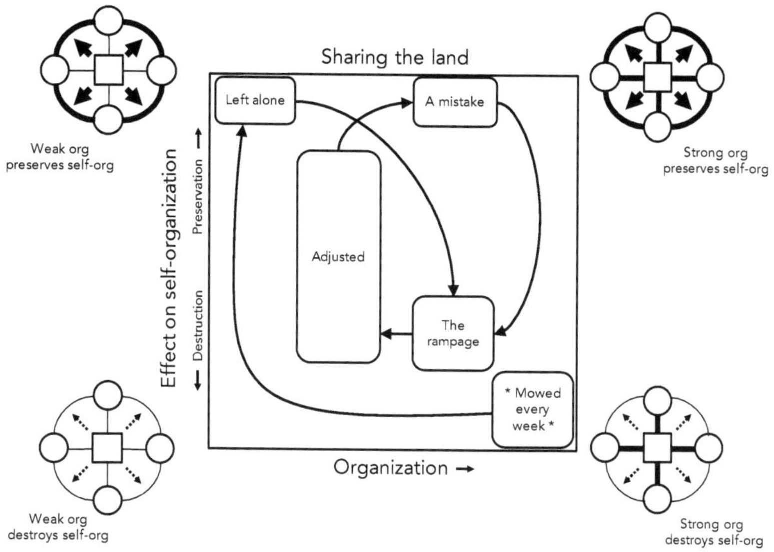


## What lies beneath

As I was writing this little story about my yard, I kept feeling like something was lurking just under the surface of the story. Then I realized what it was. When I talked about the upper-left hand corner of the inundation space (on page 84), I mentioned that industrial disasters often happen when people mistake self-organized patterns for organized plans.

In my reading about self-organization over the past few decades, I've noticed something strange about the way people describe situations in which organization and self-organization flow together. They seem to describe *just the organized parts* of the situations. You know how people say on the internet, "pics or it didn't happen"?[30] Sometimes it seems like people say *organization or it didn't happen*. And that's a problem. We can't preserve what we can't see, and we seem to have a blind spot when it comes to self-organization.

My accident with the leafy spurge was small and easily fixed. Massive, devastating disasters have grown out of the same mistakes as I made: thinking I knew what I was doing, not bothering to check, not noticing how quickly things were getting out of hand. The industrial disasters at Bhopal and Chernobyl and Wittenoom differed only in scale and impact.

Organizers do best, I think, when we *look* at what is going on in the self-organized patterns around us and *limit* the scope of our organized plans. This does not mean we should never attempt to organize self-organization. It means we should do it carefully, at small scales, with many safeguards, and with the humility to admit we might be wrong. Because we can never trust our sense of control when it comes to regulating self-organization.

# 8 The Mix

*Thinking about how organization and self-organization interact*

In the previous two chapters, we considered how self-organization inundates organized plans and how organizers regulate self-organized patterns. Now we will consider how both forces push on each other at the same time.

Our thinking space combines the axes of influence from the two previous chapters to define a space of *mutual* influence.

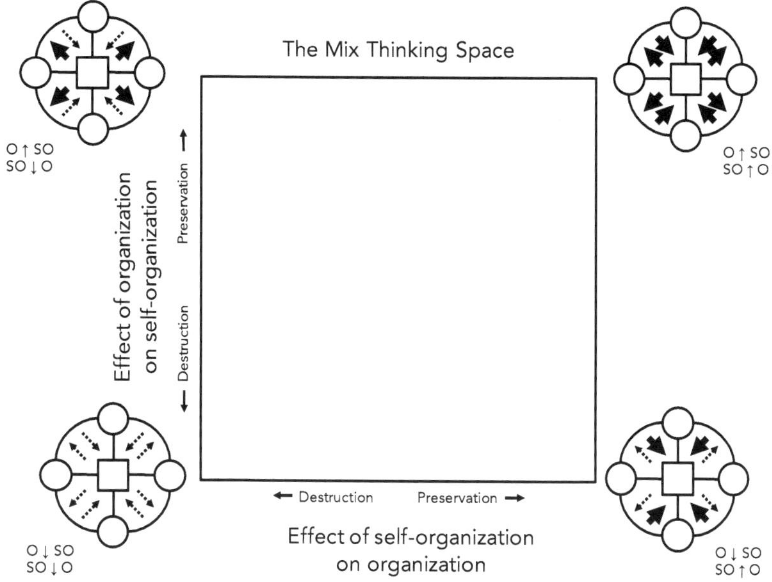


Toward the left side of the space, self-organization *tears apart* organized structures and plans. On the right, self-organization *preserves* existing structures and supports the creation of new ones. Near the top of the space, organization *preserves* self-organized patterns. Near the bottom, organization *destroys* self-organized patterns. Exactly in the middle, neither force has any impact on the other—or the forces of preservation and destruction are perfectly balanced.

For a quick orientation to the space, consider a situation you read about two chapters back: vines on a wall. When a wall is well maintained, the wall and its vines help each other, so the situation belongs in the upper-right corner of this space. When the wall is not well maintained, vines and wall damage each other, and the situation moves to the lower left.

## The world in a story

Once upon a time, when I was a child, in an annual ritual only a true nerd could appreciate, I would go to my school library, find Hans Christian Andersen's *Fairy Tales for Children*, bring it home, settle in to my favorite spot near the fireplace, and reverently reread every story. One of the first things I bought with my own money was my own copy of the book. I can see it on my shelf now, along with about sixty similar collections. I love to wander through them mapping patterns in stories told yesterday and a thousand years ago in every part of the world.[1]

For the past few decades I have had a growing suspicion that folk tales and self-organization have something to do with each other. When I drew this chapter's thinking space for the first time and folk tales came tumbling out of it, I knew it was time to explore the idea. It would take a year to go over every book in my collection again, so with great regret, I picked out just six of my favorite books, one per region, and read them again, this time looking explicitly for connections to self-organization.[2] I found enough to convince me—and hopefully, you—that one of the reasons we tell folk tales is to learn how to live in a world where organization and self-organization intermingle and interact.

I mentioned folk tales in the chapter on organization ("The Plan"), and I will mention them again when we consider weak connections (in "Connecting the Dots"). But those are small subsets. Most folk tales live and die in the mix.

Before we start, a quick note about folk tale sources. Stories told by old folks in their kitchens and gardens are messy, rambling, and often downright weird. But because they are closer to their original purposes—passing down lessons about human life—they are more useful to our exploration in this chapter than any prettied-up, entertainment-focused, literary versions of the same stories. For that reason, all of the story collections I reread for this chapter were of stories collected from real people. None were from literary sources.

### Always further into the forest

Let's begin with a story that introduces just a *touch* of self-organization. Here is a fragment of the story of Red Riding Hood (Rothkäppchen), as it was told by Jeannette Hassenpflug to Jacob and Wilhelm Grimm in 1812.

> The wolf considered to himself, that is a good fat bite for me, how do you start it, that you get it, "listen Rothkäppchen, said he, have you not seen the pretty flowers, that stand in the forest, why do you not look around . . . you go onwards yourself as when you go in the village to school, it is so cheerful out in the forest."
>
> Rothkäppchen opened her eyes, and saw how the sun broke through the trees and everything was standing full of beautiful flowers. . . . And when she broke one, she thought, there another more beautiful one stood and ran after and always further into

> the forest. But the wolf went straight away to the grandmother's house. . . .[3]

The wolf persuaded Rothkäppchen to leave the path she would take if she were going to school—that is, the path of organized planning. He led her instead into the pathless, meandering, always-further world of self-organization. Meanwhile, he himself took the path of organization—"straight away" to her grandmother's house. As you probably know, the wolf ate both Rothkäppchen and her grandmother, but a kindly hunter cut them both out of the wolf's stomach and replaced them with stones.

Apparently, after Jeannette Hassenpflug finished telling this story, Marie Hassenpflug added a story of her own. Later, she said, another wolf tried the same trick. (It seems to me that she was referring to the same Rothkäppchen, only *after* she had been tricked, eaten, and saved.)

> But Rothkäppchen heeded herself and went straight on her way, and told her grandmother that she had seen the wolf, that he wished her good day to her but looked so bad out of his eyes.

Notice how both quotes mention eyes. The first wolf gets Rothkäppchen to "open her eyes" in a direction conveniently opposite his organized plan. In the second quote, Rothkäppchen opens her eyes herself—in the direction of the wolf. It is by her organized action that she discerns his intent and seizes control of the situation. The story's use of self-organization as a means of deception puts it just over the line into the place where organization and self-organization influence each other.

## The mix thinking space

Now let's walk around in the space looking at how folk tales represent situations in various locations. As often happens in folk tales, the situations will come in pairs: two kinds of luck, two kinds of power, two kinds of folly, and two kinds of wisdom.

### Two kinds of luck

On the horizon line that stretches across the space halfway down, organization has no effect on self-organization. Locations on the left and right sides of the line describe *conditions* in which organizers find themselves, not actions they take. On the right, helpful self-organization brings good harvests, good health, good weather, and cooperative communities. On the left, harmful self-organization brings pests, diseases, dangerous weather, and social conflict.

The fantastic world of folk tales kicks up these conditions to magical proportions. On the helpful side, cooking pots never empty, tablecloths fill themselves with feasts, and every fruit you pick from the tree of golden apples is replaced with two. On the harmful side, each giant is bigger than the last, and every time you cut off one of the monster's heads, two grow to replace it.

These magical sources of abundance and destruction run themselves. They require no effort on the part of any organizer. That's why they belong on the horizon line: the organizer has done nothing to create or destroy them.

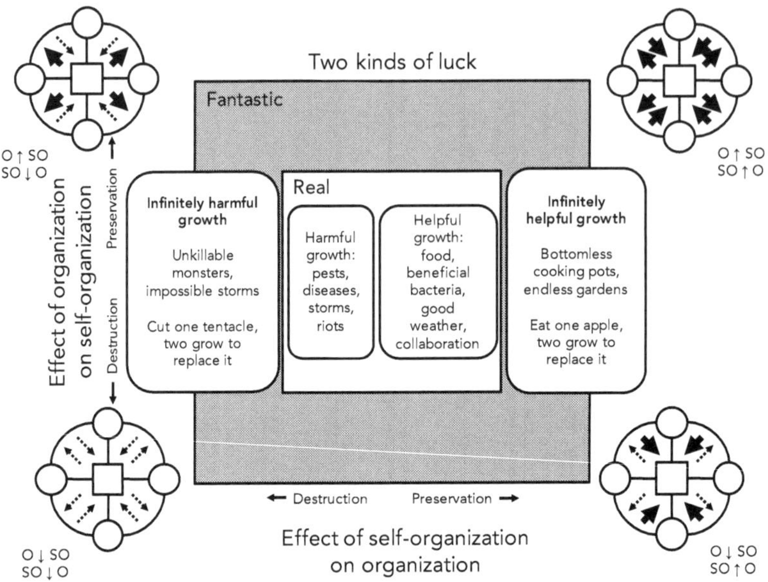


### *A whole new world*

A folk tale from Liberia tells how there was once a village of people who believed they were the only people in the whole world.[4] One day, a hunter went out into the forest and lost his way. He "did everything that he knew to do to try to return home, but he could not find the way back." After days of wandering, he found a flowing creek. He decided to follow it. On the eighth day he walked into a strange village full of strange people. They were kind to him. When he told them how he had become lost, they helped him find his village. From that day forward, the people no longer believed they were alone in the world. The hunter's journey helped them discover "the world beyond."

That doesn't even sound like a folk tale, does it? Some guy goes out hunting and wanders over to the next town? But think about it for a minute. What if *we* found people just like us living—somehow—deep under the ocean? Wouldn't that be amazing? I wanted to include this example to show that what *counts* as magic depends on context, and context depends on knowledge.

The self-organized help or harm that appears in folk tales is often given to organizers as a gift or punishment from a supernatural being or an experienced elder. But sometimes, like the strange village the hunter found, it appears for no apparent reason—that is, for no reason anyone understands. In the real world as well, self-organized patterns often appear for no apparent reason. That's what makes them so fascinating. They seem to come from nowhere, like magic. But not all magic is good.

## The horror of self-organization

Many popular books and articles have recently been written about self-organization. Most have placed nearly all of their emphasis on its positive aspects. They have told us that crowds are full of wisdom, that we can get "order for free," and that a butterfly can flap its wings and save the world.[5] But in each case the opposite is also true. The story we have been told is dangerously incomplete, and it's *definitely* not the story our folk tales have been telling us for thousands of years. What *they* tell us, quite correctly, is that self-organization can turn from sun to storm in the blink of an eye.

Social insects, for example, are often held up as examples of the wonders of self-organization. Colonies of ants, bees, and termites build intricate structures, almost like miniature cities, as if by magic. This is true. Ant hills and termite mounds *are* fascinating places. That doesn't mean they always work perfectly.

Consider the phenomenon of the circular ant mill. Army ants of the genus *Eciton* find food by following pheromone trails on the forest floor. Normally this self-organized pattern helps the colony find and exploit new food sources. But when a pheromone trail folds back on itself, army ants can become trapped in endless circles.

William Morton Wheeler described the phenomenon in 1910. He had confined some army ants in a jar, and when he removed the lid, a single-file column of ants marched over the rim of the jar and down to the table:

> . . . where it turned to the left at a right angle and proceeded completely around the base [of the jar] till it met the column at the turning point. To my surprise it kept right on over the same circumference. . . . They continued going round and round the circular base of the jar, following one another like so many sheep, without the slightest inkling that they were perpetually traversing the same path. . . . They kept up this gyration for forty-six hours before the column broke. . . .[6]

This is the horror of self-organization: that it can turn against itself and destroy what it has created. Similar ant mills have been observed by many naturalists since, and not just around artificial obstacles. In 1921, William Beebe described a huge ant mill that wound its way round and round a sinuous path, over logs and under bushes, 366 meters in circumference. The terms he used to describe the sight were almost magical in their intensity.

> All the afternoon the insane circle revolved; at midnight the hosts were still moving, the second morning many had weakened and dropped their burdens [of food], and the general pace had very appreciably slackened. But still the blind grip of instinct held them. . . . Through sun and cloud, day and night, hour after hour there

> was found no Eciton with individual initiative enough to turn aside an ant's breadth from the circle which he had traversed perhaps fifteen times: the masters of the jungle had become their own mental prey.[7]

From this perspective, self-organization sounds more like a curse than a blessing: and so it is, sometimes. Folk tales scare us with self-organized horror to remind us that though we can derive many benefits from self-organized patterns, we also have much to fear from them.

The most frightening folk tale I ever read in my life appears in those published by the Grimm brothers in 1812. It begins like this:

> Oncetime a house father had butchered a pig, that his children saw; as they now in the afternoon wanted to play with each other, the one child said to the other: you should be the piglet and I will be the butcher. . . .[8]

You don't need to read any more of that story, do you? That's the most frightening thing about it: that you can guess what is coming next. Anyone who has raised children knows that such a thing could happen in reality. In one version of the story, the mother of the children was bathing the baby when she heard the screams of the butchered "pig." She came running, pulled out the knife, and "in anger" stabbed the other child dead. The baby drowned, the bereaved mother killed herself, and the father died of grief.

This trail of runaway devastation is as shocking as any horror-movie plot. Its characters are trapped in a state of self-organization, unable to plan, think, or do anything but compulsively react—like those hapless ants compelled to walk in endless circles. We think of ourselves as masters of our world, but with a simple miscommunication we can also be reduced to our own mental prey.

There are plenty of contemporary folk tales in which similarly gruesome tragedies unfold. In one story, a babysitter who is drunk, high, insane, or some combination mistakes the baby for a turkey, cooks it, and serves it to its own parents.[9] Often there is a similar cascade of people killing each other and themselves after the crime is discovered. This is the same local-knowledge nightmare as the butcher tale and the ant mill.

### Both kinds of luck at once

Thankfully, the scary part of self-organization, just like the happy part, is only half of the story—and we have folk tales about that, too. The most famous is the Zen parable of the lucky man.[10] One day, a farmer's horse ran away. His neighbors consoled him for his bad luck. The farmer said, "Maybe it's bad luck, maybe it's good luck. Who knows?"

The next day, the farmer's horse returned, bringing with it two wild horses the farmer could tame. The neighbors celebrated the farmer's good luck. The farmer said, "Maybe. Who knows?" Then the farmer's son broke his leg while taming one of the new horses. Soon after, the king's men came looking for conscripts, and the son could not go off to war. After each event, the farmer wisely said the same thing: "Who knows?"

Here's a more recent story with the same message. Somebody drove their brand new, expensive car to a sports game.[11] While they were at the game, an earthquake struck. The car's owner walked out of the stadium to find their car missing. Later, the police called to say that the car had been found—crushed under a bridge with the thief still in it. So was it good luck or bad luck that the car was stolen?

## Two kinds of power

Halfway across the space, in a line going from top to bottom, self-organization does not help or harm organization. Situations on *this* line are defined by the actions of organizers. At the top, they stimulate and sustain self-organized patterns. At the bottom, they work to eradicate them.

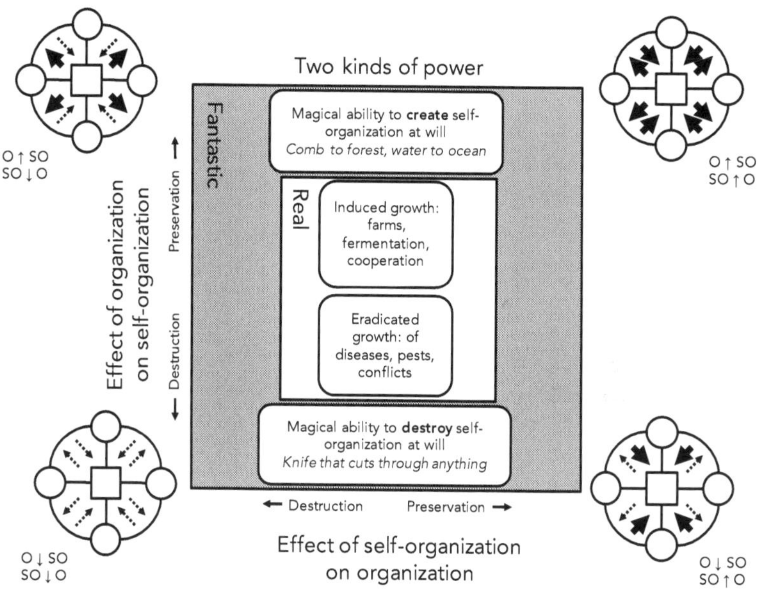


These folk tales tend to involve *super-organizers*, people who can create and destroy self-organized patterns at will and with complete control. They might be supernatural beings or wise people, or they might be ordinary people who have been given magical objects imbued with super-organizer powers.

### *Shooting up into the sky in no time at all*

One American Indian story begins by introducing a young woman who was exceptionally skilled at working porcupine quills into intricate designs.[12] Though she was an only child and had no suitor, she felt an inexplicable urge to sew a man's buckskin outfit. When she finished, she kept working until she had created seven sets of clothing, all beautifully embroidered. Then she went on a journey to find the seven brothers who would become her new family. Without knowing how or why, she traveled directly to their home. "I know about them," she told her mother, "but I don't know why." The brothers welcomed her into their tipi, especially the youngest, who said he knew she was on her way.

Soon afterwards, a buffalo calf came to the tipi and demanded that the brothers give up their new sister to the buffalo nation. They refused. The next day a heifer came and made the same demand. After the heifer came a cow, then a bull—"the most gigantic buffalo bull in the world." The bull began to chase them, and the entire buffalo nation thundered behind.

The brothers and sister climbed up into a tree. The youngest brother shot one of his "special medicine" arrows into its trunk. "At once the tree started to grow, shooting up into the sky in no time at all." This happened four more times, until the tree grew so high that the siblings could step out onto the clouds—just in time, because the giant bull had been ramming the tree, which toppled to the ground. The family stayed in the sky and became the big dipper. The girl is its brightest star, and the youngest brother is the star at the end of the handle.

In this story there are two super-organizers, five objects of power, and the application of that power to support helpful self-organization (the rapidly-growing tree). The bigger-and-bigger buffaloes represent harmful self-organization. (The story makes it clear that even when the buffaloes speak individually, they speak for the entire herd.)

### *The magic of multiplication*

This story illustrates a common motif: a magical object that causes self-organized patterns to grow rapidly. It can work in any of three ways. First, it can cause another object to *grow*, as in this case. The plot in which good people escape in a rapidly growing tree (or some other plant) turns up in many stories.

Secondly, a magical object can cause a small group of objects to *multiply*. Many folk-tale characters have been saved from attack or starvation by huge flocks of birds or shoals of fish that magically increased in number.

Thirdly, a magical object can *transform itself* into something much larger, something metaphorically linked to its shape. A sewing needle turns into a thicket. A comb or brush becomes a forest. A jar of water dumped out on the ground becomes an ocean. A line scratched on the ground with a magic stick becomes an unbridgeable chasm.

Most importantly, the thing that springs up is *never* an organized thing. It's never a city or a building or a wall. It's *always* a self-organized pattern.

Also notice that neither the girl nor her youngest brother know *why* they have the powers they have. Their gifts were not given to them by supernatural beings. These two people just are the way they are.

### *Invisible people with invisible skills*

What is it that makes one person better than another at working with self-organization? Why are some people better at handling gardens, children, crowds, fires, or marketplaces? Why do some people gravitate to self-organization while others keep their distance from it? Nobody knows. The power to understand

and work with self-organization is not something you can see from the outside. It's an invisible skill that can only be discovered through experience.

I think this is why there are so many folk tales about *strange* people who have special talents at working with self-organization. A child is born stunted, inches tall, but they can talk to animals or raise mountains into the sky. Another is born slow and unable to keep up, but they can grow huge plants or summon vast flocks of birds. In folk tales it's always the people with the least *obvious* power who have the most *hidden* power. It's always the person to whom nothing is given and from whom nothing is expected who does what is required. It's the dullard, the cripple, the beggar, the outcast, the very person nobody thinks will ever amount to anything, who saves the day.

## The power to destroy

At the bottom center of the space lies the power to destroy self-organized patterns. This power is both greater and more dangerous than the power at the top. We ourselves are self-organized patterns, so the price of this form of magic is the risk of blowback.

A Scottish folk song tells the story of a girl who became friends with a magical elf who lived under a hill.[13] The girl's mother and three brothers treated her badly. They made her work long hours cutting peat for fuel with a blunt knife. When she met the elf, her life improved. Every day she would walk by his hill, and he would lend her his magical knife, which could cut through anything. Now the girl got through her work quickly and came home happy. On her way home, she would stop at the hill and knock twice, and the elf would reach out so she could return his knife.

After some time, the girl's mother realized that someone must be helping her do her work so quickly. So she set the girl's brothers to watch her. They soon saw what was happening. The next day, they followed the girl, attacked her, and took the knife. Then they went to the elf's hill, knocked twice, and "as the good elf stretched out his hand, they cut it off with his self's own knife." The elf, believing his dear friend had betrayed him, drew back his wounded arm, sunk down under the ground, and disappeared forever.

What I find most interesting about this story is that it seems to be a cautionary tale for *elves*, not girls. The elf is the only character who makes any choices in the story. The girl accepts his help because she needs it and he offers it. The mother and the brothers make no decisions either. They act as would be expected given their initial characterizations. The lesson of the story seems to be: if you have destructive power, don't let it be turned against you.

Like the elf in the story, we have the power to destroy self-organization, and that power can be turned against us. Unlike the elf, we are our own adversaries. You have only to look back at the previous chapters of this book to see how some of the weapons we have used to destroy self-organized patterns in our bodies, cities, and farms have backfired. And unlike the elf, we have no magical world to which we can retreat.

## Both kinds of power at once

Is there an equivalent to the Zen tale of good and bad luck along this vertical line? Of course there is. The ability to *combine* the powers of creation and destruction is the most unbeatable power of all.

My favorite story of this type is a European tale about a man who acquires a series of magical objects.[14] First he finds a tablecloth that fills itself with food. It just happens to be sitting under a tree in an endless forest. The man has a wonderful meal, picks up his new tablecloth, and walks on.

Soon he comes across a collier who is burning wood for charcoal and eating potatoes without fat. The collier offers to share his meager meal, which is friendly, so our hero opens his tablecloth and shares his abundant meal instead. Impressed, the collier offers to trade his magical knapsack for the tablecloth. When you knock on this knapsack, "a corporal comes out with six man soldiers with over and under rifles." Our hero agrees, and the trade is made. He walks off a little way, knocks on the knapsack, and sends the corporal and his six man soldiers back to get the tablecloth.

There's a lot more of that sort of thing, but you get the point, I think. If the answer to the question "Good luck or bad luck?" is "Maybe," the answer to "Creation or destruction?" is "Yes please."

## Two kinds of folly

The four corners of the space break most easily into two diagonal pairs of approaches to managing self-organization: a wise pair and a foolish pair. Let's look first at two kinds of folly.

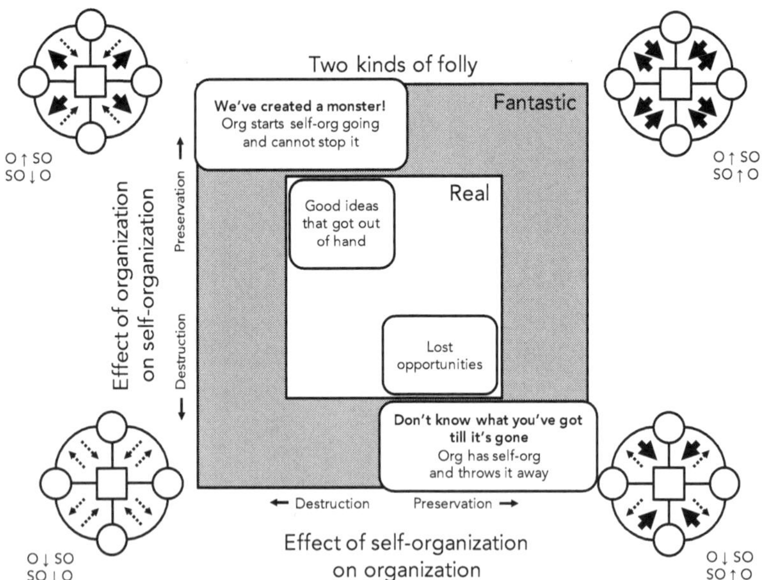

## We've created a monster

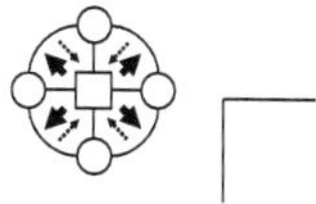

In the upper-left corner of the space, organization preserves self-organization that is destroying it. That seems like a bad idea, right? Throwing fuel on a burning house? How do people end up in predicaments like that? Because fire *warms* a house, and it can be hard to guess what a fire—or any self-organized pattern—is going to do next.

Remember those magical objects that create self-organized patterns, like the comb that turns into a forest? In most stories where they appear, they are used against adversaries. You throw the comb down *behind* you as you run away, and it stops your pursuers from following you. When you want to use self-organization for your own benefit—that is, *without* running away—you have to be more careful.

### *Yes, I can do that*

The story of the sorcerer's apprentice was first written down by Lucian of Samosata (in present-day Turkey) in the first century CE. It was probably passed down orally for centuries before that. In the story, a man named Eucrates met a man named Pancrates on a sailboat journey up the Nile.[15]

Notice the two names. Eucrates means "true rule" and Pancrates means "rule of all." Thus the story contrasts authority over organized plans (note the emphasis on authenticity) with authority over *everything*—that is, over organized plans *and* self-organized patterns. In other words, Eucrates is an organizer, but Pancrates is a super-organizer.

Eucrates saw right away that Pancrates was "no common man," so he asked if he could join him in his travels. Pancrates accepted his companionship. Whenever the two would come to an inn, Pancrates would utter an incantation that would enchant a broom or pestle to act as a servant. "It would go off and draw water, buy and cook provisions, and make itself generally useful." When they were ready to leave the place, Pancrates would utter a second incantation, and the broom or pestle would return to its previous state.

Eucrates, curious, hid where he could overhear the starting incantation. Then, when Pancrates went away to the market, Eucrates ordered a pestle to become a water-carrier. Right away it brought him a pitcher of water. He asked it to stop, but because he did not say the correct incantation, it did not stop. "It went on drawing water the whole time, until at last the house was full of it." In desperation, Eucrates cut the pestle in two, whereupon both halves began to fetch water. Finally Pancrates returned, uttered the necessary incantation, and "withdrew himself" from Eucrates, apparently in disgust.

At the end of the story, a listener asks Eucrates if he can still make a pestle come to life. "Yes, I can do *that*," he says, "but that is only half the process: I cannot turn it back again into its original form; if once it became a water-carrier, its activity would swamp the house."

***Every kind of knowledge?***

Another story in this corner is an Indian tale of four Brahmans who "had amassed every kind of knowledge."[16] Walking in the forest, they came across the bone of a tiger. The first Brahman said, "I can make a whole skeleton out of this bone," and he did. The second said, "I can put flesh and blood on those bones," and he did. The third said, "I can do better than that! I can bring those bones and flesh to life." The fourth Brahman, "who was not half as learned as the others," said, "Wait, don't give it life." The others scoffed at this, so the fourth Brahman climbed a tree and waited. The third Brahman worked his magic. "As soon as it came to life, it was hungry"—and I think you can guess what happened next.

Even though the story says the four Brahmans "had amassed every kind of knowledge," three of the four lacked an understanding of self-organization. A hungry predator is an organizer with a goal, but *hunger itself* is a self-organized phenomenon. Even in cellular assemblages that have no organs or brains (such as slime molds), a state of collective hunger is an emergent pattern that drives movement. So even though the Brahmans might not have feared the tiger they brought to life, they should have feared its hunger.

This story also highlights the fact that knowledge about self-organization never gets the respect it deserves. The fourth Brahman was the wisest, but he was "not half as learned as the others." This is clearly meant ironically. The overall message is that because the ability to deal with self-organization is an invisible skill, it is both easy and foolish to disdain it.

***Self-organization gets its revenge***

I haven't told a contemporary tale in a while, so lest you think this type of story is no longer with us, here is a recent example. A sadistic person rigs an animal with explosives for fun.[17] Once the fuse is lit, the animal runs directly to where it can do the most damage, either to the person's property or to the person themselves. This is one of many contemporary "careful what you wish for" stories, most of which involve self-organization in the form of fire, animals, diseases, or self-organized aspects of human society (fads, mobs, gangs).

**Comedy and regret**

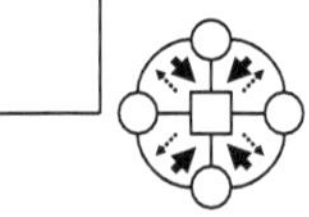

Now let's journey down to the bottom right corner, where organization destroys helpful self-organization. This is the story of killing the goose that laid the golden eggs. It's the story of the fisherman's wife, who kept sending her husband back to demand bigger and bigger wishes from the magical fish until they lost everything. It's the fool who looked a gift horse in the mouth.

While the stories in the upper left are usually tragic, stories in the lower right often paint their protagonists as comic fools. In an American Indian story, for example, the trickster Coyote decides to save time by cooking his corn *before* he plants it, "so I won't have to bother to cook it when it's ripe."[18]

There is one type of story in this corner that is not so funny. These are the stories of turning back. There are many folk tales in which a person is granted entry to a magical world, a place where their dreams can come true. In that world they have a chance to be happy, escape a problem, or save a loved one. They are always told not to look back as they enter the place, and they *always* look back. And the other world always disappears, or they are whisked away from it. So this corner is not a scary place, but it can be a place of regret.

### Both kinds of folly

Just as there are folk tales with both kinds of luck and both kinds of power, there are folk tales with both kinds of folly. Here's a European tale that fits.

There was once a king who was so wasteful that he ran through all of his money until he, his wife, and his three daughters had nothing to eat but potatoes.[19] The king went into the forest to look for food. He found nothing and got himself lost besides, so he sat down under a tree.

Just then a huge bear came storming up. He declared that the king was sitting under *his* honey tree and therefore deserved to be eaten. However, if the king would agree to give the bear his eldest daughter, the bear would spare the king's life. Plus, he'd throw in some gold to sweeten the deal. The king, cornered, said, "You shall have her, leave me only in peace." Satisfied, the bear showed him the way home, saying, "In seven days I come and get my bride."

Back at the castle, the king had his servants lock every door and window. But the bear didn't come back as a bear. He came back as a handsome prince with a magnificent carriage. The king's eldest daughter opened the door, was charmed, and went off with the prince, who turned back into a bear the next day—and as it turned out, six days out of every seven. The king was heartbroken that he had after all given his daughter to a bear. But then again, the bear did give him the promised gold. He burned through that, then went back to the forest, and—suffice it to say that all three daughters were married off to beasts.

Then, lo and behold, the queen gave birth to a son named Reinald. Everyone considered him a "wonder-child" because his birth was unexpected. (It seems to be implied that the queen was too old to bear a child. This is important, because it means Reinald fits into the category of strange, unlikely people, who always understand self-organization better than most. Also, "Reinald" means "ruler's advisor," implying that the boy was born to correct his father's errors.)

Unlike his father, Reinald was patient, selfless, and brave. When he turned sixteen, he set off to visit his sisters in their dens and nests. He soon found out that their animal husbands were actually brothers under a spell. The beautiful sister of the three brothers was trapped by the same spell in an enchanted sleep. Reinald woke the sister, broke the spell, and reunited the family.

Why did the king believe that a threat from a talking bear could be so easily dismissed? Conversely, why did he not realize that having a bear for a son-in-law might represent an opportunity? And why did he not visit his daughters? Because he was focused only on his own organized plans.[20]

#### *Folk tales, magic, and self-organization*

Is this story about self-organization? It's hard to say. Are the animal husbands super-organizers? I don't think so. They don't make any self-organized patterns appear or disappear. They are organizers, in the sense that they are human beings. But they aren't central to the story. You could replace them with other enchantments and the story would work just as well. Reinald's sisters could be covered in boils, trapped in caves, or shrunk to the size of mice.

At the heart of the story is the spell that changed the brothers into beasts. Reinald breaks the spell by shattering a "black board" (in some versions a slate) into a million pieces. The spell was cast long ago by a magician who was spurned by the sleeping sister. He was a super-organizer, because he had the power to control many things. Does the black board represent a self-organized pattern, one that is hidden, powerful, and hard to destroy? Maybe.

Sometimes the magic in folk tales clearly points to self-organization, as when swarms or herds magically coalesce. But sometimes there is no such connection. I think it's safest to say that folk-tale magic represents the entire *universe* of mysterious, surprising, and hard-to-predict phenomena, and that self-organization is one element in that universe.

### *Once is never*

So many folk tale characters ignore magical threats and opportunities that it has to be a message about the folly of ignoring *any* hard-to-predict phenomenon, including self-organization. In one story, for example, a mother gave birth to four little monsters. When she was confronted by her family, she pushed away their concerns, saying, "These children will turn out all right, by and by."[21] They didn't. They ate people. Lots of people.

In another story, a man was warned to stay away from a particularly rowdy tavern. "But once, upon a Sunday, he hears, how merrily it was in there, thought, once is never, went in, danced, and was happy."[22] And paid a price.

Once *can* be never in the world of organized plans. You can make a mistake on a blueprint, scratch it out, and start again. Plans are under your control. That's what makes them plans. But when it comes to self-organized patterns, once can never be never, because once can set a ball rolling that can't be stopped. Anyone who has ever tended a fire in a fireplace knows that. It only takes one ember on a woolen rug to start a house fire—if you aren't paying attention.

## Two kinds of wisdom

Now it's time to think about people who do self-organization right. They know how to work with it, how to work against it, and when to do both things.

### Winning with self-organization

The upper-right corner of the mix is a win-win situation. You know how to work the world, the world works for you, and you help the world work better.

In the world of folk tales, there are four ways to get to this corner: through innate talent; through long experience; by getting help from a magical being (who has innate talent); or by getting help from a wise person (who learned through long experience). In other words, it comes down to talent and time.[23]

***Deep in the mountains, high in the clouds***

One of the most common sources of help is from super-organizers who live in special places. Protagonists journey to unreachable locations where impossible secrets are commonplace understandings. Inside mountains and caves, under lakes and rivers, and above the clouds live whole communities of people who know how to shape the world around them as well as we know how to walk and talk.

Anyone who spends time in such a place, if they are deemed worthy, comes away changed. There is always some kind of barrier, ordeal, or price for visiting one of these special places. Time, for example, often runs differently inside them. People go in for a day and come out a year later. Or they are there for years, but when they return only a day has passed. They may come back crippled or burned or blind, or they may return only partly human, perhaps with wings or scales. But they always return with secrets they could not have accessed in any other way. Those secrets often have something to do with self-organization.

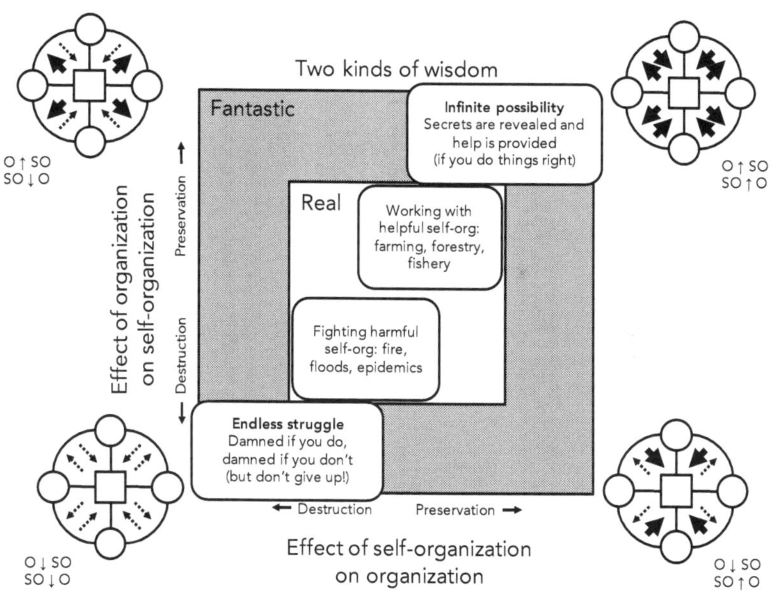


One American Indian story tells how, in an ancient time of drought, when "the earth itself was starving," a medicine man chose a woman to help him save his people from starvation.[24] The two walked for many days to a great mountain where the man believed they would find the answers they sought.

> At last they came to a vast, dark forest from whose center rose a cloud-wreathed mountain reaching far into the sky. . . . They came to a large rock at the foot of the mountain, rolled the rock aside, and discovered an entrance. They went inside the mountain

> and, closing the opening behind them, found themselves in the mountain's great medicine lodge, which was wonderful to behold.

Inside the mountain lived the Creator and his helper Great Roaring Thunder. The man and the woman lived in the mountain for four days, during which time the Creator taught them how to "perform the ceremonies in the right way." They were also given *issiwun*, a magical and sacred buffalo hat "which had the power to control the wandering animals . . . the buffalo, the antelope, the elk, the deer." They listened attentively, learned well, returned home, and performed the ceremonies without a flaw. "All was well again," and ever since then, the people have never failed to respect the secrets they were given.

***We will remember and repay***

Another source of help is from self-organization itself, as in this European tale. A curious young man, after accidentally learning the secret of animal speech, went out into the world to make his fortune.[25] As he rode along on his horse, he heard three fish caught in a pipe lamenting their demise. He stopped, picked them up, and carried them to open water. The grateful fish called out, "We will remember and repay."

Later, he heard an ant king exclaim that a horse was stepping on his ant hill. The young man led the horse away, and the ant king said, "We will remember and repay." Next he came to some young ravens who had left the nest but were too weak to feed themselves. He got off his horse, stabbed it dead, and gave it to them. (I told you some of these stories were weird.) The ravens looked up from their meal and said, "We will remember and repay."

Eventually he arrived at a great city where suitors were vying for the hand of a beautiful princess. Any man could attempt to perform the tasks she had chosen. She promised to marry the first man who succeeded. All who failed would be executed. It just so happened that the three tasks the princess chose could not be accomplished by any human being in the time provided. But they were short work for a school of fish (find a ring thrown into the ocean), a colony of ants (retrieve every grain of millet thrown into grass), and a flock of ravens (bring an apple from the tree of life, which was . . . probably somewhere high up; it doesn't say). Our hero called in his favors, accomplished the tasks, married the princess, became king, and ruled the city with great wisdom.

This story belongs to what I call the "grateful groups" genre. Each animal group belongs to a species whose self-organized patterns are obvious to human observers. Fish school, ants swarm, ravens flock. Other species that appear in similar stories are social insects (bees, wasps, termites), herd animals (buffalo, deer), other flocking birds (ducks, geese, crows), and snakes. If an animal gathers in groups that move as one, it shows up in stories of reciprocal aid.

Animals that *don't* move together in groups, such as bears and foxes, are more likely to appear in folk tales as organizers or super-organizers. Also, animals that work together in coordinated packs, like wolves, never appear in these stories, nor do domesticated animals.

### *Watch and learn*

A related genre is what I call a "watch the animals" story: a protagonist finds a solution not by communicating directly with animals but by observing and copying their behavior. There are folk tales about people learning to farm by watching boars root in the soil[26] and by watching deer scratch the ground with their antlers.[27] Another story tells how a young man made the first wooden flute after watching a woodpecker tap holes in a hollow branch.[28]

In some watch-the-animals stories, protagonists learn from swarms or flocks rather than individuals. The swarms or flocks often resemble the animals of which they are made. In one American Indian story, for example:

> Suddenly there came an awesome noise . . . like the beating of a thousand giant wings. . . . Out of the clouds, circling lower and lower, flew the great mystery bird of the heavens, a hundred times as big as the largest eagles. . . .[29]

If you have stood and watched a flock of birds twisting and shifting in the sky, you know that it *can* look like a giant bird. The same goes for columns of ants that look like the legs of giant insects and masses of fish that move like one giant fish. People today speak of self-similarity (self-organized patterns that look the same at different scales) as though we had only just discovered it. But we have been telling stories about self-similar patterns for millennia.

## Thwarting self-organization

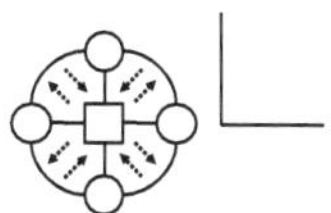

Now let's swing down to the lower-left corner, where organization and self-organization destroy each other. If the upper-right corner was a win-win situation, this is an all-out war. Nobody goes here on purpose. It's always an accident, an attack, or a mistake. These are still stories of wisdom, though, because those who make it *back* out of this corner have much to teach us about self-organization.

### *Something for nothing*

The story I like best in this corner is an Indian tale about a rich miser.[30] He was frustrated by his workmen, who worked too little, he thought, and asked for too much in return. So he was enthralled when a holy man told him how to summon a magical demon, a *brahmarakshasa*, who would work for nothing. He must repeat a certain mantra day and night for three months. He did this, and the demon appeared and said, "What do you want from me, master?"

The miser was terrified at the sight of the monstrous demon, but he gathered his wits and ordered the demon to obey his commands. "That's why I'm here," said the demon. But he warned the miser that he must keep supplying him with work. "I can't be idle even for one second," he said. "If you fail to give me work, I'll have to kill you and eat you. That's my nature."

The miser set the demon to work on his large farm, giving him task after task to complete. He had the demon clear fields, sow crops, plant trees, and build houses. But each task was finished in a matter of hours, even tasks that would have taken a dozen workers years to carry out.

As the miser began to run out of tasks, he grew worried. He consulted his wife. "Don't lose courage," she said. "When you really run out of jobs, send him to me." Finally the man found that there was nothing left for the demon to do.

> Just then, his wife herself came that way, a long curly black hair in her hand. She had just pulled it out of her head. She said to the demon, "Look here, *brahmarakshasa*, I've a small job for you. Take this hair and make it straight, and bring it back to me."

The demon tried and tried to straighten the hair, but "no matter what he did, it was still curly." He thought that if he heated it in a fire, as metalworkers do, he could pound it straight with a hammer. The hair went up in smoke, and the demon, having failed to complete his task, ran away, never to return.

In this story it is the miser's wife who understands the secrets of self-organization. By assigning the demon "a small job" that she knows will force him to grapple with a pattern similar to his own, she turns self-organization back onto itself. It's like she nudged a line of army ants into an endless circle.

### *Personification? Or super-organizer?*

Does the demon in this story represent self-organization? Or is he a super-organizer? The two character types are similar—both are powerful—but there are a few critical differences between them.

First, a super-organizer can *command* self-organized patterns, but a personification *is* a self-organized pattern. The demon in this story does not plow the farmer's fields by directing an army of invisible workers; he plows them himself, and all at once. Personifications can often split themselves into many pieces, becoming swarms or flocks as the need arises. Super-organizers may *summon* flocks, but they never *become* them. Imagine Pancrates, the super-organizer in the story of the sorcerer's apprentice (on page 153), becoming a marching army of water-carriers. He couldn't do that.

Secondly, characters that personify self-organization are always described as infinite or immeasurable in some way. They grow to fill the sky or sea, or their hunger or thirst can never be satisfied, or they work without tiring. In this they symbolize the surprising speed and scope of self-organized patterns, which seem to rise from nothing and cover everything in an instant.

Thirdly, personifications of self-organization are always associated with some kind of numinous force, like the wind, the sea, or the mysteries of life and death. In Hindu mythology, *brahmarakshasas* are the spirits of Brahmins (priests or teachers) who suffer in death for misdeeds in life. So while the demon was once a man, he is now a mysterious force.

### Both kinds of wisdom

What about stories that cover both kinds of wisdom? Here's a good one. In an American Indian tale, a young woman loved to bathe at a certain spring.[31] But it was a sacred spring, and she should have known not to use it.

The owner of the spring, Kolowissi, the powerful and dangerous Serpent of the Sea, decided to punish her for her misdeed. He transformed himself into a tiny baby. Seeing the baby, the young woman was entranced. She took it home and played with it in her room.

> On hearing this [her] father was silent and thoughtful, for he knew that the waters of the spring were sacred. . . . "Do you suppose any real mother would leave her baby in a spring?" he said. "This is not as simple as it seems."

Soon the baby began to expand. He grew and grew until he became a massive serpent, and he coiled himself tightly around the woman. She cried out for help. Her father came running. He recognized Kolowissi and assured him that atonement would be made. The great serpent released his captive.

The elders of the tribe gathered together and performed ceremonies of honor to Kolowissi. They ruled that the young woman must atone for her misdeed by going with the serpent to his watery home.

Sadly the young woman accepted her fate and said goodbye to her family. The two set out walking, the great snake uncoiling as they went. As they walked, the serpent transformed himself again, this time into a handsome young man. The woman was staring at the ground and did not notice.

After a time, the young man asked the woman if she was tired. She did not respond. "Why don't you speak?" he said. "I am filled with fear and shame," she replied. Reassured that she was sorry for her act of disrespect, the young man told her that he had come to love her. She looked into his eyes, "quite forgot her sadness," went willingly with him, "and lived with him ever after."

That's an up-and-down story, isn't it? A vulnerable infant turns into a threatening monster and then into a loving husband. Notice how Kolowissi, like the *brahmarakshasa,* personifies self-organization. He does not transform himself into multiple beings, but it seems like he could do so if he wanted to. When he expands into a serpent, it is implied that he *could* go on expanding much further. That's why the elders of the village "performed ceremonies of honor" to him: because they knew he could destroy the entire village. And his association with the sea connects him to numinous forces.

The way the human characters behaved in this story reminds me of the story of Reinald the wonder-child (page 155). The fathers in the two stories could not be more different. Reinald's father ignored both threats and opportunities. This young woman's father paid attention to both possibilities. When he said, "This is not as simple as it seems," he meant that he could not be sure whether the situation represented a threat, an opportunity, or both. So he waited, watched, and was ready to respond. It was his balanced negotiation with Kolowissi that turned the tide of the story. This father didn't need a wonder-child to fix his mistakes; he was wiser than that.

## Crossing the mix: Good and bad learners

Now I would like to introduce one of my favorite types of folk tale plot, one I call a "good and bad learners" plot. Stories with this plot can be found in every culture, and some are thousands of years old. Of all the stories that have something to do with self-organization, these connect with it the most.

### The canonical plot

The story's protagonist is always a young, inexperienced person who is worth little in the eyes of others. They might be the youngest child in a family, or they might be orphaned, poor, disabled, or just a little strange.

The story starts when the protagonist meets a helper who (unknown to them but crystal clear to us) is a bona fide super-organizer. This helper might be a supernatural being such as a god, demon, or saint; an elf or other magical creature; a talking animal; a wise old man or woman; or another outcast like the protagonist but older and more experienced. Rarely is the helper anyone who is not old, strange, or magical in some way.

Next the protagonist helps the helper. They might stop to help an old woman carry her burden, listen to an old man everyone else is ignoring, share their meal with a lame beggar, or spare the life of a talking animal. In one way or another, the protagonist shows compassion to an apparently helpless character.

In return, the helper gives the protagonist a set of instructions. Sometimes the protagonist asks the helper for instructions with a specific goal in mind, but in many stories there is no definite goal. The protagonist follows the instructions and is rewarded beyond their wildest dreams. Sometimes the reward is a fixed quantity of riches (typically gems or gold) and sometimes it is an infinite boon, like a sack of grain that never gets empty.

Next another person—the *bad* learner—finds out about the protagonist's reward and tries to get it for themselves. This person helps the helper, but with a transparent intent that doesn't fool the helper (or us) for a second. The helper gives them the instructions anyway, treating them fairly even though they don't deserve it. The bad learner follows the instructions carelessly. As a result they receive no reward but are horribly punished, usually by a self-organized horror: boils, snakes, fire, that sort of thing.

### Variations on the basic structure

Sometimes the bad learner comes *before* the protagonist. In many European folk tales, for example, the first and second brothers or sisters meet the helper, fail the test, are given the instructions anyway, fail the instructions, and are trapped or lost or turned to stone. Then the third brother or sister arrives, passes the test, receives the instructions, follows them faithfully, is rewarded, and saves their siblings.

In other stories, the protagonist starts out as the *bad* learner. The helper gives them multiple chances to follow the instructions, and the protagonist transforms themselves into a good learner over time.

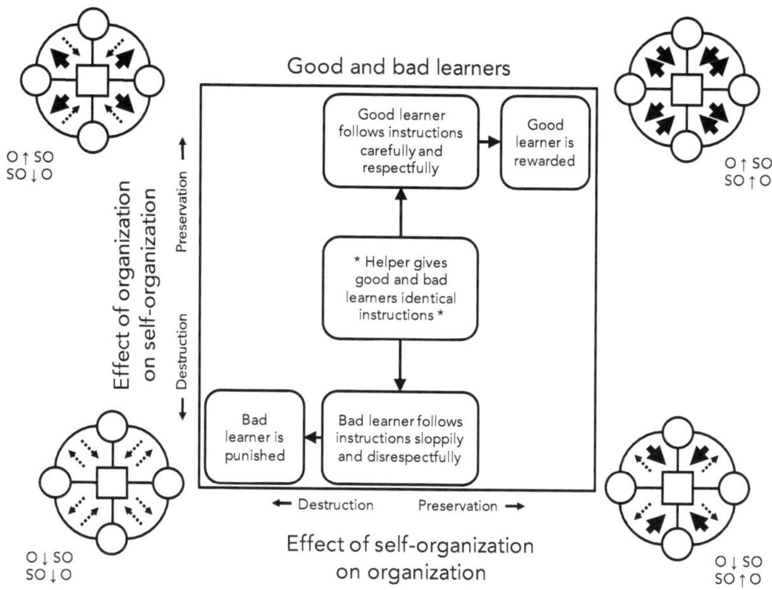


So what are these instructions? Six distinct elements tend to appear, and they fall naturally into three pairs. In the realm of *information,* you must be teachable and observant. When it comes to *action,* you must be patient and creative. When it comes to *relationships,* you must be humble and respectful.

**You must be teachable**

The instructions must be carried out exactly as given. There are to be *three* drops of magical potion given to the sleeping princess, not two and not four. Exactly five flowers must be picked, and only the ones that are sighing. The bronze door must be opened only after the wooden door has been closed. Good learners are apt pupils. They always listen carefully, and they always carry out the instructions to the letter. Bad learners half listen and miss critical details.

***The woman who turned into a tree***

In one Indian story, a young woman developed the power to turn into a flowering tree.[32] She taught her husband how to carefully pour a full pitcher of water over her, gently harvest some of her beautiful blossoms, then pour another full pitcher to change her back into a human being. All was well until the husband's pampered younger sister discovered the secret and demanded some flowers of her own. Reluctantly the young woman explained what to do. The sister-in-law half listened, poured some of the water over her, mangled her branches, scattered the second pitcher of water around at random, and ran off, leaving behind a shapeless mass with a woman's face.

Over the next several months, kind strangers took pity on "the Thing" the woman had become. They fed her, carried her, and tended her wounds. At some point her face was recognized by her husband's elder sister. This more responsible sister-in-law reunited "the Thing" with her husband, who had been wandering "like a crazy man" since she disappeared.

Her husband immediately asked what he should do. The woman had been unable to speak for months, but her speech suddenly returned, and she gave her husband new and detailed instructions. He listened carefully, followed her instructions perfectly, and restored her to full health. The younger sister-in-law was thrown into a pit of burning lime.

The woman who became a tree was the giver of instructions in this story. Her husband was the good learner, and his younger sister was the bad learner. Her inattention was not only careless but evil, and ultimately suicidal.

**You must be observant**

Learners are often given tasks that require them to watch for subtle signs. They will hear a specific bird call out, or they will see a particular flower bloom. Good learners keep their eyes open and their wits about them. They notice every detail and are ready to act when they receive their cue. Bad learners let their attention wander. Sometimes they fall asleep and miss the signal.

**You must be patient**

The instructions often include an admonition to *wait* a certain period of time before taking action. Many learners are told to wait before they open something—a box or satchel or bottle—until they have reached a particular point in their journey. Bad learners refuse to wait and are punished.

In an African story, two young women crossed a sacred river to a holy village.[33] They went to the village because they were required to cook and clean for its magical old people before they would be allowed to marry.

Fatu performed her work with patience and diligence, but Hawa was careless and lazy. When they left to return home, they were each given a quantity of gold tied up in a handkerchief. But they were "strongly advised not to untie the handkerchiefs until they had crossed back over the river." An old man from the holy village escorted them to the river. He said he would transform himself into an alligator to carry them across. Hawa, "who was very eager to know the amount of gold that she possessed," hid behind a bush and opened her handkerchief, thinking no one saw her.

The alligator carried Fatu to the other side of the river, but he first tested her faith by carrying her up and down the river a few times. Fatu waited patiently, and the alligator delivered her to the other shore. Then he returned for Hawa. Knowing that she had looked at her gold, the alligator carried Hawa back and forth for a longer time than he had carried Fatu. Finally she lost patience and yelled, "What is this old man trying to do?" Immediately the alligator and his passenger sank under the water, never to return.

**You must be creative**

Sometimes learners are asked to do something on their own: solve a riddle, pass a test, or work their way past an obstacle. The helper provides them with a hint, like "pick out the real princess," but that is all. The learner's own skills must carry them through the test. Usually the solution requires creativity, or what we today would call out-of-the-box thinking.

In an American Indian story, the trickster Coyote walked into a cave.[34] But it wasn't a cave. It was the mouth of a giant as big as a mountain. Inside he met a group of weak, starving people who explained that Coyote had now become trapped, as they were trapped long ago, in the belly of the giant.

"If we're really inside this giant," said Coyote, "then the cave walls must be the insides of his stomach. We can just cut some meat and fat from him." Why didn't the starving people think of that? Because they weren't Coyote.

Once the people were fed and feeling stronger, they began to wonder if Coyote could help them get out of the giant. They asked him what to do. Coyote said he would stab the giant in its heart, and he asked them where it was. One of the people pointed out that there was a volcano "puffing and beating over there." The person said, "Maybe it's the heart." That sentence is the crux of the story, because it shows that Coyote's lateral thinking had taken root in the formerly helpless people. He was the helper of the story, and his instructions were provided by example. The people were the bad, then good, learners.

**You must be humble**

There is always a humbling aspect to the instructions, and it has two parts. First, the learner is often asked to *lower* themselves: to do something only a servant would do, like clean the pus-filled wounds of an old man or woman, wash a filthy floor, or endure a boring conversation with an apparently worthless person. The good learner carries out these tasks with modesty and selflessness, even if they are of royal blood. (In folk tales, the youngest of royal children are often considered worthless by their families.) The bad learner considers themselves above such tasks and refuses to do them or does them badly, without care and with scorn.

Second, the learner is often told to *choose* among multiple rewards. The instructions are always to choose the *worst* prize: the wooden chest, not the silver or gold; the ugly old nag, not the beautiful prancing stallion.

The good learner always chooses the worst prize, as instructed. This is not because they are sure they will gain the best reward as a result; they are not sure of anything. But they value something else more than any of the prizes. That "something else" is the reason they are on the journey in the first place. They want to save someone or achieve something, or they want to better themselves in a general sense. They are able to look past what is immediately in front of them and see the larger picture. When the good learner gets home, the worst prize always turns into something far better than any of the prizes they were offered, including the best one.

The bad learner always picks the best prize. They may believe they are entitled to the best, but more often they act out of short-term thinking. It makes sense to get what they can while they can get it. After all, there it is, a golden chest full of gems, standing right in front of them. Why should they listen to some old nag and take a wooden chest full of stones when they can *see* and *feel* the gold? Of course, when the bad learner gets home, the best prize always turns into a pile of stones, a nest of snakes, or a pit of fire.

### *If you would only listen*

In one European folk tale, a gardener's third son was sent by his king to find a golden bird.[35] On his journey he received instructions from a talking fox. Significantly, his elder brothers fell into a trap after refusing to speak to (and shooting arrows at) the same fox. "What can an animal give me as good council?" said the eldest brother.

But the third brother did speak to the fox, and things went better for him, at least at first. The fox told him where to find the golden bird, but said that he must take it away in its ugly wooden cage, and not move it into the beautiful golden cage that happened to be hanging right next to it.

The gardener's son found the golden bird right where the fox said it would be. But he couldn't bear to carry it to his king in such an ugly cage. So he moved the bird—which woke up, screamed bloody murder, and woke up the soldiers, who threw our hero into jail.

Next the king (different king) told the gardener's son that he could save his life if he could find and bring back a golden *horse*. So off he went on a new quest. The fox reappeared and told him where he could find the golden horse. But he had to put an ugly leather saddle on the horse, not the beautiful golden saddle sitting right next to it. I think you can see where this is going.

At one point in the story, after four or five similar mistakes, the fox said to the gardener's son, "If you would only *listen*." At long last he did and was rewarded. His brothers were saved, and the fox was transformed into the queen's long-lost brother, who had been under a spell.

The hero's mistakes in choosing the golden cage and saddle were obvious. His deeper mistake was harder to see but more important to the story's lesson. He lacked the humility to take the fox's advice seriously. He thought he knew better than a fox what sort of cage or saddle was acceptable. What he didn't understand was that he was dealing with magic, and magic has its own rules.[36]

### You must be respectful

This last instruction tends to play out in one (or both) of two ways. First, the learner has to show respect for people who are not normally respected in the society to which they belong. Humility requires that the learner lower themselves; respect requires that they *raise* someone else to their own level. And this, I think, is the more challenging task.

There are many respect instructions, some realistic and some magical. Learners might be asked to kiss a frog, embrace a snake, or serve a family of gnomes. There is never an immediate or obvious reward for doing this, but it pays off in the end.

Secondly—and this is the hardest instruction of all—the helper sometimes asks the learner to do something the learner believes to be wrong. They must *disrespect* someone, or destroy something precious. In the most extreme cases, the learner is asked to kill the helper. In a surprising number of folk tales, the helper asks the learner to execute them and cut off their head, hands, and feet (and tail, if they have one). When these instructions are given, even the good learners tend to refuse for a long time. But eventually they do as they have been asked, in sorrow and in pain, out of a deep respect for the wishes of their beloved helper. Bad learners feel neither sorrow nor pain, but usually can't be bothered to exert themselves. When the good learner has done the dreaded deed, the helper is transformed into a young, healthy, beautiful human being. That's how the talking fox got his happy ending.

### An instruction manual for working with self-organization

I believe that this particular group of folk tales, taken together, constitutes a set of instructions for organizers who seek to work with self-organized patterns. If the manual had a summary, it would be something like this.

> Dealing with self-organization is never easy. It is a journey full of twists and turns. Luck plays a big part. Finding a mentor will smooth your path. If you fail, don't give up. Pick yourself up and try again. Most of all, you must be teachable, observant, patient, creative, humble, and respectful.

Let's test my theory by applying the instructions to a few real examples. Two will deal with self-organization, and one will deal with organization.

### Applying the instructions to gardening

Let's say you have a vegetable garden or a small farm, and you want to grow food to support your family. What do you need to do to make your garden work for you? What qualities must you cultivate within yourself to succeed?

#### You must be teachable

When you grow a garden, you can't ignore what it says on the seed packets and plant whatever you want whenever and wherever you want. If you plant your peas in the hottest part of the summer, you won't get many to eat. And you can't just litter your bean seeds on the surface of the soil. If you don't plant them one inch deep, they won't germinate. Gardeners who ignore good advice don't grow much food.

#### You must be observant

You can read every gardening book in the world and you still won't know what to do for *your* garden, not until you spend some quality time in it: watching, pondering, discovering. Gardens have plenty to teach those who are willing to learn. Sure, you can garden by throwing around some seeds and walking away. But gardeners who observe their gardens closely grow more food.

#### You must be patient

There are no quick fixes in gardening. If you think you have found one, it only means you have not yet realized what you have given up to get it. As Fran Sorin, author of *Digging Deep*, put it, "A garden has to go through a few cycles before it will reveal what else it requires. It needs a gardener who is willing to give it a chance to grow into itself."[37]

**You must be creative**

Gardening is creativity personified. If your garden isn't a new experiment every year, you don't have a garden. Trying new things and seeing what happens is how gardening works. To quote the essayist Paul Gruchow, "Farming the land was always new work, not repetitious but experimental, always unfolding, destined to never be completed."[38] You could even say that creativity is the reason gardening exists, because it is how we came to be able to grow food.

**You must be humble**

The world of gardening is full of talking foxes. The question is, which are the *right* ones? To whom should you listen? To authorities? Experts? Advocates? Friends? I say, listen to everyone, but let your *garden* have the last word.

I can't find it again, but in one of the books I read for the previous chapter,[39] there was a story about an advocate who was trying to convince farmers to change their methods. When they disagreed with his claims, he would say, "Okay, prove me wrong." He was confident that when they tried his ideas on their own land, they would see for themselves that his claims were sound. He lowered himself to the level of their land by inviting them to listen to it instead of him. He seems like the right kind of expert to listen to.

Building the fertility of your soil can seem pointless and even deluded when everyone around you seems to be doing fine without paying attention to it. It's like choosing a wooden chest full of stones over a golden chest full of gems. After all, there it is, a field ready for planting, standing right in front of you. Why should you listen to some ecologist and plant a cover crop when you can see your neighbor's cash crop one field over? But by the time an extractive farmer has grown old, their best field will be transformed into a barren wasteland, just as the bad learner's golden chest is transformed into a pit of vipers.

**You must be respectful**

To get food from the land, you must raise it in your mind from the level of *dirt*—disgusting filth you literally crush underfoot—to the level of *soil*, a thriving community of living things, worthy of awe and even admiration. There is no immediate or obvious reward for doing this, but it pays off in the end.

What about the instruction to kill your own helper? Surely that has no analogue in a garden. But of course it does. Anyone who has ever gardened knows that sometimes you have to destroy a plant you love for the good of the garden you love. Sometimes you plant something, love it, enjoy it, and watch it get out of control. Remember (on page 140) when I told you about the leafy spurge plants I had to kill? I *liked* those plants. They were beautiful, with their delicate green flowers and their soft leaves that turned orange and purple in the fall. But when I'm out walking, I can see that the place where I found the plants growing years ago is now covered with leafy spurge and nothing else.

## Applying the instructions to activism

Now let's think about a completely different example of working with self-organization. Let's say you are an activist, and you want to change the world by working with self-organization in human society. What qualities must you have if you want to put things right in the world?

### You must be teachable

Any successful activist will tell you that one of the factors in their success was contact with helpful coaches, mentors, or teachers. There may not be any talking foxes around these days, but effective activists know that finding experienced people and listening to their good advice makes a difference.

### You must be observant

When you are trying to create social change, it can seem like you are the butt of some cosmic comedy routine. First nobody pays attention; then everybody does, but they misunderstand or attack you; and then nobody cares again, and you're left confused. How do you ride such waves of change? The same way surfers do: with practice. You can't control self-organized patterns in human society, but you can learn to become more aware of what is happening around you, and you can use that awareness to prepare for the next moment of crisis or opportunity. Then, when the moment arrives, you can let everyone think it was the crisis or opportunity that drove the change. *You* will know that you were ready to spring into action.

### You must be patient

Patience can seem like an ugly word when you want to change the world *right now*. It's true that there is power in passion and even anger as a motivating force. On the other hand, creating and sustaining a social movement depends on clear thinking, calm planning, and renewable energy. You can't change minds overnight, no matter how strongly you feel, so you must pace yourself if you are to carry your work to completion. The more strongly you focus on urgency, the less likely you are to get it.

### You must be creative

Creativity in activism can be a wonderful thing, as long as it's *deep* creativity and not superficial spectacle. Gimmicks get people's attention, but they provide only a temporary sideshow to a public that will rush off to the next shiny thing without ever engaging with your issue. Superficial spectacle is more likely to put you in the upper-left corner (supporting self-organization that hurts you) than the upper-right (supporting self-organization that helps you).

A different way to think about creativity in activism is to think of creative ways to listen to, learn from, and connect with your supporters. There is more creativity in your self-organized network than there ever could be in your own head. How much do you know about your supporters? What are their creative ideas? If you think about them and a dozen of their ideas don't spring to mind, maybe you need to listen more and brainstorm less.[40]

**You must be humble**

The hardest thing for an activist to do is to admit that it is *perfectly reasonable* for people not to care about the things you care about. Even if you can prove to them that the issue you care about affects them, and even if they *agree* that the issue affects them, it is not the *only* issue that affects them. They may have other priorities than you do.

Lower yourself to their level by realizing that you are no different than they are. After all, there are issues *you* don't care about that other people care about. So how are you different? How are you better? You aren't. You have made choices about where to put your energy. So have they. Blaming people who don't support you will not cause more people to support you.

What is the activism equivalent of choosing the worst reward? Choose the worst supporters. It is tempting to stay in the center of your support bubble and never venture out to the places where it grows thin. But it's in those thin places where you can have the greatest impact. Push yourself out to where people question everything you say, put you down, talk over you, and ignore you.

This is not only because you need to reach out to more people. You also need more people to reach *in* to your own thinking. The worst supporters provide the best challenges to your vision. They can tell you more about its limitations and weak points than your best supporters can. If you don't have a clear view of those things, you might be in for some nasty surprises. The best place to keep your shining vision of the future might be in an old wooden box.

**You must be respectful**

Respect in good-and-bad-learning folk tales is about raising another person to your level. What does that mean for activism?

In the center of your support bubble, it means sharing control of your work with a group of like-minded people. This means that sometimes you have to let people do things the way they think is better *even though you think your way is better*. You can have complete control, or you can have a collaborative community. You can't have both.

In the rest of your support bubble, raising people to your level means telling them what they want to know, not what you want them to hear. Some activists try to manipulate their supporters with artificial crises or guilt trips or gushing praise. The sad thing is that people who play these tricks often believe their attempts at manipulation are working, when probably the reverse is true and people are supporting them *despite* their attempts at manipulation.

Time spent manipulating people is time lost educating people. Some of your supporters *must* want to know more about your issue and what you are doing to support it. Putting your energy into informing people rather than manipulating them requires a leap of faith, but it pays off in the long run.

Outside your support bubble, raising people to your level means respecting their right to disagree with you and to work against you. Even if you believe a person's thinking is wrong to its core, it will work in your favor to give them the minimal amount of respect due to any human being. They have the right to exist, so you can't wish them away or put them into an "other" category whose opinions don't count. They have the right to make their own choices, so you can't say (without evidence) that they are demented or evil.

Writing off those who disagree with you will not help you succeed. What *will* help is to think of them as *respected adversaries*. After all, it is entirely possible to respect a person while doing your best to make sure they never achieve their goals. In fact, doing so may give you an advantage over them. When you respect those who do not respect you, you can think more clearly and strategically than they can. That's an edge you can use.

What is the activism equivalent of killing your own helper? Remember, this is because the helper has *asked* you to kill them, not because *you* think it's a good idea. Has an activist ever been asked by their own supporters to work *against* their cause? Probably not. But there have surely been times when activists have been asked to stop using a specific argument or approach. If you were such an activist, and you were convinced that your approach was the right one, it *could* seem like your supporters wanted you to kill the very thing you cared about. But if you asked your supporters *why* they wanted you to make the change, you might learn something. Listening can't make you wrong any more than it can make someone else right. What it *can* do is help you understand where people are coming from.

### Applying the instructions to an organized task

Have we proven that this list of instructions helps us deal with self-organization? Maybe. Let's see what happens if we use them in a different situation, one as far from "working with self-organization" as we can get.

How about this. You just bought a thing that came in a box, and you can't use it until you put it together. It might be a little thing, but it might be a big thing. You can buy multi-story buildings in boxes nowadays. Let's say it's a nice, high-quality wooden cabinet: small enough to assemble in a few hours, but big enough and expensive enough that you don't want to screw it up.

You take the instructions out of the box.

#### Should you be teachable?

Yes. Absolutely. This aspect is the same. Read the f-ing manual.

#### Should you be observant?

Of what? Nothing is going to happen unless *you* do it. Yes, of course you will start by observing the quality of the materials, whether anything is missing, and whether the instructions are readable. But you wouldn't have bought the thing if it had bad reviews. Besides, those tasks take place before you start the assembly process, and you don't have to keep checking to see if the parts have run off while you build the thing.

#### Should you be patient?

With yourself, yes. But there is no point being patient with wood and screws. They aren't going to do anything no matter how long you wait. They're just going to sit where you put them. That's why it says right on the box how long it will take to put the thing together: because it's *possible* to say that.

**Should you be creative?**

No. If you want the thing that is pictured on the box, there is only one way to get it: *don't think outside the box*.

It is true that people sometimes buy kits in order to use their parts to build other things, but that is not the situation we are talking about. In this situation, you are probably going to be upset if what you build doesn't look like the picture on the box.

**Should you be humble? Should you be respectful?**

That's up to you. You can assemble your new cabinet while brimming with self-important pride, or you can assemble it while meditating on your cosmic insignificance. It won't make a bit of difference. And you can behave just as disrespectfully as you like. The wood and screws are not going to wither if you neglect them or scatter if you insult them, no more than they are going to grow more abundant with your support or appreciate your praise.

Of course, doing these things might have an effect on *you*. Being humble might make you more careful. Being respectful might make you less likely to break the thing you are trying to build. But you are a self-organized pattern, not an organized plan, and we aren't talking about you.

**Back to gardening and activism**

Now let's say you have finished building your cabinet. It looks just like the picture on the box, and you are pleased. You're looking at it and you think, "I know what would look perfect on top of my new cabinet. A house plant."

So off you go to the garden store to get a pot, some dirt, and a lovely little plant. When it comes to your new plant, can you treat it like you did your new cabinet? Or should you be observant, patient, creative, humble, and respectful? You had better be, if you want to keep your plant alive.

Some time later, you find out that the family-owned business that manufactured your cabinet is suffering from the recent economic downturn and may have to go out of business. You think this is a shame, and you want to do something about it. You decide to start a campaign to get people to support this lovely little company. When it comes to your campaign, can you proceed as you did when you were building your cabinet? Or should you be observant, patient, creative, humble, and respectful? You had better be, if you want to help the company and not hurt it.

## Good and bad learners today

You may be wondering if there are any contemporary good-and-bad-learner stories. Yes, sort of, but they are more like remnants of the original form than examples of it. Most contemporary tales that involve instructions focus only on the bad learners, and often the instructions are not given to the person at all, but are things people are *expected* to know without being told.

For example, in one contemporary folk tale a child copied Superman by jumping off a roof, with disastrous results.[41] In another, a family received a package from overseas relatives containing nothing but a mysterious powder. Assuming that the powder was some kind of tea or instant soup, they boiled some water, added the powder, and drank it. Later, a delayed letter explained that the package contained the cremated remains of a relative.[42]

Another story describes a driver who, having bought a camper van with cruise control, set off on a highway, turned on the cruise control, and strolled into the back of the camper to have a cup of tea.[43] These are all bad-learner stories, but there is no helper to give the instructions.

There are also good-learner tales today, about people who escape danger by keeping their wits about them. The story of the hairy arm, which I told on page 60, is one. But these protagonists rarely receive any instructions.

What happened to the strange helpers? I have two theories. One is that all good-and-bad-learner stories start out as good-learner stories or bad-learner stories, and they acquire the contrasting structure, and the helpers, later on, perhaps hundreds of years later. If that is true, some of the stories being told today will pick up contrasts and helpers as they continue to be retold.

My second theory is that we pay less attention to self-organization today than we did in the past. When you live in a world in which eighty percent of people grow their own food, sew their own clothes, and teach their own children, self-organization is likely to be a bigger part of your everyday life. Today, most of us are more engaged with *organization* than with self-organization. We don't think about floods and flocks; we think about checklists and deadlines. So we tell fewer and simpler stories about working with self-organization.

But our lives are still affected by it, by diseases and uprisings and weather. It's not something we can safely ignore. It never was, and it never will be.

## Why we need folk tales about self-organization

If folk tales teach us how to deal with self-organization, the next question is: Why do we need *folk tales* to tell us this? Don't we know already?

Yes and no. We know a self-organized pattern when we see one, and we have *some* sense of how they work. We aren't completely baffled, for example, when we see a flock of birds, a crowd, or a traffic jam. But we often guess wrongly when we predict what self-organized patterns are going to do *next*. In that respect, our intuition is notoriously, dangerously incorrect.

### Lines and curves

Let's say you are carrying out a purely organized task. Say it's cutting cookies out of dough. You cut one cookie, then you cut the next, and so on. If it takes you five seconds to cut one cookie, it will take fifty seconds to cut ten. A graph of your cookie-cutting output looks like this.

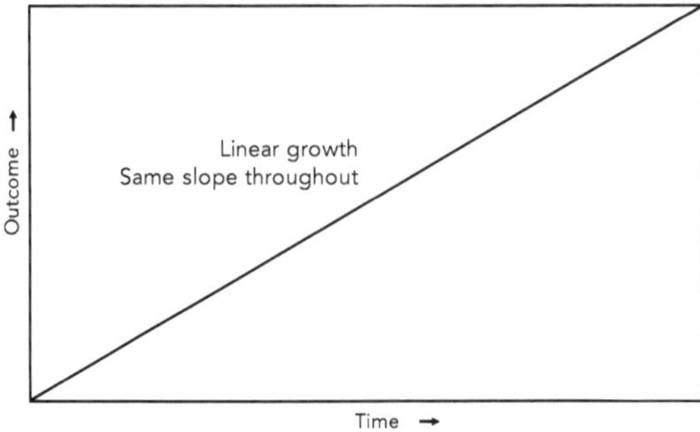


The slope of the line is set at the start of the process and never varies. Your progress is linear whether you keep up a consistent effort in every time interval or put all of your effort into the first time interval—to start up an automated cookie-cutting machine, for example.

Now let's map the growth of a purely self-organized pattern. It could be the biomass in a wildflower meadow, the spread of a fad, or the onset of an epidemic. Self-organized growth tends to follow an S-shaped curve like this.[44]

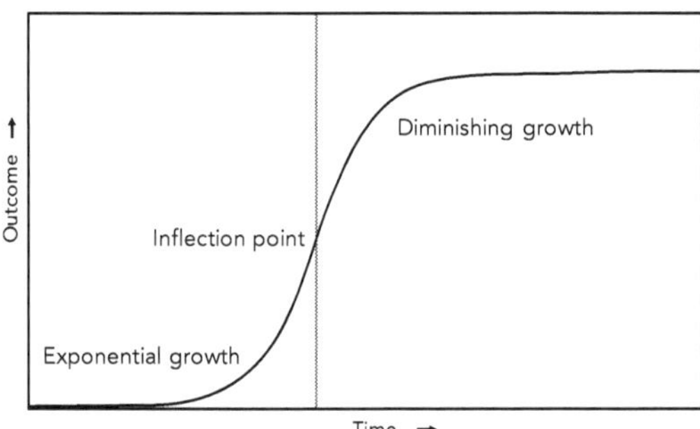


From the start of the graph to the inflection point, the growth of the pattern is roughly exponential, which means that the slope of the line increases in each time step. At the inflection point, growth begins to slow down because it has hit some kind of constraint. Growth in a wildflower meadow slows down due to competition among plants for light, water, and nutrients. Fads die out because they run out of people to whom they seem exciting and new. Viruses run out of hosts to infect, whether it's because people have died, are staying away from each other, or have developed immunity. Then at some point, growth diminishes to the point that the curve flattens out.

Among all the species on this planet, we humans are exceptionally good at making and carrying out organized plans. But because we are so focused on those plans, we tend to see organization where it isn't, and we tend *not* to see self-organization where it is. We focus on the straight line and ignore the curve.

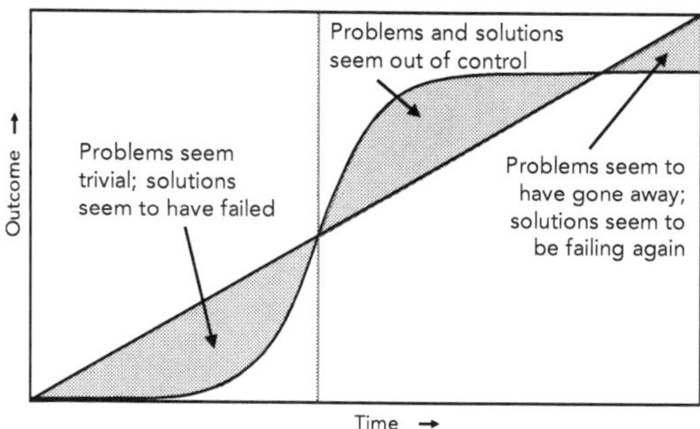


In the first part of the curve, the straight line we *expect* to see is higher than the imperceptibly increasing curve we *don't* see. As a result, growing problems seem like trivial matters, and growing solutions seem like failures. In the second part of the curve, reality exceeds our expectations, so we perceive both problems *and* solutions as too much, too fast, and out of control. When the curve levels out, our expectations again rise higher than reality, so we believe our problems have disappeared and our solutions have stopped working.

If this was our only problem, we could fix it by paying more attention to self-organization. But it's *not* our only problem. Even when we *know* a pattern is self-organized, we *still* get it wrong, for a different reason.

The *availability heuristic* describes our tendency to pay the most attention to information we can easily recall, which is usually about things that happened recently, noticeably, and nearby. In some situations, this instinct can be life-saving. If you are attacked by a predator, the last thing you want to do is spend precious moments listing the characteristics of every predator you've ever seen or heard about. But when it comes to self-organized growth, our instinctual focus on *what just happened* can lead us to the wrong conclusions.

Say we are monitoring a known self-organized pattern, like a fad, a storm, or an epidemic. At each time interval, we attempt to guess what will happen next. Our guesses are shown in the diagram below by the black arrows. Say our look-back time frame of readily available information is three intervals long. This is shown by the gray lines, which determine the slopes of the black arrows.

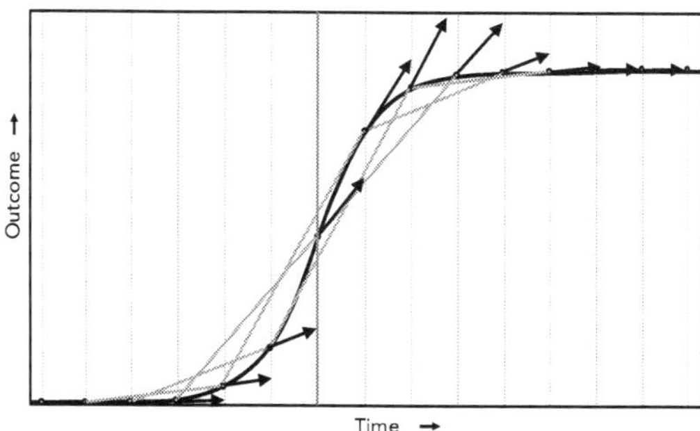

Our estimates lag behind the slope of the curve in each time interval. Even at the inflection point, our estimate is still quite a bit lower than the actual growth rate. Later, the situation flips, and our estimate is too high. This series of linear approximations is closer to the actual curve than the one I showed you before, the one in which the linear approximation stretched across the entire curve. But it's still pretty far off. The fact that both estimates are wrong means that we don't have to mistake a self-organized pattern for an organized plan to get it wrong. Even when we *know* a pattern is self-organized, the availability heuristic holds us back from seeing it as it truly is.

Of the three parts of the S-curve, the worst one to get wrong is the *first* one. You can't fix what you can't see. Our universal tendency to underestimate exponential growth has been so well studied that it has its own name: *exponential growth bias*, or EGB.

## Lilies on a pond

The fragrant water lily *Nymphaea odorata* forms dense vegetative colonies, each with hundreds or thousands of individual plants.

One day, in a certain pond, a single water-lily seed fell from the feather of a migrating bird. The seed germinated, and the plant established itself. Soon a second plant grew from one of its roots. The growing vegetative colony doubled in size roughly once per month.

Now it's four years later, and the surface of the pond is completely covered with water lilies. Not a space remains to be filled. When would you guess the pond was *half* covered with water lilies? After two years? Three?

The pond was half covered *one month ago*, in the forty-seventh month.

There's a good chance you've already heard some version of that story, so let me ask you another question. In what month did the lily pads cover *one percent* of the pond? Don't find a calculator, and don't count backwards on your fingers. Just make an *intuitive* guess.

What month did you pick? Ten? Twenty-four? I picked twenty-four. The answer is the forty-second month. After three and a half years of growth, ninety-nine percent of the pond's surface was still empty.

### A strange feeling

Doesn't that seem *strange* to you? Even when you *know* the answer, it *still* seems strange, doesn't it? Why is that? Why do we have such a hard time making *intuitive* sense of exponential growth? I'm not talking about whether we can *answer* the question. I'm talking about the *feeling* of it, the strangeness. Where does that feeling come from?

As I said before, we pay a lot of attention to our organized plans. But that's not the only factor. We are also primed to pay attention to the organized plans of potential predators—because we used to be prey. For hundreds of thousands of years, the biggest threat to our survival was the megafauna who surrounded us and hunted us.[45] Today, most of us are threatened as much by *self*-organization—in the form of diseases, accidents, economic downturns, and weather events—as we are by organization. But our brains are still looking for monsters. The idea that a small, slow, quiet growth could harm us as much as a big, fast, loud beast doesn't make sense to our prehistoric brains. But it can.

### Little jumps, big jumps

If exponential growth bias is caused by the availability heuristic, we should be better at estimating the progress of *reverse* exponential curves, because our look-back time frames will encompass larger changes.

Consider the following two sequences. Can you guess what each index will be in the tenth year? Take a moment to think about it. And if you can, notice *how* you think about it. Listen to your internal dialogue as you look at the sequences.

| Year | Index 1 | Index 2 |
|---|---|---|
| 1 | 3 | 22,026 |
| 2 | 7 | 8,103 |
| 3 | 20 | 2,981 |
| 4 | 55 | 1,097 |
| 5 | 148 | 403 |

The answer is that the end value of each sequence is the start value of the other. At Year 10, Index 1 will be 22,026. Index 2 will be 3.

Did the end point of the downward-moving index make more sense to you? It did to me. When I looked at the "Index 1" column, I thought, "Oh, those are little jumps. There will be more little jumps." Then I saw the number 22,026, and I thought, "*What?* That's not a little jump." I was surprised—not intellectually, but instinctually. When I looked at the "Index 2" column, I thought,"Oh, those are big jumps. There will be more big jumps." And there were. So I was *not* surprised when the number quickly jumped down to three.

That's exactly what Han Timmers and Willem Wagenaar found when they showed these number sequences to people and asked them to predict the values for the tenth year. Presentation of the downward progression (Index 2 only) resulted in a "considerable reduction of underestimation" of the growth curve.[46]

Did you notice *why* I made the mistake I made? I paid a lot of attention to the *beginning* of each progression, and I paid much less attention to its end. After the first three numbers, my exact thought was "okay, more numbers, whatever." *That's* the availability heuristic. We all do that.

### What looks like a solution is just another part of the problem

Maybe *you* don't do that. You know about math, and you are a careful thinker. But consider this. Might there be times when you are tired, stressed, upset, or in a hurry? Might there be topics you don't know about and don't care to learn about? Might there be situations in which you find it necessary or preferable to avoid spending your precious time and energy working out detailed predictions? Do you think you might fall back onto your general intuition at any of those times? Of course you might.[47]

Believing you are immune to EGB is just another part of EGB. Not only do we consistently fail to accurately predict exponential growth; we consistently fail to realize that we are doing so. In a 2017 study, Matthew Levy and Joshua Tasoff found that "individuals with greater EGB exhibited greater overconfidence" and that "those who would benefit the most from advice or tools have lower demand for these things."[48] Thus the more EGB we have, the *less* likely we are to seek help to improve it. That makes us doubly vulnerable.

## Where stories come in

And this, I believe, is the answer to the question I asked myself at the start of this chapter. *This* is the "something" that folk tales and self-organization have to do with each other. *One of the best ways to teach someone a lesson they think they already know is to embed the lesson in a story.*

Stories are engaging, memorable, and motivating. They draw us in and encourage us to consider arguments and perspectives we would dismiss if they came to us in any other form. Folk tales teach us how to deal with self-organized growth despite the fact that we think we already know how to deal with self-organized growth. They are a cultural solution to a cognitive limitation, one that has been helping us make sense of the world for thousands of years.

## The magical lily pond

One piece of evidence for my argument (in addition to those I have already shown you) is the fact that the examples we use to talk about exponential growth, even in our science and mathematics classrooms, have all the hallmarks of folk tales. For example, consider the lily pad story with respect to the characteristics common to all folk tales.

### Folk tales have nebulous origins

When you try to trace a folk tale back in time, it always fades out into oblivion. No one knows where or when or by whom it was first told. If you look up the lily pond story on the internet, you will find that most people call it "an old French riddle." (Some add "taught to children.") The story is almost always called "old" or "classic," whether it is called a riddle, a story, or a brain teaser. But if you try to trace the story back to its supposedly "old French" origin, the trail grows faint. I have not been able to find any published version of the story prior to the 1970s. It is difficult to pin down, like all folk tales.

### Folk tales teach essential lessons

All folk tales are about real life, even if they take place in fantastic locations or include impossible events. Sometimes the application of the lesson is obvious, as in the "morals" of Aesop's fables, and sometimes the lesson is oblique. But the lesson is always there. It is the reason the story exists.

The lesson of the lily pond dominates the story so completely that perhaps it is not a story at all. But in many versions of the story, there are protagonists, a plot, and consequences. Sometimes named or unnamed people watch over the pond. Sometimes the audience is asked to pretend that they own the pond ("You have a pond") or would enjoy visiting it ("Imagine a beautiful pond"). Sometimes the eventual fate of the pond (being covered with lily pads) is presented as a disaster to the frogs or fish that live in it, and the goal of the protagonist (the audience) is to save them. Each of these characterizations sets up a situation in which finding the right solution to the mathematical problem has an effect on the fate of someone or something. That's a story.

### Folk tales are both constant and constantly changing

Every folk tale has some deep elements that never change (usually those associated with the essential lesson) and some superficial elements that are open to change, such as what is in the endless sack or where the monster lives.

In the lily pad story, the element of doubling never changes, and the story always takes place in a pond. It is never a lake, river, or ocean.

But sometimes it is not a *colony* of lily pads that grows; sometimes it is one giant lily pad that gets bigger and bigger. And once in a while, the "old riddle" is from China, not France, and the plants are duckweed or water hyacinth plants. For example, a 1979 paper describes the story as a "fable about the Chinese mandarin who as a youth planted some duckweed in a pond."[49]

### Folk tales exaggerate

Folk tales blow things out of proportion to get and keep our attention. It's not a small man; it's "a small man who lived in a nutshell."[50] It's not a big meal; it's a meal in which "however much they ate, there was always more."[51] Things don't happen quickly; they happen "quicker than it can be told."[52] Exaggeration makes folk tales lively and memorable.

The lily pond story I told you is not one you will find on the internet. Because I'm a biology nerd, I told you about a vegetative colony of a particular species of water lily, and I set the doubling period at one month, which is fairly realistic. Most versions of the story, whether it's about a "patch" of lily pads or one weirdly giant lily pad, set the doubling period at *one day*. That's impossible.

But even my story contained quite a bit of fiction. Lily pads would never actually fill up an entire pond. They have many predators, from fish to ducks to beavers, and they would be subject to the same competition for light and nutrients as the flowers in a meadow. The actual population growth of lily pads on a pond would follow an S-shaped curve, not an exponential curve that hit a wall at full saturation. But the riddle would be a lot harder to solve if the growth curve didn't follow a simple doubling progression. The *lesson* of the story is what matters, not whether it is factual. In that sense, the lily pad story is no different from any folk tale of monsters and magic.

### Folk tales include formulaic expressions

All folk tales include formulas: unique phrases that are preserved intact across many tellings. Such formulaic expressions are often used as shorthand references to stories. In many cases you need only repeat one phrase, such as "the goose that laid the golden eggs," to tell the whole tale.

The number of doubling periods in the lily pad story is usually thirty (the number of days in a month); twenty-four, thirty-six, or forty-eight (multiples of twelve months); or sixty-four (the number of squares on a chess board). And the question "How long will it take for the pond to be covered halfway?" (or "On what *day* will the pond be covered halfway?") is consistent among tellings. Lester Brown's 1978 book *The Twenty-Ninth Day* has even come to be a sort of shorthand reference to the story.[53]

### A prince plays a game

I could tell you several more folk tales about exponential growth,[54] but I will choose just one: an ancient story about the origin of chess.[55]

An Indian prince rose to the throne quite young. His tutor, Sissa, was concerned that his young pupil lacked the experience to govern wisely. But he "saw that there were virtues in the monarch which required only the culture of reason to bring them into life." So he created a game to help the young prince learn how to lead his people.

Sissa embedded his lessons in a game so that they "should appear the result of the prince's own reasoning, rather than the instructions of another." Also, he didn't *show* the new game to the prince. He had it "spread abroad among some of the leading men." Eventually "the prince heard of it" and wanted to play.

Sissa carefully designed his game so that the king was "the most important of all the pieces, but yet the easiest to attack, and the most difficult to defend." And he "took reasonable occasions to point out the dependence of the king on the pawns." According to this ancient story, then, chess was designed as a ritualized, gamified lesson about the ways in which organized plans (intentional movements of the chess pieces) interact with self-organized patterns (iterative interactions and influences among the pieces). Fascinating, right?

Even more fascinating is that the story of Sissa and the prince ends with an explicit warning about exponential growth bias.

> The prince, eager to recompense the bramin [Sissa] for the great good derived from his ingenuity, required him to demand what he thought competent. The bramin asked only a gift of [barley] corn, the amount of which should be regulated by the number of houses, (or squares) on the chess-board, putting one grain on the first house, two on the second, four on the third, and so on in double permutation to the sixty-fourth house.
>
> The apparent moderation of the demand astonished the king, and he, unhesitatingly, granted it; but, when his treasurers calculated the amount of his donation, they found that the king's revenues were not competent to discharge it; for the corn of 16,384 towns, each containing 1024 granaries, of 173,762 measures each, and each measure to consist of 32,768 grains, could alone answer the demand!

There are many versions of this story, some of which were first written down about a thousand years ago.[56] The man who created chess is variously given to be Indian, Arab, or Persian. The items placed on the chessboard are grains of barley, rice, or wheat. The king is always surprised, and the creator of the game is usually rewarded. Sometimes he becomes the new king. In one version, however, the inventor is executed for having proven himself more clever than the king. (Which is its own lesson.)

### Truly ancient

But stories about exponential growth may go back much further than that. In the ruins of the ancient Semitic city-state of Mari, archaeologists found a treasure trove of over 25,000 cuneiform tablets. Among them is this one:

> A barley-corn to a single barley-corn I added, then
> 2 barley-corns in the 1st day
> 4 barley-corns in the 2nd day
> 8 barley-corns in the 3rd day . . .
> 2 thousand 7 hundred 37 talents 1/2 mina 2 1/3 shekels 4 barley-corns in the 30th day.[57]

The words "I" (personal pronoun), "added" (past-tense verb), "then" (time sequence indicator), and "day" (time reference) prove that this was a *story*, even if it was also a math problem. Note also the number of days: thirty, as in many contemporary versions of the lily pad story.

The tablet on which this story was written has been dated to the eighteenth century BCE. People have recognized the need to help people who think they already understand self-organized growth understand self-organized growth for at least four thousand years.

## The other side of the mix

Now it's time to look at the mix from another point of view. For each pair of story types about organizers dealing with self-organization (two kinds of luck, power, folly, and wisdom), there is a second pair of story types told from the opposing perspective. Remember the young man who stopped his horse from stepping on a colony of ants? These are the stories told by the ants.

I did not go hunting for these stories; they found me. As I read through my folk-tale books, they kept popping up. They didn't fit into any of my groups, so I put them in a set-aside pile and kept moving. After a while the pile began to divide itself, and I realized that a mirror image was taking shape.

Why do we tell stories from the ant point of view? Because we *are* ants. We like to think of ourselves as organizers, but we are also interactors to the extent that we have local awareness, muddled intentions, limited access to power, and collective strength and resilience. The more we know about how self-organization works, the more we can stop organizers from organizing us.

Who wants to organize us? In olden times, it was kings, ministers, priests, and magicians. Today it's governments, corporations, teachers, judges, and doctors, all of whom are embedded in partly-organized systems: the justice system, the educational system, the health care system, and so on.

Did you ever hear someone say, "You look like ants from up here"? That's a way of saying, "I am an organizer, and you are not." Every time someone says that to us (maybe in different words, like "your call will be answered by the next available operator"), these stories can help us regain our collective strength and resilience. Let's look at some folk-tale examples of self-organized power, luck, folly, and wisdom.

## Two kinds of collective power

Halfway down the space, what looks like luck from an organizer's point of view looks like power from a crowd's point of view. Locations on this line describe collective movements in support or subversion of organizers.

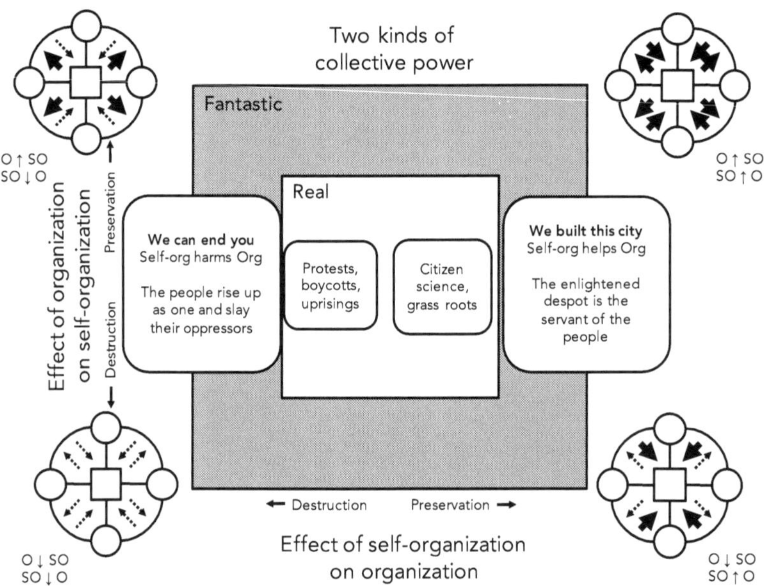


On the right, self-organized networks keep organized forces alive with their time, money, energy, and compliance. On the left, self-organized networks drain energy from unpopular organizers with protests, boycotts, and a refusal to go along quietly. The Helen Reddy song "I am woman, hear me roar, in numbers too big to ignore" is an anthem for both forms of collective power.

### *The public gets its revenge*

A folk tale that fits here is the story of the Emperor's new clothes.[58] A vain emperor was convinced by swindlers to sponsor the creation of a suit of clothes made of fabric so fine that only those who were fit for their positions were able to see it. The emperor saw nothing, but he pretended to see the outfit out of fear. So did his ministers and staff. Finally the marvelous garment was complete, and the emperor paraded through the city, naked as the day he was born. "But he hasn't got anything on!" said a little child. The bubble popped, the emperor was humiliated, and the swindlers were nowhere to be found.

Hans Christian Anderson published this story in 1837. He read it in *Tales of Count Lucanor,* a collection of Spanish folk tales written by Don Juan Manuel in 1335. In that version the ruler was a king, and the person who spoke up was "a negro" who had "nothing to lose."[59] Manuel probably read it in the *Līlāvatīsāra,* an epic poem composed by Jinaratna in 1036, which recounted Indian folk tales from an earlier oral tradition. In that version "the citizens, not being acquainted with the new science, asked whether the King had become a naked ascetic."[60]

In every version of the story, the collective strength of the people exposed the swindle. Those with the least power spoke up first, but the crowd turned the tide. In the 1335 version, after the "negro" spoke, the king "commenced beating him" for his outburst. But "others were convinced of its truth, and said the same," and the king "and all with him lost their fear of declaring the truth." Also notice the ironic "not being acquainted with the new science," an echo of the Brahman "who was not half as learned as the others" (page 154), only from the other side of the mix.

#### *Revenge reborn: Clever consumers*

A recent example of a story in this group is the expensive-recipe story.[61] Someone called a corporation that sold baked goods and asked for the recipe for a famous cake or cookie. The caller was told that the recipe would cost some number that seemed small, like "two-fifty." So they agreed to pay that amount on their credit card. They received the recipe in the mail, then found out that "two-fifty" was the number of *dollars,* not cents. In revenge, they distributed the recipe to everyone they knew and encouraged them to keep spreading it to undermine sales of the commercial product.

This is a "we can end you" story: a self-organized network (the public) demonstrated its power to disrupt the plans of an organizer (a corporation). The fact that the organizer changed (first it was the Nieman Marcus department store, then the Mrs. Fields Cookie Company) while other aspects of the story did not (there was always a mix-up about the price) marks this as a folk tale.

### Two kinds of collective luck

Halfway across the mixed space, self-organization neither helps nor harms organizers, so these situations are defined by the actions of organizers. To a self-organized network, however, the actions of organizers look a lot like good and bad luck. At the top of the space, organizers promote and sustain self-organized networks. At the bottom, they work to eradicate them.

One folk tale in this group is the story of the pied piper.[62] One day, a man wearing multicolored (pied) clothing came into a city, claiming that for a price he would lure its many rats into a river using his magical flute (pipe). The people, overjoyed, agreed to the deal. But when the rats were gone, the people of the city saw no reason to pay the piper; he seemed powerless to do anything to enforce their agreement. In revenge, the piper lured the children of the city to a cave under the ground, never to return.

Three children were left behind. One was deaf and could not hear the pipe; one was blind and could not see where to go; one was lame and could not keep up. The three remaining children told the adults what happened.

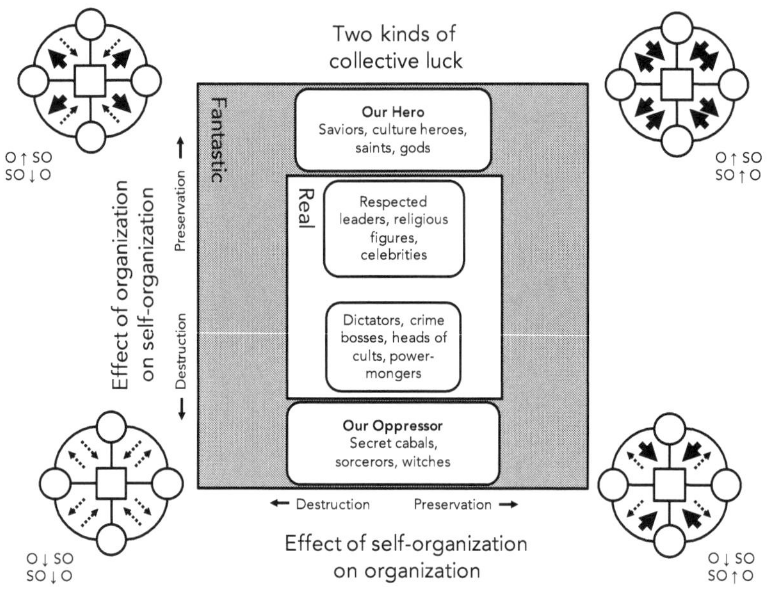


The story of the pied piper dates from the middle ages. Some believe it refers to any of several historical incidents, from plagues to crusades to bouts of mass hysteria. In any case, it is a cautionary tale about the dangers of relying on a super-organizer. The pied piper had the power to control self-organized swarming in any group. (At least he could *start* it; we never find out if he could stop it.) He offered the people of the city an opportunity to benefit from his power. But they discounted the danger he posed, and this led him to unleash his power against them. He was transformed from the city's hero (at the top of the space) to its oppressor (at the bottom) in an instant.

It is symbolic that the piper took the children to a cave under the ground, to a place in which the hidden powers of self-organization were strong. He forced them to become interactors by taking away their powers of organization: awareness, intent, and access. But he could not take awareness from the deaf and blind children, and he could not take access from the lame child, because they never had those things to begin with.

***Pied pipers everywhere***

Today's folk tales are replete with pied pipers. The folklorist Gary Alan Fine coined the term "the Goliath effect" to describe stories about being under the thumb of corporations, governments, and other partly-organized bodies.[63]

The most common Goliath-effect stories are contamination stories, which tell how every kind of packaged and restaurant food contains large quantities of mice, worms, snakes, spiders, horse meat, sawdust, cardboard, human body parts, and human bodily secretions. A similar set of stories describes the many secrets that are being kept from us. The machines we buy could run faster or more efficiently, but they don't—unless you belong to an elite group chosen by the manufacturers. Other stories tell of miraculous medicines available only to a select few. In many of these stories, the antagonists are super-organizers who have impossible amounts of power over reality.

Some Goliath-effect stories reflect historical power imbalances. For example, there was for some time a rumor in the African-American community that Church's Fried Chicken was owned by the Ku Klux Klan. This group, it was said, caused the chicken sold at these fast-food restaurants to be laced with chemicals that caused impotence in Black men. There is no factual basis to either of these claims, but there is abundant proof that African Americans were the targets of organized plans in the past, from Jim Crow laws to the infamous Tuskegee syphilis study. As a recent article explains,

> It wasn't until a whistleblower, Peter Buxtun, leaked information about the study to the *New York Times* and the paper published it on the front page on November 16th, 1972, that the Tuskegee study finally ended.[64]

That's not ancient history, it's the recent past; and folk tales about such dangers, even if they are fictional, serve useful purposes. The message of all such stories is "don't trust those in power to use it on your behalf."

## Two kinds of collective folly

On the organized side of the mix, we explored how people make mistakes when dealing with self-organized patterns. Now we will consider how the interactors in those patterns make mistakes collectively, as a crowd.

But *can* a crowd make a mistake? Is that even possible? I don't think so. Only an organizer can make a mistake. Folly is more of a wistful feeling on this side of the mix. Any interactor in a crowd may regret what the crowd does, but they usually can't prevent it—not without becoming an organizer.

### There's a sucker born every minute

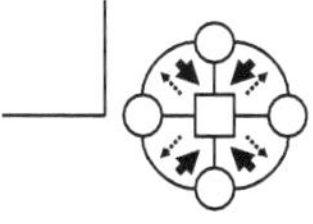

In the lower-right corner, interactors allow organizers to herd them into self-organized patterns that are helpful to the organizers but harmful to themselves. These are not wise crowds; they are easy marks for clever swindlers.

#### *The news spread far and near*

In a Liberian tale, a man named Genotee discovered a hidden cave under a waterfall on the Geno Creek.[65] After exploring the cave, Genotee decided to trick his neighbors into thinking that he had gained access to a magical underwater world of long-departed ancestors. To prove his claim, he disappeared under the water, then reappeared minutes later, unharmed.

The people were convinced, and they bestowed Genotee with gifts for the ancestors. Their gifts made Genotee a rich man. To keep people away from the waterfall, Genotee claimed that anyone who approached it (other than himself) would be turned into a person of the opposite gender. The ruse went on for the rest of Genotee's life. Even after he died, people continued to avoid the site. They told their children that Genotee still protected it.

> Then one day a group of daring schoolboys went fishing in the Geno Creek. When they got to the waterfall, one of the boys said, "One of these days, I shall jump right into this waterfall." Another brave boy replied, "Let's jump right into it now-o!"

The boys told the people about the cave, but they did not believe it. "Even today the townspeople make sacrifices on Geno Creek by Genotee's waterfall."

It is clear in the telling of the story that Genotee was only partially responsible for what happened. The story says that "within two days the news of Genotee's visit to his people who had died long ago and now lived under the water of the Geno spread far and near." That is an indictment of the *people*, not of Genotee. It's a cautionary tale about the folly of believing the claims of super-organizers who seek to control the collective beliefs of the community.

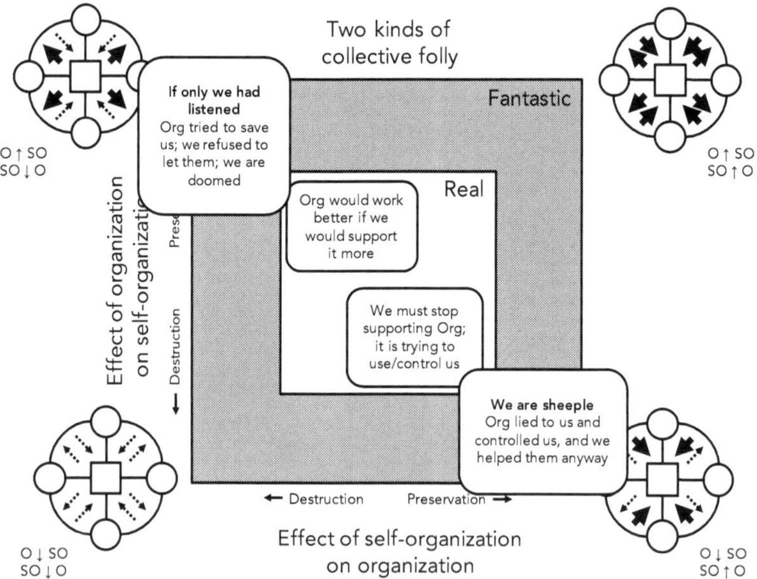
Two kinds of collective folly
Fantastic
Real
If only we had listened
Org tried to save us; we refused to let them; we are doomed
Org would work better if we would support it more
We must stop supporting Org; it is trying to use/control us
We are sheeple
Org lied to us and controlled us, and we helped them anyway
Effect of organization on self-organization
Destruction
Effect of self-organization on organization
← Destruction
Preservation →
O ↑ SO
SO ↓ O
O ↑ SO
SO ↑ O
O ↓ SO
SO ↓ O
O ↓ SO
SO ↑ O

### ***Wanna buy a bridge?***

George C. Parker was a confidence man who lived in New York City in the early twentieth century. His scam was to "sell" New York City landmarks—the

Brooklyn Bridge, the Metropolitan Museum of Art, the Statue of Liberty—to gullible foreign tourists and immigrants. It is said that he claimed to have sold the Brooklyn Bridge at least twice a week for decades.

Here's how Parker worked his Brooklyn Bridge scam. Wearing a smart suit, he would approach people who looked foreign, confused, and wealthy. He would claim to be the builder of the Brooklyn Bridge. He would say that while he loved building bridges, he had no interest in taking tolls, and he was looking for a partner to handle that part of the business. He would then bring the visitors to his official-looking office and sell them forged documents of ownership. His dupes found out that they did not in fact own the bridge when police showed up to remove the toll booths they were building.

That's the *story*, anyway. Much of what has been said about Parker has been offered without evidence, so his story might be a folk tale in the process of forming. It's hard to say how many times Parker actually "sold" anything, and he was only one of many grifters wandering the streets of New York City at the time. The only piece of hard evidence I found about Parker was a snippet from a 1928 newspaper that reads, "George C. Parker, who startled the world by 'selling' the Brooklyn Bridge to a 'hick' . . . was today sent to Sing Sing [prison] for life." Tellingly, the paper goes on to say:

> Twenty years ago on New Years Day, Sheriff Flaherty, who had just taken office, arrived at Raymond Street Jail to greet the workers and prisoners. He took off his overcoat and hat. Parker, a trusty [trusted prisoner] then, donned them. One of the guards actually salaamed [greeted] him as he walked unmolested out of the jail, bidding all a Happy New Year.[66]

That already sounds like a folk tale, doesn't it? It has exaggeration, humor, and colorful visuals, and it seems to fit within the "outlaw" tradition of tall tales. Parker's story has even developed a formulaic shorthand reference: "If you believe that, I've got a bridge in Brooklyn to sell you."

Regardless of whether the stories about George Parker are true or false, they have some interesting things to say about this corner of the mix. Parker searched for interactors who had limited awareness, confused intentions, and restricted access. (Though many of the foreign visitors he swindled had money, they rarely had connections.) Then he put on the appearance of an organizer: a snappy suit, an official-looking office, fancy documents—and most importantly, the *confidence* of an organizer: well informed, determined, and capable.

But surprisingly, Parker is not the person who gets the blame in these stories. Most of the mentions of Parker's deceptions I have found on the internet have been incredulous not that Parker deceived people, but that people *allowed* him to fool them. There seems to be a feeling that the "suckers born every minute" of the past century were more to blame than those who tricked them. (We, of course, are different.)

## Biting the hand that feeds us

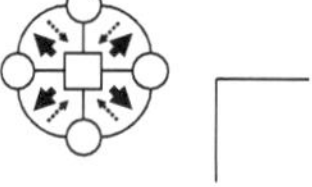

In the upper left corner, self-organized networks destroy organizers that might have preserved them. A category of story that works well in this corner has to do with out-of-control litigation. Such stories are a particular specialty of the United States. Here is a typical specimen.

> A man picks up his power mower while it is running, intending to use the machine to trim his hedge. Instead, the tips of all his fingers are cut off; his thumbs, being on the outside of the blade housing, are intact. He sues the manufacturer for failing to publish a warning about using the mower in this way, and he wins a large judgement.[67]

This story, and many more like it, show that the public can be its own worst enemy when it comes to burdening manufacturers of necessary products with lawsuits that drive up prices for everyone. Though such stories are fictions, they represent a deeper truth. Jumping to the conclusion that every organizer must be out to get us simply because they *are* an organizer is just as foolish as falling for a swindler's cheap trick.

## Two kinds of collective wisdom

Finally we arrive at situations in which robust and resilient self-organized networks win the day, either by working with organizers or by fighting them.

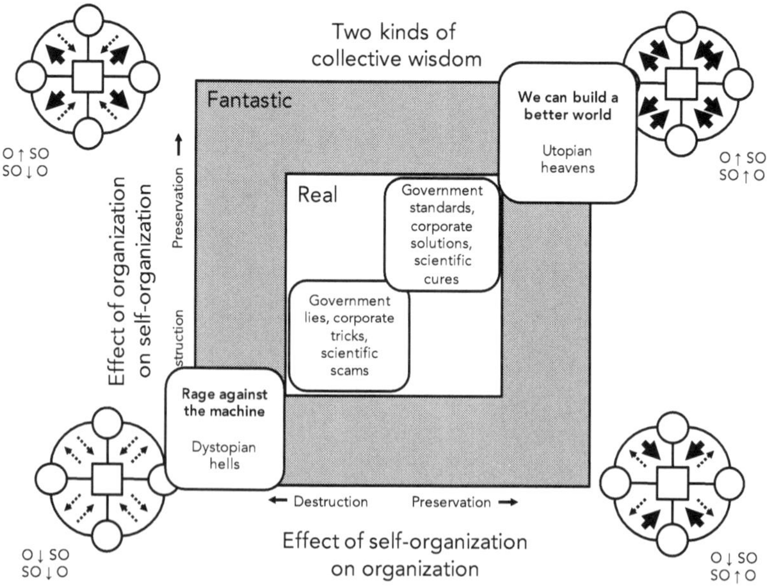

## Mutual aid

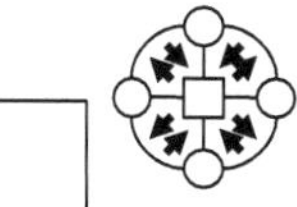

In the upper-right corner of the space are stories in which organization and self-organization work hand in hand—not because either force has perfect control over the other, but because they build on each other's strengths.

Many years ago, a Japanese farmer stood near his house on a hill, high above the village below. There had recently been an earthquake, and he was surveying the damage. Then he looked out over the ocean. Far in the distance, he could see a thin, dark line: a tsunami was forming. The people in the village below could not see what was coming. How could he get word to them in time? He could not run down the hill fast enough. He could not call out loud enough.

The farmer knew what he had to do. He went into his house, took a burning stick from the fireplace, came outside, and set his harvested sheaves of rice burning. The fire spread, and soon his whole field was alight. The people of the village came running up the hill to help. As they arrived, the farmer counted heads, making sure every last villager was there. Then he pointed out to sea, and the villagers watched as the huge wave crashed into the shore, destroying the village. The people cried out in alarm at the destruction of their village, and then they cried out in gratitude to the man who had saved their lives.

This is a true story. After the Great Ansei Earthquake of 1854, a tsunami struck the village of Hirogawa. Goryō Hamaguchi, head of the Yamasa Corporation, was visiting his country home at the time. It was indeed at the top of a hill, and he did set his rice sheaves on fire, which caused the villagers to run up the hill and escape the tsunami. After the disaster, Hamaguchi helped rebuild the town, and he paid the wages of the workers who built a new seawall to protect the town from future tsunamis.

The first step in the transformation of this real-life incident into a folk tale was when Patrick Lafcadio Hearn told the story in his 1897 book *Gleanings in Buddha-Fields*. In Hearn's telling:

> Hamaguchi watched [the villagers] hurrying . . . up from the village, like a swarming of ants, and, to his anxious eyes, scarcely faster; for the moments seemed terribly long to him."[68]

Here are organization and self-organization working hand in hand. Hamaguchi acted to organize the people of his village. In response, they ran up the hill "like a swarming of ants" to save him, and were themselves saved. Hamaguchi was an organizer, but he didn't try to control the villagers; he asked for their help. If the people of the village had not responded as one body to Hamaguchi's apparent need, they would have perished.

What is even more fascinating about this story is that its second layer is also a demonstration of cooperation between organization and self-organization. The folk tale has been incorporated into educational materials meant to help people who live on ocean shores avoid tsunamis. For example, it is included in materials distributed during the celebration of the UN's World Tsunami Awareness Day, the fifth of November.

## The ants fight back

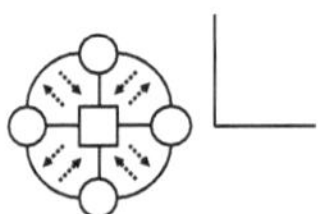

Our last corner, the lower left, covers situations in which a self-organized network rises up to defeat an organized foe. A good story of this type is from a collection of Indian folk tales called the *Panchatantra*, which was written down sometime between 200 BCE and 300 CE, drawing its tales from an older oral tradition.[69]

There was once a flock of doves whose king was named Gay-Neck because his royal neck was painted in bright colors. One day Gay-Neck and his retainers discovered grains of rice magically scattered all over the branches of a banyan tree. As they rushed to partake of the unexpected meal, a crow flew up to warn them that it was a trap. He had watched a hunter scatter the grains after carefully placing a net in the branches.

Gay-Neck and his followers ignored the crow's warning, "greedily sought to eat" the rice, and were caught in the net. The hunter advanced, smiling at his good luck, and the doves shook in fear.

> But the king, with much presence of mind, said to the doves: "Have no fear, my friends. . . . We must all agree in purpose, must fly up in unison, and carry the snare away."

Then he told them a story about two birds who shared one belly. One ate poison and both died. Convinced, the whole flock flew up together, taking the net with them. They flew until they found a mouse friend named Gold.

Gold was a nervous little mouse, and he was not sure how much he trusted Gay-Neck. So he devised a test of character. If Gay-Neck failed it, Gold would run away and save himself.

Gold began to cut Gay-Neck free, saying, "servants follow the master." But Gay-Neck stopped him, insisting that Gold cut his followers loose first. Gold replied, "It was to test you that I said what I did. Now I will cut the bonds of all." The mouse cut the net to pieces, and the birds were free.

In this story, the strength and resilience of the self-organized flock overcame the organized plans of the hunter. Importantly, this outcome was achieved because Gay-Neck did not *order* the flock to fly up. Instead, he *convinced* them to work together by telling them a story. Then Gold tested Gay-Neck by giving him the chance to accept special treatment. A second time Gay-Neck refused to use his power, and his reliance on the collective power of the self-organized network saved the entire flock.

Gay-Neck's actions in this story were much like Hamaguchi's in the story of the tsunami. By sacrificing some of his own organized power, and giving more power to his followers, he saved himself and his flock.

## These are your instructions

Thank you for tolerating a long, slightly weird, and possibly boring conversation with a strange but maybe wise older woman. In gratitude for your patience and respect, I will now give you some instructions.

Improving your ability to work with self-organization through engaging with folk tales is a self-organized process. Understandings will emerge through iterative interactions among the stories you read, your thoughts, memories, and emotions, and the people around you. The journey will have its twists and turns, but if you follow these instructions your path will be made smoother.

### You must be teachable

Go to a library, a bookstore, or the internet, find some folk tales, and read them. Avoid "literary tales" written by individual authors based on their own ideas. Those stories are not as connected to the lesson-passing-on purpose of traditional folk tales, so they are less likely to help you learn about self-organization. Look instead for collections drawn from oral interviews or historically accurate sources. If a collection provides no explanation of where its stories came from, it will not serve your purpose.

A good place to start is with one folk tale collection from your own culture and one from a culture you don't know well. Once you have that foundation in place, branch out. Read one book of stories from each continent. When you have done that, start looking at cultures within each continent. Then look back at older stories written down thousands of years ago. Develop a sense of the folk tale landscape over the millennia and around the world.

Once you have read some folk tales, come back to this set of instructions and read it again. Keep going back and forth.

### You must be observant

As you read, pay attention to the emerging patterns you see. Let the stories clump and cluster into groups. Do you see recurrent themes? What about contradictions? Take notes or draw diagrams. Make sense of what you are reading, not just in each story but across the body of stories as a whole.

Pay attention to aspects of stories that relate to organization and self-organization. When you see words like "rose up" or "rushed forth" or "swarmed round," prick up your ears and pay attention. How do the people in the stories deal with self-organized patterns? How do they support them? How do they fight them? How are they helped and hindered by them? What happens when the protagonists *are* self-organized networks? You can use the structure of this chapter to group the stories you read (and maybe you can improve on it).

### You must be patient

Don't read five stories. Read fifty. Read five hundred. You won't see the benefit of your journey until you have crossed many rivers and scaled many mountains. Don't expect answers right away. Let the stories fall on you like rain. Get used to the feel of them. The insights will arrive when the time is right.

### You must be creative

Think about how the stories you read connect to your own life. What can they teach you about your own circumstances and choices? Let them bubble up as you think about things that have happened to you and decisions you face.

Do you know a person who lets you go on at length about things you find interesting? As you read, pick out some of your favorite stories and tell them to that person. As you become more confident, start telling your favorite stories to other people. Without changing the essential lessons of the stories, make them your own. Add your own style and flavor. In time, you may become a strange but maybe wise older person who passes on folk tales that help a new generation learn how to work with self-organization.

### You must be humble

Lower yourself to the level of the characters in the stories you read and the people who told them. Don't put down folk tales just because the people who told them didn't know about basic hygiene or DNA or computers. Appreciate what you have in common with the people in the stories and the people who told them, and see what you can learn.

Choose the worst stories. Many old folk tales contain racist and sexist language. Some are simply unreadable. Establish your own threshold of tolerance for abhorrent language and plots. If a story goes too far for you, put it aside. For example, I will *never* read any of the horrible stories spread by the Nazis about the fictional crimes of the Jewish people, even for historical purposes. Other stories in which people are abused or treated as property I find difficult to read (though some stories relate abuses without condoning them).

As a reader, you have the right to walk away from any story at any time. But be careful not to place your threshold of tolerance *too* low. Remember when I said (on page 171) that listening can't make you wrong any more than it can make someone else right? The same is true when it comes to folk tales.

### You must be respectful

Many folk tales would make terrible novels. They can be tedious, rambling, even pointless. Sometimes you'll read a folk tale and you'll think, "What was *that*?" But don't let their superficial flaws blind you to their deeper messages, which can be valuable.

Here's one of my favorite folk tales. Once a lamb was drinking from a stream.[70] A tiger came rushing up and said, "Why are you muddying my stream?" The trembling lamb said, "How can I muddy your water? I'm down here and you are up there." "But you did it yesterday," growled the tiger. "I wasn't even here yesterday," replied the lamb. Then the tiger tried to blame the lamb's mother and father, but the lamb was an orphan. Finally the tiger said, "I don't care. It must be your grandfather or great-grandfather who has been muddying my stream. So I'm going to eat you." And he did.

When I read that story some twenty years ago, it stuck with me. There were a hundred stories in that book, and I've read many other books, but that one story has stuck with me ever since. I don't know why it matters to me, but it matters to me.

As you read folk tales, you will find stories that matter to you. They will become markers on your map, places you go when you need to think things through. It is hard to overestimate the value of such resources. But here's the thing: you can never tell in advance which stories are going to matter to you. Raise every story you read to your level. Take it seriously, no matter how strange or stunted it appears, because it might be the story you need.

My final instruction to you is to *kill these instructions*. When you don't need them anymore, stop using them. Develop your own guide to working with organization and self-organization. When you are ready, pass on your instructions to someone else who needs them. And the great wheel of human understanding will continue to turn.

# 9 Connecting the Dots

*Thinking about what happens when both forces are (or seem) weak*

In this last chapter of the book, we will consider what happens when organized plans and self-organized patterns are weak and isolated—or when they only *seem* so. This is the most powerful of the seven spaces. It is also the most challenging to use in practice. That's why this chapter is longest and last.

## Nothing to see here?

At first glance, this thinking space seems like it should be about situations with *indisputably* few connections: states of emptiness, voids. There are such situations, and people do study them. Astronomers study sparse molecules in space. Oceanographers search the deep sea floor for signs of life. Practitioners of meditation learn to empty their minds of thought.

But as anyone who understands these situations will tell you, they are far from empty. The vastness of space is filled with waves of electromagnetic energy and the swelling curves of spacetime. Encounters among solitary animals on the ocean floor, though rare, can have lasting impacts. When a male deep-sea anglerfish encounters a female of its species, it latches on and remains attached for the remainder of its life. And meditative practices do quell roving thoughts, but they do it by maintaining strong self-regulatory neural patterns. It turns out that emptiness is only empty when you don't know what to look for.

So the most important thing about low-connection situations is not emptiness. It is *perception,* the work we do to connect what we see into coherent explanations we can use. Dots, after all, are unconnected by definition. When we say we have "connected the dots" to arrive at a conclusion, what we really mean is that we have *built* connections between the dots. We have chosen to act *as if* the dots were connected, even though we *know* they are not, because we think doing so will help us in some way. For each connection we build, the question we ask is not "Is there a connection here?" but "To what extent would a connection here be *useful,* right here and right now?"

For example, in this image, is the downward-pointing triangle real? It depends on what you mean by "real," doesn't it? In a literal sense, the triangle does not exist. The circles and lines are unconnected. But in another sense it *does* exist, in the *relationships* among the circles and the lines. Whether the triangle is real or imaginary is a *choice,* not a condition.

The triangle that is and isn't there is called the Kanizsa triangle.[1] It was created by Gaetano Kanizsa in 1955 to demonstrate the phenomenon of *perceptual completion*, or the tendency to fill in gaps in fragmented images. Perceptual completion has been experimentally confirmed in insects, birds, and mammals.[2] It helps us make sense of connections that may or may not *actually* exist, but seem to exist *enough* to merit our attention.

## Do these dots really belong together?

Connecting the dots has obvious survival advantages. Wary prey survive; watchful predators eat. But the instinct is vulnerable to manipulation.

Polyphemus moths have pigmented spots on their back wings that resemble the eyes of the great horned owl, a predator of the mice and small birds that feed on them. When these moths are threatened, they rapidly open and close their wings, causing the eyespots to flash into view. Their predators connect the dots into patterns of danger and leave them alone.[3]

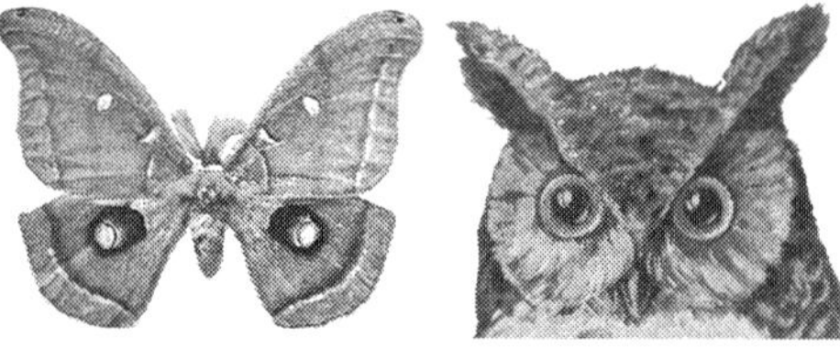

There are two competing explanations for the fact that moth predators avoid prey with eyespots. According to the *mimicry* hypothesis, they believe they are actually seeing the eyes of their own predators. According to the *conspicuous signal* hypothesis, they believe no such thing; they are simply alarmed by the unexpected colors and shapes. Experimental studies have shown mixed results. Square and triangular spots seem to alarm moth predators about as well as eye-shaped spots. But spots that are not in pairs or that appear in the wrong places (i.e., not where the eyes should be) tend not to elicit avoidance responses.[4]

It is possible that both hypotheses are correct.[5] If you could *ask* a mouse whether it thought it was seeing an owl or just some bright spots, its answer might be equivocal. It might say, "I'm not sure what's going on here, but I do know it's making me nervous. I'd better back off." If a vague sense of peril saves a mouse's life often enough—that is, if the bright spots *are* the eyes of an owl once in a while—the instinct to flee will be passed on, as will eyespots.

In human affairs, we often say that the great scientists who brought health and prosperity to billions of people "connected the dots" when they found solutions to longstanding problems. For example, August Kekulé famously claimed that he discovered the ring shape of the benzene molecule during a nap in which he dreamed that he saw a snake seizing its own tail. Less often noted is his addendum to the story: "We must take care, however, not to publish our dreams before submitting them to proof by the waking mind."[6]

As Rob Brotherton pointed out in his book *Suspicious Minds*, conspiracy theorists also claim to have "connected the dots" when they tell us that our lives are being controlled by secret government plots, globalist cabals, or alien visitors. Says Brotherton: "A brain biased toward seeing meaning rather than randomness is one of our greatest assets. The price we pay is occasionally connecting dots that don't really belong together."[7]

We are all being told every day that one pattern or plan is real and another is not, and we all need to connect the dots as we decide what to believe and what to do. Which candidate is telling the truth? Which corporation does what it says it does? Which choice is better for our families? Exploring whether the dots we connect, and the dots other people connect, "really belong together" is something we could all use some help with.

## The connecting-the-dots thinking space

This thinking space explores situations in which *anyone* believes that *any* connection does or does not exist enough to merit attention. This includes situations in which one person or group sees one connection as indisputable and another sees a different connection as equally indisputable.

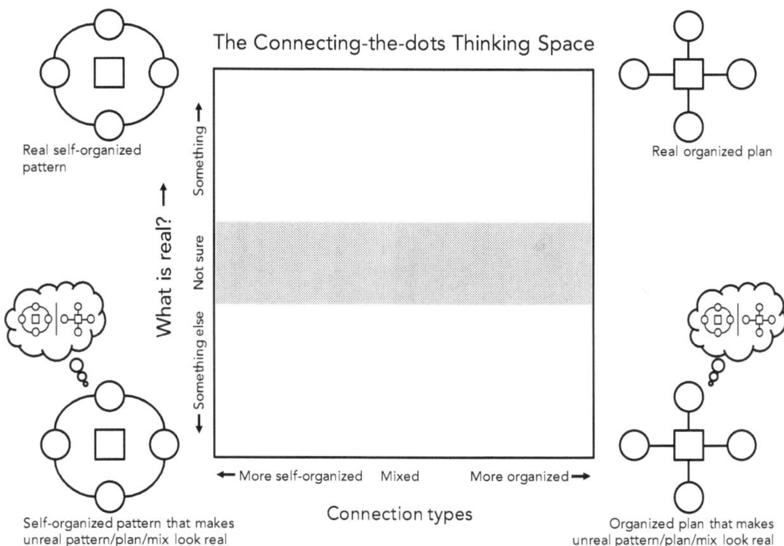


The horizontal dimension of the space compresses the two axes of the confluence space into one: more self-organized towards the left side, more organized towards the right side, and mixed in the middle.

The shaded area that runs across the middle of the space is not a dividing line. It is a broad twilight zone of doubt and uncertainty across which ambiguous situations wander. The further our perception moves from the zone of uncertainty, the stronger our perception of truth or falsity becomes.

Above the shaded area, a self-organized pattern (on the left), an organized plan (on the right), or a mixture of both (in the middle) gathers strength as it ascends. For example, you might look up into the sky and see a flock of birds (on the left), a flight of airplanes (on the right), or both (in the middle). As you move up the space, you become more and more convinced that what you are seeing is real, with absolute certainty at the very top.

Below the shaded area, a self-organized pattern (on the left), an organized plan (on the right), or a mixture of both (in the middle) *creates the appearance* of a pattern, plan, or mix. For example, you might look up into the sky and see floaters on your eye that look like birds or airplanes (on the left), a giant painting of birds or airplanes (on the right), or both (in the middle). As you move down the space, you become more and more convinced that what you are seeing is not real but has been *caused* by something real.

Note that we are mapping the *cause* of the appearance, not the appearance itself. Thus the bottom corner diagrams show real patterns or plans that create false perceptions (in the thought bubbles) of real-*seeming* patterns or plans. On the left are unintentional causes: illusions, misperceptions, delusions. On the right are organized, intentional causes: lies, scams, hoaxes, jokes, works of art or fiction. In the middle are causes that involve both forces, such as a scam that capitalizes on confusion or a misunderstanding of a joke.

### This space is unique

Among the seven spaces in this book, this one is unusual in three ways. First, it explores an intentional act (perception) rather than a state of affairs. Second, it has a marked zone in the middle.

Third, in the exercise materials for this space, the upper Y axis label is blank. On that label you must write an *assertion*, a statement of fact or belief that the top of the space represents as real, true, or right. Without an assertion to define the top of the space, you run the risk of talking past each other.[8]

### Some quick examples

Now I'll give you an example of placing some perceptions of what is real and unreal on the connecting-the-dots space. Then I'll ask you to do the same.

#### Example one: Climate change

Here are some things you might hear people say about climate change. The assertion that defines which way is up is that *climate change is real.*

1. "Climate change is a real disaster, but no one is to blame, and we all must pull together to fix it." This statement is very close to the upper left corner. From this point of view, climate change is real, but it's not an organized plan. It's an entirely self-organized phenomenon.
2. "I don't know what's going on, but I'm worried about my grandchildren." This one goes right into the middle of the space, in the zone of uncertainty.

3. "Climate change is a misunderstanding, a sort of mass hysteria. It's going to blow over soon, you'll see. People have their fads." This one belongs in the lower left. It's not real, but it's not a lie or a trick. It's a misperception.
4. "Climate change, or 'global warming' as they used to call it, is a massive hoax whose goal is to extract power and money from the gullible masses." Lower right—climate change is a lie, and we've been tricked into believing it by people who are carrying out organized plans.
5. "Oh, it's real, and I know what caused it: greed. The people in power saw it coming, and they chose to keep making it worse for their own enrichment." At the top, and closer to the right than the left. The problem is real, and though it was not caused by an organized plan, it was made worse by one.

**Example two: Racism**

Now you try one. This time we will look at some things you might hear people say about systemic racism. The assertion for this group of statements is that *systemic racism is a real, pressing problem* that needs to be fixed.

1. "I know people from all different backgrounds, and we all get along fine. Sure, some people are struggling, but, you know, people are people wherever you go. It's a small world."
2. "Ethnic minorities are treated unfairly in housing, in hiring, in education, in the justice system. This is no accident. The system was *designed* to work this way. And it's working fine—for some. The good news is that it can be *redesigned*. We can build a more equitable society."
3. "I'm just trying to live my life. I try to get along with everybody. I'll go along with what other people think is right."
4. "What do things that happened hundreds of years ago have to do with my life today? I think some people play the race card to get a free ride."
5. "People are tribal. It's built in to the human psyche. It only makes sense that people want their own tribe to have the most power and money. May the best tribe win, I say."

The exercise is to place these statements based on how they fit into the space *as defined by the assertion at the top*. Whether you or I agree or disagree with the statements does not affect their placements.

**Example three: Inequality**

This third example is a little harder. It has more statements, and they aren't as easily classifiable. The assertion this time is that though extreme income inequality exists, it is not a *real* problem, and it requires no solution.

1. "Income inequality will always be with us to some extent, but we can set limits. Everyone should have the right to affordable health care, child care, retirement, and higher education. Of course, by 'affordable' I don't mean free. People shouldn't be getting handouts."

2. "The rich get richer and the poor get poorer. I like it that way, because *I* plan to get rich. Someday."
3. "People have been unequal since the beginning of time. We are *born* unequal. Income inequality, even when it's extreme, is *natural*. There's no point trying to *do* anything about it. It's just the way things are."
4. "Right now I'm just trying to make it to the next paycheck. I sure would like some help, though. Seems like people like me don't get a fair shake."
5. "What does it mean to be rich or poor? I mean, some 'poor' people have strong communities, and you can't buy that. We need to look beyond petty things like money and focus on more important things, like friendship."
6. "I am a strong proponent of Universal Basic Income."
7. "I worked my way up to where I am today. Sure, I had some help getting started. But I worked hard. I don't see poor people working hard. Most of them sit around all day watching TV and eating junk food. Lazy bums."
8. "Unfettered capitalism is a disaster. The problem is, the only people who can change it are the people who benefit most from it. And *they* aren't going to do anything about it! It suits them just fine. The only real solution is to hold the moneyed classes accountable, regulate the markets, and pass critical economic reforms."

People everywhere have a mix of perspectives on these issues. Some of us have staked out a claim near one of the corners and don't plan to budge from it anytime soon. Some of us wander through the space, up and down, left and right, tacking this way and that from one day to the next. All of us are going to have to live with whatever comes next, and nobody can predict the future.

## A model of dot-connecting strategies

Have you ever seen a mirage? On a sunny day when the pavement is hot, the road looks like a lake? You've seen that, right? Of course you have.

What a strange question that would have been if I had asked it of you two hundred years ago. It would have been as if I had asked, "Have you ever walked on the moon? You've been there, right? Of course you have."

Before we had so many paved roads, mirages were rare enough that most people knew nothing about them, and those who had heard of them weren't sure they were real. Few people ever saw one for themselves. Sailors did, and desert nomads, and people who lived on particular shores, but hardly anyone else did. When people did see a mirage for the first time, they were not mildly amused, as we might be; they were frightened. Today, most of us can see a mirage on just about any hot summer day, if we bother to look. I've seen dozens, and you probably have too.

Isn't it amazing how something can be so rare in one age as to seem unreal, yet so common in another age as to seem trivial? Though things can also move in the opposite direction, from trivial to unreal. When I read the medieval-history novel *The Pillars of the Earth*, I had to laugh when one character asked another, "Do you know how to weave?" and the other replied, "Of course. Doesn't everyone?"[9] I laughed because I am one of the relatively few people today (at least where I live) who *do* know how to weave.

I saw a mirage a few months ago. That's where I got the idea to write about mirages in this chapter. My son and I were sitting on a bench next to our local lake watching the sunset. Across the lake, we could see a small peninsula that stuck out into the water. The trees on this little spit of land were reflected in the water. But the reflection was broken. It looked as if the tops of the reflected trees were hovering in the air.

It was a fascinating sight, like a glimpse of another reality, and it meshed perfectly with my thoughts about how we connect the dots as we try to make sense of uncertainty. When I got home, I started reading about mirages and how people have interpreted them over the ages.

As I read, it dawned on me that when different people saw the same mirages differently, it was not because they knew different things. It was because they were inclined toward different ways of deciding whether or not what they saw was real. *They had different dot-connecting strategies.* A model began to form in my mind, a model of how people decide what is real. And not only real: smart, normal, reasonable, correct, permitted.

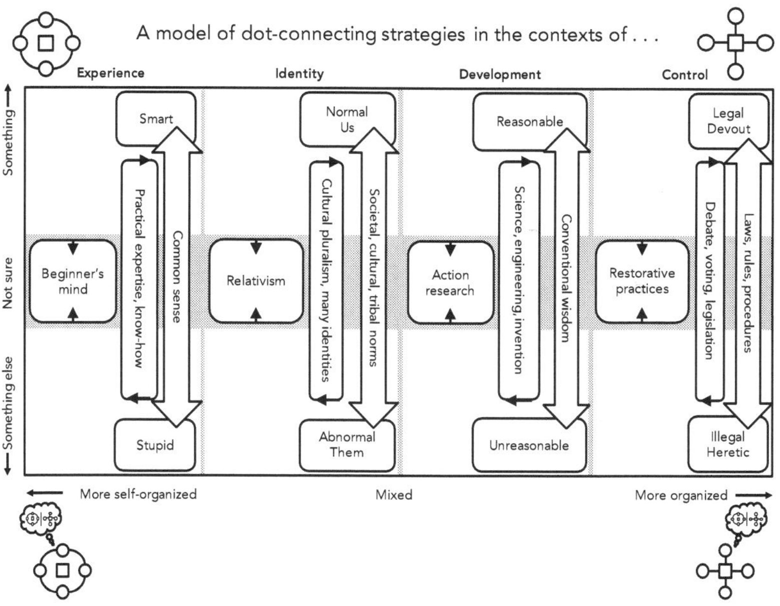


As you can see, I have divided the connecting-the-dots thinking space into four *contexts* within which we make sense of whether the things we see are real, true, and good. Any one of us might find (or place) ourselves in any one or more of these contexts at any time. Moving from self-organized on the left to organized on the right, the four contexts are as follows.

### The context of experience

As interactors, we work with limited information, but our interactions repeat over time, so *we learn from the patterns we see*. Individually, the context of experience rests on the solid ground of our biological existence: our sensations, impressions, and habits. Collectively, experience is shaped by our nature as a communal, collaborative species. It includes gossip, folklore, and folk wisdom.

### The context of identity

As interactors who also organize, *we make sense of who we are*. Individually, we negotiate our intersecting memberships in the groups to which we belong, those we have chosen to join and those we cannot escape. These identity memberships influence the choices we make by telling us how "people like us" do things. Collectively, the context of identity refers to cultural norms that negotiate the complex boundary between what is normal and abnormal within each group, within each society, and among all human beings.

### The context of development

As organizers who also interact, *we make things work better*. Individually, we improve our lives, families, homes, and jobs. Collectively, we improve our communities, organizations, and societies. Development includes scientific research, engineering, technology, and innovation; aspects of creative improvement such as art, music, and literature; and aspects of spiritual improvement such as meditation and religious study.

### The context of control

As organizers, *we shape the world* to suit our needs and desires. Individually, control means making decisions, establishing and enforcing boundaries, maintaining self-discipline, and expressing our opinions. Collectively, it includes governmental, cultural, military, and religious institutions, laws, political campaigns, diplomatic agreements, and wars.

## Three strategies

Within each context, moving along the vertical axis of the model, we can choose among three strategies: shuttling, spiraling, and focusing.

There are no shuttl*ers*, spiral*ers*, or focus*ers*. Strategies are not people. They are choices, and we all make many choices every day. We may shuttle with respect to one task or issue, spiral on another, and focus on a third.

### Shuttling

When we shuttle, we skip over the zone of uncertainty as a child would skip over a bad-luck crack on a sidewalk. We defer to sources of authority such as common sense, cultural or tribal norms, conventional wisdom, or the laws of the land. These sources of authority are often represented by specific people: teachers, doctors, therapists, religious leaders, political figures. They tell us that some ideas and actions are smart, normal, what "we" do, reasonable, legal, or devout. They tell us that other ideas and actions are stupid, abnormal, what "they" do, unreasonable, illegal, or heretical.

I call this strategy shuttling because when we do it, we are like a weaving shuttle that stops only on either side of the warp, at what is definitely true and certainly false—and nowhere in between.[10] We go to these positions because our preferred sources of authority are there, and they are there because they are sure. Any location near the middle of the space involves uncertainty and doubt, so we never stop there. We only shuttle from one certainty to another.

When an authority we follow tells us that something that *was* good is now bad, or vice versa, *we move with them,* and without a second thought. We might, for example, stop eating a particular food, or start, because our favorite doctor or fitness instructor has made a recommendation. Or we might go to a particular university or restaurant for no reason other than that a respected friend or relative went there. "That's reason enough for me," we might say.

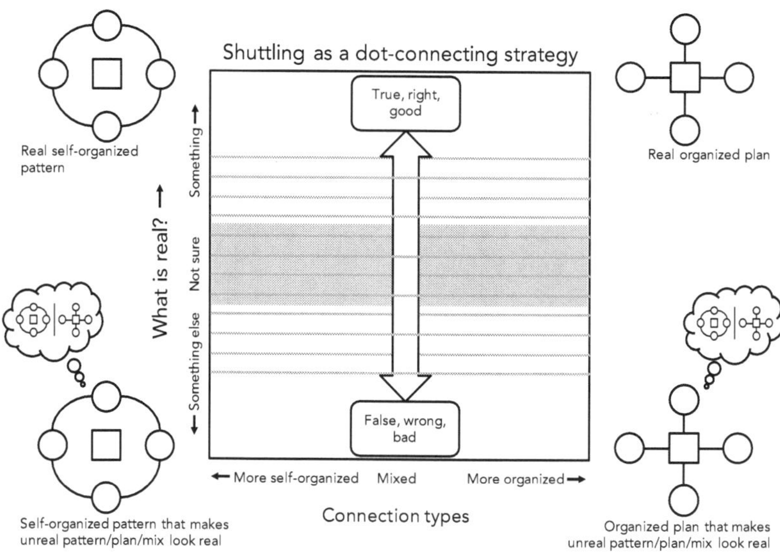


Do authorities have doubts? Of course they do; but they don't *express* them. That's what makes them authorities. "Authority" is one of those words, like "money," that doesn't come apart into roots when you look back in time. In ancient Latin, an *auctoritas* was . . . an authority, someone who gets to say what is true, and *does* say so. Some things never change.

One quick way to tell if you are shuttling on a topic is to make a list of people or resources you rely on when it comes to determining what is true and right on the topic. If you can rattle off such a list in a few seconds, it's a good bet that you have been shuttling on that topic. For example, if I'm in the grocery store and I see a favorite brand logo on a bottle of cleaning solution or a box of crackers, I put it right into my cart, barely noticing that I am doing it. If you asked me why I always choose that brand, I wouldn't have a ready answer for you. I must have made a decision about it a long time ago, but I can't recall it. I don't need to. It's a no-brainer, an action that requires no thought.

***Shuttling is easy***

Shuttling is a low-risk, low-responsibility option. That's what makes it so attractive. When we shuttle, we don't have to make any decisions on our own. We can just open up a can of our favorite brand of pre-made decisions and pour some out. If the decisions we pour out don't work well, it's not *our* fault; it's the fault of whoever made them.

Shuttling is also easy in that it is open to everyone. Nothing is required but our consent. We don't need to learn anything or pass a test or face scrutiny. We can simply say we did as we were told. It is true that authorities sometimes become discredited to the point that continuing to follow them results in criticism. But such moments are rare, and they are easily remedied by switching to another authority. Luckily, because authorities tend to benefit when people use their shuttles, there are always plenty around to choose from.

***Shuttling is oracular***

In ancient times, oracles in religious temples spoke in the infallible voices of the gods. Any apparent inaccuracies in their prophecies were taken to be failures on the part of those interpreting their words, not of the oracles themselves. The ancient historian Herodotus tells how Croesus, the emperor of Lydia, asked the oracle at Delphi whether he should send his army against the Persians. The oracle replied that if Croesus sent an army against the Persians, he would destroy a great empire. So Croesus sent his army. He did destroy an empire. It was his own.

Oracular sources of authority may be omniscient, but they are also opaque. You can't ask *why* they say what they say—well, you *can* ask, but you will receive a tautological response: what we say is right because it's right, and it's right because we say it's right. You can't ask an oracle what they want from *you* and whether they might be manipulating you to get it.

***Shuttling is constraining***

Shuttling frees up time and energy, but it also constrains us, in three ways. First, it's over-simplified. Authoritative answers are coarse-grained answers, and they usually don't address specific problems. Most of us have had the experience of falling between the cracks of government bureaucracy: too rich for one solution but too poor for another, eligible for help for one reason and ineligible for another. If you want an answer or a solution that is specific to your unique situation, you will not get it from shuttling.

Shuttling is also constraining because it relies on instruments of social control. Common sense, cultural norms, conventional wisdom, and laws give us only a *subset* of all possible answers. Because other answers are possible, we must choose what to believe about the things we have been told to believe. To what extent were we given these answers because they are truly the best answers—for us, right now? To what extent were they given to us in good faith, but in error? And to what extent were they given to manipulate us, to exploit us, to keep us in line?

Making *these* choices also takes time and energy. So in practice, most of us carve out *portions* of our decision-making universes within which we feel comfortable shuttling, and portions within which we don't. Few people would spend dozens of hours per week investigating the safety of each bottle of cleaning solution and box of crackers they find at the grocery store. But most people would take a few minutes to look up a medication their doctor recommended. And if their doctor suggested something more serious, like surgery, they would spend some serious time considering its pros and cons, and they might ask another doctor for a second opinion.

Finally, shuttling is constraining because it is not always available. It requires a certain degree of social stability to work. When even the most reliable authorities are out of answers, shuttling is not an option. Becoming too comfortable with shuttling can leave us unprotected in emergency situations.

## Spiraling

The strategy of spiraling is to energetically explore reality and unreality, moving in cycles or waves, plunging into the zone of uncertainty and out again on the other side, splashing part of the way into certainty each time—but never *too* far, to avoid becoming trapped in error. When we spiral, we seek answers through exploration, not consultation.

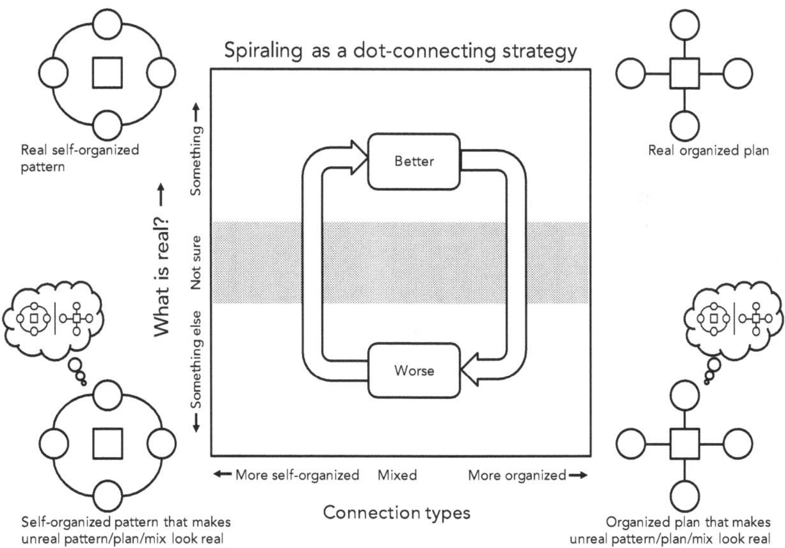


In the context of ***experience***, we spiral individually when we build hands-on skills such as gardening or hunting, and we spiral collectively when we pass on skills to new generations, accumulating knowledge over the centuries.

In the context of ***identity***, we spiral individually when we learn to balance our intersecting memberships: our gender, race, class, sexuality, religion, profession, and so on. We spiral collectively when we explore the multiplex connections among our social groups, celebrating our unity as human beings while respecting our cultural differences.

In the context of ***development***, we spiral individually when we enter into a serious course of study to improve our lives, spending years developing expertise in a field, experimenting and innovating. We spiral collectively when we develop research institutes, universities, and professional networks to learn together through cooperation and exchange.

In the context of ***control***, we spiral individually when we find new ways to motivate ourselves, relieve stress, manage anger, and be the people we want to be. We also spiral when we inform ourselves about the issues of the day in order to evaluate those who claim to be authorities. Collectively, we spiral when we debate issues, investigate problems, and come together in support or protest.

***Spiraling is progressive***

The aim of spiraling is continual, or at least periodic, improvement. Each level of the spiral is meant to be closer to an imagined positive future. Spiraling is powered by hope, ambition, and hard work.

***Spiraling is difficult***

When we spiral, we spend years or decades improving our skills and understandings. The solutions we seek elude us as we journey through wastelands of misinformation and swamps of confusion.[11]

But the work of spiraling is just one part of what makes it difficult. There are also entry costs, physical, financial, and intellectual. If you want to become an expert rock climber, for example, you must be in good physical shape before you can even begin to learn the art of climbing. And you must have equipment and free time you can devote to your passion.

The same is true in many careers. Take science, for example. When I was younger, I spent nine years working to become a scientist. But I never became one—not in my mind, and not in the minds of most scientists—because I never finished my Ph.D. That's a hard pill to swallow, but it's the way spiraling works. Nobody gets to say they're on level twenty when they're actually on level one.

Not only are there entry costs and barriers to spiraling, but anyone who spirals is subject to constant scrutiny. Rock climbers assess each other's skills. Chefs rate each other's meals. Parents evaluate each other's child-rearing practices. Scientists decide whether other scientists should be hired or fired.

You have scrutinized this book, and rightly so. I have been deeply aware of your scrutiny in every sentence I have written. It has made the book better.

Scrutiny is the irritant that creates the pearl of knowledge. It makes spiraling difficult, and it makes spiraling possible. Working without scrutiny may *look* like spiraling, but it isn't. It's more like pseudo-spiraling, believing you are making progress without actually getting anywhere.

Why is spiraling so hard? Because when we spiral, if we do it right, we gradually turn into the authorities who create the rules that are followed by those who are shuttling. Anyone who cannot spiral themselves up into greater and greater levels of skills and understandings on a topic cannot and should not gain the trust of those who want answers they can rely on.

### *Spiraling is dissonant*

The hardest part of spiraling is not jumping through hoops or living under the burning gaze of critical observation. It's *cognitive dissonance,* that awful feeling we get when our thoughts or beliefs break apart into clashing fragments. Seeking out cognitive dissonance means leaving behind comfortable certainties as we prepare for our next crushing plunge into the sea of uncertainty. And it is doing this not once but many times.

In my career I have developed what I call my "embarrassment rule." It says that if I can look back on something I wrote or said a few years ago and I am not embarrassed by it—if I do not cringe—it is a bad sign, because it means I am not making progress. I do actually look back on things I wrote in the past *looking* for embarrassment, and when I don't find it, I work on creating it. You should have seen me grimace when I read what I had written about organization and self-organization years ago. I could barely stand to look at it.

When I look back, I am always glad to discover that I have made excellent progress. But that doesn't mean I *like* being embarrassed. I hate it. I do not abide by this rule because I like it; I abide by it because without it I cannot get to where I want to go. And I only use it where it is absolutely necessary, for the things I care most about, like this book.

Anyone who spirals in any area of their life chooses to endure and even seek out the pain of being wrong, so they can move through it to something better. If you have never cringed, you have never spiraled.

## Focusing

The word "focus" was originally synonymous with a hearth or fireplace, the center of any ancient home. It was first used metaphorically in the seventeenth century to refer to a point of convergence, such as between rays of light in a lens. When we focus, we concentrate our attention on the central zone of uncertainty, the point of convergence between reality and unreality.

The best description of focusing I have ever read is in the book *Arctic Dreams* by Barry Lopez.

> No culture has yet solved the dilemma [of] how to live a moral and compassionate existence when one is fully aware of the blood, the horror, inherent in all life, when one finds darkness not only in one's own culture, but within oneself. If there is a stage at which an individual life becomes truly adult, it must be when one grasps the irony in its unfolding and accepts responsibility for a life lived in the midst of such paradox. One must live in the middle of contradiction, because if all contradiction were eliminated at once,

> life would collapse. There are simply no answers to some of the great persistent questions. You continue to live them out, making your life a worthy expression of a leaning into the light.[12]

When we focus, we lean into the light that lies between reality and unreality. We accept that our lives are being lived in the midst of paradox, and we *stay with* that acceptance. We don't run away from it, and we don't try to resolve it. We just live with it.

This is the third answer to the question of what is real. The first answer is "*I* can tell you; listen to *me*." The second answer is "Let's figure it out." The third answer is "I don't know, but this floor isn't going to mop itself."

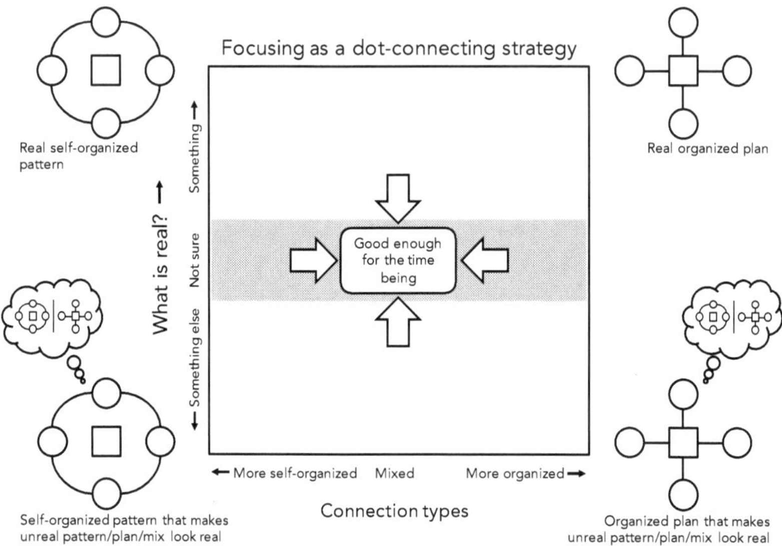


Focusing is a natural fit for situations whose contradictions cannot be easily resolved. If you care for children, for example, or improvise music, or provide health care, or train animals, or work in law enforcement, or facilitate dialogue, or even write books, you won't get far if you don't know how to focus.

Everyone is talking these days about jobs computers and robots can do better than we can. Focusing is what's left over: the things we still do best. Computers and robots excel at shuttling, and they are getting better at spiraling. But by the time they are able to focus as well as we can, they will essentially *be* us, and they'll want the rights we have, and we'll be back to square one again.

***Focusing in the context of experience***

The ancient Zen practice of *beginner's mind* calls for emptying our minds of the things we know and suspending our beliefs about what is real and right so we can see things anew. This does not mean *abandoning* our beliefs, but it does mean getting some distance from them so we can see them more clearly.

In the words of the Aikido master Seigo Yamaguchi:

> The ancient masters stated that we must not be content to pluck out only our bad habits. Our good habits as well, must be eradicated. Our bad habits . . . are easily recognized by all. . . . Compared with this, our good habits are firmly assumed to be definite attributes and real virtues. The harmful effects of these are seldom realized. No matter how good we may believe we are, let us remain aware that we are still immature and imperfect.[13]

That seems like a tall order. Eradicate your *good* habits? Yes, to find out if they are flawed. It makes perfect sense, but it's not easy.

A related concept is *negative capability*. Just as negative space is what we see between objects in an image, negative capability is what we use when we linger in the space between reality and unreality. This is not an ancient tradition, and it's not a school of thought. It's just a few tantalizing words. The poet John Keats mentioned negative capability in an 1817 letter to his brothers. He was talking with a friend when:

> [I]t struck me what quality went to form a Man of Achievement . . . I mean Negative Capability, that is, when a man is capable of being in uncertainties, mysteries, doubts, without any irritable reaching after fact and reason—Coleridge, for instance, would let go by a fine isolated verisimilitude . . . from being incapable of remaining content with half-knowledge.

A *verisimilitude* is a thing that might or might not be true, but is useful in either case. A novel about a family, for example, can help us think about families even though the family in the novel does not exist. Negative capability is itself a fine isolated verisimilitude, a hint at what might be possible, and it has been bouncing around in people's heads ever since Keats jotted it down. It's not exactly the same thing as beginner's mind, but it lives in the same city of thought, and it fits into the same spot in my model.

***Focusing in the context of identity***

In the context of identity, shuttling draws our attention to the differences between cultures. Spiraling favors cultural *pluralism*, which attempts to reconcile those differences within a single set of universal human values. The focusing approach to identity is cultural *relativism*.

From a relativistic perspective, we can say nothing about a person's beliefs, choices, or actions without understanding the details of their life. What seems real and right to one person can seem strange and wrong to another *without either person being strange or wrong*.

Relativism is often misunderstood as a belief that "anything goes," even such obvious evils as slavery and genocide. But "anything goes" is a universal claim that no relativist would make. Instead, they would say that from their perspective, in the context in which they live, slavery and genocide are obvious evils. But a relativist would add that had they lived in another place at another time, they might have said something different.

To some extent, this is a freeing prospect. I am a person who lives in a specific time and place, and I cannot be expected to understand everything and make every decision perfectly. But it is also frightening. Who would I *be* in another time and place? How would I behave? Would I *like* myself?

To a relativist, *all truth is verisimilitude.* That is, whether a particular statement is true or false matters less than whether it is useful or useless. A true relativist would apply the same logic to relativism itself. Understanding the details of a person's life before judging their beliefs and actions seems like the most useful thing to do—or at least it seems so to me, right here, right now.

***Focusing in the context of development***

When you want to study natural phenomena like storms or waves, spiraling is the strategy of choice. Its careful attention to detail leaves no stone unturned. But studying *people* is different. Studying people *changes* people. It's impossible to conduct research on people without them reacting to it. If I knew I was part of a study on how people exercise, I could not help but exercise differently, even if I had no idea what aspect of exercise was being studied.

Traditional sociological and psychological research attempts to minimize "experimental contamination" using a variety of tests and checks, ensuring validity, reliability, and repeatability. *Action* research takes a different stance. Instead of trying to pull research and action away from each other, it pushes them together by pursuing learning and change at the same time.

For example, traditional social research separates people into three groups: those who are studied (the researched), those who carry out the study (researchers), and those who fund or support the study (the researched for). Action research brings all of these people into *one* group of co-researchers. It asks each participant to bring their goals, assumptions, and ideas to the table so they can create a project that will help everyone.

Action research can get messy. Conflicts can arise and discussions can get heated. But a mess can be a good thing. It can mean that necessary, if difficult, discussions are finally taking place, and that people are able to move forward together in ways they never could before. As researcher Tina Cook put it:

> Engaging in action research, research that can disturb both individual and communally held notions of knowledge for practice, will be messy. Investigations into the 'messy area', the interface between the known and the nearly known . . . reveal [the mess] as a vital element for seeing, disrupting, analysing, learning, knowing and changing.[14]

Action research is a sort of collective beginner's mind. A community can use an action research project to examine its habits, both bad and good, and take a fresh look at the way things are and the way things could be.

***Focusing in the context of control***

In the context of control, shuttling means obeying and enforcing the laws of the land. Spiraling means debating and voting on those laws. Focusing means looking *beyond* laws to the underlying conditions that make a community healthy and strong. Restorative practices seek to bring back the health of damaged communities while preventing conditions that could cause further damage. The best known such practice is restorative justice.

In communities with restorative justice programs, victims and offenders are given opportunities to talk to each other about what has happened to them. They speak in safety—only in person if both agree—with a trained facilitator who knows how to support and prepare each of them for the process. As they speak, whether it's face-to-face or via letters or videos, the victim expresses their anger and fear, knowing that the offender is listening. The offender attempts to explain why they did what they did, and the victim gets some answers to their questions. Even if those answers are messy, awful, unsatisfying answers, they are still better than no answers at all. Both victim and offender are helped to make some sense of what happened. And eventually, sooner this way, both people may once again become capable of contributing to the community.

According to one participant in a restorative justice process, a man who was brutally attacked:

> Restorative justice introduced an element of humanity into a situation which had dehumanised both [my attacker] and myself. The process may seem difficult, but I think victims and offenders can get so much out of it. The only way to resolve conflicts between people is to sit together, talk, and find a way to move forward.[15]

Like many other forms of focusing, restorative justice is not easy. It requires courage on both sides, and a positive outcome is in no way guaranteed. But many participants have said it lessened the weight they had to carry.

***Focusing is universal***

Focusing is open to everyone. There are no entry costs, no barriers, and no tests. You have only to step into the zone of uncertainty and learn as you go.

***Focusing is humbling***

Focusing is a different experience for everyone who uses it, every time they use it. You can get better at focusing, but you can't "level up" in the same way you can with spiraling. In fact, you can only begin to succeed at focusing once you *give up* the idea of finding a single solution that will work in all situations. If you try to find such a thing, focusing will keep setting you back to square one. Ask any experienced teacher if they've ever encountered a student who made them feel like they knew nothing about teaching. Or ask anyone who deals with messy, uncertain situations for a solution that will work for everyone, everywhere, all the time. They will just laugh and tell you to get back to work.

Focusing is also humbling because it renders you vulnerable to attack. When your answer to "What do you do?" is "Whatever works," it can seem to the uninformed like you're saying you don't know what you are doing. What you *actually* mean is the opposite, but it can be hard to explain.

Still, focusing is rewarding for the same reason it is humbling: you're right there in the action, and that can feel wonderful. Leaning into the light never gets old. When you focus, at least you know you are alive.

#### *Focusing is surprising*

Focusing is one surprise after another. If you think you've been focusing, and you haven't been surprised, you haven't been focusing. Unlike shuttling and spiraling, focusing both expects and welcomes surprise.

Shuttling eliminates surprise by rewriting the past. In the 1940s, for example, when everyone suddenly stopped dressing baby boys in pink and started dressing them in blue, not only did the style change; the *history* of the style changed. Today, few people are aware that pink was once considered a manly color and that blue was seen as the color of maidenly purity. A similar thing happened with wedding dresses, which only recently have always been white. The retroactive elimination of surprise is taken to an extreme in George Orwell's *1984*, in which the Ministry of Truth endlessly rewrites history to conform to the current party line.

Spiraling works to *avoid* surprise by methodically exploring every possible outcome. It's fueled by cognitive dissonance, but dissonance is not surprise. Musically speaking, dissonance is a clash between notes that exist but don't belong together. Focusing is more like the hum of a summer forest or a milling crowd. You might sometimes hear a hint of harmony or dissonance, but it's hard to be sure exactly what you are hearing.[16]

### Looking for balance

You may have noticed that as I described these three strategies, my sections kept getting longer. To some extent this has to do with familiarity. I don't need to tell you how to do what authorities tell you to do; they tell you that themselves. And most people are familiar with the spiraling that goes on in universities and research institutes. Focusing took longer because I wasn't sure how much you would know about it.

However, you could interpret the length of the previous sections as an attempt to *promote* focusing and spiraling over shuttling. You would be correct in that interpretation. This whole book is an invitation to spiral and focus more and shuttle less. I designed its thinking spaces and group exercise to help you improve your ability to work in and near the zone of uncertainty.

#### A world of shuttlers

What would the world be like if everyone shuttled all of the time? Well, obviously, *everyone* couldn't shuttle at once; one brave soul would have to *build* the shuttles everyone else used. That very solution has been tried several times in history. It's called *enlightened absolutism*, rule by one good and smart person, and it has not always been a complete failure.

The Holy Roman Emperor Joseph II famously followed the motto of "Everything *for* the people, nothing *by* the people." He believed that he ought to make every decision for every one of his subjects. And it worked—sort of. Joseph's reforms were enlightened by today's standards. He freed the serfs, improved education, granted religious freedoms, abolished brutal punishments, supported a free press, and promoted the arts.

But Joseph II was hampered by unrealistic beliefs about his power to single-handedly revise longstanding cultural norms. He was *so* sure he knew best that he paid no attention to signs of discontent that were obvious to everyone else. And his orders could be contradictory. He supported freedom of expression while harshly repressing those who criticized his policies. And he sometimes rushed headlong from one extreme solution to the next. Most of his reforms fell apart. Still, some historians argue that his unilateral actions eventually led to more substantial reforms than might have taken place without his influence.

### A world of spiralers

What would the world be like if everyone spiraled all of the time? At first glance, that sounds fine. We wouldn't have to deal with decisions other people made for us, and we'd all keep on learning every day. But learning about *everything* would use up a lot of time. Every little thing would balloon out into its own decades-long investigation.

Say it's time for breakfast, and you decide to have some oatmeal. But wait—*is* oatmeal the best thing to eat for breakfast? Have you read every word of every medical, scientific, and historical document that pertains to oatmeal and its effect on health, society, and the environment? And where did you *get* that oatmeal? From your local store? Do you trust it? Why? What brand is that oatmeal? Do you trust that brand? Why? Are you sure that oatmeal was grown and processed in the right way? What *is* the right way? And what's the best way to *cook* oatmeal? How does your microwave or stove work? Could you build one from scratch? Should you be using a machine you can't build from scratch? And what do those machines run on? Do you know how electricity works? Could you generate it?

Oh my. This is exhausting, and we've only started on one decision. No, spiraling all the time won't work either. We have to take *some* things for granted.

### A world of focusers

What about focusing? What would happen if everyone in the world focused on the zone of uncertainty all of the time? On the good side, all of our decisions would be our own. And we wouldn't waste years of our lives ramping up skills in every possible area. We could eat our oatmeal in peace. Every time we had a choice to make, we would look at our options, recognize that it was impossible to say which was *actually* better, pick the one that seemed best at the moment, and move on. To a perfectionist like me, that sort of life has a simple appeal.

But if everyone focused all the time, if everything was local and contingent, I would never have written this book. In such a world, we would need only *one* book, and it would be one sentence long. It would say: *Do what works for you right now.* There would be no point writing anything else.

In a focusing-only life, we would still make decisions, solve problems, and resolve arguments. But *we would never think big.* We would never formulate hypotheses or gather data. We wouldn't see any reason, for example, to develop microscopes and use them to look at tiny organisms. And we wouldn't study those organisms to see if they might be related to the times when we suddenly get sick and die. We'd just say "there's no way of knowing" and move on.

A beginner's mind is only useful as long as it's taken seriously but not literally. If a magical being came to you and said, "I can wipe out your knowledge, and you will remember nothing," would you *want* them to do that? I wouldn't. I've put in a lot of work to get where I am today, and though I know I'm far from perfect, I would not want to start all over again. Would you?

To have a mind that is both open *and* useful, we need to *balance* the three strategies. One way to improve that balance is to think about how, where, and when we shuttle, spiral, and focus, and ponder whether we need to make any changes. We can also use the three strategies to better understand how *other* people think, especially when they seem to think in ways that make no sense.

## Castles in the sky

Now let's return to the subject of mirages. As I said at the start of the chapter (page 201), my dot-connecting-strategy model emerged out of reading historical explanations of mirages. I noticed that different people did not simply place mirages in different areas of the connecting-the-dots space. They used the whole space differently. That observation led me to the strategies of shuttling, spiraling, and focusing. Now let's explore how the strategies apply to mirages.

Since ancient times, people have interpreted mirages in a variety of ways: as tricks of the light, hallucinations, deceptions, and glimpses of supernatural places and beings. These four interpretations fit into the four corners of the connecting-the-dots space. (That's another exercise for you: which goes where?) Let's start by going over the scientific explanation.

### It's electric

A wave is a rhythmic pattern that carries energy through matter or space. All waves, whether of light, sound, water, or the motions of subatomic particles, exhibit similar properties. One of those properties is that the speed of a wave is influenced by the environment through which it is moving. When a moving wave reaches a *boundary* between two mediums, it may slow down or speed up, depending on how its interactions with objects in the new medium compare to its interactions in the old medium.

Imagine that you and I go out walking one rainy day. At some point we walk right across our local town square. Because it's a rainy day, the square is empty of people, and we move at a brisk pace. The next day we walk across that same square again. But now it's a nice sunny day, and there are clumps of people scattered all around the square. We move more slowly now, *even if no one is in our way*, because we look at people and people look at us. Our speed is an emergent property of the interactions we participate in as we walk.

A light wave is an electromagnetic pattern that consists of two oscillating components: an electric field and a magnetic field. When a wave of light enters a pane of glass, its electric field interacts with the electric fields of electrons in the glass. The interacting fields create a *merged* electric field, which causes the light wave to move at a slower speed and with a shorter wavelength through the glass. In the same way that our sunny-day walk was different from our rainy-day walk, a light wave that has crossed the boundary between air and glass is no longer a light-and-air wave; it's a light-and-glass wave. When the wave leaves the pane of glass on the other side, it becomes a light-and-air wave again. (If there's air there.)

The same thing happens to ocean waves. When they near the shore, they bunch up and slow down because they begin to interact with the ocean floor. You could say that an ocean wave near the shore is not a water wave at all, but a water-and-rocks-and-sand wave.

### Turn and face the strange ch-ch-changes

Now we arrive at another property common to all waves: refraction. When a wave enters a new medium straight on, at a perfectly perpendicular angle, it keeps right on moving in the same direction, though its speed may change. But when it enters a new medium at a non-perpendicular angle, one side of the wave slows down (or speeds up) while the other side is still moving at its previous pace in the old medium. As a result, the wave turns, or *refracts*.

When you and I walked across that square full of people, every time you came close to a clump of people before I did, you slowed down, but I kept on walking at the same speed for a while, and our little wavefront turned.

You can watch refraction happening at the ocean shore. In the open ocean, waves move in all directions. When they approach the shore, they turn until they are roughly parallel to the beach. But this only happens in places where the beach profile is relatively shallow. Cliffs that rise steeply out of the sea are struck by waves from every direction—until they erode enough to build up a terrace or platform that slows down and refracts the waves that come in.

In the same way, light waves that travel from the sun to the earth pass through increasingly dense air as they approach the surface of the planet. Every wave that does not move at a perpendicular angle to the density gradient (that is, straight downward) gets refracted, curving towards the surface of the earth. This is called *standard atmospheric refraction*. It is most obvious at twilight, when many light waves are moving on non-perpendicular trajectories. That's why the sun and moon look a little squashed when they are rising or setting.

Because standard atmospheric refraction is familiar, we don't pay much attention to it. Astronomers pay attention to it; they have to adjust their telescopes to account for it. But most of us don't. Mirages are *non-standard* atmospheric refractions, which really just means that few people see them often. Throughout history, how people have made sense of mirages has been influenced by what was familiar—or standard—to them. This is still true today.

## Floating in the sky

There are two main categories of mirage: inferior and superior. An inferior mirage appears below an object, and a superior mirage appears above it.

Say you are out strolling along your favorite beach and you see this.

It looks like the boat is floating in the sky, but it isn't. The light waves that look like they are coming from *below* the boat are coming from *above* it.

Inferior mirages happen when the air very close to the ground is quite a bit warmer than the air higher up. Picture a summer day when the sand or pavement is so hot you can't walk on it with your bare feet. Or picture a crisp autumn day when the air is cold but the ground still retains some of the warmth of summer. Warm air is less dense than cold air, so the usual lower-is-denser gradient is reversed near the ground.

Light waves come into the atmosphere from space and bounce off dust particles and water droplets in the sky. If the air near the ground was not extra warm, the light refraction would be standard—that is, refracted downward, just a bit—and you wouldn't see the light waves that come from above the boat. However, because the light waves are refracted *up*, you can see them. As a result, in the place where you thought you'd see light waves that bounced off the *water*, you see light waves that bounced off the *sky*.

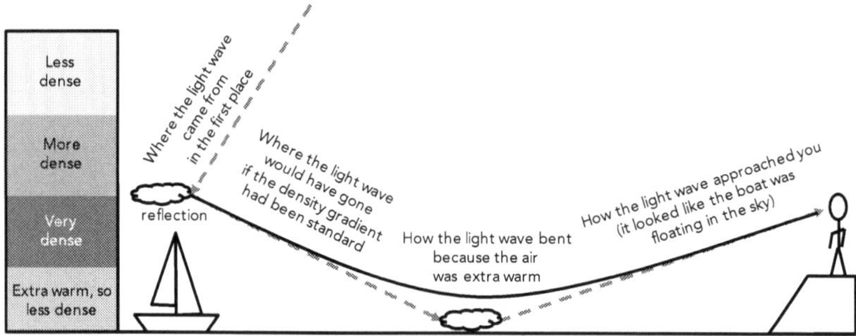


The mirage my son and I saw at the lake (page 201) probably happened because the water in the lake was warmer than the air above it, as would be likely in the fall. When light waves from the sky reached the extra-warm air near the water, they bent upwards, toward the bench we were sitting on. If that bench had been one meter higher or lower, we would not have seen the mirage, and this chapter would have gone in a different direction. That makes mirages an even more perfect example for a chapter about uncertainty.

## Hanging in the air

In superior mirages—which are less often seen, thus more mysterious—some number of "extra" images appear above an object. Usually at least one of the images is upside-down.

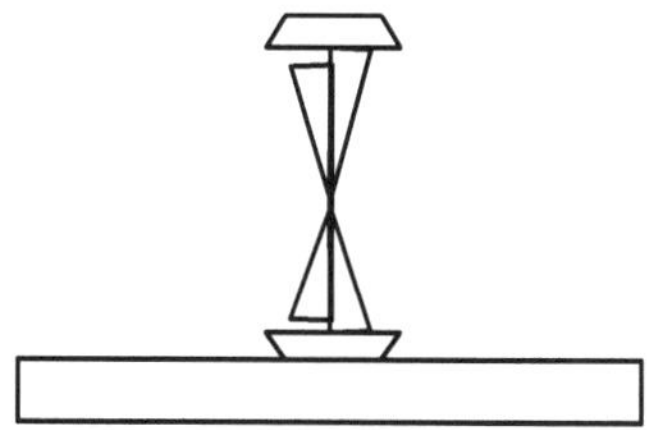

Superior mirages happen when the air very close to the ground is *colder* than the air above it. In this situation, the usual density gradient is not reversed; it is *intensified*. A light wave that bounces off the boat in our example would normally shoot into the sky, but because of the stronger-than-usual density gradient, it bends down to where we can see it.

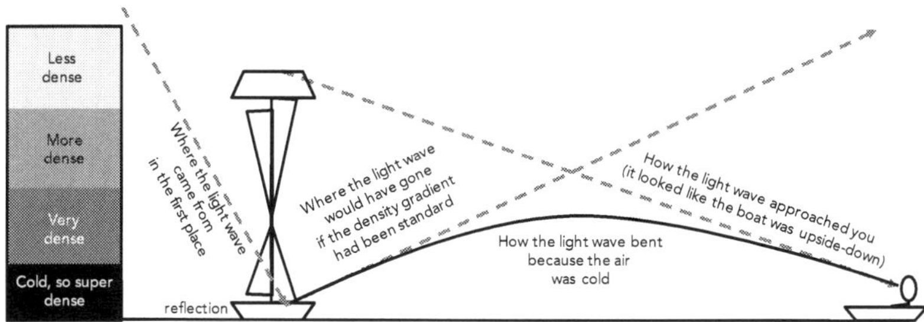


Why is the extra boat upside-down? Because the light waves that bounced off the top and bottom of the boat *crossed paths* on their way to you. It's like what happens when you look at your reflection in a spoon. The image is reversed.

Why can you still see the boat? Because light waves are bouncing around at *lots* of different angles. Some of them came from behind you, traveled over to the boat, and bounced right back at you. They were not refracted because they approached the density gradient in parallel, not at an angle.

Superior mirages can be much more complex than this. They can include four or more images, some inverted and some not, some elongated and some squashed. Some images may be magnified to the extent that objects seem much closer than they actually are. And mirages *move*. They shift up and down as temperature and density gradients change. It can seem as though a giant is tossing around buildings and trees, or as if the mountains themselves are walking around. Complex superior mirages are called *fata morganas*, after the European folk-tale character Morgan le Fay (of whom we shall speak later in the chapter).

Here is a 1907 newspaper account of a complex superior mirage:

> The passengers on the American liner Philadelphia bound for New York were recently treated to the unusual sight of a mirage of the French liner La Lorraine, which was at the time twenty-five miles ahead of the Philadelphia and slightly off the starboard bow. The reflection was of an inverted vessel sailing across the sky with smoke pouring from her stacks and with passengers walking about on her decks. So clear was the likeness that those on the Philadelphia could make out the officers on the bridge and the captain pacing up and down.[17]

I've never seen people walking upside-down in the sky. Have you? I've watched videos of superior mirages on the internet, but I don't think I've ever seen a video that captures the experience of seeing one in person. I'll bet it still feels mystical to see one, even when you know what's happening.

### Which one is real?

When you see a composite image like the right-side-up and upside-down boats, the obvious question is: Which is the *real* image? Which is the real boat? They're *both* real. They're both real images of a real boat. They just come to us riding on different waves of light. We're not used to that, so we think we must be seeing multiple boats. But the truth is, we never see *any* boats. We see waves of *light*, and we *interpret* those waves to figure out where there might be boats.

The best explanation I've ever heard of how we see things was given in an interview by the physicist Richard Feynman in 1983. The whole interview is worth watching, but this excerpt should give you the gist of it.

> If I'm sitting next to a swimming pool . . . I think of the waves, these things that have formed in the water. And when there's lots of people that have dived into the pool, there's a very great choppiness of all these waves all over the water. . . . [I]n those waves, there's a clue as to what's happening in the pool. . . . [S]ome sort of insect or something, with sufficient cleverness, could sit in the corner of the pool . . . and by the nature of the irregularities and bumping of the waves, have figured out . . . what's happening all over the pool.
>
> And that's what we're doing when we're looking at something. The light that comes out is waves, just like in the swimming pool, except in three dimensions. . . . And we have an eighth-of-an-inch black hole into which these things go. . . .
>
> Now it's easy to think of [the light waves] as arrows passing each other, but that's not the way it *is*. Because all it *is* is something shaking. It's called the electric field, but we don't have to bother

> with what it is. It's just like the water height is going up and down. ... There's this *tremendous mess* of waves all over in space.... and yet we can sort it out with this instrument.[18]

The reason we can see the world around us is because we are constantly making sense of the "tremendous mess" of light waves that come to us from all directions. We connect the dots every time we open our eyes.

A mirage is like an echo. It's a pattern that seems out of place until we understand where it is coming from. Echoes don't confuse or surprise us, because they are familiar. If you were walking in a canyon or a church, and you heard people talking in a place where they could not possibly be, such as high in the air, you probably wouldn't think you were hearing floating people. You'd just think the sounds of real people talking were bouncing around, as they do. And you wouldn't wonder *which* of the people were real. You'd know that they are *all* real; you were just hearing their voices coming from different locations.

Children *are* surprised and confused by echoes. That's why, when we take them to canyons and churches, they're always yelling "Echo-o-o!" By the time children grow up, though, they stop doing that, because echoes have become familiar to them. The same thing is *starting* to happen with inferior mirages, because children see them and ask about them as they are being driven around in cars on roads. *Superior* mirages are still rare enough that most adults either don't know they exist or don't know what to make of them.

## You aren't just seeing things

One thing mirages are *not* is optical illusions. They are optical *phenomena*, but they are not illusions. The Kanizsa triangle you saw at the start of this chapter was an optical illusion. A mirage is not.

An optical illusion is something *you* can see but a camera cannot. When you see a triangle in the Kanizsa image, you also know that according to the mathematical definition of what constitutes a triangle—a polygon with three edges and three vertices—*there is no triangle* in the image. That's what makes it feel so uncanny. If you fed the Kanizsa image to an image processing algorithm, it would not detect a triangle—unless you redefined the parameters by which the algorithm recognized a triangle, rendering them inconsistent with thousands of years of mathematical definition.

This image is called the Ponzo illusion.[19] An image processing algorithm programmed to detect lines of identical length would pick out the two white lines with perfect speed and accuracy. But we hesitate. That's because the apparent difference in the length of the lines is not in the image itself. It is in our minds. More specifically, it is in our use of contextual cues such as apparent distances to decide what we should "make" of what we see. Cameras see things differently than we do because *they aren't trying to survive in a dangerous world.*

This photograph shows both inferior and superior mirages. It is of Black Island in Antarctica.[20] It was taken three months before I wrote these words.

In the photograph, the tops of the mountains appear to be spread out; they look like plateaus rather than peaks. Those are light waves that bounced off the mountains part-way down, moved upward, bent downward, and got in front of the light waves coming from the mountain tops.

Under the mountains you can see an inferior mirage, with a messy inverted image of the mountains on the snow in front of them. Those are light waves that bounced off the mountains part-way up, moved downward, bent upward, and got in front of the light waves coming from the snow.

It's a fascinating image, and it's perfectly real. The photographer saw it; the camera saw it; I saw it; you saw it. There's no illusion about it.

Good photographs of complex mirages like this one are still hard to find. That's because mirages are short. If you hold up your index finger sideways at arm's length, it will be taller than most mirages. Mirages are also short in duration. Many can only be seen for a matter of minutes before the temperature gradients shift. Also, most mirages are fuzzy, and most photographs don't do them justice. This photograph happens to be exceptionally clear, but I was lucky to find it. A few months ago it didn't exist.

So that's the current scientific explanation of mirages. It belongs near the upper left corner of the connecting-the-dots space. Mirages are real, natural, self-organized phenomena, not organized actions. All other hypotheses than non-standard atmospheric refraction have been discarded for lack of evidence.

Now let's look at how mirages fit into my shuttling-spiraling-focusing model. We'll consider spiraling first, because that's what we've been doing.

### Spiraling on mirages

Where did the current scientific explanation of mirages come from? Mostly from spiraling. It came from people making observations, asking questions, testing hypotheses, and plunging into the zone of uncertainty over and over, each time learning a bit more and fixing a few errors.

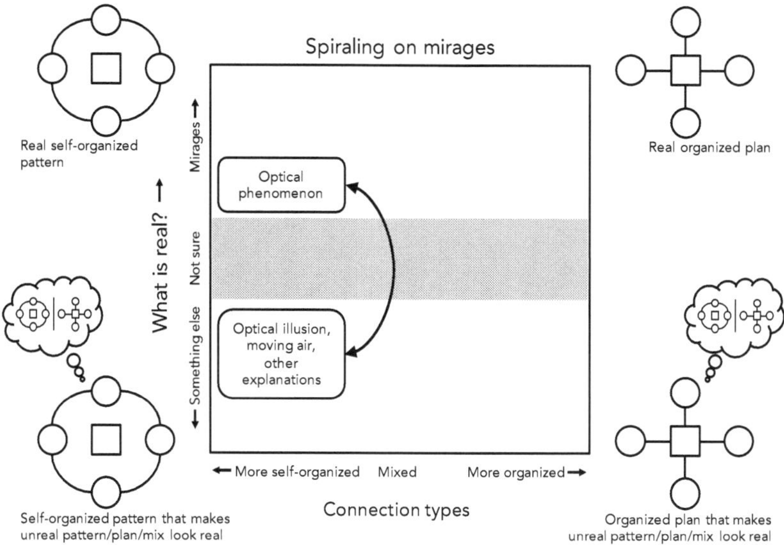


Popular articles about mirages often claim that "before the scientific revolution," they were unexplained mysteries. That's not exactly true. People had some pretty good guesses about them ages ago. Aristotle wrote in 350 BCE:

> Distant and dense air does of course normally act as a mirror . . . when there is an east wind promontories on the sea appear to be elevated above it and everything appears abnormally large. . . .[21]

If you consider refraction analogous to reflection in a mirror, that's not a bad description of a mirage. Also notice the mention of dense air as a cause.

The historian Quintus Curtius Rufus, in the middle of a story of Alexander the Great fighting barbarians, added this parenthetical note in 40 CE:

> Then too a mist, aroused by the excessive warmth of the ground, obscures the light, and the aspect of the plain is not unlike that of a vast and deep sea.[22]

An inferior mirage is not a mist, but it *is* aroused by the excessive warmth of the ground. More importantly, Quintus Curtius Rufus was not a scientist. His casual yet mostly-accurate reference suggests that mirages were not universally misunderstood even in ancient times.

Still, things did pick up quite a bit during the scientific revolution. In 1507, Antonio de Ferarris wrote:

> [A]s the strong south wind ceases . . . as it is warm, it raises tenuous mists, which reflect images of cities, flocks, and other things like a mirror. And like the vapors, those images are moved, as things are

> seen moving in mirrors that are moved.... [T]hose that are oblique and turned produce images, which we also see turned, as also in water we see the tops of mountains and roofs at the bottom.... For the lines of shadows do not proceed directly, but are transposed and intersect in the middle. This same thing happens in a concave mirror....[23]

Our current understanding of non-standard atmospheric refraction dates to the early nineteenth century. David Brewster's 1832 book *Letters on Natural Magic* covered a variety of optical and auditory phenomena. On the subject of mirages, he described an experiment in which one could produce an artificial mirage by creating density gradients in water and looking through them.

> [I]f saline substances, soluble in water, are laid at the bottom of [a] trough, the density will diminish upwards, and the figure [seen through the water] will undergo the most curious elongations and contractions.... [B]y thus creating as it were an atmosphere with local variations of density, we may exhibit the phenomena of the mirage and of looming, in which the inverted images of ships and other objects are seen in the air....[24]

Today, such demonstrations are carried out in every university physics course. If you want to see one in action, you can find videos of them on the internet, and you can set up your own demonstration at home.[25] I wonder how many of the people who watch such demonstrations today realize that they were first worked out two hundred years ago.

***Flashes of reflected light***

I will close this section with my favorite example of spiraling on mirages. An 1895 article in the *Detroit Free Press* described a dilemma faced by engineers who were surveying a sight line across Lake Superior. They needed to connect two stations on opposite sides of the lake, a distance of over sixty miles.

The engineers knew that "a straight line connecting the two would pass under the water for a considerable part of its length." However, they also knew that under certain conditions, atmospheric refraction across the lake was exceptionally strong. That is, *they knew there would be mirages*. So they placed mirrors at the two stations and waited for a mirage to happen. After two weeks, they were rewarded by seeing flashes of reflected light.

> The sun flash seen at one station from the other presented numerous peculiarities. It would sometimes appear single, then would split up into three, four, and even five different flashes—one over the other in a vertical line. Sometimes flashes would appear white, at others they would take the different colors of the rainbow. The line could be seen across generally after a storm, when the wind

> changed to northwest and cleared the atmosphere out. The conditions were the same as those attending the mirage which is frequently seen, especially on Lake Superior.[26]

People are still spiraling on mirages. A recent article in *Science Daily* explains how researchers created a "cloaking device" by heating thin sheets of carbon nanotubes with electrical stimulation. The carbon transferred heat into the medium immediately surrounding the object, which created a mirage-like refraction of light waves around the object, obscuring it.[27]

## Focusing on mirages

Now let's think about a different way of looking at mirages. Remember that bench my son and I sat on when we watched the mirage at our lake? Imagine how we would have experienced the mirage if that bench had been at our kitchen table. We would not have seen it once; we would have seen it dozens of times, at all times of the day, in all weather conditions, and in all seasons. And we would have had a detailed understanding of what the lake looked like when there was *no* mirage, so we would have known exactly what was distorted and how.

People who live in places where mirages happen often build up fine-grained experiential knowledge about them. Such knowledge is local and contingent, and people don't usually write it down. So it's difficult to find *direct* accounts of mirages written by people who were focusing on them. You can find *echoes* of such accounts, though, in the writings of people who were spiraling on mirages, because they sometimes *compared* themselves to people who were focusing. Scattered among the descriptions of mirages written by intrepid explorers are many parenthetical references to unimpressed locals.

It's easy to sense the exasperation in the words of explorers who traveled halfway around the world to see amazing sights, only to encounter people to whom the amazing sights were no more strange than what the explorers could see at home. In 30 BCE, for example, Diodorus Siculus described "marvellous" mirages in the desert, then grumbled that "the natives, who have often met with such things, pay no attention to the phenomenon."[28]

### *Come and see*

I think we can all recognize ourselves in Antonio Minasi's 1773 description of people rushing to see a mirage:

> So much is the joy that the vague spectacle produces that all men and women, ignorant and learned, rush to the sea to observe it as soon as the first "Morgana, Morgana" is called out.[29]

People who call out to each other that there's a mirage to be seen are most likely used to seeing them. Otherwise they would cry out other things, like, "What the heck is *that*?" Indeed, Minasi's story reminds me of times when people in my own family have said to each other, "Hey, come and look at this rainbow!"

Or, "Listen, I think I can hear an echo!" That's the kind of everyday familiarity I'm talking about, the kind that can only come from focusing.

Minasi went on to say that he had only seen three mirages in his life, and that he would rather see one again than "all of the most beautiful glances of the theatres of Europe." It must have seemed to him as if the people who considered mirages to be interesting but ordinary events were wasting something precious. I'll bet *they* didn't see it that way. To them, Minasi probably seemed to be wasting something *else*, something *they* didn't have, like maybe money.

You can see the conflict between spiraling and focusing when I add focusing to the connecting-the-dots space. It adds only one irritatingly small spot, and it's filled with uncertainty.

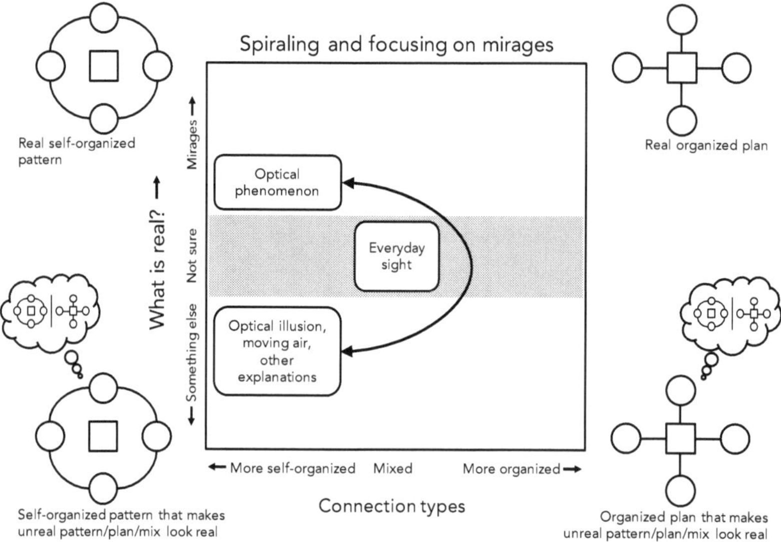


Keats would like that spot, but a lot of people wouldn't, and haven't—and we are all the better for it. Not wanting to stay in that spot led Minasi, Brewster, and many other scientists and scholars to ask questions that led to useful answers. After all, the science of optics brought us many of the technological wonders we rely on today.

On the other hand, if none of the available explanations of mirages helps you catch more fish, one is as good as another.

Even though I'm a big fan of spiraling, I tend to take the side of the locals in these who-is-wasting-their-time stories. That's because it bothers me that so many of the intrepid explorers exaggerated what they saw to impress the folks back home. Some of the drawings they brought home were of sights they could not possibly have seen. Consider, for example, this image from an 1896 book, *The Half Hour Library of Travel, Nature and Science for Young Readers*.[30]

No mirage has ever appeared that high in the sky, and no mirage has ever been that tall. Any local resident who saw such a drawing would laugh at it. That's one of the many difficulties of spiraling: it doesn't work if you don't stick to the facts. You can't level up on shaky ground.

**The nonchalance of deep experience**

I want to show you one more example of people focusing on mirages. In 1941, the German battleship *Bismarck* was sunk by the British cruisers *Norfolk* and *Suffolk*. Popular accounts of the battle claim that a fantastic mirage caused soldiers on the British ships to suddenly see the *Bismarck* steaming directly toward them at great speed. They changed course in alarm, only to see the phantom ship fade away into nothing.

That's quite a story, so I went looking to see what the sailors on the ship had to say about it. I was lucky enough to find the log entries written on the *Suffolk* during the incident.[31]

> 16. 0325 (B). Enemy appeared to be altering course to starboard, so circled to northward to open the range to 15 miles, and continued shadowing by sight from enemy's starboard quarter. (Norfolk known, and B.C.S. assumed to be to port of enemy).
>
> Note.- During the turn at 0325 the wind, now force 6, carried away the securing gear of the controls of the only aircraft on board, which was on the catapult, causing damage necessitating extensive repairs which took some days to complete. The aircraft was thus wholly unserviceable at a time when it might have been of decisive value.
>
> 0330 (B). Appreciated that enemy's alteration of course at 0325 must have been a small one to port, not a large one to starboard, though appearances had at first suggested the latter. Enemy's new course proved from the plot to be 220°, 27½ knots.

That doesn't sound like alarm, does it? Of course, it's a log entry, so it's supposed to be boring. But note the frustration in the middle section about damage due to high winds. Clearly log entries express alarm when it is warranted. Later in the log (at entry 0542) it says this:

> Enemy appeared to be approaching, and in case he had reversed course at 0538 (being "turned" by the Battle Cruiser Squadron), Suffolk circled to keep northward of enemy. It was soon realised, however, that the enemy was not approaching, the appearance being due to mirage, which also explains the similar (false) appearances at 0325.

I don't know about you, but "the appearance being due to mirage" sounds ordinary to me, as if you were to say, "I thought I heard something, but it was an echo." The choice of words is especially surprising given that the mirage *caused* the accident by which "the only aircraft on board" was damaged. My guess is that these sailors saw the uncertainty of mirages as a normal aspect of life at sea. (Which reminds me of a book from a previous chapter: *Normal Accidents*.) The nonchalance of deep experience is a sure sign of focusing. When you know something on a day-to-day basis, you're not amazed by it. You just *know* it.

## Shuttling on mirages

Spiraling on mirages is a group activity. People who are spiraling learn from each other, even if they live centuries or continents apart. Focusing on mirages is a one-person experience; it's just you and the mirage. Shuttling on mirages is a two-party affair. Someone makes the shuttle, and someone else uses it. Shuttle makers are some of the most important players in the knowledge ecosystem, because when shuttle makers fail, shuttling fails.

There are at least five groups of mirage-shuttle makers. We've already covered two of them. First are the *scientists* who do the spiraling we talked about before. Second are the *locals* who learn to live with mirages and pass on what they know to those who bother to ask them what they've learned.

### Curious minds want to know

The third group of shuttle makers is the *instructors*. These are people who explain mirages to other people, not because mirages are their life's work or they see mirages often, but because they explain *lots* of things to other people. Teachers, writers, and encyclopedists fit into this group.

To the technology-jaded, where-are-our-jet-packs people of today, getting worked up about optical phenomena seems as nonsensical as staring in amazement at the forks and spoons in our silverware drawers. But in the nineteenth century they were all the rage. People lined up in droves to see public lectures and demonstrations of things we barely notice today. Microscopes, telescopes, movie projectors, cameras, light bulbs, engines, and everything optical, electrical, or magnetic: it was all exciting once.

Is anything exciting today? Of course! Plenty of things are exciting today, but that's not my point. My point is that, even when people were excited to learn about mirages, many of the shuttles on offer were sloppily made. Here's a snippet from a newspaper article written in 1894:

> A wonderful mirage was visible in Buffalo recently, and it is remarked that scientists, with all their learning, have never yet been able to determine concisely the cause of a mirage.[32]

That's ridiculous. Brewster's book *Letters on Natural Magic* was published in 1832. And in it, Brewster mentioned that "It is only within the last forty years that science has brought these atmospherical spectres within the circle of her dominion."[33] So in 1894, when that newspaper article was written, the physics of mirages had been well established for nearly a *century*.

Can you imagine someone saying today that "scientists have never yet been able to determine" the cause of something that was described in a popular science book sixty years ago and considered by scientists to have been well understood *one hundred* years ago? Actually, scratch that, I can think of several topics on which people seem to be doing exactly that. But I'll let you ponder the question on your own.

Are mirage shuttles better today? Yes. But at the same time, people are still saying a lot of stupid things about mirages. The internet is littered with misconceptions about them. I had to wade through vast fields of stupid to put together the explanation I wrote for you. If you ever find yourself writing anything that claims to represent an authoritative, scientific view of any phenomenon, *check your work* using the abundant evidence left behind by those who have been spiraling on the subject for decades. The nerds are out there. Use them.

### Tell me a story

The fourth group of mirage-shuttle makers is the *storytellers*. Every region in which mirages often appear has its own stock of folklore about them.

Sadly, many travelers have misunderstood the function of folklore in the societies they visited. Antonio de Ferraris famously described the mirage folk tales he heard as "childish fantasies and senile ravings."[34] This was a deep misunderstanding caused by an *absence* of spiraling in a different direction.

Folk tales about mirages do not exist to explain the causes of mirages. Like all folk tales, they convey lessons about human life. When a folk tale says a mirage is a magic city in the sky, a doomed ghost ship, a demon who lures sailors to their deaths, or a delusion that torments thirsty travelers, every listener is free to take the story literally, symbolically, or in any mixture they like.

The uncertainty that is a vital part of all folk tales is neither a flaw nor an accident. It is a method of exploring uncertainties that cannot be resolved. Mirages, as uncertain images that lie between land and sky, provide valuable opportunities to explore *other* uncertainties of life, such as those that lie between gods and mortals, humans and animals, men and women, youth and age, health and illness, safety and danger, thought and action, kindness and cruelty, life and death. And no matter how well mirages are understood and explained, mirage folk tales will continue to provide such opportunities for many years to come.

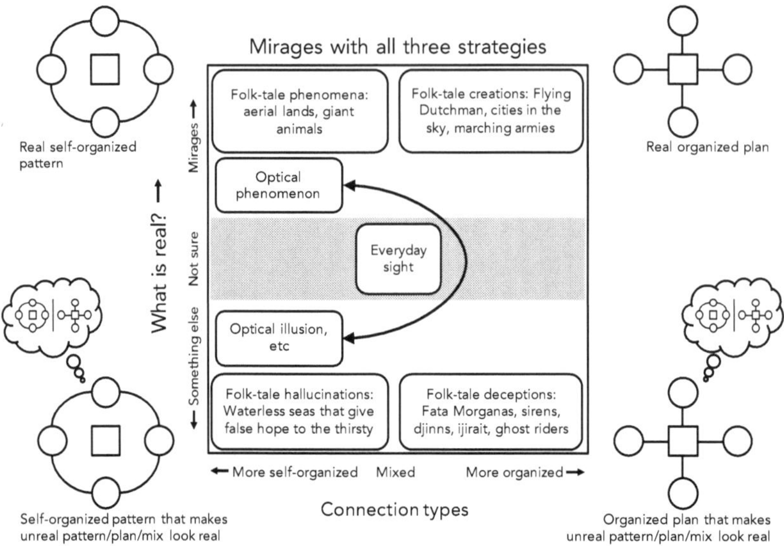


These are some of the most common lessons conveyed by folk tales that seem at first glance to be about mirages.

***Don't get too comfortable***

The most common lesson of mirage stories is that *life is contingent*. You'd better not expect too much stability in your life, say these stories, because strange things happen in the world. Folk-tale demons, fairies, and other supernatural beings don't just cause mirages; they are equally culpable for a variety of other uncertainties, such as the dangers of childbirth, earthquakes, storms, wars, and mental breakdowns. Such stories help people avoid becoming complacent in good times and despondent in bad times.

In Inuit mythology, a mirage is a sign that a supernatural being called an *ijiraq* might be nearby. *Ijirait* live suspended between the worlds of life and death, and their presence is said to confuse travelers and cause them to forget events. It is easy to say that such beliefs make no literal sense, but no one could argue that learning to accept the unpredictability of life has no utility.

Supernatural beings connected to mirages are often morally ambiguous. According to a web site on Inuit legends, "Some elders argue that these land spirits are not inherently evil, but rather misunderstood. . . . [They] believe that the *Ijirait* often appear to bring messages to travelers."[35]

Morgan le Fay, the European folk-tale fairy whose name has been associated with complex superior mirages since medieval times, is similarly ambiguous. Her connection to mirages derives from her deep magic, which allows her to change her shape as she flies through the air—and to control the air, the sea, and the minds of people. Her famed ability to heal wounds is matched by her equally famed ability to manipulate and deceive.

***The truth is out there***

Another common lesson of mirage stories is that *things are not always as they seem.* This theme may lie behind the many contemporary representations of mirages as hallucinations (seen only by those in distress) or illusions (seen only by those too gullible to question what they see). If that's true, while such accounts are factually inaccurate, they may be part of a long and honorable tradition that goes back thousands of years.

The *Yoga-Vasishtha Maharamayana,* an ancient Indian collection of wisdom, includes many references to mirages as metaphors for the impermanence of human existence and the need to ponder deeper truths.

> As the mirage appears to be a sheet of water to the thirsty deer, while it is known to the intelligence to be the reflexion of the solar rays on the sandy desert; so does the reality appear as unreal and the unreal as real to the ignorant; while in truth there is neither the one nor the other here, except the images of the Divine Mind.[36]

The popularity of the *Matrix* movies is a contemporary manifestation of the same need to explore differences between what is actually real and what only *seems* so. Now that inferior mirages don't work as well as they did to explore "life lived in the midst of such paradox," we need new stories—but the needs themselves have not changed.

***What goes around comes around***

Some of the stories that surround mirages convey the message that they exist to punish bad people and reward good people. For example, in 1811, John Leyden described the mirage "spectre-ship" called the Flying Dutchman thus:

> The crew of this vessel are supposed to have been guilty of some dreadful crime, in the infancy of navigation, and to have been stricken with the pestilence. They were hence refused admittance into every port, and are ordained still to traverse the ocean on which they perished, till the period of their penance expire.[37]

Today, the story of the Flying Dutchman has been replaced with new stories that fulfill the same function. This is most noticeable in the recent proliferation of stories about superheroes whose strengths flow from their friendships and their fair dealings. Like the crew of the Flying Dutchman, comic-book super-villains are often stricken with grotesque disfigurements and refused admittance into society.

***There's a land that I heard of***

A fourth message in mirage folktales is that *we need to hold out hope,* because we may find some measure of happiness someday. This positive message lies behind mirage stories in which people claim to have seen fantastical mountains, cities, and islands in the sky.

In 1817, Anne Plumptre described local folklore in Northern Ireland:

> At Rathlin a belief prevails that a green island rises every seventh year out of the sea between their island and the promontory of Bengore. The inhabitants assert that many of them have distinctly seen it, and that it is crowded with people selling yarn and engaged in various other occupations common to a fair.[38]

Did the people of Rathlin actually believe they were seeing people selling yarn on an island that appeared only once every seventh year? Or did a mirage help them *imagine* a place they wished they could visit? Maybe it was both.

In 2015, a grainy photograph of a city in the sky was posted on Facebook. It was said to be a superior mirage seen by hundreds or even thousands of people. But no details surfaced and no witnesses spoke up. Based on the unrealistic height of the image, experts concluded that the "floating city" was not a mirage but a photoshopped hoax. Still, it's a fascinating *story*, and its viral spread points to the continuing need to find hope for a better future—in the clouds or on a computer. In today's urban societies, mysterious manipulations of digital images fulfill the same function that mirages once did.

**Faraway places with strange-sounding names**

The last group of mirage-shuttle makers is the *politicians*. These people are like storytellers in that they use mirages as opportunities to spread messages. But their messages are of a political rather than cultural nature. In his book *The Waterless Sea*, Christopher Pinney explores both cultural and political conflicts in historical interpretations of mirages. Says Pinney:

> Mirage often has a politics: it is rarely if ever only the product of atmospheric optics. The narratives that attach to mirages and the exact nature of what beholders believe they can see reflect, in part, the concerns and anxieties of their times.[39]

Pinney highlights conflicts between "territorializing" representations of mirages, which are tied to particular cultures and places, and "de-territorializing" representations of mirages, which attempt to bring the entire world under the control of a context-free "global space of science."[40]

These two points of view seem to match my model categories of focusing—locally meaningful explanations built from lived experience—and spiraling—globally valid explanations built from meticulous observation and experimentation. This brings up the fact that focusing and spiraling can *compete* for dominance in shuttle creation. And that brings up thoughts about conflicts and compatibilities between scientific and indigenous knowledge cultures. I'm not going to explore the idea further, but I can tell you that scholars have been thinking about it for some time.[41]

## Connecting the dots of conspiracy thinking

Believe it or not, I had originally planned to write about several examples in this chapter. But I started on the first one (mirages) and fell down a rabbit hole. I suppose that's par for the course when you're writing about uncertainty.

Speaking of rabbit holes, I will finish the chapter by exploring how conspiracy theories fit into the connecting-the-dots space.

I will start with a disclaimer. I am no expert on conspiracy theories. I have read a few popular books and a few dozen articles about them, but that is all. I wanted to write about them because they connect so well to the topic of this chapter. Also, recent events have led me, along with many other people, to think about conspiracy theories more than I usually would.

I didn't want to prolong this book project by spiraling for the months or years that would enable me to speak with authority on the subject. So I'm *not* speaking with authority on the subject. Please take what I have written here as a set of intriguing connections for *you* to research—from one spiraling journey to another—and not as a shuttle, that is, an authoritative treatment of the topic. If you want an authoritative treatment of the topic, read the books I cite, or do some searching of your own.[42]

### Aspects of conspiracy theories

In his book *Conspiracy Theories,*[43] the philosopher Quassim Cassam describes six aspects of conspiracy theories that make them dangerous. When I read his book, I noticed right away that his six aspects connect to movements on my connecting-the-dots space. I also noticed that they can be combined into a useful mnemonic: ESCAPES. Conspiracy theories are Esoteric, Speculative, Contrarian, Amateur, Plan-oriented, and Self-sealing. (The second E is secret.) Also, conspiracy theories are escapes in that they offer an easy way out—out of uncertainty, and out of the effort required to figure things out on our own.

#### Everyday conspiracy thinking

You don't have to participate in a conspiracy *theory* to indulge in conspiracy *thinking*—that is, believing what you want to believe based on scant or nonexistent evidence. This style of thinking is also called *motivated reasoning.* Every time we try to guess what a person is "really up to," and our fears or desires about that person—or that *type* of person—creep into the guess we make, we are engaged in conspiracy thinking.

To some extent, the wariness that lies behind such thinking is a useful survival instinct. But wariness is only useful up to a point. "There is a fine line," says Rob Brotherton, "between healthy suspicion of potential threats and overzealous, unwarranted perceptions of sinister intent."[44]

Conspiracy *theories* come about when groups of people *coordinate* their conspiracy thinking, gathering around a specific set of beliefs. They are closer to political movements than to any other social phenomena. And like all political movements, they are created, spread, and maintained by networks of people who interact in both organized and self-organized ways.

Conspiracy thinking may seem like something only "strange people" do, but we all dabble in it, even if it's just a little. If you read about the topic, as I have been doing, it will only be a matter of time before you will run up against something *you* believe to be perfectly normal thinking that someone else considers to be conspiracy thinking. It happened to me, and it will happen to you. You'll be reading along, thinking "oh, those strange people," and then *you will recognize yourself.* I am not going to tell you what caused my own hey-wait-a-minute moment, but I suspect the experience may be universal.

But let's say you are absolutely certain your thinking is perfect, airtight, iron-clad. Conspiracy thinking is something you have never indulged in, not even a little bit. You could read every word of every book on conspiracy theories and never once recognize yourself. You may be correct in that assessment. In that case, consider this: people who get caught up in conspiracy thinking do not believe their thinking is conspiracy thinking. They believe their thinking is perfect, airtight, iron-clad.

It follows, then, that learning how conspiracy thinking works and how we can get ourselves out of it is something we should all do *just in case we are wrong*—and if not now, in the future. Consider it a form of mental insurance, like doing crossword puzzles now to keep your mind sharp in old age.

As I said, however, I am of the opinion that every one of us indulges in conspiracy thinking from time to time. Is there a person alive who has never thought *someone* was scheming against them?

### *The pen-stealing monster*

I remember a time, let's say I was thirteen, when I became convinced that another girl in my class had stolen my special set of colored pens. She even kept using them right in front of me—twisting the knife in the wound, I thought. With righteous fury I conspired with my friends to steal the pens back. As they kept watch over the empty classroom, I opened the evildoer's desk and snatched my pens out of it. But as soon as I had the pens in my hands, I could see that they were not my pens at all, though they did look an awful lot like them. In a state of shock, I put the pens back and checked my own desk again. My pens were there, in the back of the desk. They had fallen behind some books.

I learned an important lesson that day, and I never forgot it. I can still remember how *certain* I was that I was right, that the monster who had stolen my pens had to be stopped before she could strike again. And I remember the moment when I realized that *I was the monster,* that I had placed blame on an innocent person, that I had hurt someone by my rush to judgment. As an adult, the memory of that mistake has prevented me from entering into many other attractive certainties of much greater importance.

Have *you* ever been certain of something and then found out you were wrong? What was that like? Would you want to avoid being that wrongly certain again? Of course you would. We all need to guard against conspiracy thinking.

So I've included a few instructions to avoid falling into the trap of unwarranted certainty. There are many better resources than what I have written; but if you read nothing else, these hints should help you on your journey.

**The architects of conspiracy theories**

The people who conjure up conspiracy theories are no ordinary shuttle makers. Their shuttles are made of lies. Most of them are after money, fame, and power. Those few who lie with a greater purpose in mind, and the even fewer who believe their own lies, are, like their followers, looking for an easy way out—out of the need to convince people on the honest merits of their arguments, and out of the responsibility to seek out cognitive dissonance.

But conspiracy theories cannot be built out of nothing. Not every lie will shuttle well. So those who seek to create them search for *seeds of collective anxiety* they can encourage to grow. Like parasites, the builders of conspiracy theories feed on our inescapable concerns about future accidents, diseases, attacks, and losses. And we all have some of those.

The danger of falling prey to conspiracy mongers gives us a second reason to improve our skills at avoiding conspiracy thinking. We can't walk away from our anxieties about the future, but we can walk away when people try to *use* our anxieties to achieve their goals without having our best interests at heart.

Now let's look at Cassam's six aspects of conspiracy theories.

**Conspiracy theories are Esoteric**

Conspiracy theories draw some of their power from the special terms they use. Esoteric language, known only to those in the know, makes the claims of conspiracy theorists seem more valid to *them* while simultaneously making the claims seem more strange and suspect to those outside the circle of jargon.

Jargon can be a positive force. Cryptic language has been used to create entry barriers to specialist communities for thousands of years, in areas ranging from medieval alchemy to contemporary philosophy to knitting. Like a cell membrane, the shared language of jargon helps communities maintain a coherent sense of purpose and identity. Shorthand references to complicated concepts save time and energy that can be invested in common goals.

But a well-functioning cell membrane is not just a barrier. It is an active nexus of exchange between the cell and its environment. A network of pores, pumps, channels, and gates filters the passage of molecules through the membrane with as much bureaucratic red tape—and as much in-the-moment bargaining—as any political border crossing.

In the same way, healthy specialist communities cooperate and coordinate with a surrounding matrix of popular writers, documentary filmmakers, journalists, and teachers. These mediators stand between specialist communities and the general public, representing and negotiating the meanings of jargon terms, such as "standard atmospheric refraction."

In conspiracy-minded specialist communities, those who attempt to fill the mediator role do not find cooperation or coordination. Instead, their work is discouraged or even actively sabotaged. Why? Because those who build conspiracy theories seek to maintain *impermeable* barriers that prevent people (and their money) from *leaving* the community. The jargon of conspiracy-theory communities makes them easy to get into and hard to get out of.

***Function and dysfunction***

Before I show you how I have mapped esoteric jargon (and all of Cassam's six aspects) on the connecting-the-dots space, I need to explain some of the terms I will use on my diagrams. (See, I'm mediating my jargon.)

Some situations are certain, like sitting at your kitchen table eating breakfast. Some are uncertain, like driving late at night in a snowstorm. Our *perceptions* of those situations, our interpretations of them as certain or uncertain, can be *functional*—that is, they work, they make things easier for us—or they can be *dysfunctional,* causing us to make painful and costly mistakes. For example, it would be a mistake to spend your whole day deciding what to eat for breakfast, and it would be a mistake to assume that nothing could possibly go wrong while setting out to drive late at night in a snowstorm.

Combining the two dimensions of situation and perception, and pretending for the moment that such binary states exist, we arrive at four combinations:

| | |
|---|---|
| **Functional certainty**<br>Sure of what is certain<br>*Eating more vegetables will help you live longer.* | **Functional uncertainty**<br>Unsure of what is uncertain<br>*Which doctor is the best one for me?* |
| **Dysfunctional certainty**<br>Sure of what is uncertain<br>*Every government worker is corrupt!* | **Dysfunctional uncertainty**<br>Unsure of what is certain<br>*Are government workers actually human beings? Or are they aliens?* |

How can *uncertainty* be functional? Isn't it necessary to resolve uncertainties in order to make decisions? Not really. We all make decisions in the absence of certainty every day. For example, you've probably heard people say they are *weighing their options* or *sifting through the facts* or *looking at the pros and cons.* When people say those things, they mean that they are trying to make a decision knowing that they will *never* arrive at a state of perfect certainty. Have you ever weighed your options, and have you ever made a good decision because of it? If you have, you have experienced functional uncertainty.

Benjamin Franklin famously invented a pros-and-cons decision-making tool for precisely this situation. In a 1772 letter, he wrote:

> When these difficult Cases occur, they are difficult chiefly because while we have them under Consideration all the Reasons pro and

> con are not present to the Mind at the same time.... To get over this, my Way is, to divide half a Sheet of Paper by a Line into two Columns, writing over the one Pro, and over the other Con. Then during three or four Days Consideration I put down under the different Heads short Hints of the different Motives that at different Times occur to me for or against the Measure.... [I]f after a Day or two of farther Consideration nothing new that is of Importance occurs on either side, I come to a Determination accordingly.

Franklin called his approach "Moral or Prudential Algebra." Today it is usually called a *decisional balance sheet*. There are many variations on the basic form, some with additional columns and some with named rows. The tool is widely used in therapy to help people make difficult life decisions in the face of ambiguity. I've used it myself, and maybe you have too. The fact that Franklin's idea caught on so well and grew to such an extent shows that people must—and can—make decisions *without* resolving uncertainties.

What if you need to choose among several options, not just pro and con? There's a method for that too. I first encountered it in Richard Nelson Bolles' *What Color is Your Parachute*[45] and have used it many times since then. Bolles calls his method a *prioritizing grid*. Here's how to use it.

Place your options as both rows and columns on a table. For every unique row-column combination, compare the two options and write whichever one is better in the cell. When you have gone through all the option pairs, *count* the number of times you wrote each option. The one with the highest count is the best choice. For example, say I wanted to choose between four vegetables for dinner. I could make a table like this.

| | *beans* | *squash* | *broccoli* | *asparagus* |
|---|---|---|---|---|
| *beans* | - | squash | broccoli | asparagus |
| *squash* | | - | squash | asparagus |
| *broccoli* | | | - | asparagus |
| *asparagus* | | | | - |

It looks like I will be having asparagus for dinner, maybe with some squash. Methods like these help us deal with functional uncertainty every day.[46]

***Situations and perceptions***

So now we have four situation-perception pairings (from the previous diagram) to combine with Cassam's six aspects of conspiracy theories. That would give us twenty-four combinations. I don't know about you, but that's too many for *my* patience. So I will consider only one *contrast*: between functional uncertainty and dysfunctional certainty.

Why this particular combination? Because it offers the strongest contrast. Functional certainty is the optimal situation, but it is rarely possible. Beyond death and taxes, there aren't many things in life of which we can be absolutely certain. Maintaining a well-functioning sense of *uncertainty* seems the best practical option. Functional uncertainty leads to openness, and openness leads to learning—which may in time lead to some degree of functional certainty.

Of the two *dysfunctional* situations, dysfunctional certainty seems the worst. When we believe a situation is uncertain, we are more likely to be willing to learn about it. But when we are dysfunctionally *certain*, we are not interested in learning, and we may even be hostile to it.

So for each of Cassam's aspects, I will consider only the contrast between functional uncertainty and dysfunctional certainty.

***Mapping the influence of jargon on conspiracy thinking***

Conspiracy thinking begins with an *attractive possibility*: something that may or may not be *actually* true but is compelling to our emotions and desires. It could be a positive or negative thing, but it is always attractive. If the possibility is only trivially attractive, we may push it this way or that for a short time, but we soon forget about it, and it drifts into functional uncertainty. But if the possibility *matters* to us, if it connects to our identity or anxiety, whether we push the situation towards functional uncertainty or dysfunctional certainty depends on how much Cassam's six factors affect our thinking.

In the case of jargon, when we choose to use it—and refuse to explain it—we shrink the pool of people we can talk to about the attractive possibility. This gives us a safe space to express our anxieties, but at the same time, it reduces our opportunity to learn by being exposed to other points of view.

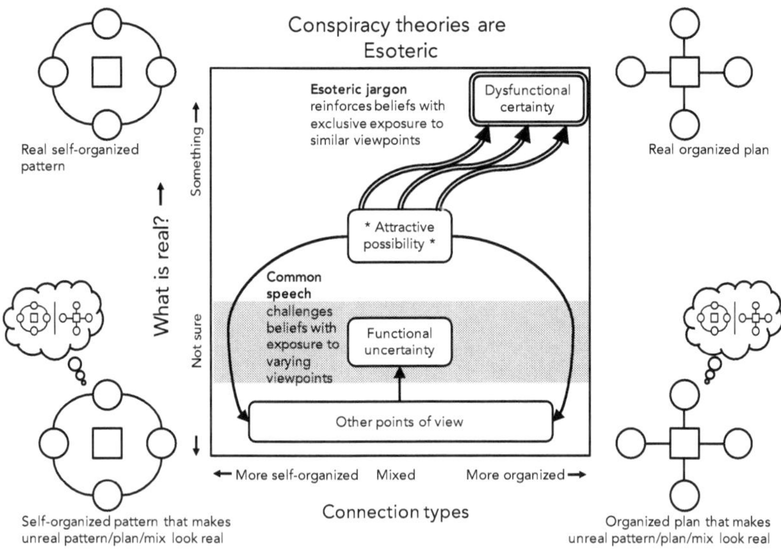


When we avoid or explain jargon, we can speak to *anyone* about the attractive possibility. And when we do that, we hear things that surprise us, leading us to question the validity of our perception. That moves us down into the space of cognitive dissonance—where we might be wrong—which helps us arrive at a helpful state of functional uncertainty. (Why is the dysfunctional certainty box in the upper *right* hand corner? I will explain that later.)

> ***Practice mediating your jargon***
>
> In a few sentences or paragraphs, describe a topic you care about. Explain its major issues and points of contention. Write what you would like to see happen with respect to the topic in the future.
>
> Now look at what you have written. How much jargon did you use? How many of your words would be confusing to people who don't already know about the topic? What do you think this means about your thinking on the topic?
>
> Next, *replace* each jargon term with words everyone can understand. If you need help, search the internet for a "thousand most common words" list, and replace any words in your description that do not appear on it.
>
> Finally, compare your two descriptions. Which do you like better? Why? If you were to use less jargon, how do you think it would change your conversations and your thinking?

## Conspiracy theories are Speculative

When we are engaged in conspiracy thinking, we create what-*if* scenarios and fail to notice that they have morphed into what-*is* explanations. Conspiracy theories are stories we make the mistake of taking literally rather than seriously.

People have been telling and listening to stories to make sense of their lives and communities for thousands of years. And in a sense, conspiracy theories are a form of modern folklore. We look at folk tales people told hundreds or thousands of years ago and think they couldn't *actually* have believed that they would find fairies and giants and dragons when they ventured outside their villages and farms. But some people probably did. Most people, though, probably *played* with the possibility of such magical beings, allowing them just as much actuality as was useful, and no more.

You could argue that people do the same thing with conspiracy theories today. A small number of people at the dense center of the theory believe it fully, and everyone else believes it just a bit—not the weirder parts, of course, but some of the outer, tamer layers. The earth isn't flat, but scientists can be condescending. Politicians aren't aliens, but they can be self-serving. The government isn't poisoning us, but we need more transparency and accountability.

The development and spread of stories about forces we can't control, and the constant renegotiation of those stories as those forces change over time, is a natural and healthy societal response to uncertainty. And it helps all of us—as long as most of the stories *stay* within the realm of fiction. In other words, it's all fun and games until somebody gets hurt.

### *Tales of (and for) the gullible*

To reduce the extent to which fiction impinges on reality, every folk tale tradition includes some stories about gullible people who jump to conclusions based on stories, lies, hearsay, and scant evidence. Such stories act as a brake to keep fictional explorations from getting out of hand.

One of my favorite gullible-fool stories is an Indian tale about a foolish shepherd. As the story is told in *Folktales from India*,[47] one day a shepherd was sitting on a branch while cutting it. A Brahman came rushing up, crying out, "Hey, you! You'll fall down! You're cutting the branch you're sitting on."

The shepherd, surprised, asked the Brahman how he could possibly know what would happen in the future. The Brahman tried to explain by suggesting that the shepherd put a *cloth* on a branch, then cut the branch. The shepherd did this, and to his amazement the cloth fell, just as the Brahman had predicted!

Now fully convinced that he had met a soothsayer, the shepherd asked the Brahman to tell him when he was going to die. The Brahman said he could do no such thing, but the shepherd insisted. Finally, annoyed, the Brahman told the shepherd that he would die when his nose began to shrink and his eyes began to sink into his head.

One day, months later, the shepherd was sitting with his flock and waiting for his wife to bring his dinner. He absent-mindedly measured his nose with his finger. It seemed shorter than he remembered. Alarmed, he felt his eyes. They seemed sunken. Convinced that he was either dying or already dead, he went home. "He came into the house, held in his breath, and sat against the wall. He sat on his haunches, without breathing, I don't know how."

The shepherd's wife and relatives decided that since he was not speaking or breathing, he must be dead. So they buried him, only to run away in panic when he rose up covered with dirt and asked for food. The poor man walked all over the village for days, but everyone ran from him, afraid of the ghost he had become. Finally he went back to his wife, who at last summoned the courage to take a good long look at her foolish ghost of a husband. She let him back into the house, cleaned him up, fed him, and sent him back to his flock.

The very first sentence of that story tells you that the whole thing is a joke as well as a cautionary tale, because nobody sits on a branch while they are cutting it. Later on, the "I don't know how" sentence amplifies the joke—and makes the lesson more memorable—by pushing events just over the line into the impossible. The fact that the shepherd's mistake spreads to the whole community, who believe that a man who is obviously able to walk around and demand food is dead, shows that the story is not just about one person jumping to conclusions. It's about *lots* of people jumping to conclusions together. And the fact that the wife finally solves the problem by looking past her fears and taking a long and unflinching look at reality gives the problem a remedy and the story a moral. This story—and many more like it in every folk tradition—was *designed* to stop conspiracy thinking in its tracks.

Are there stories like this one today? Yes, but there could be more. Some of the people who leave cults and get out of conspiracy thinking give interviews and write books. They perform a valuable public service, and we all should thank them. But we need more of them to speak out. Most of the people who get over conspiracy thinking are too embarrassed to talk about it. That's natural, but we have a mechanism to deal with embarrassment: fiction. More television shows and movies about people coming out of conspiracy thinking would be good, but personally I'd like to see more folk tales moving around society about people who saved themselves and their families by taking a long and unflinching look at reality. Let's get those stories moving, people.

## Why we do it

Before we talk about alternatives to speculation, I'd like to ask an obvious question. *Why* do we slide into conspiracy thinking? What causes it? Is it personality? Is it upbringing? Is it genetic?

We slide into conspiracy thinking because we BLEED: we have Biases, we are Lonely, we are influenced by our Experiences, we crave Excitement, and we have Desires. In other words, we are human beings. Every one of us is susceptible. Let's take a moment to go through each cause.

### *We have Biases*

Of all the cognitive biases that have been studied, two are most relevant to conspiracy thinking. *Confirmation bias* is our tendency to pay more attention to evidence and arguments that confirm our existing beliefs. This explains why we discount the information we see in news sources we don't like, *even when it is identical* to the information we can find in news sources we do like.

The *fundamental attribution error* is our tendency to attribute our own actions to situational influences and the actions of others to dispositional influences. In simpler terms, I'm a good person who is having a bad day, and you're just a bad person.

Like the availability heuristic (page 175), these cognitive biases save us time and energy in the short term *and* lead us astray in the long term. We can't escape them, but we can become *aware* of them and work around them, like a person with a limp can still walk up stairs, only maybe sideways.

### *We are Lonely*

Loneliness interacts with conspiracy thinking before, during, and after involvement. Say I've moved to a new city or gone through a divorce. For whatever reason, I'm feeling especially alone. So I look for connections.

I happen to run into some people who are engaged in discussions of a conspiracy theory. On entering the group, I feel a rush of excitement. Suddenly I have friends who are eager to spend time talking to me—as long as it's about the conspiracy, but I don't pay much attention to that, not at first. As time goes by, I start to lose faith in the conspiracy theory. Its inconsistencies pile up, and I have a harder and harder time making myself believe it.

Eventually I leave the group. Now I feel worse than ever. Not only have I lost my new friends, but I've also broken ties with old friends and family members, who I tried to bring into the fold when I was sure about the space aliens or whatever. From the outside, my conspiracy thinking seemed like it was a matter of belief, but it was really a matter of belonging. Stories like this one have played out for millions of people over thousands of years.

### *We are influenced by our Experiences*

The influence of experience is the hardest to counter of the five causes, because it is not always an unreasonable position. We *should* be suspicious of official accounts that contradict our experiences and those of our loved ones. I can think of several people I know who tend to be suspicious of specific categories of institutions, for example in the medical, government, police, corporate, or educational arenas. For each of those people, their suspicions are based on real—not imaginary—mistakes and improper actions of those who were in positions of authority and were neither transparent nor accountable. Even when people give such suspicions unwarranted attention, it does not help matters to dismiss them as insignificant.

Every time a person in authority disregards their ethical responsibility, every time a public institution does things to people without their consent, and every time a politician knowingly lies to the public, conspiracy thinking grows. And most of the blame does not lie on the people who wrongly believe they are being harmed. It lies on the people who gave them cause to believe it.

### *We crave Excitement*

Conspiracy theories are like superhero movies, except *you're* the superhero. Even someone like *you* can make a difference and save the day. To a person who feels that society has left them behind—for whatever reason—this is indeed an attractive possibility. Every one of us knows what it's like to feel like we don't matter, that nobody cares what we think, that nobody is listening to us. It's an understandable response, but it's not a useful one. The energy we put into conspiracy thinking is wasted energy.

I remember how I felt when I came out of the movie theater after watching *Raiders of the Lost Ark* for the first time, probably in 1981. I had so much energy to *do* something—*anything*. I should have realized that what I was already doing, learning, was the best place to put my energy.

In contrast, I recently enjoyed watching the television series *Homecoming*. The aspect of the story I liked best was the character of Thomas Carrasco, a mid-level bureaucrat who saved the day by doing his job with integrity and diligence. We need more stories like that, I think, to show us that *superheroes can save the day by checking their work*. Careful nurses are superheroes, as are observant farmers, calm police officers, kind teachers, patient parents, and friends who work on their listening skills.

### *We have Desires*

If conspiracy thinking is about making up stories, why do we make up such *awful* stories? Why don't we believe in *happy* conspiracies? Because the conspiracy isn't the point of the story. The *thwarting* of the conspiracy is the point. And the thwarting *is* happy. Every superhero story needs a supervillain, but the story is never *about* the supervillain. Their function in the story is to provide a challenge for the superhero to overcome.

The beating heart of every conspiracy theory is a set of *desires*, things we want to have or have happen. The villains of our conspiracy-theory stories are chosen—and to some extent *designed*—to suit those desires. If we believe, for example, that our government is being run by a secret cabal, we want transparency and empowerment—because that's what we'll *get* when the conspiracy is thwarted. If we believe that people have been breaking into houses on our street, we want to feel secure in our homes. If we believe that corporations have been slipping mind-control chemicals into their products, we want to know more about those products, and we want better choices.

Surrounding the heart of desire is a layer of beliefs about trust, responsibility, and blame. What sorts of people can we trust? Whose responsibility is it to make sure that our children are safe? Who is to blame when we lose our jobs? And what should happen when people break the rules? The answers to these questions are *political* in nature. They explain *why* our desires have not been met. This second layer of political belief transforms conspiracy theories from desires into causes. To quote Quassim Cassam:

> What purpose do Conspiracy Theories serve, if not to tell the truth? And why do people continue to peddle Conspiracy Theories that have virtually no chance of being true? *Because Conspiracy Theories are first and foremost forms of political propaganda.* They are political gambits whose real function is to promote a political agenda.[48]

It's a mistake to think political propaganda comes only from politicians and political parties. We are all active generators of political propaganda, and sometimes we use it on ourselves. We generate it every time we read the headline of an article, glance at the author's name or photo or affiliation, and think to ourselves, "Oh, of course someone like *that* would say that." We generate it every time we hear about something bad happening and think to ourselves, "I'll bet *those people* are behind this." But again, *those people* are not the point; the point is *what we want.* We fall into conspiracy thinking because we want the world to be the way we want it to be.

Has anyone, ever, believed in a conspiracy theory that, if the conspiracy was thwarted, would *hurt* the people who believe in it? For example, has there ever been a conspiracy theory that a secret cabal is going around paying people's bills? Or that corporations have been conspiring to make their products better and cheaper? Or that doctors have been secretly meeting to become better listeners? What kind of a conspiracy theory would any of those conspiracies make? A lame one, and nobody would believe it—not because it was unlikely, but because it would not suit the purpose for which conspiracy theories exist.[49]

### *The path to Narnia*

When I was eighteen years old and just starting college, I was reading a lot of fantasy fiction. In particular, I read C. S. Lewis' *The Chronicles of Narnia* over and over. One day I went out into the woods, found a dry spot to sit down, and tried my hardest to go to Narnia—for real. I know it sounds ridiculous, but I had managed to work myself into a state where I truly believed it might be possible. After several attempts, I gave up and moved on. But if I had been surrounded by people who believed what I believed, maybe with a nasty supervillain thrown in for good measure, I could have ended up trapped in a conspiracy theory.

Looking back, I can see why I got so caught up in my Narnia fantasy. If you consider my state of mind at the time, you can see all of the BLEED aspects in it. I was *Biased* toward fantasy because I had spent years reading fantasy novels. I was *Lonely* because I had recently started commuting to college, where I made no friends. As for *Experience*, well, I was an imaginative child, and growing up Catholic, I found plenty of ideas to feed my imagination, probably in ways more sensible Catholics didn't. As a nerd with poor social skills, I experienced significant parasocial *Excitement* as I became imaginary friends with the Pevensie children. Most importantly, I had a desperate *Desire* to become a biologist—and being a perfectionist, I wanted to be the best biologist ever.

The truth is, I wanted an easy way out. I wanted to study animal behavior, and in Narnia, *all the animals talked*. If I could *go* to Narnia, I would be effortlessly transformed into the best animal behaviorist who had ever lived. I wouldn't have to *study* animals; I could just ask them questions. It was absolutely ridiculous. But it was so very *attractive*.

You might wonder why I am using these examples from my own life. I'm doing it on purpose, and for two reasons. First, I want to drive home the point that it is not only "strange people" who indulge in conspiracy thinking. We are all vulnerable to it.[50] And we are much more vulnerable at difficult times in our lives—when we are making transitions, facing challenges, or dealing with losses. (Like when I was going to college for the first time.) That's yet another reason to work on our thinking *when we are relatively unstressed*: to prepare ourselves for times when it may not be as reliable as it usually is.

Secondly, I've been telling these teenage stories because I want to highlight the fact that *conspiracy thinking comes in all sizes*. It's easy to think that if you don't believe in any of the *big* conspiracy theories we've all heard about, the poisons and the lizard people and so on, you don't engage in conspiracy thinking. That would be a mistake. *All* unchallenged conspiracy thinking hurts people, relationships, and communities, whether the conspiracy you believe in involves multinational corporations or your neighbors across the street.

## Alternatives to speculation

If speculation is guessing what *could* be true and then sliding into believing it *is* true, what can we do instead? Three things, and of course I've made them into a handy mnemonic: SEE. We can Simulate, Estimate, and Experiment.

### *Simulation*

Cognitively, storytelling is a means of simulation. It's a way to play out possibilities *as if* they were real without actually going through the events of the stories. So, instead of speculating about conspiracy theories, we can *play* with them, treating them as if they were folk tales or novels or movies.

You know how you watch a movie and then talk about it with your family or friends? You say things like, "That plot hole was so big you could drive a truck through it." And you talk about how *you* would have made a better movie if you had been in charge of it. You work out alternative plots, cast other actors, build better sets and costumes, improve the clichéd ending—you know. So why don't we do that with conspiracy theories? Why don't we *mess with them*? It would help us think through the issues we are trying to use them to explore, and it would do it without hurting anyone. That's what stories are for.

For example, in my thirteen-year-old pen frenzy, if I had stopped to think about *why* I believed that particular girl had stolen my pens, I might have been able to explore some issues that were important to me at the time. I seem to recall that I got the pens for my birthday, and that the girl who stole them was one of the "town girls" who lorded their higher social status over us "bus kids" from out in the country. She was also one of the richer girls in my class, the ones who didn't wear hand-me-down clothes and had allowances to buy pens with. My rush to judgment was probably fueled by a desire for social justice. I could have worked through those feelings by playing with a number of stories—if I had known that was an option.

### *Estimation*

When we are caught up in conspiracy thinking, we tend to think in absolute terms. The evil villains in our conspiracy stories are *completely* evil, and the heroes are completely good. So what would happen if we stopped using absolute terms? What if we started *estimating* evil?

Again, I'll go back to the infamous pen caper as a case study. What if someone had stepped in and asked me to estimate how popular multi-colored pen sets were that year (very), how similar the sets available for purchase in my local area were likely to be (very), and how many students must have had similar-looking pen sets (many)? What if they had asked me to estimate the *probability* that two girls in the same class might have similar-looking multi-colored pen sets (high)? Such questions would not have changed my perception of social injustice, but they would have poked a gaping hole in my conclusion that theft was the only reasonable explanation. Why didn't I ask those questions of *myself*? I don't know. I was thirteen. The good thing is that there are lots of thirteen-year-olds alive right now, and we can teach *them* how to estimate.

### *Experimentation*

My third alternative to speculation is trying things out, and I have another teenage story for you about that. I was a socially anxious child, always on the lookout for another reason to freak out. One day, probably around fifteen, I decided to wear the same clothes to school two days in a row. I thought I would be ridiculed by everyone who saw me. But to my amazement, *nobody noticed*. I remember walking through the halls of the school as if seeing the people around me for the first time. I started conducting other experiments. One day I would wear all black, and the next all white. Nobody noticed. All blue: nothing. All green: nothing. Blue and green in alternating patterns: nothing. One experiment at a time, I destroyed the fearful speculations I had built.

Conspiracy thinking is like a train riding on a track. It only follows one path, and its light reveals only the track ahead. Experimentation takes the train off its track and pushes it in every direction. Its light shines all over the land and reveals details we had not seen before.

In the case of my stolen pens, I could have experimented with the situation by complimenting the thief's pens and watching to see how she responded. I could have asked her where she bought them. I could have had one of my friends ask the same question, and then compare the two answers. I could have asked if I could *borrow* the pens so I could examine them more closely. An experimental attitude could have brought me to a new understanding of what was going on.

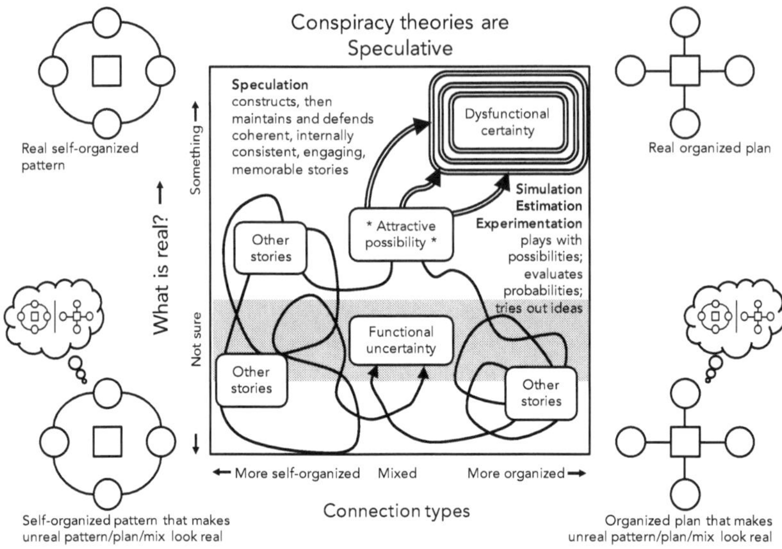


### *Practice your alternatives to speculation*

Make a list of topics about which you are willing to admit that you have at times speculated on scant evidence. They will probably be topics about which you feel you have not been treated fairly.

Choose one of the topics and write a list of *desires* related to it. What do you want and need? Why do you *not* have those things? Who or what is standing in your way? What *should* happen? Who bears responsibility? Who is to blame? Who can you trust? Who can't you trust? Why?

Now run some *simulations* on the topic. If the situation was perfectly ideal, what would happen? If it was perfectly horrible, what would happen? What if it was just okay? Tell about an injustice related to the topic. Tell about a hero who saves the day. What can you learn by playing with fictional stories about the topic?

Write down some things you think are true and false about the topic. Give them numbers. *How* sure are you about each thing, as a percentage measure? Fifty percent sure? Ninety? What percent of people in your family, community, and country agree with you on those points? Why? What does that tell you?

On that same topic, think of a few *experiments* you could run. Maybe you could ask someone a question, look something up on the internet, or say something and see how people respond. What could you do to *test* your beliefs on the topic? Now try one of the tests you thought of. What did you learn?

This last option is difficult, so only do it when you're rested. Sit down in a nice quiet place with a mug of something hot, and start making up stories. Conjure a scenario in which you are wrong. And not just wrong; wrong in a way that hurts the people you care about. Play out the scenario for as long as you can stand it. It might be a few seconds or a few minutes. But work it out. Watch it happen like it's a movie. Then return to reality and realize that you're probably not *actually* wrong. But you might have thought of a few things you want to look up on the internet.

## Conspiracy theories are (narrowly) Contrarian

Conspiracy thinking is opposite-world thinking. If everyone says something is true, we say it's false, and vice versa.

But the contrarianism in conspiracy thinking is of a special kind: it's *narrow*. It confines itself to challenging only *some* assertions. People who have gotten involved in conspiracy theories famously claim that they are "following the money" and "asking questions," but that's not universally true. They are only following *some* of the money, and they are *avoiding* many of the questions they *could* be asking. But, I'll say it again, we all do this, if only a little. We *say* we are contrarian, but we're actually partisan.

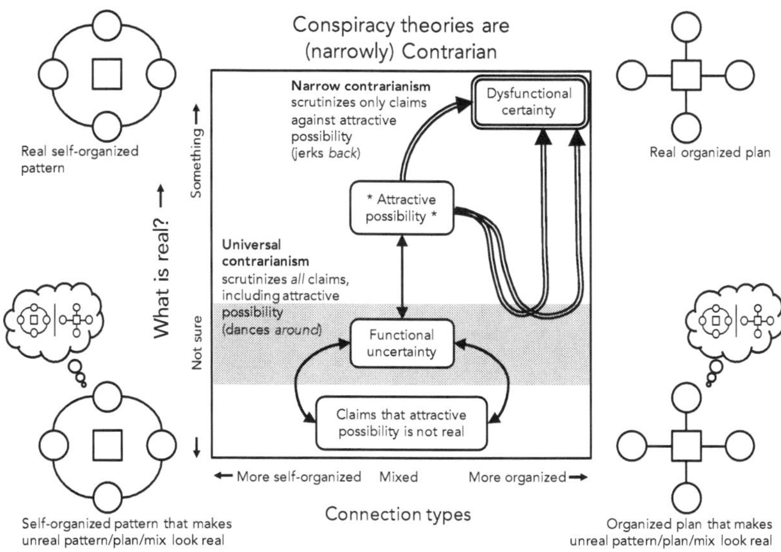


When I read this part of Cassam's book, I felt challenged by it. I've always thought of myself as a contrarian, ever since I was a child. Every time anyone says anything, my first thought is always, "And what's the opposite of *that*?"

After some thought, I realized that, in my opinion, Cassam's characterization of contrarianism could use a wee bit of refinement.

Conspiracy thinking is not just contrarian; it's narrowly contrarian. *Universal* contrarianism is perfectly healthy, though it does take a certain amount of self-awareness and self-discipline to *keep* it universal. But contrarianism is definitely dangerous if it *stops* being contrary when it runs into something it fancies. (Though as a universal contrarian, I'm not *entirely* convinced that universal contrarianism is a good idea.)

***Knee-jerk thinking***

One day a few years ago, I was sitting with my son looking at the news on the internet. I saw one of those click-bait headlines, "So-and-so said this awful thing." I was upset by it. I said to my son, "Look, So-and-so said this awful thing. They *would* say something like that, wouldn't they?"

But then, out of some deeply buried research-nerd instinct, without noticing what I was doing, I *copied* the awful thing So-and-so said, pasted it into a search engine, and hit Enter. Right away a whole slew of fact-checking articles came up, proving that So-and-so never said any such thing.[51] I said, "Oh, wait, that's not true. It's a lie, and it's being spread around by the people I like."

Looking back, I am *so* glad my son saw me do that. In the midst of a bout of knee-jerk narrow contrarianism, I had a moment of *universal* contrarianism. The whole thing took less than thirty seconds, but I managed to bounce myself out of my comfortable belief that everything was simple and clear, that the good guys were good and the bad guys were bad. And I leaned into the light of universal contrarianism.

I wish I could say that after that blessed day I never looked at the news in a knee-jerk way again. But of course I did, and do. Still, that moment of discovery, and many others like it, comes into my mind every so often, and it helps me avoid being sure I am right—at least some of the time.

That's an interesting metaphor, isn't it, "knee-jerk" thinking. It's an apt description of narrow contrarianism, and for two reasons. First, the knee is a hinge joint. It only moves in one direction. And once it's bent, it has only one place to go: back to where it came from. The hip joint, on the other hand, is a ball, and it moves in all directions. Can you imagine anyone condemning *hip-jerk* thinking? It wouldn't make sense.

The second and more important reason the knee is a fitting metaphor for narrow contrarianism is that *somebody else can make it move*. When we go to the doctor, they test our reflexes by hitting our knees with little hammers. No matter how hard we try, we can't make our feet stay still.[52] In the same way, narrow contrarianism is *assignable* contrarianism. When we make a habit of knee-jerk thinking, we render ourselves vulnerable to deception and exploitation by people who don't have our best interests at heart.

***Practice your universal contrarianism***

Find a source of news you would never look at in a million years. Look at it. If you can't bear to read the articles or watch the videos, or if you don't want to give credence to bad reporting, *just read the titles*. Read lots of titles. Get an idea of some of the things people are saying that you would never know about because you don't read that stuff.

Now look at some of the news articles in your regular news feed or reports on your regular news program. *Disagree with every one of them*. Do not leave out a single article or report, especially the ones you like best. As you do this, notice how easy or difficult it is to disagree with each one. Do you see a pattern?

Go to Wikipedia and click "Random article" over and over. Or find a web site that delivers random YouTube videos. Or go to an internet news reader, find the search bar, look around you, and type the first thing you see: chair, stapler, cat. Or type something that happened recently: a flat tire, a hooting owl, tripping on a laundry basket. Read the news articles that come up. Agree and disagree with them.

Write down a list of authorities you respect: people, groups, and institutions. Go to an internet search engine, and one at a time, type in the name of each authority, plus one of these words: *wrong*, *lying*, or *fake*. See what comes up.

## Conspiracy theories are Amateur

For this one aspect, I am going to leave behind my "we all do this" stance, because amateurism has more to do with social patterns than it has to do with individual attitudes.

Very few people who have achieved high levels of knowledge and competency in any area believe in conspiracy theories centered on that area. Such people may believe in conspiracy theories about *other* areas, but few *bona fide* experts can be found among the ranks of conspiracy theorists. People who believe in conspiracy theories may have spent dozens or even hundreds of hours studying specific topics, but with few exceptions, they have not spent *tens of thousands* of hours.

More importantly, they have not embraced the relevant scrutiny that comes with true spiraling: undergoing comprehensive courses of study, passing exams, submitting articles for critical review, making presentations, fielding questions, defending dissertations. And they have not gone looking for cognitive dissonance as a means to achieve their goals. Usually they have avoided it.

Instead, the scrutiny that is commonly applied in conspiracy-theory communities is *irrelevant* to the topic. People are respected not because they know the topic well, but because they speak often or well or with passion—or worse, because they're celebrities, or good-looking, or wealthy. These things have nothing to do with actually understanding a topic. Irrelevant scrutiny leads to over-confidence, which leads to misinformation. Psychologists call unearned confidence the Dunning-Kruger effect, after the social psychologists David Dunning and Justin Kruger, who studied it in 1999.

If you put your ear to the side of any conspiracy theory, you will hear the Dunning-Kruger effect spinning inside it like a turbine, providing energy that keeps the community going. But the Dunning-Kruger effect can't actually *go* anywhere; it can only run in circles. If you have opinions about epidemiology, for example, and you can't give a factually-correct hour-long lecture on how viruses spread through communities and how, why, and when various types of mitigation efforts work, you have not earned the right to a credential in that area.[53] If you have opinions about the government, and you can't give a factually-correct hour-long lecture on its history, structure, and rules, you have not earned the right to a credential in that area. It doesn't matter if you speak with passion when you don't know what you are talking about.

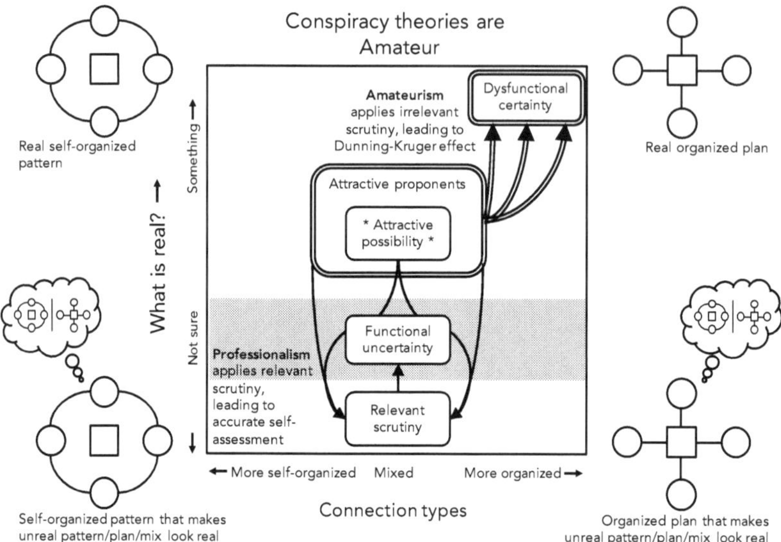


None of this means we can't have opinions and make decisions that affect our own lives and families. But it does mean we should *check our work* before we hold forth on a subject we don't know well. It's why I wrote a disclaimer at the start of this part of the chapter. I have credentials in biology and in organizational and community narrative.[54] I have spent many thousands of hours learning about those topics. I do not have credentials in the area of conspiracy theories, and I *should not* have credentials in that area, because I have spent something like fifty hours learning about it.

That is why I expect—no, I *demand*—that you take everything I say in this section as an *exploration*, not an explanation. If you want to learn about conspiracy theories, read Cassam's book, and read *Suspicious Minds* by Rob Brotherton. Those are the books I found most useful in what I read. Of course I would love to tell you that I am an expert on conspiracy theories, but no one would *believe* me if I did, and rightfully so.

The word "credential" comes from the Latin *credentia*, or belief. Credentials are packages of belief. We earn them so we can show them, and we show them so we can avoid having to prove over and over that we know what we are talking about. Yes, credentials are bound up with power structures in society, and they can be given out unfairly. On the other hand, we need *some* form of belief packaging for society to function, and it must be a form that is *relevant* to the subjects about which people claim to have knowledge. Otherwise all that matters is who can shout the loudest and wear the craziest hat.

***Practice avoiding amateurism***

Make a list of topics you know very well and a list of topics you know less well. Choose one of the topics that you know very well. Find a popular article about it. Laugh at its flaws. Map the shape of its ignorance. Think about the people who have been reading that article and believing they understand the topic. Think about how much more *you* know about it.

Now choose one of the topics on your list that you *don't* know well, one you would like to learn more about. Set aside some time to learn about it, say five or ten hours. Read some introductory articles or a popular book about it.

Find an article written for experts in that area, people who have spent tens of thousands of hours learning about it. Try to read it. Are you in over your head? What does it feel like? Is it frustrating? Motivating? Both? Read some more. Map the shape of your ignorance. Develop a *respect* for it. Understand how it is like and unlike the knowledge of the truly knowledgeable. Go back and learn some more.

## Conspiracy theories are Plan-oriented

Of Cassam's six aspects, this one is the most connected to organization and self-organization. This aspect of conspiracy theories finally explains why, in all six diagrams, I have drawn dysfunctional certainty only in the upper *right* corner of the space: because it tends to be accompanied by a propensity to overestimate the influence of intentional plans.

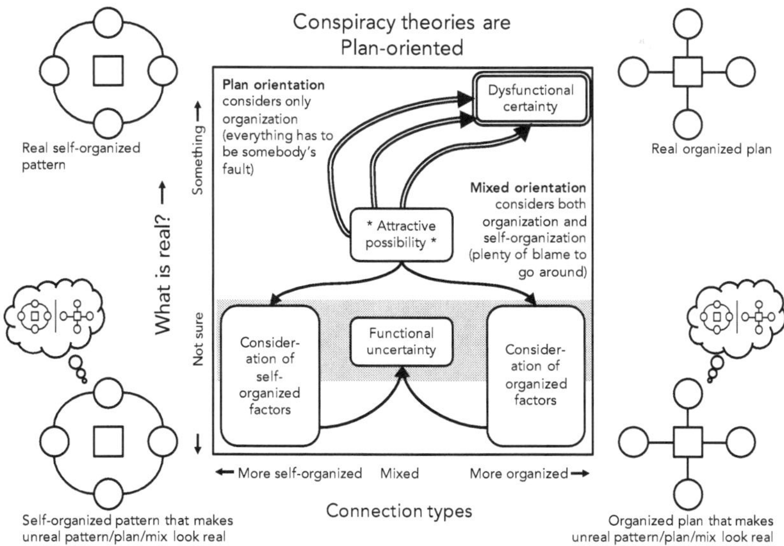

I've mentioned in previous chapters that our perceptions of events seem to drift toward attributions of agency. Remember when I said (on page 84) that industrial accidents are often caused by people mistaking self-organized patterns for organized plans? Remember when I said (on page 141) that people seem to think "organization or it didn't happen"? I was talking about this.

Actually, Cassam does not use the term "plan-oriented." That is my term. He calls this aspect "premodern" and describes it as "the view that complex events are capable of being controlled by a small number of people acting in secret."[55] With respect, I don't think this is the best way to frame the aspect. People have been thinking in healthy and unhealthy ways about organization and self-organization since the beginning of people, and they will continue to do so until the end of people. There's no time arrow to it.

Conspiracy theories have been with us since at least Roman times, and conspiracy *thinking* has probably been with us for tens of thousands of years. Conspiracy theories (and demagogues) tend to gain influence when social norms and institutions begin to change in unsettling ways. Such waves of collective anxiety, and the fact-free explanations that grow out of them, will probably continue to rise and fall in human societies far into the future. So instead of Cassam's "premodern" term, I will speak of an orientation towards *planning*.

***The gods of complexity-speak***

I've been watching people talk about self-organization, complexity, and chaos for the past thirty-some years. I've noticed that some of the people who are shuttling on these topics speak of these phenomena as if they were supernatural beings. People seem to seize upon the most easily personified of the various names for complex and chaotic phenomena, such as strange attractors, fractals, and the "edge of chaos." When they use these terms, people sometimes sound like they are invoking the names of god-like mystical powers. You can hear it in their voices, and you can see it in their eyes. This worries me.

I have a special dislike for the term "complex adaptive system," because there are no such things. First, as I hope I have shown in this book, organization and self-organization are rarely found separately in any situation that involves people, and very few situations we care about don't involve people. In reality, most of the things people say are complex—cities, traffic, health care, education—are *complexicated*, with complex (self-organized) and complicated (organized) aspects intermingling and interacting. Keeping self-organization walled off from organization helps render it amenable to personification.

Secondly, the word *adaptive* pushes away the unpleasant fact that *maladaptation* is just as likely an outcome. As I have pointed out several times in this book, self-organization does not always lead to wonderful things. Sometimes it leads to disaster. But the word "adaptive" doesn't mean "sometimes better and sometimes horribly worse." *It just means better*. A more useful word would be "reactive." Swarms and flocks react to perturbations. Sometimes they adapt, sometimes they crash, and sometimes they dissipate into things that are no longer swarms or flocks. "Reactive" doesn't imply a positive outcome. Chemicals react, and nobody thinks every chemical reaction turns out well.

What about *system*? Of the three words, I dislike it the most. "System" comes from the Latin *systema*, meaning "an arrangement," and from the Greek *synistanai*, meaning "to place together." Thus the word once implied the *intentional* creation of a bounded frame. And in truth, it still *does* mean that. It's just that we have forgotten that we *built* the frames we see.

That's why I don't like to use the word "system" in a general sense. A system is not a thing; it's a *choice*, a choice that included some things and excluded others, a choice bounded in time, space, and perspective. Ask anyone what is included in the "health care system" or the "educational system" or the "legislative system," and you'll get as many answers as people. What's more, if you ask the same people a year later, you'll get different answers.[56]

What concerns me most about the word "system" is that I've seen people use it in the same way they use the word "god." I worry about what that means for the future of thinking about complexity. For example, systems theorists often use the saying "the purpose of the system is what it does." *They* know what they mean by it. They mean that when events happen, we should consider any self-organized patterns that influenced those events, such as network effects, before we rush to praise or blame organized actors who "pulled the strings."

The problem is that *sayings travel*, and as they travel they become distorted. Sometimes the intended meaning of a useful saying can get flipped around so that it works *against* its intended purpose. If you know nothing at all about complexity, and you hear "the purpose of the system is what it does," the only part that makes any sense to you is "it *does*." It sounds like agency. It sounds like a "system" is some kind of supernatural being that *does* things. Big things. Things we want.

### *Having our complexity cake and eating it too*

The words we use to talk about complexity point to an underlying pattern of motivated reasoning. Understandably—but dangerously—we want to keep the fun parts of complexity and pretend the not-so-fun parts don't exist.[57]

Consider the word "agent." Decades ago, the simulation of self-organized patterns was called "*individual*-based modeling." But somehow the term morphed into "*agent*-based modeling." The difference is telling.

The word "agent" comes from the Latin *agentem*, which meant "powerful." It still means that. Agency is power, and agents have it. But in a self-organized pattern, *the power is in the network*, not its members. In other words, agency is precisely what interactors *don't* have. Saying "agents have limited agency" is like saying "gods have limited power." By definition, *they don't*. The first word overpowers the rest of the statement and flips it upside-down.

If you add together the opaque jargon of complexity theory, its many poor translations of specialist terms, and its soft underbelly of implicit denial, you have a *recipe* for a source of deliverance we have been denied, in secret, by nefarious forces. Complexity could fit into the same slot as the aliens the government won't allow to help us, the amazing medicines we could have if the elite weren't hoarding them, and the money and power we could enjoy if only the globalists and the immigrants weren't taking them from us.

Anyone who builds shuttles that have anything to do with complexity has a responsibility to be aware of this danger and work to avoid such misunderstandings. Don't throw around complexity jargon without making sure people understand what you mean by it. Don't go around telling people that complexity will give them "order for free"—because it won't, not really. The cost will just shift around, and they will discover it later, when it's too late.[58]

Complexity can "do" wonderful things. But it can also tear people apart. Literally. So let's be careful. Somebody could get hurt.

***Practice questioning your plan orientation***

Make a list of some recent events that you believe happened because specific people or groups caused them to happen. Think at multiple scales: in your family, in your community, in your country, in the world. Then, for each of those events, list all the ways in which either self-organized or random occurrences *could* have played a part in what happened.

Now think of an event from history that interests you, something that happened hundreds or thousands of years ago. Find a good book, article, or web site about it. Better yet, find *two* books with competing perspectives on it. As you read, think about the planned and unplanned aspects of the event. Did weather patterns play a role? How about social networks? Infectious diseases? Mental illnesses?

When you feel that you fully understand the historical event you chose, go back to the recent event you thought about earlier. Does it seem different to you now? Might you have attributed some elements of the situation to planning when they were at least *partially* influenced by self-organized or chance conditions? Are there questions about the event that you would like to investigate?

## Conspiracy thinking is Self-sealing

Attempts to counter conspiracy theories with facts often backfire, causing them to grow even stronger. Why does this happen? Because *conspiracy theories aren't theories*. They are points of view, ways of seeing the world, and you can't disprove a point of view.

In my diagram for this aspect, I drew the dysfunctional certainty box as not only thick-skinned but also partly *outside* the space. When we practice conspiracy thinking, we slide partway into the realm of fantasy—or faith, depending on how you see it. That's why conspiracy theories can seem like religions: because they share characteristics with traditions of religious belief.

But I would like to propose a more mundane explanation for the self-sealing aspect of conspiracy thinking: defensiveness. It is the shield and the burden we all carry.

We all have our soft spots, the aspects of our identity we hold most dear, and we will go to great pains to protect them. Withdrawing into wishful thinking can help us feel safe in a world that can seem as if it was designed to attack us.

Unfortunately, defensiveness is just another form of attack, because it hurts us more than it hurts anyone else.

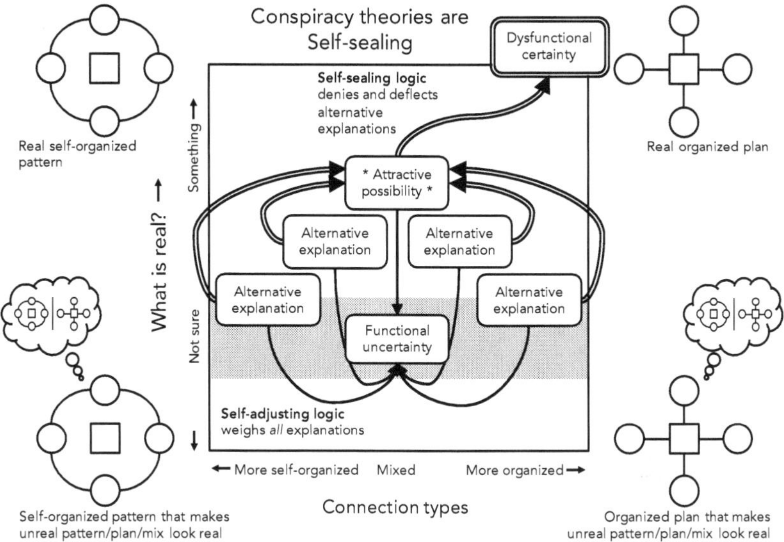


### *The warmth of the sun*

Thoughts of defensiveness and attack remind me of a story. It was passed on for probably hundreds of years before it was written down by Aesop about 2500 years ago. This version is from a 1912 collection of Aesop's fables.

> A dispute arose between the North Wind and the Sun, each claiming that he was stronger than the other. At last they agreed to try their powers upon a traveller, to see which could soonest strip him of his cloak. The North Wind had the first try; and, gathering up all his force for the attack, he came whirling furiously down upon the man, and caught up his cloak as though he would wrest it from him by one single effort: but the harder he blew, the more closely the man wrapped it round himself.
>
> Then came the turn of the Sun. At first he beamed gently upon the traveller, who soon unclasped his cloak and walked on with it hanging loosely about his shoulders: then he shone forth in his full strength, and the man, before he had gone many steps, was glad to throw his cloak right off and complete his journey more lightly clad.[59]

The man in the story represents all of us. But the story is not about the man; it's about the wind and the sun. We are like the wind when we attack people who have fallen into conspiracy thinking, forcing them to wrap the cloaks of their beliefs even more tightly around themselves. We are like the sun when we *listen* to their fears and desires and help them find healthier ways to explore and express them.

***The power of love***

This brings me to my final mnemonic. The best way to avoid or reduce self-sealing thinking is with LOVE. We can Learn, get Outside, Volunteer, and Empathize. And we can help other people do those things.

This last mnemonic is not from spiraling. It's from focusing, from being alive. So take it for what is: my point of view.

***Learning***

We can reduce our self-sealing thinking by learning in two directions: inward and outward.

When we focus our learning inward, we can better understand the motivations that drive our reasoning. We can examine our fears, histories, and hopes, and we can think about the effect each of these factors has on the way we habitually think. We can find the pillars that support our sense of identity and purpose. We can study what holds them up and what pulls them down. Then, when we understand ourselves better, we can put aside the question of whether our beliefs are *true* and ask whether they are *functional*—whether they help or hurt us, our families, and our communities. And we can ask whether there might be other, better ways to explore and express our points of view.

When we focus our learning outward, we can spiral on the topics we care about, such as politics, law, medicine, immigration, or the economy. But to succeed at spiraling, we have to admit—if only to ourselves—that we have made mistakes in the past. As John Caddell put it in *The Mistake Bank*:

> When something you're working on goes wrong, many parties may have a role. Yet focusing on all those external parties distracts you from what you can control—yourself and how you react to situations. Believing that you can manage your life requires that you take responsibility for your actions and deal with their consequences. That requires forgetting about other influences and owning the result.[60]

Now *that's* an exciting thought. Leaving conspiracy thinking behind and owning our mistakes can give us *real* control, control that is *actually* available to us, instead of a fantasy of control that was never real.

Once we have learned enough to recognize our mistakes, own them, and forgive ourselves for them, we can let our cloaks of defensiveness hang more loosely about our shoulders. We can feel anxious or even threatened without jumping to simplistic explanations. We can realize that there can be bad actors in an industry, even *many* bad actors, without the *entire* industry being bound up in a vast conspiracy. We can realize that there can be systemic mistakes and flaws that can and should be fixed, without anyone having put them there on purpose. Or even if someone *did* put them there on purpose, we can realize that there were probably also people who worked against that purpose.

The more we learn, the more functionally uncertain we can become. We can reach for decisional balance sheets and prioritizing grids rather than kill switches. Our thinking joints can change from knees to hips, and we can dance.

### *Getting Outside*

In his book *Liminal Thinking*, Dave Gray explains how we avoid changing our views of what is real, right, and good.

> The obvious is not obvious. It is constructed. We work together, as individuals and in groups, to construct the obvious every day. We band together in "obvious clubs" that defend competing versions of reality. When you walk into your obvious club, you will find people reading the same books, watching the same news channels, and talking to the same people, all of which tends to reinforce the same version of reality.[61]

We can walk *out* of our obvious clubs in four ways: in the air, in our media habits, in our communities, and in the world.

- When we get outside in the air, we can open ourselves up to self-organization and reduce the impact of organization on our existence. Our self-organized bodies work better when we move around in the world, and our self-organized minds work better when we look at self-organized patterns: in the sky, in the grass, in the trees, in the water. A regular dose of self-organization can help us keep our attributions of agency and contingency in balance.
- When we get outside our normal diet of news and media, for example by watching movies and reading books in categories we rarely experience (because they are for audiences we do not consider ourselves to be part of), we can learn new things about ourselves and about other people.
- When we get outside our circle of family and friends and meet other people in our cities and towns, we can learn about people who are unlike us. By doing this, we can learn that *nobody* is unlike us. Every person on this planet is like us in *some* way, even if it's not obvious. Even a person who disagrees with us on every single topic might still love their children or talk to their plants or appreciate good cooking. The more we learn about people who are superficially unlike us, the harder it gets to blame them—especially groups of them—for the things that happen to us.
- When we get outside our usual geographic area, we can learn the same thing about cultures as we learned about people: every culture is unique, and every culture is the same. We can also see our own culture from the outside, giving us new perspectives on the way we live.

All of these ways of getting outside loosen up our shells, let in some fresh air, and give us room to grow.

### *Volunteering*

It's a Sunday afternoon, and for the past hour you have been listening to an old friend, a widower, reminisce about his lovely wife and the pancakes she used to make. Your friend's wife and her pancakes had nothing at all to do with the system that is keeping *you* down right now. When you leave that conversation and return to your own concerns, your strong feelings of injustice may have abated a little. Maybe they have abated to the point where you are ready to do some spiraling on what makes that "system" work.

Stepping outside our own misfortunes and into the misfortunes of others can loosen the hold our misfortunes have on our thinking. That's why volunteering is such a win-win situation. When we focus on someone else's problems, our burden can seem a little lighter than it was. And when our burden is lighter, we are less likely to use it as a shield.[62]

### *Empathizing*

Arno Michaelis, a former white supremacist who now works to combat racism, describes his journey into and out of the hate-filled conspiracy theories of white supremacy in his book *My Life After Hate*.

When I read Michaelis' book, I was struck by a contrast between two stories about children. Early in the book, as he is describing his indoctrination into a self-sealing worldview, he recalls a meeting at a bonfire.

> The roaring flames of the bonfire reflected in our eyes as we stood sweltering in its heat. . . . [T]he men . . . gathered around one of their infant daughters, raising their arms as we were as they swore an oath to protect her and all white children from the horrors of the mud races. . . . Adrenaline surged through my body at the thought of tearing the [Jewish and African-American people] from limb to limb with my bare hands.[63]

Michaelis began his turn toward empathy when his own daughter was born. He recounts an epiphany when he picked her up from her day-care center.

> A young black man about my age walked in to pick up his daughter, who leaped into his arms and hugged him, the same way my little girl hugged me. The smile on his face as he listened to his child relate her day in a gleeful, excited stream was the same smile my daughter gave me on a daily basis.
>
> I thought of all the people I had hurt, whether with my own hands or by lighting some psychopath's fuse. Those people had moms and dads and brothers and sisters. How did their loved ones feel when they saw this person who was so special to them battered and broken? How horrible would it be to have my daughter exposed to such violence in the slightest aspect?
>
> Love for my child thawed a dormant empathy for humanity that I was never aware of.[64]

Love is not a new-age hippy joke; it is the beauty that will save the world.[65] The so-called Darwinist idea that we live in a world where survival of the fittest matters more than cooperation is neither correct nor Darwinist. In his book *Darwin's Lost Theory*, David Loye describes his content analysis of Darwin's writings. In *The Descent of Man*, Loye writes, "Darwin wrote only *twice* of 'survival of the fittest,' but *95 times of love*."[66]

We humans are a suspicious lot, but we are also capable of love. And it's never too late to get better at loving each other. The first step is learning to love ourselves. When we can do that, we can take a long, unflinching look at our flaws and fears, stop sealing ourselves off from the world, throw off our defensive cloaks, and complete our journeys more lightly clad.

***Practice opening up your self-sealing thinking***

For this exercise you will need a partner, someone you disagree with and trust. First, *choose an issue* to discuss, something you both know you disagree about.

Next, agree that each of you will listen to what the other person says. *Do not move forward unless you both agree to listen.* Once you agree, both of you, answer the following questions, either in writing or by recording yourself speaking.

1. What do you *believe* about this issue?
2. Was there a time *before* you believed that? If so, what did you believe then, and what caused your belief to *change*?
3. When you think about this issue, how do you *feel*?
4. What do you *wish* would happen? What do you hope *never* happens?
5. When you feel that your belief on this issue is being challenged, or when you worry that you could be wrong, what points of *evidence* and sources of *authority* do you turn to? What do they tell you?
6. When you think about this issue, what are you *curious* about?

When you are both done, exchange your answers. *Do not read or listen to them together.* Instead, each of you, when you can be alone, take some time to read or listen to the other person's answers. Give yourselves a few days or weeks to reflect.

Next, decide whether you want to talk about the answers. *If either person doesn't want to talk, don't talk.* Just push the answers into the back of your minds and move on with your lives. But if you both want to keep talking, answer *these* questions:

1. When you read or listened to the other person's answers, how did you *feel*?
2. What did you *learn* about the other person?
3. What are you *curious* about now?

Then decide if you want to talk about *those* answers. Or think of more issues and exchange more answers. You can keep doing this for years *without ever talking directly about your answers.* You will end up talking about them indirectly, here and there, but you never need to *confront* each other on these points.

You can use this exercise to understand the issues you explore in ways you could not understand without the help of the other person. You can help each other *because* you disagree. That's a gift you can give to each other.

# Postscript

To bring this book to a close, I would like to pass on to you the best piece of advice I ever heard in my life. Overheard, actually. I was riding on a train, and I heard a young woman talking to an old man. The young woman was trying to decide whether to get married.

"I don't know what to do," she said. "I don't want to make a mistake."

"Oh, you'll make a mistake," he replied. "You'll make a mistake if you marry him, and you'll make a mistake if you don't. The only thing you can do is make the best mistake you can make."

Right here, right now, this book is the best mistake I can make. I hope it helps *you* make the best mistakes you can make.

# Acknowledgements

Many people helped me write this book. If you and I ever talked about organization and self-organization over the past thirty-some years, you helped me write this book. If you and I ever worked on a project together that touched on these topics, you helped me write this book. If I read your book or paper about organization, self-organization, or both, or about any of the topics I explored in this book, you helped me write this book.

But my debt of gratitude goes back much further than that. The people who came up with the concepts of yin and yang, the five elements, and the medicine wheel helped me write this book. The people who passed down and wrote down folk tales helped me write this book. Going back thousands of years, every person who ever passed on an insight, discovery, or thought about organization and self-organization helped me write this book. Thank you all.

In my earlier years of work on this topic, the people I spoke most with about my ideas were Sharon Darwent, Paul Fernhout, Harold van Garderen, Lev Ginzburg, Tom Graves, Charlie Janson, and Dave Snowden.

More recently, after I finished writing this book, my "early readers," a diverse group of friends, family members, and colleagues, read the book and sent feedback. All of these people helped me improve the book by seeing it through their eyes. They are: Sue Batson, John Caddell, Lella DeBonis, Karen Dietz, Beverly Folmer, Keith Fortowsky, Harold van Garderen, Dave Gray, Jeff Hallen, Wendy Hallen, Sherry Johnson, Mary Klinger, Adelle Kurtz, Cyril Kurtz, Theresa Kurtz, Tatiana Feitosa Correa Lima, Yeu Wen Mak, Lily Martens, Murray McGregor, Thaler Pekar, Caroline Rennie, Stephen Sillett, Geert Sturtewagen, Carl Tolbert, and Bruce Waltuck.

Before any of those people read the book, my husband Paul Fernhout and my son Elliot Fernhout listened to me read the whole thing out loud, chapter by chapter. And before that, they listened to me talk about organization and self-organization, then about the thinking spaces I could build, then about the topics I could explore. Through it all, they pointed out flaws, suggested ideas, and helped me improve my thinking. This is a much better book than I could have written without their help.

# Exercise Materials

On the following pages are materials you can use to work with the seven thinking spaces in this book.

To use the materials, you can:

- photocopy pages from the printed book
- download the materials from cfkurtz.com/confluence and print the pages you need
- copy the labels onto sticky notes by hand

Instructions for using the materials are in Chapter Three.

## Confluence (Chapter Two) - Axes and Corners

### Axes

***Horizontal axis***

| Organization → | |
|---|---|
| ← Weak organization | Strong organization → |

***Vertical axis - rotate before placing***

| Self-organization → | |
|---|---|
| ← Weak self-organization | Strong self-organization → |

### Corners

Weak organization
Strong self-organization

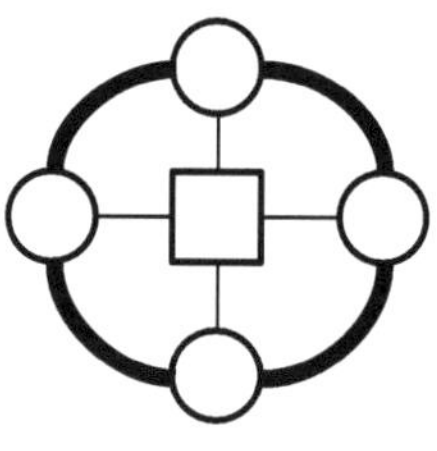

Strong organization
Strong self-organization

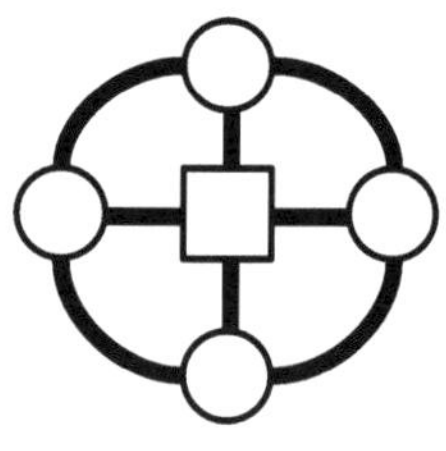

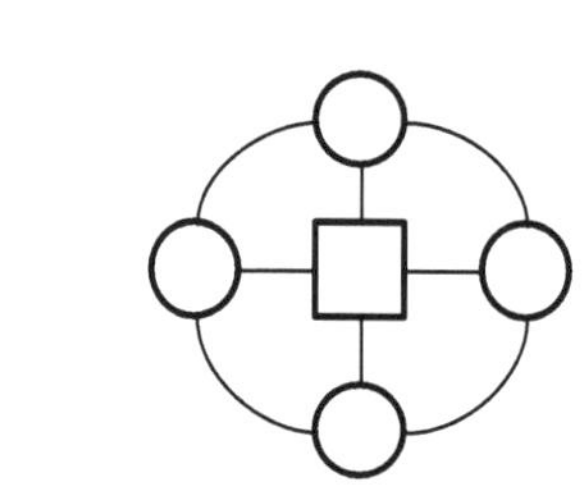

Weak organization
Weak self-organization

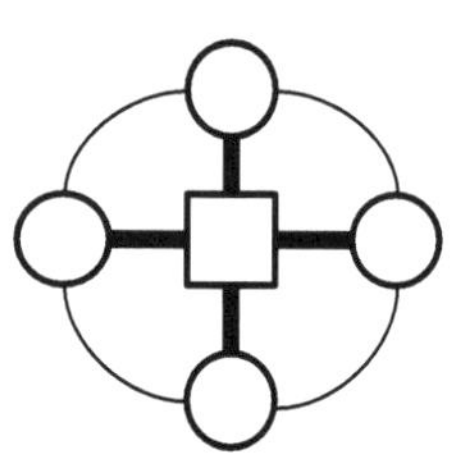

Strong organization
Weak self-organization

## Confluence (Chapter Two) - Example situations

| A beaver builds a dam | A crew builds a road | A couple plans a wedding |
|---|---|---|
| Children play in a park | Teenagers hang out | Old folks reminisce |
| A tornado hits a house | A city holds an election | A gardener pores over a seed catalog |

## Confluence (Chapter Two) - Proverbs

| Birds of a feather flock together | Each to their own | Variety is the spice of life |
|---|---|---|
| If you fail to plan, you plan to fail | Many hands make light work | Measure twice, cut once |
| A chain is only as strong as its weakest link | If you want something done right, do it yourself | It takes all kinds to make the world go round |

## The Jungle (Chapter Four) - Axes and Corners

### Axes

*Horizontal axis*

Resilience →

← Low resilience

High resilience →

*Vertical axis - rotate before placing*

Strength →

← Low strength

High strength →

### Corners

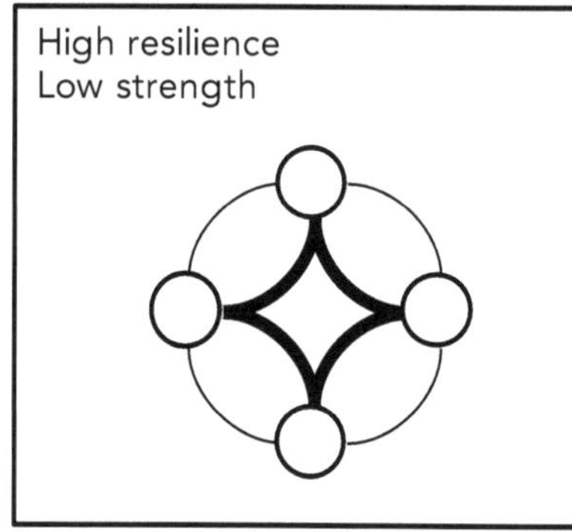


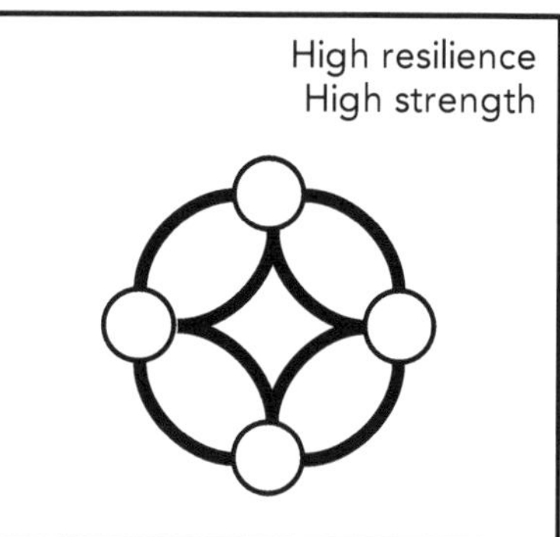


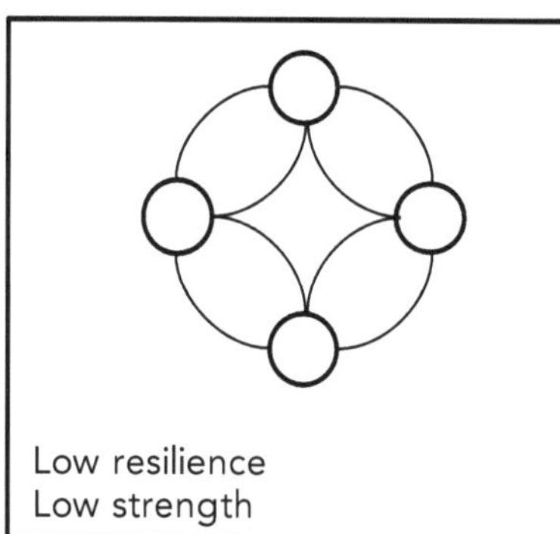


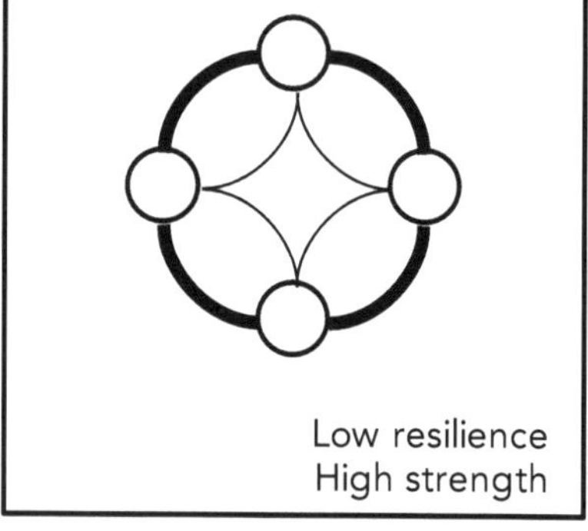

### The Jungle (Chapter Four) - Example situations

| | | |
|---|---|---|
| A crowd cheers at a sports event | A congregation sings in a church | A reading club meets in a library |
| A fern grows in an old growth forest | A fern grows in a managed forest | A fern grows in a botanical garden |
| Bacteria grow on a public bench | Bacteria grow in an operating room | Bacteria grow in a school cafeteria |

### The Jungle (Chapter Four) - Proverbs

| | | |
|---|---|---|
| Fall seven times, stand up eight | Too many cooks spoil the broth | Still waters run deep |
| People who live in glass houses should not throw stones | A friend in need is a friend indeed | You can lead a horse to water, but you cannot make it drink |
| Tell me who your friends are, and I'll tell you who you are | Laugh and the world laughs with you, weep and you weep alone | The longest journey starts with a single step |

## The Plan (Chapter Five) - Axes and Corners

### Axes

#### *Horizontal axis*

| Effort → |
|---|

| ← Low effort | High effort → |
|---|---|

#### *Vertical axis - rotate before placing*

| Awareness → |
|---|

| ← Low awareness | High awareness → |
|---|---|

### Corners

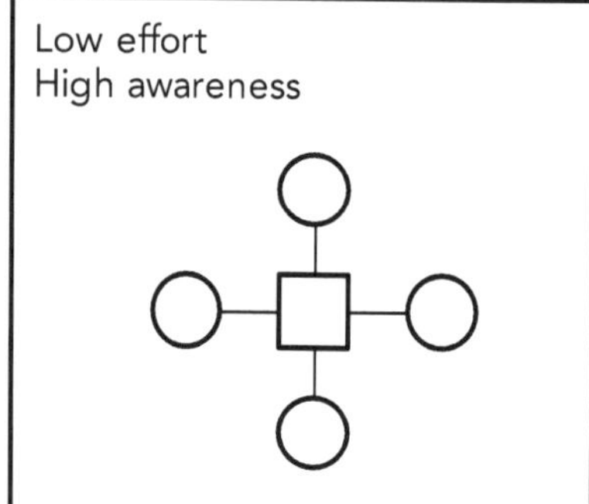


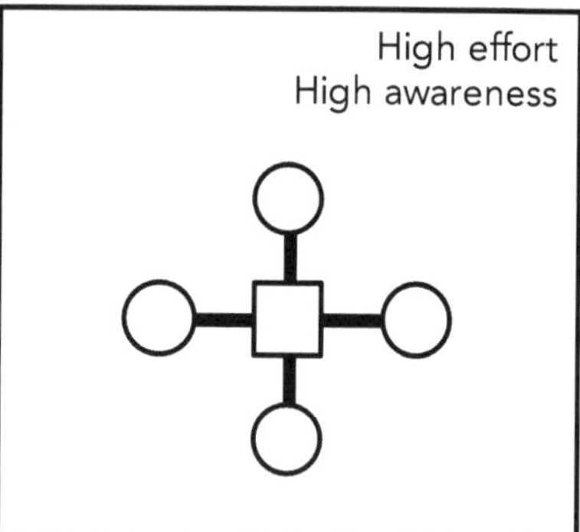


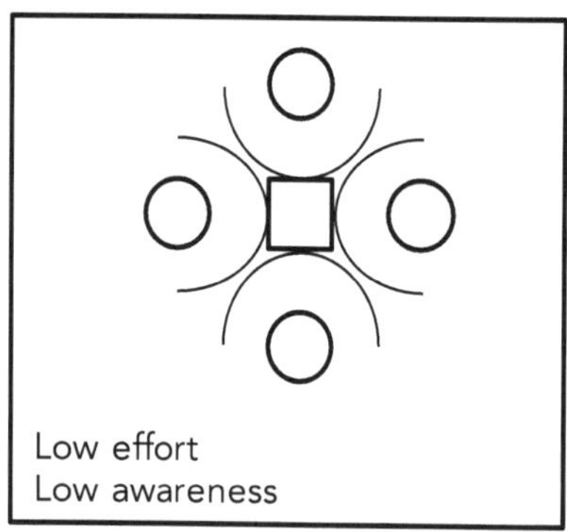


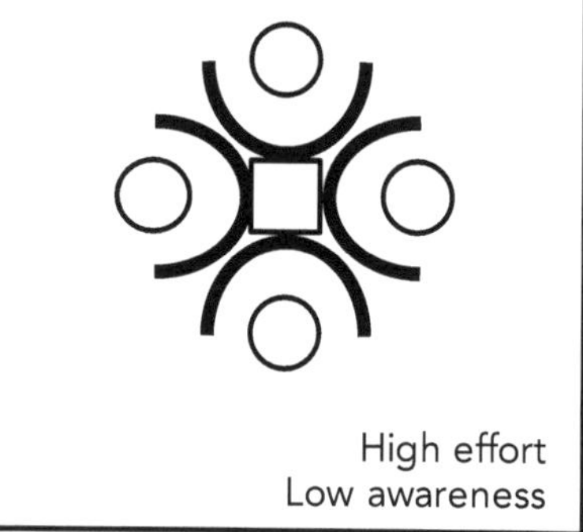

## THE PLAN (CHAPTER FIVE) - EXAMPLE SITUATIONS

| | | |
|---|---|---|
| A government enforces a curfew | A police officer listens to a wiretap | A social service sets up an anonymous tip line |
| Two dogs sniff each other | A dog growls and snaps at another dog | Two dogs fight |
| A road is blocked due to an accident | A sign warns drivers of trouble ahead | Drivers hear a *bang* and slow down |

## THE PLAN (CHAPTER FIVE) - PROVERBS

| | | |
|---|---|---|
| Take the bull by the horns | Fools rush in where angels fear to tread | In the kingdom of the blind, the one-eyed man is king |
| Don't burn your bridges | What you don't know won't hurt you | You're never too old to learn |
| A little learning is a dangerous thing | Fortune favors the bold | Don't throw the baby out with the bathwater |

## Inundation (Chapter Six) - Axes and Corners

### Axes

***Horizontal axis***

| ← Effect on organization → | |
|---|---|
| ← Destruction | Preservation → |

***Vertical axis - rotate before placing***

| Self-organization → | |
|---|---|
| ← Weak self-organization | Strong self-organization → |

### Corners

Organization destroyed by strong self-organization

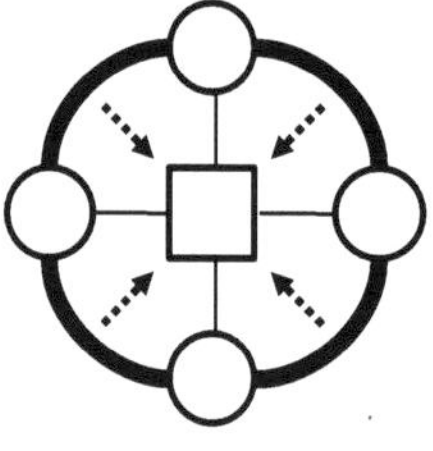

Organization preserved by strong self-organization

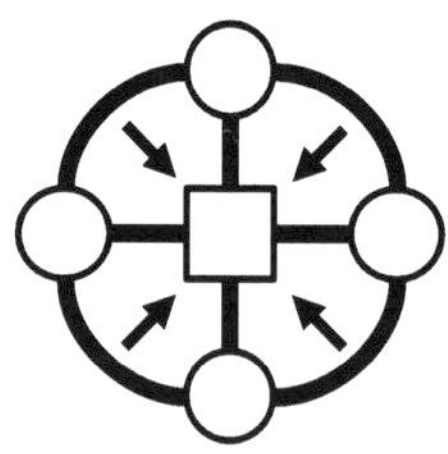

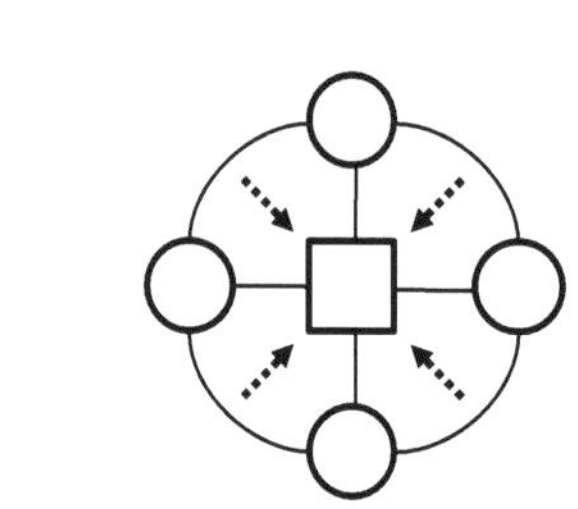

Organization destroyed by weak self-organization

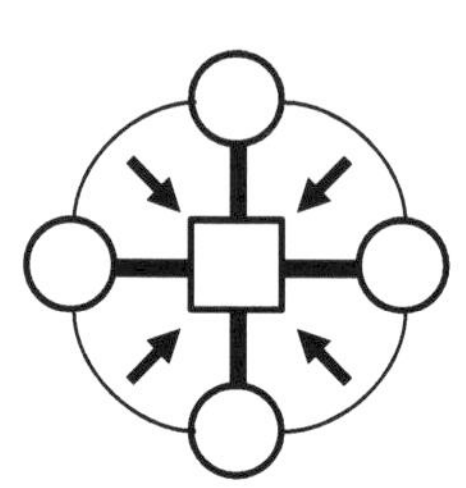

Organization preserved by weak self-organization

## INUNDATION (CHAPTER SIX) - EXAMPLE SITUATIONS

| | | |
|---|---|---|
| A dandelion grows in a sidewalk crack | A sidewalk ices over in the winter | A sidewalk is swallowed up by a sink hole |
| People rush to a bank to take out their money | People avoid a restaurant after reports of illness | People build a park in a city center |
| A city becomes popular | A city goes through an epidemic | A city is bombed |

## INUNDATION (CHAPTER SIX) - PROVERBS

| | | |
|---|---|---|
| If wishes were horses, beggars would ride | Better the devil you know than the devil you don't | All good things must come to an end |
| Be careful what you wish for; you just might get it | Good fences make good neighbors | Don't count your chickens before they hatch |
| What can't be cured must be endured | The more things change, the more they stay the same | Let sleeping dogs lie |

## Regulation (Chapter Seven) - Axes and Corners

### Axes

#### *Horizontal axis*

Organization →

← Weak organization

Strong organization →

#### *Vertical axis - rotate before placing*

← Effect on self-organization →

← Destruction

Preservation →

### Corners

Self-organization preserved by weak organization

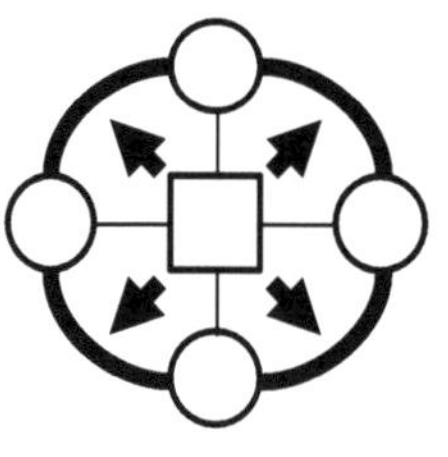

Self-organization preserved by strong organization

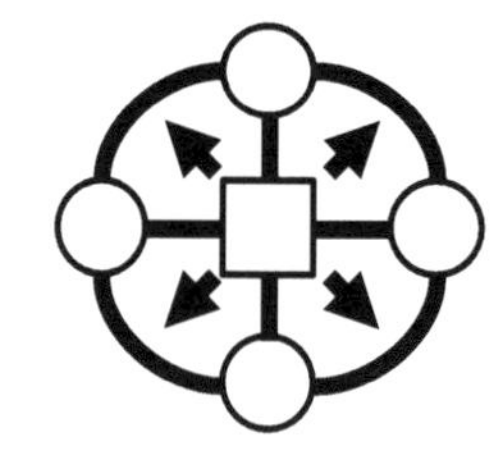

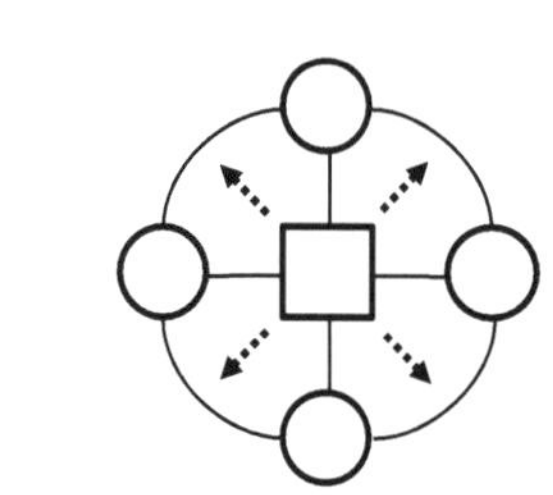

Self-organization destroyed by weak organization

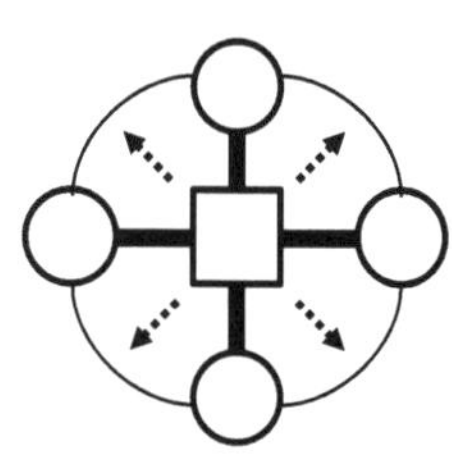

Self-organization destroyed by strong organization

## Regulation (Chapter Seven) - Example situations

| | | |
|---|---|---|
| A police officer watches an intersection | A bird eats a berry | A teacher listens to a child tell a story |
| A store manager checks a display | A parent reprimands a child | A town board meets to discuss an issue |
| A grandparent pushes a child on a swing | A trail crew maintains a trail | A gardener picks a flower |

## Regulation (Chapter Seven) - Proverbs

| | | |
|---|---|---|
| If it ain't broke, don't fix it | No pain, no gain | You can't get blood out of a stone |
| Attack is the best form of defense | Don't try to walk before you can crawl | If anything can go wrong, it will |
| Never look a gift horse in the mouth | Better safe than sorry | An ounce of prevention is worth a pound of cure |

## The Mix (Chapter Eight) - Axes and Corners

### Axes

#### *Horizontal axis*

| ← Effect of self-organization on organization → | |
|---|---|
| ← Destruction | Preservation → |

#### *Vertical axis - rotate before placing*

| ← Effect of organization on self-organization → | |
|---|---|
| ← Destruction | Preservation → |

### Corners

SO destroys O
O preserves SO

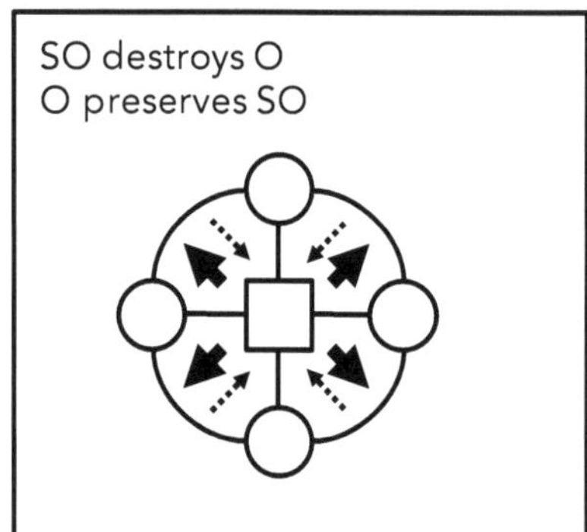

SO preserves O
O preserves SO

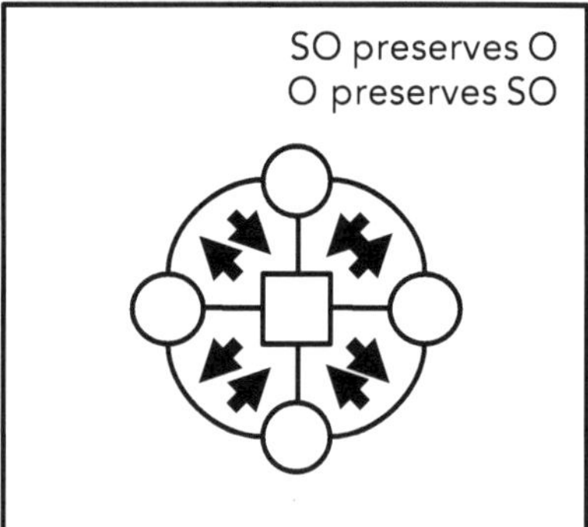

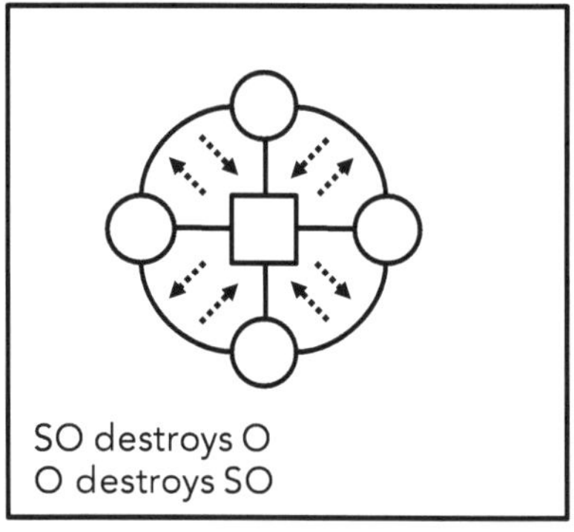

SO destroys O
O destroys SO

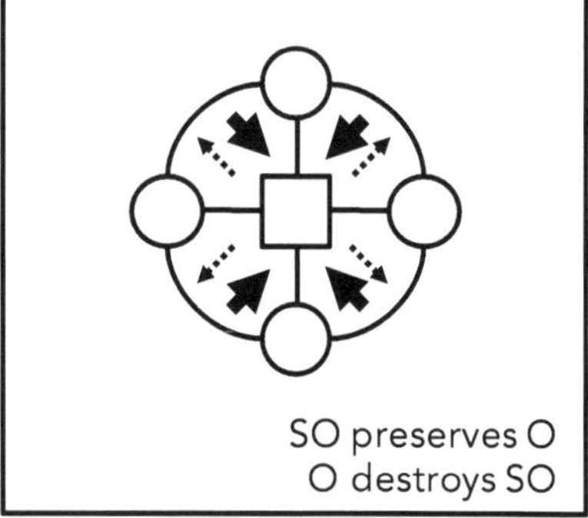

SO preserves O
O destroys SO

## The Mix (Chapter Eight) - Example situations

| | | |
|---|---|---|
| A farmer is encouraged by a good harvest | A homeowner fixes a mildew problem | An advertisement goes viral |
| A teacher wins a lottery | A gardener waits for the right time to plant a seed | A tax rate increases |
| A used car is sold for a very good price | A child helps with dinner | A crowd listens to music |

## The Mix (Chapter Eight) - Proverbs

| | | |
|---|---|---|
| Hope springs eternal | United we stand, divided we fall | Curiosity killed the cat |
| Opportunity never knocks twice | A rolling stone gathers no moss | Hindsight is always twenty-twenty |
| All good things come to those who wait | Cross the stream where it is shallowest | Don't rock the boat |

## Connecting the dots (Chapter Nine) - Axes and Corners

### Axes

*Horizontal axis*

| ← Connection types → | |
|---|---|
| ← More self-organized | More organized → |

*Vertical axis - rotate before placing - fill in assertion*

| What is real? → | | |
|---|---|---|
| ← Something else | Not sure | → |

### Corners

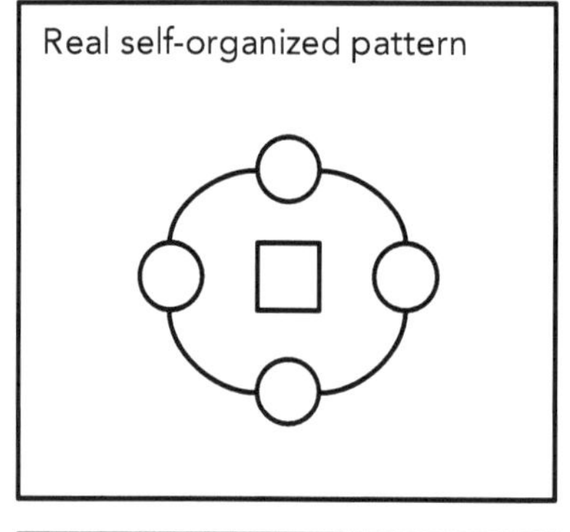


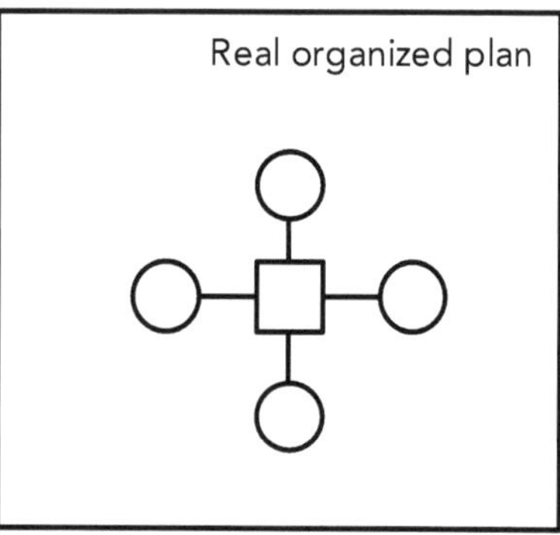


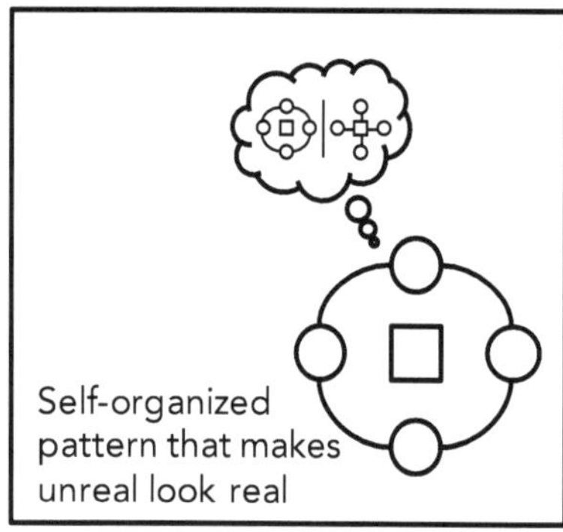

Self-organized
pattern that makes
unreal look real


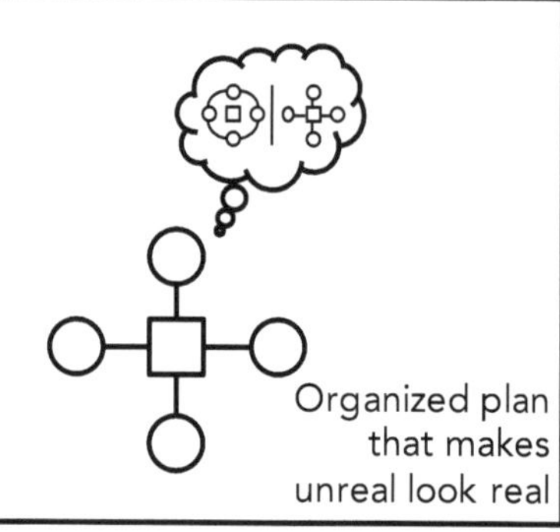

## Connecting the dots (Chapter Nine) - Example situations

| | | |
|---|---|---|
| An unidentified flying object | An alien spacecraft | A weather balloon |
| A movie model of an alien spacecraft | An alien spacecraft designed to look like a movie model | A movie model of a weather balloon |
| A cloud that looks like an alien spacecraft | An alien spacecraft that just happens to look like a cloud | An alien spacecraft designed to look like a cloud |

## Connecting the dots (Chapter Nine) - Proverbs

| | | |
|---|---|---|
| All that glitters is not gold | Even from a foe a man may learn wisdom | False friends are worse than open enemies |
| Many a true word is spoken in jest | An apple a day keeps the doctor away | Cleanliness is next to godliness |
| A fool and his money are soon parted | You pays your money and you takes your choice | Big fish eat little fish |

# Notes

## Notes for Chapter 1 – Introduction

1. Who is the *self* in *self*-organization? It's the *collective self* of the group (which organizes *itself*), and it's the pattern that forms (which forms *itself*). By the way, my all-time-favorite starter book for understanding self-organization is *Turbulent Mirror* by John Briggs and F. David Peat, published in 1989 by Harper Perennial. The science is a bit dated at this point, but it's still the best introduction to the topic that I've found.
2. If you want to read more about how piles of sand suddenly fall down, and how lots of other things that fall down (like avalanches) follow similar patterns, look up "self-organized criticality." My favorite starter book for understanding self-organization in nature is Philip Ball's *The Self-Made Tapestry: Pattern Formation in Nature,* published in 1999 by Oxford University Press.
3. My favorite starter book for understanding self-organization in biology is *Self-Organization in Biological Systems* by Scott Camazine, Jean-Louis Deneubourg, Nigel R. Franks, James Sneyd, Guy Theraulaz, and Eric Bonabeau, published in 2001 by Princeton University Press.
4. Why did we want to minimize the distance between ourselves and our closest neighbors? Because we all wanted the people around us to protect us from whatever made the loud noise. The instinct to bunch together in times of danger is common to all social species. It's the reason flocks, herds, crowds, and cities form: for mutual protection. My favorite starter book for understanding self-organization in people is *Small Groups as Complex Systems* by Holly Arrow, Joseph E. McGrath, and Jennifer L. Berdahl (published in 2000 by Sage Publications).
5. If you want to learn about the history of the term "self-organization," check out *Invisible Hands: Self-Organization and the Eighteenth Century* by Jonathan Sheehan and Dror Wahrman, published in 2015 by the University of Chicago Press.
6. To watch fish doing this, search the internet for "fish circular mating mound." Cichlid fish and pufferfish are two groups of fish that build circular constructions.

## Notes for Chapter 2 – The Confluence Thinking Space

1. I developed this first thinking space in 2001, at IBM, in response to Dave Snowden's early work on his Cynefin framework. (This 2001 drawing shows my first version of the space's four corner diagrams.) My "version" of Cynefin drew on my previous work on self-organization and decision making. (See Kurtz, C.F. 1991. The evolution of information gathering: operational constraints. In *From Animals to Animats*, eds. Meyer, J.A. and S.W. Wilson. Proc. 1st Int. Conf. on Simulation of Adaptive Behavior, Paris, MIT Press.) With help from Sharon Darwent, Dave and I tested and refined both versions of the framework in a series of discussions and workshops. (See Kurtz, C. & Snowden, D. 2003. The new dynamics of strategy: sense making in a complex and complicated world. *IBM Systems Journal* 42(3): 462-483.) In 2010, I renamed my version of Cynefin "the Confluence Sensemaking Framework" and added four more spaces to it. In 2019, when I started work on this book, I improved all of my diagrams and some of my axes, and I added two more spaces.

2. For an interesting discussion of spider cognition, see "Do Spiders Think?" by Mary Bates, on the *Psychology Today* blog, posted March 7, 2019. Accessed February 2021 at https://www.psychologytoday.com/us/blog/animal-minds/201903/do-spiders-think.
3. See, for example, "Ancient Mongolian nests show that dinosaurs protected their eggs" by Jonathan Lambert, *Nature*, volume 571, pages 308-309. Accessed February 2021 at https://www.nature.com/articles/d41586-019-02174-7.

4. What if an organizer believes it has awareness but is mistaken in that belief? I would still call it an organizer, because it is at least *attempting* to organize the world around it. But the two categories are not mutually exclusive; it is possible to be both at once.
5. How do we know the fish's construction represents *intentional* arrangement, and not just a side effect of an unrelated behavior? Well, for one thing, each male fish *maintains* the circularity of its mound until mating has taken place. (See for example, Kawase, H., Okata, Y. & Ito, K. 2013. Role of Huge Geometric Circular Structures in the Reproduction of a Marine Pufferfish. *Sci. Rep.* 3, 2106.) Pufferfish may use simple rules to construct their mating mounds (See Mizuuchi, R., Kawase, H., Shin, H., Iwai, D., & Kondo, S. (2018). Simple rules for construction of a geometric nest structure by pufferfish. *Scientific reports*, 8(1), 12366.). However, to my mind, this does not make the mounds any less organized—as opposed to self-organized—because each fish creates its mound by the deliberate actions it takes, even if those actions are simple. For a fascinating photographic exploration of animal constructions, see *Animal Architecture* by Ingo Arndt and Jürgen Tautz, published in 2013 by Harry N. Abrams.
6. Throughout this book I use the "singular they," a gender-neutral pronoun that is both grammatically correct and hundreds of years old.
7. "Plastic Bag Found at the Bottom of World's Deepest Ocean Trench" by Sarah Gibbens, published July 3, 2019 as a *National Geographic* Resource Library article. Accessed July 2020 at https://www.nationalgeographic.org/article/plastic-bag-found-bottom-worlds-deepest-ocean-trench.
8. The *One Small Square* series, by Donald M. Silver and Patricia Wynne, includes a backyard, woods, seashore, pond, cave, tundra, savanna, desert, night sky, rain forest, swamp, and coral reef.
9. Could a situation be purely self-organized if the human interactors in it have only *local* intentions and plans? Yes. But that almost never happens. As soon as one person in a traffic jam makes a call to the city to complain, or honks their horn loud enough for dozens of other drivers to hear it, the pattern stops being purely self-organized. My crowd-bunching-up story was *close* to pure self-organization, but that's because it took place over a few seconds. If the emergency had gone on for even another minute, *somebody* would have tried to organize the crowd.
10. Cleanroom standards are massively complicated. The Wikipedia page on cleanrooms is a pretty good introduction to the topic. See https://en.wikipedia.org/wiki/Cleanroom.
11. You can find the "Life After People" television series on the History Channel web site at www.history.com/shows/life-after-people.
12. All of the quotes in this paragraph are from the book *History of Clarion County, Pennsylvania*, edited by Aaron J. Davis, published in 1887 by Record Press. Accessed February 2021 at http://sites.rootsweb.com/~pacchs/davis/44.htm.
13. The question of whether a ghost town must be *completely* uninhabited is a matter of debate.
14. Reading the pioneering work of Jane Jacobs on self-organized patterns in city life is a wonderful way to become more familiar with these issues. As she said on page 57 of her 1961 book *The Death and Life of Great American Cities*, "Formal public organizations in cities require an informal public life underlying them, mediating between them and the privacy of the people of the city."
15. The writings of Ralph Stacey and Manuel de Landa are particularly useful in these areas.
16. The concept of "positive deviance" is relevant here.
17. This widely-cited quote is from *Time Magazine*, 12 February, 1979. However, it is quoted out of context there. It is on the second page of the "People" section of the magazine. (I accessed it in February of 2021 at http://content.time.com/time/subscriber/article/0,33009,920116-2,00.html.) Because the *Time* quote is introduced with the words "Eugene McCarthy, former Senator and now author," it must be drawn from a book or article written by McCarthy prior to February 1979. However, he published seven books (and who knows how many articles and speeches) between 1960 and 1979. So to find the original quote in context, I would have to read every possible source. I did not do that.
18. An excellent source of information about life in medieval monasteries is *A History of Private Life, Volume II: Revelations of the Medieval World*, edited by Philippe Aries and Georges Duby, first published in 1987 by Belknap Press.

## Notes for Chapter 3 – Using the Confluence Space

1. If you are using the "Connecting the Dots" space, you need to use at least the Y axis labels. Fill in what you want the space to represent as real (or true or right) on the upper Y axis label. See that chapter for details.
2. If you are working online, download the slide-set version of the exercise materials from cfkurtz.com/confluence. Then open the file and add sticky-note boxes to it. If you have a sharing workspace where everyone can see everyone else's cursors, you can all work on the document at once. Otherwise, have one person share their screen while they act as a scribe, typing into the sticky-note boxes and moving them around on request.
3. If you are working online, you can simply move the example situations and proverbs into the space as you talk.
4. If you are working online, write down your situations separately, on your own devices. Keep your thoughts separate until you merge them.
5. If you are working online, now is the time to type all of the situations into sticky-note boxes. Put the boxes outside the space until you place them into it.
6. If you are working online, use the annotation tools at your disposal to mark up the space.
7. If you are working online, write your wrap-up list items on your own devices first. Then share them as you retype them into your common space.
8. Consultants, like therapists, have to be good at keeping secrets. I often help people find out things they don't want to share with the world. In fact, the more I am able to help people discover, the less they want me to tell anyone about what they found out. Hence the fictional walk-through, which illustrates what generally happens in workshops without revealing any private details.
9. Where did the situations in my fictional walk-through come from? I drew them from a set of eighty stories I made up to demonstrate the use of *NarraFirma*, my software that helps people work with their stories. You can read all eighty stories in the example project on narrafirma.com.
10. Are more situations *always* better? No. At some point, diminishing returns begin to set in. At around 80-100 situations you usually stop finding new patterns. At that point, if you want to keep exploring, it's best to start over with a new space or a new topic.
11. You might want to discuss whether people can move sticky notes other people placed, especially if you don't know each other well. I learned this tip from Michael O'Bryan, an experienced facilitator.
12. If you want some advice on running participatory workshops, check out *Participatory Workshops* by Robert Chambers (first published by earthscan in 2002). It's the best book I know on the topic.
13. I used to say "Native American." Now I say "American Indian," because I read that native peoples prefer the latter term. "American Indian" is what it says on the treaties, and the treaties matter.
14. If you wonder what these ancient sources of wisdom have to do with organization and self-organization: read about them. You'll notice the connections.
15. If you know of a method or framework you think I should add to this list, let me know. To be included, it must *explicitly* address how organization (intentional plans) and self-organization (spontaneous patterns) flow together in situations. Methods or frameworks that consider only organization or only self-organization do not qualify. If I agree that the method or framework you suggest meets this criterion, I will add it to the book's web site.

## Notes for Chapter 4 – The Jungle

1. Of course, some of these measures of network strength also relate to network resilience. For example, multiplex networks bounce back faster than networks with only one type of connection.
2. The movie *The Shining* takes place in a hotel.
3. Song YY, Zeng RS, Xu JF, Li J, Shen X, Yihdego WG. 2010, Interplant Communication of Tomato Plants through Underground Common Mycorrhizal Networks. PLoS ONE 5(10): e13324. Accessed February 2021 at https://doi.org/10.1371/journal.pone.0013324.
4. See "Deep-sea mining could find rare elements for smartphones — but will it destroy rare species?" by Alessandra Potenza in *The Verge*, January 22, 2019. Accessed February 2021 at https://www.theverge.com/2017/10/3/16398518/deep-sea-mining-hydrothermal-vents-japan-precious-metals-rare-species.

5. See "Kudzu, Japan's Wonder Vine" by Kristen Hinman, published in *American History*, June 2011. Accessed February 2021 at https://www.historynet.com/kudzu-japans-wonder-vine.htm.
6. Finch, B. 2015. The True Story of Kudzu, the Vine That Never Truly Ate the South. *Smithsonian Magazine*, September 2015. Accessed December 2020 at www.smithsonianmag.com/science-nature/true-story-kudzu-vine-ate-south-180956325.
7. USDA Forest Service Southern Research Station. 2011. Southern Forest Futures Project Technical Report 178. Accessed December 2020 at www.srs.fs.usda.gov/futures/technical-report/15.html.
8. See "What to Do About Kudzu" by Kelly Holland, published in July 28, 2019 in the "Habitat at Home" column of *Conserving Carolina*. Accessed February 2021 at https://conservingcarolina.org/get-rid-of-kudzu/.

## Notes for Chapter 5 – The Plan

1. The story of the boy who put his finger in the dike is not a folk tale, nor is it Dutch. It was made up by U.S. author Mary Mapes Dodge, who told it in her 1865 novel *Hans Brinker, or The Silver Skates*. Today, so many people *think* the story is an old Dutch folk tale that it might be turning into a folk tale—but not a Dutch one. As many people have pointed out, Dutch dikes are mostly made of clay, not stone, and you can't plug leaks in them with little things like fingers.
2. The wu-wei quote is from page 22 of *Zhuangzi: The Essential Writings*, translated by Brook Ziporyn, published by Hackett Publishing Company in 2009.
3. Slingerland's 2015 book *Trying Not to Try* was published by Broadway Books.
4. This is a reference to *Finite and Infinite Games* by James P. Carse, my second-favorite book. It was first published in 1987 by Ballantine Books.
5. From page 470 of *American Indian Myths and Legends*, selected and edited by Richard Erdoes and Alfonso Ortiz, published in 1984 by Pantheon Books.
6. From page 115 of *Mayan Folktales*, translated and edited by James D. Sexton, published in 1992 by the University of New Mexico Press.
7. From page 184 of *Encyclopedia of Urban Legends* by Jan Harold Brunvald, published in 2001 by Norton.
8. You can find Fénelon's quote on page 128 of the book *Selections from the Writings of Fénelon* (under the heading "The Spirit of God Teaches Within"), published in 2014 by Whitaker House.
9. The where-the-wheel-isn't quote is from my favorite translation of the *Daodejing*, by Ursula K. le Guin. It was reissued in 2019 by Shambhala Publications as *Lao Tzu: Tao Te Ching*.
10. An interesting take on the "Footprints" story can be found in the essay "Enter Sandman," published in *Poetry* magazine on March 19th, 2008. Accessed December 2020 at https://www.poetryfoundation.org/articles/68974/enter-sandman.
11. Here's one source: http://www.online-literature.com/anton_chekhov/1260/.
12. From page 124 of *Anton Chekhov: The Complete Short Novels*, translated by Richard Pevear and Larissa Volokhonsky, published in 2004 by Vintage Books, a division of Random House. All of the quotes in this section are from the same translation.
13. From page 215 of *Anton Chekhov: The Complete Short Novels*.
14. From page 230 of *Anton Chekhov: The Complete Short Novels*.
15. From page 234 of *Anton Chekhov: The Complete Short Novels*.
16. You can find Fröbel's quote on page 85 of *Friedrich Froebel: A Selection from His Writings* by Irene M. Lilley, published in 1967 by Cambridge University Press. 188 pages.
17. From section 36 of the chapter "Some Thoughts Concerning Education" in *The Educational Writings of John Locke*, published in 2018 by Forgotten Books.
18. UN Declaration of the Rights of the Child. Accessed February 2021 at www.ohchr.org/documents/professionalinterest/crc.pdf.
19. From page 12 of Bowlby's 1988 book *A Secure Base*, published by Routledge.
20. The Piaget quote is from the chapter "Some Aspects of Operations," which starts on page 15 of the book *Play and Development: A Symposium with Contributions by Jean Piaget, Peter H. Wolff and Others*. The editor was Maria W. Piers, and the book was first published in 1972 by Norton.
21. Huxley's quote is from his book of essays, *Technical Education*, which was published in 1877.

22. See, for example, "Learning by Observing and Pitching-In and the Connections to Native and Indigenous Knowledge Systems" by Luis Urrieta, Jr. Published December 2015 in *Advances in Child Development and Behavior* 49:357-379.

## Notes for Chapter 6 – Inundation

1. This section benefited from my reading of the book *Response to Disaster: Psychosocial, Community, and Ecological Aproaches*, edited by Richard Gist and Bernard Lubin, published in 1999 by Routledge.
2. Nuestadt, R. E. and May, E. R. 1986. *Thinking in Time*. Free Press.
3. Trost, Z. et al., 2012, "Cognitive dimensions of anger in chronic pain." *PAIN*, volume 153, pp 515-517. Accessed February 2021 at sullivan-painresearch.mcgill.ca/pdf/abstracts/2012/Pain_153_515-517.pdf.
4. From page 75 of *Normal Accidents*, published in 1999 by Princeton University Press.
5. From page 33 of Dietrich Dörner's *The Logic of Failure*, published in 1997 by Basic Books.
6. From the blog post "Amidst the ruins of Bokor Hill Station," posted November 14, 2012 on the blog "What's Dave Doing?" Accessed February 2021 at https://whatsdavedoing.com/amidst-ruins-bokor-hill-station.
7. Larkham's quote is from page 33 of *Conservation and the City*, published in 1996 by Routledge.
8. From page 5 of *Saving Our Vanishing Heritage: Safeguarding Endangered Cultural Heritage Sites in the Developing World*, Global Heritage Fund, October 17, 2010. Accessed February 2021 at globalheritagefund.org/images/uploads/docs/GHFSavingOurVanishingHeritagev1.0singlepageview.pdf.
9. The Helike Project web site, www.helikeproject.gr, is full of fascinating details.
10. See for example, "Rewriting Tel Megiddo's Violent History" by Pamela Weintraub, *Discover*, Sep 30, 2015. Accessed February 2021 at https://www.discovermagazine.com/the-sciences/rewriting-tel-megiddos-violent-history.
11. The risk-hope quote is from *Doctor Who*, episode 2, season 11 ("Spyfall, Part 2").
12. The phrase "order for free" was coined by Stuart Kaufmann, who has used it to explain that self-organized patterns can appear without any effort being put into them on the part of people who benefit from them. This is true; but far less often mentioned is the fact that self-organized patterns can frustrate efforts and drain resources from those who need them most.
13. The Dickens quote is from his book *American Notes*, starting at the tenth paragraph of chapter fifteen. "Canes" are most likely lengths of bamboo or rattan called "swagger sticks," which were used to convey authority (and had to be periodically straightened). "Glazed stocks" are probably the stiff, polished leather collars worn by soldiers at the time.
14. *Ivy on Walls*, a 2017 report from Historic England, written by M. Coombes, H. Viles, and A. Cathersides. Accessed February 2021 at research.historicengland.org.uk/Report.aspx?i=15604.
15. The faulty-signals quote is from page 45 of Perrow's 1999 book *Normal Accidents*.
16. One source on the Surry accident is allthingsnuclear.org/dlochbaum/pipe-rupture-at-surry, accessed February 2021.
17. See, for example, "Rolls-Royce plans 16 mini-nuclear plants for UK" by Justin Rowlatt, BBC News, 11 November 2020. Accessed February 2021 at https://www.bbc.com/news/science-environment-54703204.
18. Where did the C128 story come from? I made it up based on what I read about Industry 4.0.
19. The flooding incident is described on page 45 of *Normal Accidents*.

## Notes for Chapter 7 – Regulation

1. Plato's *Critias*, 433 BCE, section 111b.
2. This is a line from the song "History Repeating," written by Alex Gifford and originally performed by the Propellerheads featuring Shirley Bassey in 1997.
3. "In Thailand, shifting cultivators have even been arrested for causing 'deforestation and rise in temperature'"—this is from page 25 of the 2015 FAO report "Shifting Cultivation, Livelihood and Food Security: New and Old Challenges for Indigenous Peoples in Asia," edited by Christian Erni, accessed in July 2020 at http://www.fao.org/3/a-i4580e.pdf

4. The Ohalo excavations are described in the paper "The Origin of Cultivation and Proto-Weeds, Long Before Neolithic Farming" by Ainit Snir (and several others), published in the journal *PLoS One* on July 22, 2015. Accessed July 2020 at https://doi.org/10.1371/journal.pone.0131422
5. LIDAR stands for "Light Detection and Ranging" or "Laser Imaging, Detection, and Ranging."
6. It is possible to create *conditions* under which self-organization is likely (even extremely likely) to arise. But self-organization itself can never be created, nor can it be completely or precisely controlled. People often work to shape and influence self-organized patterns, like, say, bonzai trees, but they only succeed in this when they understand the limits of their control and adapt to working within them. A bonzai master who cannot accept the limits of organized control over self-organization makes nothing but broken branches. This is what makes bonzai an art form and not a production process.
7. We also have a limited view of cities. Menno Schilthuizen's 2018 book *Darwin Comes to Town: How the Urban Jungle Drives Evolution* (Picador) delves in fascinating depth into the *non*-human life that thrives in every city. "To my biologist's eye," says Schilthuizen on page 2, "the inner city, for all its hustle and bustle and thoroughly unnatural appearance, becomes a constellation of miniature ecosystems." And so it is.
8. Plants may also feed on bacteria and fungi directly. Recent research has indicated that some bacterial and fungal cells enter into the root-tip cells of some plants, and some of them are broken up and absorbed by the plants, much as you or I would eat a leaf of lettuce. It's called rhizophagy, and it's considered a symbiotic relationship, but it sounds like a bad deal to me.
9. See Provenza, F. D. 2008. What does it mean to be locally adapted and who cares anyway? *American Society of Animal Science,* 86 (Issue Supplement 14), April 2008, pp E271–E284. Also see Provenza, F. D. 2003. Twenty-Five Years of Paradox in Plant-Herbivore Interactions and "Sustainable" Grazing Management. *Rangelands,* 25(6), 4-15.
10. See, e.g., Pimentel, D.; Edwards, C. A. Pesticides and Ecosystems. *Bioscience* 1982, 32 (7), 595-600.
11. From page 54 of *Dirt to Soil* by Gabe Brown, published in 2018 by Chelsea Green Publishing.
12. From page 239 of *Growing a Revolution* by David Montgomery, published in 2017 by Norton.
13. From page 23 of *Growing a Revolution.*
14. The information about farm size is from the FAO paper "What do we really know about the number and distribution of farms and family farms in the world?" Background paper for *The State of Food and Agriculture 2014,* by Sarah K. Lowder, Jakob Skoet, and Saumya Singh, ESA Working Paper No. 14-02, April 2014, accessed July 2020 at http://www.fao.org/3/a-i3729e.pdf
15. You may be wondering why I placed CEA to the *right* of the status quo. After all, it represents a shift to a more production-oriented mindset, and I placed production to the *left* of extraction on my model. I did this because CEA seems more organized than current extractive practices—even though past production was less organized (usually because it was on a much smaller scale).
16. The Burren quote is from the article " 'Life attracts life': the Irish farmers filling their fields with bees and butterflies" by Ella McSweeney in *The Guardian,* June 6, 2020, accessed July 2020 at https://www.theguardian.com/environment/2020/jun/06/food-will-be-a-by-product-the-irish-farmers-creating-nature-friendly-fields
17. David Montgomery's quote from his conversation with Gabe Brown is from page 174 of his book *Growing a Revolution.*
18. The quote about the Land Institute is from the "Vision & Mission" page of their web site, accessed July 2020 at https://landinstitute.org/about-us/vision-mission/.
19. From the Beacon Food Forest web site, accessed July 2020 at https://beaconfoodforest.org.
20. The "ancient Maya agriculture" quote is from pages 159-160 of *The Maya Forest Garden* by Anabel Ford and Ronald Nigh, published by Routledge in 2016.
21. The quote from Malcolm Cairns is from page XL of the Preface to the edited volume *Shifting Cultivation Policies: Balancing Environmental and Social Sustainability,* for which he was the editor. It was published in 2017 by CABI.
22. The "Yukatek Maya" quote is from page 57 of *The Maya Forest Garden.*
23. From pages 23-24 of "Shifting cultivation, livelihood and food security: New and old challenges for indigenous peoples in Asia" by Christian Erni. In the 2015 UN FAO Report *Shifting Cultivation, Livelihood and Food Security: New and Old Challenges for Indigenous Peoples in Asia,* edited by Christian Erni.

24. The swidden-and-climate quote is from an article titled "The impact of swidden decline on livelihoods and ecosystem services in Southeast Asia: A review of the evidence from 1990 to 2015" by Wolfram H. Dressler, David Wilson, Jessica Clendenning, Rob Cramb, Rodney Keenan, Sango Mahanty, Thilde Bech Bruun, Ole Mertz, and Rodel D. Lasco, in *Ambio*, volume 46, number 3, pages 291-310. Accessed July 2020 at https://www.ncbi.nlm.nih.gov/pmc/articles/PMC5347523.
25. The guilt quote is from page 79 of *Farming on the Wild Side* by Nancy and John Hayden, published in 2019 by Chelsea Green Publishing.
26. From pages 171-3 of *Half-Earth: Our Planet's Fight for Life* by E. O. Wilson, published in 2016 by Liveright Publishing Corporation, a division of W. W. Norton & Company.
27. From page 18 of *Nature's Best Hope* by Douglas W. Tallamy, published in 2020 by Timber Press.
28. The "rethink pretty" quote is from *Farming on the Wild Side*, page 7.
29. Just in case you are wondering why native plants are important: it's because they have strong relationships with other players in the ecological world, relationships that evolved over thousands of years. Non-native plants have no such ties, and that gives them an unfair advantage. When a non-native plant usurps the space of a native plant, entire networks can come crashing down. Of course, an intact ecosystem can absorb moderate amounts of invasion; but many ecosystems today are not intact, and many invasions are not moderate.
30. For the uninformed: "pics or it didn't happen" means "I am not going to believe you unless I see a photograph."

## Notes for Chapter 8 – The Mix

1. This is a proof story, a form of storytelling I talked about in Chapter Five. I don't have a degree in folklore studies, so I showed you that I know something about folk tales in a different way. Note my mention that "only a *true* nerd could appreciate" my appreciation for folk tales.
2. The folk tale collections I reread for this chapter are as follows. *American Indian Myths and Legends*, selected and edited by Richard Erdoes and Alfonso Ortiz, published in 1984 by Pantheon Books. *Encyclopedia of Urban Legends* by Jan Harold Brunvald, published in 2001 by Norton. *Folktales from India*, edited and with an introduction by A. K. Ramanujan, published in 1991 by Pantheon Books. *Mayan Folktales*, translated and edited by James D. Sexton, published in 1992 by the University of New Mexico Press. *The Original 1812 Grimm Fairy Tales, Volume I: A New Translation of the 1812 First Edition* (200 Year Anniversary Edition), translated by Oliver Loo, published in 2014 by Oliver Loo. *West African Folktales* by Stephen H. Gale, published in 1995 by National Textbook Company (NTC Publishing Group).
3. *The Original 1812 Grimm Fairy Tales, Volume I*, page 133. Note that this Grimm translation uses the pronoun "it" to refer to girls and unmarried women. I have changed these instances to "she" to avoid confusion.
4. *West African Folktales*, page 122. Note that in order to stay within the boundaries of fair use, I quoted no more than 300 words (in total) from any one of these books. You can read the entire stories in the books cited, all of which I recommend.
5. See my note on "order for free" on page 283. The "butterfly effect," as it is popularly known, inverts the original meaning of the term, which was that *it is impossible to say* what effect a single action will have in a complex network of connections. See my paper "Are We Ready for Complexity?" (cited on page 291) for a longer explanation.
6. From page 265 of William Morton Wheeler's book *Ants: Their Structure, Development and Behavior*, published in 1910 by Columbia University Press.
7. From paragraph 292 of William Beebe's book *Edge of the Jungle*, published in 1921 by Henry Holt and Company. Beebe estimated that the ant mill he observed was 366 meters in circumference, and that it took each ant 2.5 hours to complete the circle. If each ant walked round the circle 15 times, it means they walked for 37 hours without resting, eating, or drinking. That *is* insane. By the way, you might be wondering why I think the *Eciton* example shows the influence of self-organized patterns on organized plans. Ants are self-organized, aren't they? Yes, as a group. But each *individual* ant also has organized plans, which probably include not dying of starvation. Last thing: you can find videos of ant mills on the internet.
8. *The Original 1812 Grimm Fairy Tales, Volume I*, page 123.
9. *Encyclopedia of Urban Legends*, page 26.

10. This Zen parable isn't from a specific book, but it's easy to find on the internet.
11. *Encyclopedia of Urban Legends*, page 62.
12. *American Indian Myths and Legends*, page 209.
13. The elf's story was collected in Scotland by Anne MacVicar Grant and retold in the 1812 Grimm folk tales. It appears on page 43 of the 2014 English translation of the Grimm tales, along with Grant's version of the story and a fragment of the song from whence it came.
14. *The Original 1812 Grimm Fairy Tales, Volume I*, page 188.
15. From paragraph 250 of Lucian's story "Lover of Lies," which is also called "The Doubter" or "Philopseudes." Accessed October 2020 at sacred-texts.com/cla/luc/wl3/wl315.htm.
16. *Folktales from India*, page 319.
17. *Encyclopedia of Urban Legends*, page 14.
18. *American Indian Myths and Legends*, page 352.
19. *The Original 1812 Grimm Fairy Tales, Volume I*, page 384.
20. The story does not mention why the *queen* did not visit her daughters. She is what I would call a non-functional character. She makes no choices of any consequence, and she was probably only in the story to give birth to Reinald.
21. *American Indian Myths and Legends*, page 120.
22. *The Original 1812 Grimm Fairy Tales, Volume I*, page 185.
23. You may have noticed that long experience connects to the path of mastery, getting help from a magical being or wise person connects to the path of deliverance from an organized source, and innate talent connects to the path of deliverance from a non-organized source.
24. *American Indian Myths and Legends*, page 33.
25. *The Original 1812 Grimm Fairy Tales, Volume I*, page 87.
26. "The Boar with the Golden Bristles," pages 49-56 in *Dutch Fairy Tales for Young Folks* by William Elliot Griffis, published in 1918 by the Thomas Y. Crowell Company, New York.
27. I cannot remember where I read the story about the deer scratching the ground. I am fairly certain it was an American Indian story.
28. *American Indian Myths and Legends*, page 275.
29. *American Indian Myths and Legends*, page 193.
30. *Folktales from India*, page 204.
31. *American Indian Myths and Legends*, page 327.
32. *Folktales from India*, page 110.
33. *West African Folktales*, page 113.
34. *American Indian Myths and Legends*, page 223.
35. *The Original 1812 Grimm Fairy Tales, Volume I*, page 292.
36. You might think "If you would only listen" would have to do with being observant. But as I see it, the problem was not so much inattention as disrespect. The gardener's son, like his brothers, did not believe the fox was worthy of being listened to—at least not at first.
37. From Fran Sorin's blog "Gardening Gone Wild." Accessed October 2020 at gardeninggonewild.com/why-its-important-to-cultivate-patience-in-the-garden.
38. From page 19 of Paul Gruchow's book *Grass Roots: The Universe of Home*, published in 1995 by Milkweed Editions.
39. The story was either in Gabe Brown's *Dirt to Soil* or David Montgomery's *Growing a Revolution*. I didn't make a note of it. I looked, but I couldn't find it on a quick skim. I'd have to read both books again to find it. Why don't *you* find it? They are both great books.
40. This is a shameless plug for my book *Working with Stories in your Community or Organization: Participatory Narrative Inquiry*, published in 2014 by Kurtz-Fernhout Publications.
41. *Encyclopedia of Urban Legends*, page 44.
42. *Encyclopedia of Urban Legends*, page 3.
43. *Encyclopedia of Urban Legends*, page 100.
44. Two other names for S-shaped curves are "sigmoid functions" and "logistic functions." Here the term "logistic" has nothing to do with logistics (moving things around) but is in comparison to "logarithmic" (or geometric or exponential) curves, in which the slope of the line never decreases. Exponential growth and decay are embedded within the logistic function, positive at the start, and (roughly, usually) negative later on.

45. A fascinating book on the topic of our historical legacy as a prey species is *Deadly Powers* by Paul A. Trout, published in 2011 by Prometheus Books.
46. Timmers, H. and W.A. Wagenaar. 1977. Inverse statistics and misperception of exponential growth. *Perception and Psychophysics*, Vol 21(6), pp. 558-562.
47. The heading of this section was inspired by Sir David Attenborough saying, on the BBC's *Planet Earth*, Episode 4, Caves: "The flooded caverns can play tricks on you in other ways. What seems like air isn't. It's just another kind of water."
48. Levy, M. R. and Tasoff, J. 2017. Exponential-growth bias and overconfidence. *Journal of Economic Psychology*, Vol 58, pp. 1-14.
49. Wagenaar, W. A., and Timmers, H. 1979. The pond-and-duckweed problem: three experiments on the misperception of exponential growth. *Acta psychologica* 43(3), pp. 239-251.
50. *The Original 1812 Grimm Fairy Tales, Volume I*, page 185.
51. *American Indian Myths and Legends*, page 201.
52. *American Indian Myths and Legends*, page 208.
53. *The Twenty Ninth Day*, by Lester Brown, was published by W. W. Norton & Company in 1978.
54. Look for Problem 13 in the book "Propositions for Sharpening Youths" by Alcuin of York (735-804 CE). Find the rhyme that begins with "As I was going to St. Ives." Search for "penny that doubles every day." Consider the folding-paper riddle, which seems to be growing into a folk tale (a version from an internet forum: "An evil king threatens to destroy your town unless you can fold a paper in half eight times.").
55. From the article "Origin of the Game of Chess" (subtitled "From the Arabic"), pages 400-401 in *The Universal Magazine of Knowledge and Pleasure*, December, 1797.
56. By Ferdowsi (940 –1020 CE) in *Shah-nama* ("The Book of Kings"). By Abu'l-Hasan al-Uqlīdisī in Chapter 32, "On Doubling One, Sixty-Four Times," in his book *The Arithmetic of al-Uqlīdisī*, possibly written in 952 CE. Also, the Stith-Thompson Motif-Index of Folk Tales entry Z21.1 reads "Origin of chess. Inventor asks one wheat-grain for first square, two for the second, four for the third, eight for the fourth, etc. The king cannot pay." Entry Z21.1.1 reads "Wages: successive harvests from one grain of rice. Master has no fields left (Chinese)."
57. The translation of the Mari tablet (number 08613) can be found on pages 14-18 of *Unexpected Links Between Egyptian and Babylonian Mathematics* by Jöran Friberg, published in 2005 by World Scientific Publishing Company.
58. From page 64 of Hans Christian Andersen's *Eighty Fairy Tales*, published in 1976 by The Pantheon Fairy Tale and Folklore Library.
59. "Of that which Happened to a King and Three Impostors," from *Tales of Count Lucanor* by Don Juan Manuel in 1335.
60. From page 269 of *Indian Kāvya Literature: The art of storytelling, Volume 6* by Anthony Kennedy Warder, published in 1992 by Motilal Banarsidass.
61. *Encyclopedia of Urban Legends*, page 273.
62. I don't have a book reference for the pied piper story, but you can find many versions of it on the internet—along with many discussions of how the story relates to current events.
63. *Encyclopedia of Urban Legends*, page 272.
64. Ada McVean, "40 Years of Human Experimentation in America: The Tuskegee Study", an article on the web site of McGill University's Office for Science and Society, published 25 Jan 2019 and accessed in November 2020 at mcgill.ca/oss/article/history/40-years-human-experimentation-america-tuskegee-study.
65. *West African Folktales*, page 79.
66. "'Seller' Sent to Sing Sing for Life," *The Brooklyn Daily Eagle*, November 23, 1928, page 24.
67. *Encyclopedia of Urban Legends*, page 236.
68. From pages 16-27 in *Gleanings in Buddha-Fields: Studies of Hand and Soul in the Far East* by Patrick Lafcadio Hearn (also known as Koizumi Yakumo), published in 1897 by Houghton Mifflin.
69. From pages 214-221 of *The Panchatantra of Vishnu Sharma*, translated by Arthur W. Ryder and published in 1925 by the University of Chicago Press.
70. *Folktales from India*, page 92.

## Notes for Chapter 9 – Connecting the Dots

1. Kanizsa, G. 1979. *Organization in vision: Essays on gestalt perception*. Praeger, New York.
2. A review of animal research on perceptual completion can be found in the paper "Seeing more than meets the eye: processing of illusory contours in animals" by A. Neider, published in 2002 in the *Journal of Comparative Physiology*, volume 188, pages 249-260.
3. Photo credits: Moth, plate 365 of *Nature neighbors, embracing birds, plants, animals, minerals, in natural colors by color photography* by Nathaniel Moore Banta, published circa 1914 by the American Audobon association. Accessed January 2021 at https://www.biodiversitylibrary.org/page/32495640. Owl: From page 379 of *Field book of wild birds and their music; a description of the character and music of birds, intended to assist in the identification of species common in the United States east of the Rocky Mountains* by Ferdinand Schuyler, published circa 1921 by G.P. Putnam's Sons, London. Accessed January 2021 at https://www.biodiversitylibrary.org/page/13653783.
4. See, for example, Mukherjee, R., and U. Kodandaramaiah. 2015. What makes eyespots intimidating—the importance of pairedness. BMC Evolutionary Biology, volume 15. Accessed December 2020 at https://www.ncbi.nlm.nih.gov/pmc/articles/PMC4374370. Or: Skelhorn, J., Dorrington, G., Hossie, T. J, and. Sherratt, T. N. 2014. The position of eyespots and thickened segments influence their protective value to caterpillars. Behavioral Ecology, volume 25(6), pages 1-6. Accessed December 2020 at https://www.researchgate.net/publication/265124957_The_position_of_eyespots_and_thickened_segments_influence_their_protective_value_to_caterpillars.
5. An explanation of this possibility can be found in "'Quick Guide: Eyespots" by John Skelhorn, Grace G. Holmes, Thomas J. Hossie, and Thomas N. Sherratt, in *Current Biology Magazine*, volume 26, January 25, 2016, pages R52-R54. Accessed December 2020 at https://www.cell.com/current-biology/pdf/S0960-9822(15)01252-X.pdf.
6. The Kekulé quote is from page 269 of "The Scientific Imagination," *The Scientific Monthly*, Vol. 15, No. 3 (Sep., 1922), pp. 263-270.
7. From page 179 of *Suspicious Minds* by Rob Brotherton, published in 2016 by Bloomsbury Sigma.
8. You could also use the vertical axis of this space to denote something more complex than the extent of truthfulness of a fact or belief, such as how significant or surprising or relevant the fact or belief appears to be. You could also consider *changes* in such beliefs over time, and the causes of such changes. Such advanced uses of the space are worth exploring once you have learned to use it in its simplest what-is-real form.
9. The "Do you know how to weave" quote comes from page 540 of *The Pillars of the Earth* by Ken Follett, first published in 1990 by Penguin Books.
10. On a loom, warp threads are strung from front to back. Weft threads run left to right (then right to left, then left to right again) above and below alternate threads of the warp. Warp and weft together make a woven cloth.
11. Is there such a thing as *negative* spiraling? I would say no, because these dot-connecting strategies are meant to be *goals*, not outcomes. Thus they are always going to be positive. You can fail to spiral, but you can't spiral to failure.
12. From page 521 of *Arctic Dreams* by Barry Lopez, published by Open Road Media in 2013.
13. The quote from Seigo Yamaguchi is from a pamphlet given to students at a black-belt Aikido seminar, as recounted on pages 37-38 of *The Spiritual Foundations of Aikido* by William Gleason, published in 1995 by Destiny Books.
14. Cook, Tina. 2009. The purpose of mess in action research: building rigour though a messy turn. *Educational Action Research*, 17(2). pp. 227-291.
15. The restorative justice quote is from page 11 of 'Restorative justice works," published by the Restorative Justice Council in March 2015. Accessed January 2021 at https://restorativejustice.org.uk/sites/default/files/resources/files/rjc-victims-rjc-dig1.pdf.
16. You may have noticed that spiraling and focusing connect to the path of mastery, and that shuttling connects to the path of deliverance. Does the fact that I built three remarkably similar models mean that I tapped into some deep well of universal truth? Or does it simply mean that I wrote all three chapters? Probably the latter—which proves my point that these spaces can help people explore and explain their perspectives on life, the universe, and everything.

17. The "passengers walking about" quote is from page 17 of the Marine Review of Cleveland, Ohio, on July 25. 1907. Accessed January 2021 at https://images.maritimehistoryofthegreatlakes.ca/124575/page/144443?q=mirage.
18. The Feynman quotes are from the "Seeing things" section of the "Fun to Imagine" series, recorded by the BBC in 1983. This transcript is my own interpretation of what Feynman says on the video. You can find the interview by searching on YouTube.
19. Public domain image created by Tony Philips at NASA. Accessed January 2021 at https://commons.wikimedia.org/wiki/File:Ponzo_illusion.gif.
20. The Black Island image was photographed on November 4, 2020, by John Meyer for the U.S. National Science Foundation. The image can be found in the U.S. Antarctica program (USAP) photo library. I accessed it January 2021 at https://photolibrary.usap.gov and at the Wikimedia Commons at https://commons.wikimedia.org/wiki/File:2020Nov4-Fata-Morgana-Black-Island-HR.jpg.
21. The Aristotle quote is from paragraph 2 of part 4 of Book 3 in his work *Meteorologica*, written circa 350 BCE. I am heavily indebted to Andrew T. Young for his extensive bibliography of mirage quotes. His comprehensive web site on mirages and other atmospheric phenomena (https://aty.sdsu.edu/mirages/mirintro.html) is a magnificent example of spiraling as an aid to spiraling.
22. Paragraph 2 of part V of book VII of the *Delphi Complete Works of Quintus Curtius Rufus* (Kindle edition, so no page numbers), Delphi Classics, 2017.
23. From pages 92-93 of *La Iapygia* by Antonio de Ferraris, written in 1507-1509 and published in 1558. This English translation is from Andrew T. Young's bibliography of quotes about mirages and other atmospheric phenomena. Accessed January 2021 at https://aty.sdsu.edu/bibliog/bibliog.html.
24. From page 80 (paragraph 34 of Letter IV) of David Brewster's book *Letters on Natural Magic, Addressed to Sir Walter Scott, Bart.*. The book was originally published in 1832 by Harper & Brothers. The copy from which I drew these quotes was an 1842 reprint, which I accessed in January 2021 at https://www.loc.gov/resource/rbc0001.2009gen29167. Looming is the vertical elongation of objects due to non-standard atmospheric refraction.
25. To see an artificial mirage, search the internet for "refraction demonstration sugar water." You'll find lots of videos and instructions for setting up such a demonstration yourself.
26. The story about engineers on Lake Superior is from the article "Seeing Sixty Miles: United States Engineers Did it on Lake Superior," published in the *Detroit Free Press* (Detroit, MI), on July 20, 1895. Accessed January 2021 at https://images.maritimehistoryofthegreatlakes.ca/3107/data?n=18.
27. 'Mirage-effect' helps researchers hide objects, *Science Daily*, October 4, 2011. Accessed January 2021 at https://www.sciencedaily.com/releases/2011/10/111003195245.htm. If you watch the video linked in the article, you can see that the cloaking effect looks remarkably like a mirage.
28. The quote is from paragraph 4 of section 50 of Book III of Diodorus Siculus' *The Library of History*, translated by Charles Henry Oldfather. Loeb Classical Library 279. Cambridge, MA: Harvard University Press, 1933.
29. From page 4 of the 1773 printing of *Dissertazioni sopra diversi fatti meno ovvi della Storia Naturale*, Volume I, by Antonio Minasi. Accessed January 2021 at https://books.google.com/books?id=mw85AAAAcAAJ. In the Italian, it is "Tanta e la gioia che ne' riguardanti produce il vago spettacolo, che tutti uomini e donne, ignoranti e dotti, al mare accorrono per osservarlo, subito che i primi Morgana, Morgana, gridino." The English translation was provided by Google Translate, with a few readability tweaks I could not stop myself from making.
30. British Library digitised image from page 357 of *The Half Hour Library of Travel, Nature and Science for Young Readers*, published by James Nisbet in 1896, author unknown. Note that the scanned page number is not necessarily the actual page number in the publication. Accessed January 2021 at https://www.flickr.com/photos/britishlibrary/11234125713.
31. I found the *Suffolk* ship log on the "Battle Cruiser Hood" web site (http://www.hmshood.org.uk) in January 2021 at http://www.hmshood.org.uk/reference/official/adm234/adm234-509suff.htm.
32. From the *Marine Record* of Cleveland, Ohio, from October 4, 1894, pages 2-3. Accessed January 2021 at https://images.maritimehistoryofthegreatlakes.ca/64601/page/19992?q=mirage.
33. From page 140 of *Letters on Natural Magic*.
34. From paragraph 10 of part 18 of *De situ Japigiae* by Antonio de Ferraris, written between 1506 and 1511 and first printed in 1558. Accessed January 2021 at the Centro Interuniversitario Internazionale di Studi sul Viaggio Adriatico web site, at http://www.viaggioadriatico.it/biblioteca

_digitale/titoli/scheda_bibliografica.2009-03-20.2900829752. The English translation is courtesy of Google Translate.
35. Accessed January 2021 at http://www.inuitmyths.com/ijirait.htm. Italics my own.
36. Part 15 of Chapter 47 of the *Yoga-Vasishtha Maharamayana*, translated by Vihari-Lala Mitra. Accessed January 2021 at https://www.gutenberg.org/files/46531/46531-h/46531-h.htm.
37. From page 176 of the 1811 (second) edition of *Scenes of Infancy: Descriptive of Teviotdale* by John Leyden. Accessed January 2021 at https://books.google.com/books?id=XHdLAQAAMAAJ.
38. From page 21 of *Narrative of a Residence in Ireland During the Summer of 1814, and that of 1815* by Anne Plumptre. Accessed January 2021 at https://books.google.com/books?id=B0Eb4UO_FDsC.
39. From the second paragraph of Chapter 2 and the first paragraph of Chapter 6 of *The Waterless Sea: A Curious History of Mirages* by Christopher Pinney, published in 2018 by Reaktion Books.
40. Similarly, on page 80 of *Marvelous Possessions: The Wonder of the New World* (published in 1992 by the University of Chicago Press), Stephen Greenblatt refers to "a sense of the marvelous that in effect fills up the emptiness at the center of the maimed rite of possession."
41. I do not mean to imply that indigenous knowledge cultures are wholly based on focusing, nor that scientific knowledge cultures are wholly based on spiraling. Each culture mixes all three strategies, but they do tend to tip to one side. My favorite book on this topic is *Braiding Sweetgrass: Indigenous Wisdom, Scientific Knowledge and the Teachings of Plants* by Robin Wall Kimmerer, published in 2013 by Milkweed Editions.
42. In your own spiraling on this topic, if you can find a mistake in what I have written here, please tell me about it. I hope to be embarrassed by this chapter in the future.
43. *Conspiracy Theories* by Quassim Cassam was published in 2019 by Polity Press, London.
44. From page 112 of *Suspicious Minds* by Rob Brotherton, published in 2016 by Bloomsbury Sigma.
45. Richard Nelson Bolles, *What Color is Your Parachute*, new editions published every year.
46. There are many more elaborate decision support methods for the "wicked problems" that arise in uncertain situations. My husband likes Issue-Based Information Systems, or IBIS. I like my thing. The world works best, I think, when everyone can find a solution that works for them.
47. From pages 170-175 of *Folktales from India*, edited and with an introduction by A. K. Ramanujan, published in 1991 by Pantheon Books.
48. From page 6 of *Conspiracy Theories* by Quassim Cassam. The italics in the quote are his own.
49. The political nature of conspiracy theories also explains why "that's just a conspiracy theory" is sometimes used to discredit political opinions even when there is no evidence that those opinions meet the criteria that define conspiracy theories.
50. Unless, of course, I have only succeeded in convincing you that *I* am a strange person, in which case my plan has failed and . . . I made up those stories. That's right, they're folk tales.
51. This is called "lateral reading." Look it up.
52. A doctor I know had this to say: "Well, you *could* keep your foot still if you tensed your leg. Sometimes, if no reflex movement is elicited (in the knee, for example) we distract the patient by asking them to link the ends of their fingers together and pull. And sometimes we ask them to lightly tense their leg, to contract the muscle a bit so a reflex will be easier to obtain." Even though the "distraction" in this case is meant to help us, it proves my point that a knee-jerk response can be "obtained" without our intending to provide it.
53. By "credentials" I don't just mean academic degrees. There are other legitimate forms of credentials, such as track records, testimonials, accreditations, affiliations, and awards.
54. I have BS and MA degrees in biology. I do not have a degree in organizational and community narrative. I worked on it for two years at IBM Research, a respected institution, and I have done well-spoken-of project work for several dozen other respected institutions, governmental and corporate, since 1999. I have published papers on the topic in respected peer-reviewed journals, and my textbook *Working with Stories*, though self-published, is well spoken of by many professionals. What are my credentials in the area of complexity? Good question. I learned about it when I was studying ecology. My 1991 master's thesis was on self-organization in foraging theory. I worked on projects related to self-organization for roughly two years at IBM's Institute for Knowledge Management (which no longer exists but was respected at the time). Around the same time, I worked on two years-long research projects that involved stories, complexity, and decision support for government clients. Since then I have provided coaching and support on projects related to

stories and complexity for a variety of clients. I have also published a few papers on complexity in respected peer-reviewed journals.
55. From page 26 of *Conspiracy Theories.*
56. What alternatives to "system" are available? How about network, web, complex, aggregate, mix, coalescence, stream, or flow? None of these words convey the same sense of intention as "system."
57. In 2018 I published a nagging paper about these concerns. It's called "Are We Ready for Complexity?" and you can find it in *Policy and Complex Systems*, volume 4(1): pages 135-154.
58. See my note on "order for free" on page 283.
59. "The North Wind and the Sun," from *Aesop's Fables*, translated by V. S. Vernon Jones, published in 1912. Accessed February 2021 at https://www.gutenberg.org/files/11339/11339-h/11339-h.htm.
60. From page 9 of *The Mistake Bank* by John M. Caddell, published in 2013 by Caddell Insight Group.
61. From page 13 of *Liminal Thinking: Create the Change You Want by Changing the Way You Think* by Dave Gray, published in 2016 by Two Waves.
62. Cognitive behavioral therapists call the bad habit of exaggerating difficulties "catastrophizing" (or "catastrophic thinking") and recommend volunteer work to gain perspective.
63. From pages 71-72 of *My Life After Hate* by Arno Michaelis, published in 2012 by Authentic Presence Publications.
64. From page 100 of *My Life After Hate.*
65. "Beauty will save the world" is one of my favorite lines from Dostoyevky's *The Idiot*, my favorite book.
66. From page 2 of *Darwin's Lost Theory* by David Loye, published in 2007. The italics are his.

# Index

Bold page numbers refer to diagrams.

# About Me

When I was a little girl, my dad used to call me "Cynthia the guru" because I was always staring off into space, thinking. I still do that a lot. I started thinking about how organization and self-organization flow together in the late 1980s.

My career has taken me from biology (ecology, evolution, ethology) to software development to organizational and community narrative. My 2014 book *Working with Stories in Your Community or Organization: Participatory Narrative Inquiry* is widely considered a useful resource.

At the moment I work as an independent consultant, researcher, software developer, and author, and I live near Albany, New York with my husband and son.

You can contact me at cfkurtz@cfkurtz.com.

Made in the USA
Las Vegas, NV
21 May 2021